Academician, administrator, politician and author, Nitish Sengupta studied at Presidency College, Kolkata, securing first class in both BA (Hons) and MA and winning a gold medal for his master's in history. He began his career as assistant professor of history in Presidency College and joined the Indian Administrative Service (IAS) in 1957. He held key posts in the Union government including Revenue Secretary and Member-Secretary, Planning Commission. He completed his doctorate in management from Delhi University and lectured at several universities and leading management schools in the country. After his retirement, he was director-general of the International Management Institute, New Delhi.

Nitish Sengupta has represented India at various UN bodies and was elected chairman of the UN Commission on Transnational Corporations. He joined politics in 1996 and was elected to the thirteenth Lok Sabha, where he served as member of several key committees, notably the Public Accounts Committee. He was also general secretary, All India Trinamool Congress. Currently, he is chairman, Board for Reconstruction of Public Sector Enterprises, New Delhi.

Sengupta has been a regular columnist in leading dailies and is the author of fifteen books, including several related to management. As a historian, his notable books are *History of the Bengali-speaking People, Dr B.C. Roy: Biography* and *Land of Two Rivers: A History of Bengal from the Mahabharata to Mujib.* His other books include *Unshackling of Indian Industry, Government and Business, Inside the Street Frame* and *My Times: A Civil Servant Remembers.*

He is based in Delhi.

BENGAL DIVIDED

THE UNMAKING OF A NATION
1905-1971

NITISH SENGUPTA

PENGUIN BOOKS

PENGUIN BOOKS

USA | Canada | UK | Ireland | Australia
New Zealand | India | South Africa | China

Penguin Books is part of the Penguin Random House group of companies
whose addresses can be found at global.penguinrandomhouse.com

Published by Penguin Random House India Pvt. Ltd
7th Floor, Infinity Tower C, DLF Cyber City,
Gurgaon 122 002, Haryana, India

First published in Viking by Penguin Books India 2007

Published in Penguin Books 2012

ISBN 9780143419556

Typeset in Minion Regular by SÜRYA, New Delhi
Printed at Repro India Ltd, Navi Mumbai

www.penguinbooksindia.com

*Dedicated to the memory of all those valiant soldiers in the
Bangladesh Mukti Bahini and in the Indian Army
who laid down their lives in the war for
Bangladesh's independence in 1971*

CONTENTS

PREFACE

There is no parallel in history to the paradox that while in 1905 a majority of the people of Bengal rejected the British-directed partition of their land and fought against it, only four decades later, in 1947, the same majority asked for a partition of Bengal between Muslim majority and Hindu majority areas. The explanation lies in nearly six decades of interaction between the Hindus and the Muslims of Bengal in the course of which the two communities, after coming close to each other on several occasions, eventually drifted apart and asked for partition.

The 1905 anti-partition nationalist movement in Bengal also led to heightened communalism. In a way it both hastened the end of British rule and laid the foundation for the second partition of Bengal in 1947. The annulment of the partition in 1911 was not to the liking of the majority of East Bengal Muslims. Along with the loss of Dhaka's privileged position, the shifting of the imperial capital from Kolkata to Delhi was a big jolt to Bengali pride in general. What Berlin is to the Germans, Kolkata is to the Bengalis, both Muslims and Hindus.

Notwithstanding the 'highs' and 'lows' of the India–Bangladesh relationship, the cultural unity and interaction between the two Bengals have remained steady. Also, there is a fair amount of cross-border, often strictly illegal, movement of people, leading to people-to-people contact. Interestingly, West Bengal has still kept the adjective 'West' in her name despite suggestions from time to time to follow the Punjab pattern of having an Indian Punjab and a Pakistan Punjab. Clearly, many Bengalis in West Bengal still like to fondly cling to the vague idea that they constitute the western part of a greater Bengal in the cultural sense. In that belief while remaining as two political entities, Bangladesh and West Bengal can have close cultural links and freedom of movement among themselves. These issues will have to be addressed by the leaders of India, Bangladesh and West Bengal.

As a matter of fact, there is and always has been a great deal of cultural interaction between the two Bengals. Bangladesh is at present facing a serious challenge from Islamic fundamentalism. Hopefully the nationalist feelings, still very strong, will be able to overcome it. What is not noticed is that, despite the surface tension between the two countries—India and Bangladesh—from time to time, a great deal of fellow feeling and mutual understanding between the common people of the two Bengals remains beneath the surface. This is reflected from time to time in events like the wave of jubilation that prevails in Bangladesh when Amartya Sen, the economist, wins the Nobel prize, the joy and pride with which the news of Mohammad Yunus getting the Nobel peace prize is greeted by people at large in West Bengal, or the fact that Fazlul Huq's centenary is celebrated with equal solemnity in West Bengal. Or the people of Bangladesh taking much pride in the achievements of Saurav Ganguly as a cricketer and also feeling sorry when his career crashlands. Television and radio channels treat the two Bengals as their common market and the same interaction is noticed in music and films. All this makes one feel that despite the fact that politically they are two different countries, culturally Bengal had always remained one and will ever remain. This author will consider his labour amply rewarded if this trend is strengthened as a result of the publication of this study.

It is well established that a sort of composite Bengali culture developed prior to the advent of the British and there was hardly any communal animosity. The unity of language was a key factor in the emergence of Bengal as a distinct political and cultural entity right from ancient times through the Turkish conquest and the Turkish phase of Bengal's history, the period of Mughal rule to the British conquest in the eighteenth century and the period of British rule. It was only after the advent of British rule in Bengal that a wide divergence developed on account of a variety of factors, the most important being the policy of divide and rule followed by the rulers. Paradoxically, the great Bengal Renaissance and Hindu Reformation Movement of the nineteenth century, which lifted up educated sections of Hindu society, accentuated the divide between the upwardly mobile Hindu community and the numerically larger, but 'withdrawn' Muslim community.

The nineteenth-century resurgence among the people of Bengal was, by and large, confined to the Hindus for a long time. The Muslims, smarting under their replacement as the rulers of Bengal, progressively withdrew to a kind of cocoon, not even wishing to accept the English language and the lifestyle induced by British rule. A kind of divergence was created between the mainstreams of the two communities. The promised 'nation in making' of the nineteenth century remained an unrealized dream and was, in fact, followed by a process of the unmaking of a nation. On the one hand, the Muslims' contempt for English education as a passport to jobs under the government and, on the other hand, their disregard of modern professions like law, teaching and government jobs created a kind of duality or divergence of interests. The community's subsequent romance with English education, thanks to reformers like Abdul Latif and Amir Ali, led to a clamour for government jobs, till then a preserve of the Hindu Bengalis. This further intensified the divergence.

There was indeed a high noon of Hindu–Muslim camaraderie in Bengal in the first two decades of the twentieth century climaxing under the charismatic leadership of Deshbandhu C.R. Das. Except for a handful of zamindar-type sections of Bengalis, Muslims and Hindus were, by and large, united under his leadership. His untimely death was a great tragedy, all the more so because the more vocal section of the Hindu public opinion repudiated his legacy, like the Bengal Pact. Thus, from this high noon, there was a climb down of substantial sections of Muslims to communalist positions, leading to the return of separatist politics which lasted until the tragic partition of 1947.

I am indebted to a large number of friends and professional academicians who have encouraged and helped me to undertake this study. I particularly remember that the suggestion to carry on after 1947 until the emergence of Bangladesh came from a large number of people from Bangladesh who were present at the launch of my book *History of the Bengali-Speaking People* at London School of Oriental and African Studies in 2006. I recall their suggestions with gratitude. I thank Mr Santosh Kumar Mukherjee, formerly of the Oxford University Press, for going through the first draft and giving some useful suggestions. I also thank my daughters Mekhala and Tamali for their unfailing assistance, my granddaughter Chandika Gupta for providing me invaluable computerized data for finalizing the maps, Professor Arindam Banik for helping me to get useful materials, my personal secretary Nirmaljit Singh for his secretarial assistance and Shri Ravi Singh and Ms Manjula Lal of Penguin Books India and Abantika Banerjee for their invaluable suggestions and assistance at every stage. Above all, I must recall with gratitude the fond memory of my late wife Sunanda, who encouraged my return from the world of management and economics to history as a subject. But for the turning point she gave me, the book may not have been there.

NITISH SENGUPTA

NEW DELHI
16 OCTOBER 2006

PART I

ONE BENGAL

Last Phase

1

GENESIS OF SEPARATISM

Islam came to Bengal towards the end of the twelfth century, but spread rapidly in the next three centuries, so much so that the Muslims considered Bengal as a Muslim-dominated area. It is paradoxical that while the region around Delhi and Agra, which was the centre of Muslim rule in the subcontinent, never lost its predominantly Hindu character, the outlying Bengal province became a Muslim majority area, where the Muslim ruling elite came in close contact with the common people. After the initial few centuries of conquest and conversion, the rulers of Gaur from Hussain Shah onwards settled down to a policy of promoting a liberal national monarchy, treating both Muslim and Hindu subjects alike and appealing to the loyalty of both.

Meanwhile, Islam's doctrine of universal brotherhood and direct communion with God together with reverence for a whole range of local deities and customs rapidly spread among the local people. Islamic preachers helped the Bengalis assimilate Islam in their life not by doing away with local traditions and practices but keeping them alive as far as possible, while inculcating among the common folk the essential religious, social and legal aspects of Islam. The large number of Buddhists in Bengal, already facing persecution by Hindu orthodoxy, found it easier to get assimilated into Islam.

In general, people dissatisfied with the oppression of a caste-ridden society and vulgar ritualism turned to the new faith which

3

promised common brotherhood, liberation from the offensive yoke of Brahmanic oppression and considerable material incentives such as easier availability of government jobs. The process of conversion was facilitated by cruel practices of Hindu society such as closing the doors to anyone who had been forcibly fed beef or who had taken food or water from a Muslim or any woman who had been abducted by force and wished to return to her home and faith. Many members of the lower castes embraced Islam as the only way to get out of the concentration camptype of existence that Hindu society inflicted on them. There were also some special economic disabilities imposed on non-Muslims by the early Turko-Afghan rulers. These disappeared from Akbar's time onwards.

Contemporary literary pieces like Ramai Pundit's *Sunya Purana* and *Shekhasubhodaya* by Halayaudha Misra (clearly a pseudonym) illustrate how large masses of people surrendered to the appeal of Islam with its monotheism, universal brotherhood and direct communion with God.[1] It is quite clear that the Hindus in general gave unstinted loyalty to the rulers of Gaur and thereafter to the Mughal rulers up to the time of the nawabs of Murshidabad. Communal violence, as found during the British period, was practically unknown. Also, there was extensive social mixing between the two communities until the nineteenth century. Vaishnava literature referred to King Hussain Shah as the incarnation (avatar) of Lord Krishna in the *Kaliyuga*.[2] Also, Hussain Shah protected Shri Chaitanya, the great Vaishnav saint, from both the kazis and also the orthodox Brahmans. His son and successor, Nusrat Shah, had the Mahabharat translated into Bengali. Many Muslim writers like Alaol wrote extensively on Hindu themes and motifs. Both the Sufis and the Vaishnav poets wrote on philosophical aspects which had a great deal of commonality and which appealed to both the communities. All over Bengal there are shrines where members of both communities offer prayers and seek blessings. They also shared common rituals such as worshipping Satyanarayan (Satya Pir for Muslims) or Dakshin Roy in the Sunderban areas. Liberal Muslims often participated in Hindu ceremonies like Durga Puja and Saraswati Puja just as Hindus participated in Muslim religious ceremonies like

Id-ul-Fitr. The British divide and rule policy and the Hindu Reformation accentuated the divide between the upwardly-mobile Hindu community and the inward-looking Muslim community.

Roots of Muslim separatism

The roots of Muslim separatism in Bengal lay in the near-wholesale political, economic, social and educational downgrading that the Bengali Muslims suffered with the advent of British rule. Not only did they lose political power and the privileges and patronage that went with it, but the 1793 Permanent Settlement drastically reduced the number of Muslim zamindars and other large landholders. Without such exposure to commerce historically, the Muslims in Bengal could not take advantage of the economic opportunities the new era offered. Inherently suspicious and conservative, they also denied themselves the new English education, thereby leaving the stage free for the Hindu Bengalis, who were dominant in government jobs and professions like law, medicine and teaching. Slowly, they withdrew into a cocoon, having little to do with the British and with things modern. Both the Muslim aristocracy and professionals came to a precarious existence. Interestingly, Muslims in other parts of the country, including Bihar, did not quite share this experience. Nowhere else in the subcontinent were Muslims as badly off as in Bengal, just as, paradoxically, few other communities derived as much benefit from British rule as Bengali Hindus. The following true-to-life description of the state of affairs given by a famous Bengal civilian, Sir William Hunter, in his book *Indian Musalman* is worthy of note:

> My remarks apply only to lower Bengal, the province with which I am best acquainted and in which so far as I can learn, the Muhammadans have suffered most severely under British rule. I should be sorry to believe or to convey to the readers the belief that the following remarks were predictable of all the Muhammadans of India. If ever a people stood in need of a career, it is the Muslim aristocracy of Bengal. The

administration of the imperial taxes was the first source of income in Bengal and the Musalman aristocracy monopolised it. The police was another source of income and the police was officered by Muhammadans. The courts of law were a third great source of income and the Musalmans monopolised them. Above all there was the army, an army not officered by gentlemen who make little more than bank interest on the price of their commission, but a great confederation of conquerors who enrolled their peasantry into troops, and drew pay from the state for them as soldiers. A hundred and seventy years ago, it was almost impossible for a well-born Muslim in Bengal to become poor. At present it is almost impossible for them to continue rich.[3]

The publication of this book in 1870 was indeed a turning point in British policy. It took a 180-degree turn from a policy of encouraging Hindus and ignoring Muslims to one of appeasement of Muslims and discouragement of Hindus.

But a change in Bengali Muslim attitude was also underway. Like his Hindu neighbour, the Bengali Muslim was unaffected by the Sepoy Mutiny of 1857. But for him the Indigo Movement that started almost as soon as the guns of the Sepoy Mutiny fell silent was a great watershed. The peasants resisted pressure from planters to grow indigo, as it had become uneconomic in the export market. Prices had become depressed after the boom in the early nineteenth century. This carried on from 1859 to 1862, when the government took a stand in favour of the peasants. Both Bengali Muslims and Hindus shared a common platform in defying indigo planters about growing indigo. Unfortunately, this commonality was short-lived and did not become a tradition.

While Kolkata and urban Bengal were undergoing the great intellectual and cultural transformation of the nineteenth-century Bengal Renaissance and Hindu religious reformation, a massive demographic change was underway in rural Bengal—the ascendancy of the Muslims to numerical majority in relation to the Hindu community. Strangely enough, it remained largely unnoticed for a long time. It took both the British rulers and the dominant urban Hindu elite nearly three quarters of a century after 1800 to realize that the Muslims had become a majority in Bengal.

A typical observation was that of James Wise: 'When the English magistrates first came in contact with the people of Bengal, they arrived at the conclusion that the Muhamadans only comprised one per cent of the population.' A report on vernacular education by William Adams in 1839 revealed surprisingly that in Rajshahi district, there were only 450 Hindus for every 1,000 Muslims although officials had treated it as a Hindu district. Sambhu Chandra Mukherji, a journalist writing in 1882, found it hard to persuade his so-called educated Hindu brethren of districts like Rajshahi that in those districts the Mussalmans were more numerous than the Hindus.[4] It was the 1881 Census that convincingly showed for the first time that in the majority of the twenty-eight Bengali-speaking districts of undivided Bengal presidency, the Muslims numbered significantly more than the Hindus (48 per cent) and that in the three divisions of Rajshahi, Dhaka and Chittagong, they formed two-thirds of the population. It showed that the Muslims accounted for 48.7 per cent of Bengal's population, a figure significantly larger than the Hindu population. The revelation of this momentous demographic change also marked the starting point of a series of new attitudes. For the British administration, there was a new appraisal of the importance of the Muslim factor. For the marginalized and inarticulate Muslim leadership, it was the realization of their own importance and an assurance that they could not be ignored any longer. Hunter's path-breaking book, *Indian Mussalman*, symbolized the first. The second phenomenon was illustrated by Nawab Abdul Latif's Muhamadan Education Society (1863) and, a few years later, Syed Amir Ali's National Muhammadan Association of Kolkata.

The great intellectual awakening in Bengal in the nineteenth century left the Muslim community untouched except in the fringes. In the galaxy of famous names in early Bengal Renaissance we scarcely come across Muslim names before the twentieth century arrived. The century from the Battle of Plassey in 1757 to the 1857 Mutiny saw the Muslims in Bengal as a sullen, withdrawn community, unreconciled to the loss of political power and withdrawing itself, so to say, in a shell of suspicion of both the British rulers and the new Hindu meritocracy. As the Hindu upper and middle classes vigorously embraced western education and new economic and professional opportunities, the Muslims withdrew more and more. The early British strategy of making friends with the Hindus and keeping Muslims at a distance further accentuated this divide. Also, the fact that the revivalist Wahabi Movement of upper India cast a deep influence among a section of downtrodden Bengali Muslim peasantry made the Muslims suspect. Some of the leaders of the Indigo Movement were Wahabis. One of them, Amiruddin, was imprisoned for sedition in 1871. On 20 September 1871, the chief justice of Kolkata was assassinated by a Wahabi, B. Abdullah. The well-known Barasat uprising led by Titu Mir illustrated a pronounced anti-British trend among sections of Muslims in Bengal. All this alienated the British rulers. Also, the Bengali Muslims, despite their lack of support for the great 1857 uprising, had suffered from the hostility and displeasure of the British Raj for the sins of disloyalty of their co-religionists in upper India. The authorities shunned them. They also, in their turn, withdrew into a shell, so to say, keeping only a minimal unavoidable interaction with an unfriendly Raj.

A subtle change in the official attitude, as already discussed, was underway. Hindus were gradually turning seditious and, therefore, the British Raj needed to look for new allies. Only Muslims could provide this. This community could be won over through patronage in the form of job opportunities and educational support. Thus began a new policy of appeasement of Muslims. In a government resolution in 1871, Governor-General Lord Mayo regretted that 'so large and important a class possessing a classical literature replete with works of profound learning and great value, and counting among its members a section specially devoted to the acquisition and diffusion of knowledge should stand aloof from active cooperation with our educational system and should lose the advantages both material and social which others enjoy'.[5] This coincided with the Aligarh Movement led by Syed Ahmed Khan, who established the Aligarh College in 1874, and encouraged Muslims to take to western education and come to terms with British rule. Syed Ahmed was of the firm opinion that there had been uneven development of the two communities and that this had led to Hindu domination. He further believed that political emancipation without adequate safeguards for the weaker community could only mean further subjugation of the latter. This line of thinking inevitably found an echo among Bengali Muslims, whose leaders like Syed Amir Ali encouraged Muslim separatism.

Meanwhile, the Bengali Muslims remained steeped in ignorance and illiteracy. So great was their apathy to modern education that in Hooghly College, an institution started with a large endowment fund left by Haji Mohammad Mohsin, a great philanthropist, in 1836, there were only five Muslim students out of a total of 409 as late as 1850. Both the Indian Education Commission (1882) chaired by Hunter and a committee appointed by the government of Bengal in 1885 dwelt extensively on the educational backwardness of the Muslims in Bengal and recommended generous and special measures. A memorandum submitted to Lord Ripon on 6 February 1882 is of special significance. It was circulated by the Government of India to all provinces and 'assumed a kind of national significance', to quote a contemporary source and was 'deeply pathetic as coming from former conquerors and rulers'.[6] The government responded by stating in a resolution (15 July 1885) that 'the very fact that a memorandum like that has been presented with the concurrence and approval of so many leading gentlemen in Bengal and elsewhere indicates that the Muhammadans themselves have come to appreciate fully the necessity of moving with the times'.[7] While the Bengal government had reservations about the Education Commission's recommendation for exclusive schools or scholarships for Muslim students, the Government of India was more generous in its attitude and accepted most of the recommendations.

Unfortunately, the Bengal Hindu leadership, flushed with the new glory of the Bengal Renaissance and the new political awakening, remained non-responsive. It failed to appreciate that the newly revealed numerical superiority of the Muslims in Bengal had

introduced a new element of great significance in the situation and
that it was necessary to carry the Muslims with the process of
awakening if it were to mean anything for the bulk of the common
people. The comments of the *Hindu Patriot* on the Education
Commission's recommendations suggesting special measures for
special classes reflect this impervious attitude:

> But the bulk of the Hindus who pay for the whole machinery
> of government administration and education or, in other
> words, those who contribute the most and have done most
> for self-help should be denied the helping hand of the
> government, and their revenue contributions and savings to
> be affected by abolishing or reducing the educational staff
> of the colleges their children frequent must go to the
> benefit of the indolent, the discontented and the specially
> favoured. This is the upshot for which the Hindu population
> in India are to thank the government and the Education
> Council.[8]

A recurring controversy on whether Muslim school students should
receive their education in ordinary Bengali-medium primary schools
or in *maktabs* where Urdu was the medium of instruction also
obstructed the progress of education among Muslims. There was a
clear divergence of interest, on the one hand, between upper-class
Muslims, most of whom spoke Urdu, and the Bengali-speaking
peasantry and lower classes and, on the other hand, between the
largely Urdu-speaking West Bengal and Kolkata Muslims and the
overwhelmingly Bengali-speaking East Bengal Muslims. As Muslim
religious books were generally in Urdu, there was a natural pull
towards it, all the more so because Bengali literature in the nineteenth
century was overwhelmingly loaded with Hindu polytheistic
expressions, motifs and myths. Also, unlike the pioneers of Bengali
literature like Rammohun Roy and Ishwar Chandra Vidyasagar,
some of the subsequent literary stalwarts like Bankim Chandra came
to be widely perceived as essentially anti-Muslim in nature. In
particular, Muslims found it difficult to appreciate some of the
comments, observations or attitudes in Bankim Chandra's *Anand*

Math, *Rajsingha* and *Sitaram* where uncomplimentary references to *yavanas* or Muslims were made. This created scope for fundamentalist forces among the Muslims to create a prejudice among orthodox sections against Bengali literature of that epoch, which was described primarily as Hindu literature. Nonetheless, the fact remains that their efforts to make the Bengali-speaking Muslims learn the unfamiliar Urdu script and language did not succeed. Bengali-speaking Muslims did not get over their psychological inhibition to learn Urdu and, on the whole, stuck to the line of learning Bengali. Some of them concentrated on producing Islamic literature in Bengali to counter both Urdu-based Islamic literature and the predominant Hindu influence in Bengali literature. Works of Musharraf Hussain, the author of *Bishad Sindhu*, played a significant role in filling this vacuum. Another part of this controversy was the predominantly Hindu character of the district boards, which did not spend enough money on Muslim education. Also, the educational backwardness of the Muslims was reflected in their poor representation in government service. This became yet another sore point.

There was also a deep-rooted social cause. Socially the Bengali Hindu *bhadralok* looked down upon their Muslim neighbours. 'Muslims were in most respects untouchable to the Hindus', states Tamizuddin Khan.[9] Not only was all cooked food thrown away as unclean if a Muslim entered the room but Muslim tenants were seated only on the floor on *piris* (low wooden seats) when they visited landlords' offices, and not even allowed to smoke from the same *hookahs* as the Hindus. But in fairness it must be pointed out that the same treatment was meted out to Hindu lower castes by the Hindu bhadralok upper castes. 'They were as good as two distinct peoples in spite of fraternisation in certain fields of action.'[10] The Muslims resented this unequal social treatment and the resultant anguish was to lead to an inevitable backlash as and when more and more Muslims joined the educated ranks and got the upper hand politically. Thus the entire movement of Syed Ahmed Khan in north India, where Muslims were much better off, had little or no effect in Bengal. Although Sir Syed spoke on behalf of the Muslims of the whole of India, his voice had little impact in far-off Bengal. It was only after the Muhammadan Educational Conference in north India held its first session in Kolkata in 1899 under Amir Ali's chairmanship that the awareness for reorienting the education of Muslim youth in madrassas on western lines dawned on Bengali Muslims. Muslims, therefore, along with the Hindus, opposed Curzon's educational reforms, but for different reasons.

There was also a deep economic basis for Muslim separatism. The new zamindar class that Cornwallis created in Bengal was dominated by the Hindus. So also were the two other classes that British rule brought about, namely, the native bourgeoisie that sprang up with the growth of modern industry and commerce and the new professional groups: the teachers, lawyers, doctors, engineers, government officials and employees. Muslim zamindars were few, but the overwhelming number among the downtrodden peasantry were Muslim. The 1881 Census showed that cultivators constituted 49.28 per cent of the Hindu population while the percentage was 62.81 for Muslims. Hence any zamindar–ryot issue inevitably tended to take on a communal colour. Also the fact that Muslims had by and large avoided western education, industry and commerce only meant that Muslims in the new bourgeoisie and professional classes were exceptions, not the rule. Muslims, in general, seldom felt an identity of interest with the Hindu aristocracy and meritocracy clamouring for reforms and more rights. There was, therefore, an underlying class basis behind early Muslim separatism.

Inevitably the strained relationship between the oppressive zamindar and the oppressed ryot took a communal overtone. The first serious attempt by the government to offer rights and safeguards to the ryots was criticized by the zamindars vociferously through their mouthpiece—the British Indian Association. Due to their educational backwardness and general attitude of withdrawal, the Muslims remained outside the four important movements that swept over Bengal in the nineteenth century—the Renaissance, the religious reformation, the social reforms and the growth of political agitation. The British Indian Association (1851) was a landlords' body to protect their interests. On 26 July 1876, Surendranath

Banerji founded the Indian Association to form the views of the educated middle classes. Despite declaring the promotion of friendly feelings between Hindus and Muhammadans 'as one of the objects of this association' and including a Muslim aristocrat, Mir Mohammed Ali, as a committee member, the association remained primarily a Hindu association. The Bengal Muslim middle class was still in slumber. 'Consequently, for a period, the community became apathetic and indifferent, and did not exert itself towards any kind of social or political activity, lest it should arouse the suspicion of the rulers. The Muslims were at this time in the deepest depths of degradation and decay.'[11]

A small undercurrent of Muslim awakening was, however, developing outside the mainstream of the nineteenth-century's dominantly Hindu Bengal Renaissance. One of the earliest to realize the damage that the withdrawal syndrome was doing to the community was Nawab Abdul Latif (1828–83), originally from Faridpur, who founded the Muhammadan Literary Society (1863) in Kolkata in which he gathered all the upper- and middle-class Muslims of Kolkata. The society propagated that British rule was too powerful to be resisted and too useful to be ignored. He realized the great value that western education and loyalty to the government offered to his community. His role in Bengal was somewhat similar to that of Sir Syed Ahmed Khan's in north India. This society met once a month for many years at Abdul Latif's house and freely discussed various questions of the day. It also held annual conventions where leading scholars, both European and Indian, were invited to present results of scientific experiments. The purpose of these gatherings was two-fold: to create among educated Muslims an interest in the subject and second, to provide an opportunity for friendly social gathering for all classes of Muslims. At times the Viceroy, the Lieutenant-Governor of Bengal, judges of the high court and the elite of Kolkata society—European and Indian—were in attendance. Oriental artifacts would sometimes be exhibited. The Lieutenant-Governor became the society's patron in 1870 and continued to be so till 1895. The society was overtly loyal to the British government and took special care to promptly remove any trace of sedition anywhere. It was because of this that it never came anywhere near the Indian Association. But towards the close of the century, it inevitably started expressing views on important political issues of the day. Thus, it petitioned the Secretary of State strongly supporting the Indian Councils Bill, but opposing the principle of election which, in its opinion, would harm the interests of the backward Muslim community. Nawab Abdul Latif also helped in the founding of the famous Presidency College of Kolkata (1855) and helped in the reorganization of Hooghly College and his own alma mater, the Kolkata madrassa. In fact, his educational work continued till his death in 1893, after which the society gradually petered out.

Unlike the Muhammadan Literary Society, there was considerable political orientation in the next Muslim body that came up, namely, the National Muhammadan Association, founded in 1878 under the leadership of Syed Amir Ali (1849–1928), barrister and honorary magistrate. It declared that 'there was need for a bona fide political body among the Mohammedans, to represent faithfully and honestly to government, from a loyal but independent standpoint, the legitimate wants and requirements of the Mussalman community'. To Amir Ali, therefore, goes the credit for initiating Muslim Bengal into some sort of rudimentary politics, although he himself remained loyal to the British government. His association also had the support of the Hindu elite. Amir Ali acknowledged the great assistance he received from influential Hindus.[12] One of the honorary vice-presidents of the association was Raja Indra Chandra Singh of Paikpara. There were six Hindus among the honorary members, including Surendranath Banerji, Kristo Das Pal and Maharaja Jatindra Mohan Tagore, and there were twenty-nine Hindus among the subscribing members. Two even served on the management committee. Unfortunately, this healthy trend was not followed by other Muslim associations in Bengal, thereby preventing the possibility of Hindu–Muslim unity on a common social and political platform. The organizers of the association felt that 'the welfare of the Mohammedans is intimately connected with the well-being of the other races of India'. The association directed its attention to social liberation and educational activities of the Muslims. It achieved a crowning success when its memorandum on education of 6 February 1882, submitted to Lord Ripon, provided the basis for Lord Dufferin's famous resolution of 15 July 1885 on Muslim education and Muslim employment in public services. In 1883, in the Bengal Council, Mohammad Yusuf demanded reservation of seats for Muslims, but Amir Ali's association suffered an eclipse when its moving spirit was appointed a judge of the Calcutta High Court in 1890 and was forced to withdraw from public activities.

Several other organizations were formed, like the Muhammadan Reform Association (1896) devoted to the education of Muslims. With the founding of the Indian National Conference (1883) and of the Indian National Congress on 28 December 1885, it was evident that the Hindu upper and middle classes were willing to plunge into direct political action. A few like Amir Ali did feel that unless the political activities of the Muslims 'ran on parallel with that of their Hindu compatriots they were certain to be submerged in the rising tide of the new nationalism.' But, on the whole, it became clear that few Muslims in Bengal were willing to give up their loyalty to British raj and come out in support of the Congress. Most of them had become more attuned to Syed Ahmed's line of total support to British authorities and even followed Ahmed's Patriotic Association (formed in 1885) to oppose the Congress. Abdul Latif, on behalf of the Muhammadan Literary Society, regretted their inability to accept the invitation to join the Congress session in Kolkata in 1886 'as they do not anticipate any benefit to be derived from the deliberations of the Congress'. The National Muhammadan Association also sent a similar reply of regrets. Some Muslims like Abdul Hamid Khan Yusufzai, editor of the Bengali paper *Ahmadi*, criticized this attitude, but Lord Dufferin appreciated this refusal. Thus there was a clear divergence of opinion among Hindus and Muslims in Bengal on joining the Congress. 'The Muslims were conscious of the fact that the Hindus were far more advanced than themselves in every sphere of life. Hence it will be unwise for them to join hands with the Hindus in political affairs.'[13]

One important reason why the on-going process of the creation

of a 'nation in making' was frustrated was the close identification of
the activities of extremist Congress groups with Hindu motifs,
deities and rituals. This started with the Hindu Mela—no one
knows why it had to be called that rather than Bengal Mela—and
went on with Bal Gangadhar Tilak starting the Ganapati and Shivaji
festivals, both of which had repercussions in Bengal. There was a
general move to organize them on Hindu lines. The target was no
doubt British rule, but inevitably there was an unintended anti-
Muslim fallout. All appeals to the past could only mean the Hindu
past. Patriotic writers invariably glorified not merely ancient Indian
culture, but its predominantly Hindu texture. They also began to
dwell upon the struggles of the Rajputs, the Marathas and the Sikhs
as instances of early urges for freedom. As it happened, all these
people had as their adversaries Mughal rulers, and the Hindu trend
in the national sentiment was, therefore, intensified with very
unhappy consequences. The report of the Sedition Committee (1918)
commented that the religious practices of the Ganapati festival were
similar to those of Muharram. Whether in this and in promoting
the Shivaji festival, which revived bitter memories of Shivaji battling
the Mughals and other Muslim powers, Tilak deliberately wanted to
hurt the Muslims is doubtful; but clearly these had the unintentional
effect of driving the two communities apart. Muslim sentiments
were hurt by Tilak justifying Shivaji's killing of Afzal Khan, and his
strong support to the movement against cow slaughter. When no
less a patriotic leader than Bipin Chandra Pal could announce that
'in honouring Shivaji we were honouring the Hindu ideal', Bengali
Muslim sentiment found it difficult to work on a common platform.
They felt impelled to go along with leaders like Nawab Salimullah to
think that their path was different from that of the Hindus, and that
they must strive for separate safeguards for their community.

Thus a great divide had already been created when the partition
of Bengal, a sinister move to curb the influence of the anti-British
Hindu elite, took place on 16 October 1905. No doubt the anti-
partition agitation was the first of the great people's movement
against colonial rule. But, paradoxically, except for a handful like
barrister Abdulla Rasul, the majority of the Muslims in East Bengal

supported partition and viewed the great anti-partition agitation as an attempt to deny them an opportunity to have a Muslim majority province and as an all-out effort by the Hindus to continue their dominance—an aspect that has been ignored by Indian national historians. In 1904, Lord Curzon toured East Bengal and appealed to Muslim separatists. In retrospect, the anti-partition agitation, the Swadeshi movement and even the overtly Hindu armed revolutionary movement aggravated the ill will between the two communities and accentuated the great divide. It made the Bengali Muslims line up with the Muslims of upper India and the Aligarh movement, something they had not done till then. Anti-partition agitators and the terrorists were by and large Hindu bhadralok, who at times unwittingly took an anti-Muslim stance. Bengali Muslims wanted to include among the Aga Khan deputation demands that the 1905 partition of Bengal must continue. Nawab Salimullah and Nawab Ali Chaudhury threatened that in case this was not agreed to, Bengal would not cooperate with the deputation.[14]

In fact, a subtle difference between the Bengali Muslims and the upper India Muslim leadership now appeared. The latter wanted to avoid taking sides on a controversial issue like the partition of Bengal, while for the Muslim leadership of East Bengal, the continuance of the partition was necessary for protecting the interests of Muslims. Eventually, the Aga Khan deputation to Lord Minto at Shimla on 10 October 1906, comprising nobles, ministers, great landlords, lawyers and merchants, only raised the demand for separate electorates and weighted representation for Muslims in all elected bodies, and did not raise the question of partition of Bengal at all. This somewhat peeved the East Bengal Muslims.[15] The Aga Khan deputation was primarily championing the cause of the Muslim landed aristocracy and Muslim soldiers in the army. Bengali Muslims were insignificant both as zamindars and as army recruits and could thus be ignored. The Aga Khan deputation to Minto pleading for a separate electorate and larger representation in services included only five members from Bengal and one from East Bengal and Assam, all of them aristocrats.

Leaders like Salimullah now turned to other political experiments.

He successfully converted an All India Muslim Educational Conference convened at Dhaka in December 1906 into a political conference out of which was born the All India Muslim League. He had issued invitations to all members to continue sitting after the Educational Conference was formally over and circulated the outlines of a plan for a Muhammadan Confederacy and requested them to consider it. The resolution adopted at this meeting announced the following objectives:

a) To promote among Musalmans of India feelings of loyalty to the British government and to remove any misconception that may arise as to the intentions of the government with regard to any of its measures.

b) To protect the political rights and interests of Musalmans of India and respectfully to present their needs and aspirations to the government.

c) To prevent the rise among Musalmans of India of any feeling of hostility towards other communities without prejudice to the objects of the League.

On 30 December, at a Muslim Educational Conference held in Dhaka, Nawab Salimullah moved a resolution for establishing a Muslim political association—the All India Muslim League—to respectfully present their needs and aspirations to the government. The resolution also pledged loyalty to the British government. The League had its next session at Karachi in December 1907. The headquarters were shifted to Lucknow in 1910. 'Thus what was born in the soil of East Bengal came to be nurtured in the United Provinces of Agra and Oudh under the Urdu group.'[16] The seeds of separation in politics had been sown, obstructing the growth of inter-communal nationalism.

While a generally non-communal Amir Ali undertook the task of providing leadership to the London branch of the Muslim League from 1908 onwards, Muslim leaders in the Congress tried their best to thwart this growth of separatism in Muslim politics. They met in Kolkata after the Congress session held there in 1906 and formed a political association named the Indian Mussalman Association to counteract the League's separatism. One of the vice-presidents was Muhammad Ali Jinnah, a staunch nationalist at that time.

For Salimullah and his followers, the annulment of the partition in 1911 was a great blow. Obviously, for the upper Indian Muslim leadership, this was not important. In disgust Salimullah, in quest for a Muslim federal political body, persuaded Fazlul Huq, who had joined government service as a deputy magistrate, to resign and join politics. This marked the advent on the stage of a great leader who was destined to be called Sher-e-Bangal or Bengal Tiger in later years, and who was destined for four decades to play a major role in Bengal politics and thereafter in the politics of East Pakistan. Fazlul Huq, like so many others, joined both the Congress and the League and, in fact, at one time became a general secretary of the Congress. In April 1914, in the Bengal Legislative Assembly, Huq expressed his bitterness over the annulment of partition and warned that for the Muslims there may be a parting of ways. But he was soon to outgrow this phase and turn more radical. With the death of Nawab Salimullah, who had almost retired from politics after the annulment of the partition, in January 1916, the age of 'courtier upper class Muslim politicians' was over. The new, more modern type of politician was typified in Fazlul Huq. They never had much fondness for the politics of the Aligarh School, which comprised nobles, the landed aristocracy and titled gentlemen.

The growing assertiveness of Muslims in Bengal found reflection in increased quotas for Muslims in government jobs and in making a show of observing religious customs not acceptable to the Hindu community, in particular cow sacrifice in public on religious occasions. Not to be outdone, Hindus would also insist on taking their Durga immersion processions along routes where mosques stood and even played loud music near those mosques. This contributed enormously to dividing the two communities, at times erupting in communal violence. Agent provocateurs started such violence and anti-social elements took advantage. There are many theories to explain the growth of Muslim separatism. These range from the rationalist historians attributing it to the British policy of divide and rule, to the fundamentalist Islamic historians emphasizing the absurdity that the Muslims had been a separate nation from the time the Arabs came to India under Mohammed Bin Qasim in the eighth century. But there were clearly, as already noted, deep-seated economic, social and political reasons. These were not appreciated by Indian nationalists who ignored them and simplified things by pretending that these differences did not exist. But, interestingly, separatism in the political sense was unknown till the 1930s.

2

FROM CAMARADERIE TO CONFLICT

Belying signs of separatism, there was a thaw in Hindu–Muslim relationship during the second decade of the twentieth century. Following the reunion of the two Bengals in 1911, there was a new phase of rapprochement and a new attitude of acceptance of each other, with their differences and differing interests. For several years during the First World War (1914–18) and afterwards, the Congress and the League used to hold their sessions one after another in the same town, enabling common delegates to attend both. Fazlul Haq was one such. The Congress–League scheme forged at the 1916 Lucknow session of the Congress by a group of experts headed by Motilal Nehru and Jinnah was a new beacon-light for the future. From the widely accepted scheme (1916) through the Non-Cooperation–Khilafat Movement there followed an unprecedented Hindu–Muslim togetherness in Bengal, which lasted for about ten years until the drafting of C.R. Das's Bengal Pact, the high noon of Hindu–Muslim camaraderie in Bengal. Chittaranjan Das was one political leader who was acceptable to both Muslims and Hindus. A major section of Muslim leaders respected him. Despite Congress' non-cooperation movement (1920–24), dyarchy as envisaged by the Montague-Chelmsford reforms came into force and elections were held to elect the legislature where ministers were to deal with the 'transferred' subjects while the 'reserved' subjects stayed with the Governor. The working of the dyarchy for about a decade provided an opportunity for Hindus and Muslims, despite the strain, to work together.

No Congress candidate contested for the Bengal Legislative Council in 1920 in pursuance of the party's boycott decision. The liberals (formerly moderates) had a free run. In a house of 140 in which officials and nominated members numbered twenty-six, there were fifty-seven elected Hindus and thirty-nine elected Muslim members. Governor Lord Ronaldshay appointed Surendranath Banerji, Pravash Chandra Mitter and Nawab Ali Chaudhury of Mymensingh as ministers to deal with the transferred subjects. They served the full term of the Council from January 1921 till the end of 1923. The Muslim minister, Nawab Ali Chaudhury, who was elected president of the Central National Mohammadan Association after Salimullah's death, was a zamindar without any formal education. He was chosen in preference to the highly educated Abdullah Suhrawardy because he was from East Bengal. Otherwise, all three would have represented West Bengal.

An emerging difference between Hindu and Muslim legislators became evident even in the discussion in the Council on Surendranath's amending bill on Curzon's anti-democratic Kolkata Corporation Act of 1899 restoring self-government in the corporation. Taxpayers were to elect 80 per cent of the municipal commissioners, who would elect the mayor and the chief executive officer. The majority of Muslim members, led by Syed Nasim Ali of the Muslim League, demanded a separate electorate for the Muslim seats and an increase in the number of reserved seats for Muslims from twelve, which the bill had provided. This was despite opposition from Abdullah Suhrawardy and some other Muslim councillors affiliated to the Khilafat Party. Suhrawardy challenged Nasim Ali to contest any member of the Khilafat Party in any ward in Kolkata to prove his claim that the Bengal Provincial Muslim League was the true representative body of Muslims in Bengal. Eventually, the principle of separate electorates was accepted, reflecting the majority Muslim view.

A straw in the wind was the unnecessary controversy over the government grant to the newly established Dhaka University promised by the government as a sop to East Bengal Muslims, some of whom felt aggrieved by the annulment of the partition and the resultant loss of Dhaka's importance. From having been a provincial capital, Dhaka had become only a district town with the divisional commissioner's headquarters. An unfortunate agitation against it was started by, of all people, Ashutosh Mukherjee, a great educationist and judge, who felt that this would affect the standing of Kolkata University. Lord Hardinge announced, as a compromise, that the new university would cover only the city of Dhaka and a radius of 10 miles and would be essentially a residential university. While this compromise satisfied the West Bengal Hindus, some of them agitated and were successful in depriving Dhaka University of the annual contribution of Rs 5 lakh from the government of India. In that process, they created animosity between Muslims and Hindus and between East and West Bengal. Educated Hindu opinion simply failed to gauge the East Bengal Muslim's hurt feelings and to appreciate how much this new university could do in eradicating ignorance and spreading the light of education in backward East Bengal. We cannot do better than to recall the appeal made by the respected leader, Fazlul Huq, in the course of his intervention in the debate in the Council on this issue:

> To my mind the Dhaka University became an eyesore to the men at the helm of the Calcutta University ever since Lord Hardinge proclaimed its establishment, though this proclamation was merely the fulfillment of a long-promised and long-desired decision of the government that had so long been kept in cold storage. I do not want to say much but I would caution my friends of West Bengal who put up objections whenever any money is proposed to be spent for Dhaka—Beware; if you persist in this attitude, it will only create differences between the two communities which will cause serious harm to the administration. I appeal to my friends on behalf not only of the Muslims but of the people of East Bengal in general not to object to the allotment of the fund proposed for the Dhaka University.

Khwaja Muhammad Azam of the Dhaka nawab family observed:

> The major part of the total income of the Bengal government
> is collected from East Bengal but is spent for West Bengal;
> we do not object to it. What I do not understand, however,
> is the attitude of the people of West Bengal in objecting to
> the Dhaka University a few lakh rupees which was intended
> to be spent for that university but could not be spent so
> long. Nor do I understand why the Calcutta University
> should be so envious of the Dhaka University.

The meaningless controversy definitely sowed the seeds of communal division in Bengal. But there were silver linings. Many conservative Hindus supported the scheme for Dhaka University and voted with Muslims against the proposal to give women the right to vote.

By 1923, the Swarajya Party contested the Calcutta Corporation elections with the approval of the Congress leadership. With their getting a majority in the Calcutta Corporation, the spotlight shifted to the corporation. C.R. Das became mayor, H.S. Suhrawardy deputy mayor and Subhas Chandra Bose chief executive officer. Five aldermen were also elected by Swarajya Party members, including luminaries like Rabindranath Tagore and scientist Sir J.C. Bose.

The Bengal Pact, 1923

Now Chittaranjan Das, in a determined effort to break the communal deadlock and win back the general support of the Bengal Muslims, drafted his historic Bengal Pact (1923), a shining example of an instrument that could bring the Muslims and the Hindus of Bengal together. The following were the main terms:

a) The number of members of the two communities would be decided by their respective strength in Bengal's population and the two communities would vote separately to elect their members.

b) The Muslims would have 60 per cent and the Hindus 40 per cent of the seats in local self-government institutions.

c) Fifty-five per cent of government appointments would be

Muslims, but 80 per cent of the vacancies would be filled by them until the overall percentage of 55 per cent was reached.

d)   Music near mosques, usually a standard excuse for Hindu–Muslim riots, was to be banned.

e)   Killing of cows for religious purposes on Bakr-Id, a standard pretext for starting communal violence, was to be permitted and nobody was allowed to object to it.

f)   A committee with an equal number of Muslims and Hindus would be appointed in every subdivision to supervise the implementation of these terms.

The Bengal Pact, Chittaranjan's masterstroke, did win for him the support of the Bengal Muslims, but cost him substantial Hindu support. But it was rejected at the Congress session (1923) at Kakinad presided over by Mohammed Ali. Again it was endorsed by the Bengal Provincial Conference of 1924, showing that the majority of the Hindu Congressmen defied their own central leadership and preferred to go along with Chittaranjan Das in what they perceived to be in Bengal's larger and long-term interest. But the Bengal Pact, in some respects the high watermark of Chittaranjan's political career, remained a subject of heated debate. Chittaranjan was so agitated when the Kakinad Congress refused to endorse the Bengal Pact that he confided that he would wash his hands off all-India politics and confine his activities to Bengal.[1]

In the elections to the Second Legislative Council (1924–26), the Swarajya Party, a group within the Congress itching to take part in the elections under C.R. Das's charismatic leadership and fortified by Congress's approval to join the election, stormed the bastion of the Liberal Party. Surendranath Banerji himself lost to a young unknown doctor, Bidhan Chandra Roy, who fought as an independent candidate with the support of the Swarajya Party. C.R. Das became leader of the fifty-four-member Swarajya group in the Council. The Nationalist Party, led by Byomkesh Chakraborty, had nineteen members and usually voted with the Swarajists. The Muslim members usually sided with the government. Lord Lytton, the Governor, invited Chittaranjan, the leader of the largest party, although it did not command an absolute majority, to form the government. This move met with strong opposition from the British community and its spokesman, the *Statesman*. But Chittaranjan declined. After all, the Swarajya Party's avowed object was not to form any government but to oppose the government at every step and to create a deadlock and show the hollowness of the Mont-Ford (Montague-Chelmsford) reforms. In retrospect, this was perhaps an unwise decision from the bhadralok point of view. Lytton now appointed A.K. Fazlul Huq, a one-time protégé of Nawab Salimullah, but till recently a Congress leader, A.H. Ghuznavi and Surendranath Mullick as ministers, signalling the shift of political gravity in Bengal for the first time to Muslims. As Surendranath Mullick's election was set aside by the court, Huq and Ghuznavi stayed as the only two ministers and they carried on with the support of the officials, the Europeans, the old liberals and some friends. Thus it was the 1924 Council election that, for the first time, put Muslims in a dominant position in the politics of modern Bengal.

After the very first meeting of the Second Legislative Council, a resolution moved by J.M. Sengupta and eloquently supported by C.R. Das for the release of all prisoners detained under the Bengal Regulation Act of 1818 without trial was passed by seventy-six to forty-five votes. This put the government in a predicament. Law and order was the Governor's 'retained' subject. Sir Abdur Rahim, member of the Governor's Executive Council, had a dig at the Swarajists wondering how those who wanted to do away with these laws would refuse to take the responsibility for administration. Das' retort was 'I can assure Sir Abdur Rahim that we should take over the responsibility for the administration the moment the entire responsibility therefore devolves on the people.'

The Council passed two more resolutions—one urging the release of all prisoners convicted of political offences and the other calling for the repeal of all those laws under which persons had been convicted. Emboldened by such success, the Swarajists moved a no-confidence motion against the ministers, but this was defeated by one vote. Unfortunately, this incident acquired a communal overtone with agitated Muslim demonstrators rushing into the Council chamber (the Town Hall) urging members not to 'join the conspiracy for removal of Muslim ministers'. The Swarajya strategy of voting against the budget proposals with the help of others in the Opposition further heightened tensions. The Governor himself held a secret conference with some members to garner support for the budget. Das with his followers left the chamber in protest. Thereafter, the budget proposals were passed. But the Opposition took a stand on the salary of the ministers and, despite the Governor's best efforts, repeatedly disallowed the salaries. The motion was moved by Dr Bidhan Chandra Roy, who had already made a mark as a legislator. The ministers had to resign and the Governor himself took over the administration of the transferred subjects. Thus the Swarajists succeeded in their main objective of bringing the dyarchy of the 1919 Act to a halt temporarily. But in that process they had to pay a heavy price of kindling the communal flame.

Another effort was made by the Governor to make the system work when he appointed Raja Manmothnath, Raja of Santosh, and Nawab Ali Chaudhury as ministers, but the Swarajya Party moved a cut motion reducing their salary and got it passed with the support of Fazlul Huq. The government then decided not to appoint ministers any more, but to suspend dyarchy till the end of the second term of the Council (January 1927).

The basic disagreement between Gandhi and Chittaranjan Das on the issue of the attitude to terrorists continued. It came to the surface in 1924 when a young terrorist, Gopinath Saha, in trying to assassinate Sir Charles Tegart, the notorious anti-terrorist commissioner of police of Kolkata, shot dead another Englishman, Day, an officer of Kilburn & Co., by mistake on 11 January. Gopinath expressed his regret at killing an innocent man, but showed great courage when he was being hanged, declaring, 'Every drop of my blood will sow the seeds of freedom in the homes of Bengal'. Sympathy and emotion surged up all over Bengal. The Bengal Provincial Congress Committee at its annual conference held at Sirajgunge on 1 June 1924 passed a resolution acknowledging the supreme self-sacrifice of Gopinath Saha. It stated: 'This conference while denouncing and dissociating itself from violence and adhering to the principle of non-violence, appreciates Gopinath Saha's ideal of self-sacrifice, misguided though it is, in respect of the country's best interest and expresses respect for such self-sacrifice'. This was opposed by Gandhi. He moved a resolution at the Ahmedabad session of the All-India Congress Committee (AICC) condemning the killing of Day by Gopinath Saha. But Chittaranjan moved a counter-resolution reproducing the text of the Sirajgunge resolution. The AICC rejected Chittaranjan's motion and approved Gandhi's motion by a very narrow majority of seventy-eight to seventy. This reflected the strength of both sides, as also the fact that Gandhi's support base in the Congress was only a shade larger than that of Chittaranjan Das.

The disagreement between Gandhi and C.R. Das was visibly growing. The government took advantage of this situation by hitting the extremists hard. Subhas Bose, chief executive officer of the Calcutta Corporation and Das's main lieutenant, was arrested on a charge of encouraging terrorism. Even Gandhi saw through this game and hurried to Kolkata for a conciliatory dialogue with Das, which resulted in an agreement between the two.[2] All the hard work and the immense tension was beginning to tell on Chittaranjan's health. Even during the short span of life left to him he followed a mixed policy of confrontation and conciliation with the British raj. He vehemently opposed a draconian ordinance issued on 5 October 1924 for suppressing terrorists and the arrest of Subhas Bose and several others under this ordinance. He left Shimla, where he was convalescing, and rushed to Kolkata on 27 October to lead the protest demonstration. He had to be carried to the Council chamber on a stretcher, accompanied by Dr B.C. Roy and others. The Bill was defeated. From the mayor's chair Chittaranjan announced that 'Mr Subhas Chandra Bose is no more a revolutionary than I am'. But his conciliatory tone was evident both from a published pamphlet (29 March 1925) in which he condemned violence and from his presidential address at the Faridpur session of the Bengal Provincial Congress (2 May 1925) where he offered a compromise to the British Raj on his terms. These terms were:

First, government should relinquish for good the repressive powers assumed by them and, in proof of their bona fides, should release all political prisoners.

Secondly, they should make a firm commitment of complete Swaraj for India within the British Empire and this commitment should be unalterable.

Thirdly, pending grant of independence, the administrative machinery should be moulded in such a way as to serve as the foundation for the complete independence to come.

The nature and manner of moulding of administrative machinery to suit complete independence should be determined by mutual discussion.

We, on our part, shall undertake not to encourage any seditious movement by word, deed or conduct—of course this is not done now—and we shall try in all possible ways to eradicate such suicidal movements from the land.

The strength and energy that are now being misdirected against the government would find their fulfillment in full utilisation for the real good of the country.

If government would not heed our proposals for a compromise, we would generate among the masses in the whole country a general atmosphere of disobedience of the government. Vanquished in our struggle for freedom, this is the ultimate weapon in our hand—a weapon sure and unfailing.

Chittaranjan's gesture coincided with a significant change in British attitude. The British authorities realized that with Gandhi having withdrawn from active politics for a while, Chittaranjan's leadership of the Congress offered the best prospects of a settlement. There began what an observer has called a long-range flirtation between Lord Birkenhead, the new secretary of state for India, and C.R. Das.[3] Birkenhead entered into negotiations with Chittaranjan Das through Governor Lord Lytton and an intermediary.[4] In a speech in the House of Lords, Birkenhead appealed to all Indians to move forward on the lines of Chittaranjan's appeal and cooperate with the government. On his part, he expressed his willingness to lay aside all suspicions from his mind. Das had also in his memorable speech at Faridpur on 1 May 1925 declared that he was prepared to negotiate if the government divested itself of its discretionary powers and announced an amnesty for all political prisoners. But within six weeks, Chittaranjan, while convalescing at Darjeeling, breathed his last on 16 June 1925. Birkenhead's promised statement on India was still to come. Needless to say, his untimely death put an end to a strong possibility of a Congress–British political settlement. It plunged Kolkata and the whole country into unprecedented grief. To quote from his daughter's biography: 'If the country had advanced along the path indicated by my father at Faridpur with the leaders forsaking the illusion of leadership and their vanity, we would have obtained complete independence long ago and would not have to partition the country for gaining independence'.[5] Gandhi, who was at Khulna when Chittaranjan died, rushed to Kolkata and endeared himself to Bengalis by joining the funeral procession and making a number of grief-stricken statements.

Before his death, Chittaranjan Das had gifted his house to the nation 'in order to divest himself of the last vestige of wealth that he possessed in the world', to use Mahatma Gandhi's own words.[6] Even on his death-bed, he tried to solve the deteriorating communal situation over matters in the Calcutta Corporation. The burial of a Muslim *pir* inside the municipal market had created much controversy, primarily among non-Bengali Muslims. He told Mahatma Gandhi, who spent five days with him at Darjeeling 'Neither Suhrawardy nor Subhas Bose had any authority to allow the *pir* to be buried in the Hogg market. A wrong has been committed, but we cannot wound the feelings of the Mussalmans— it will be a greater wrong to exhume the body.' He asked an associate to 'go and see Sarat and ask him to speak to Suhrawardy so that everything may be smoothly done. If other communities raise the proposal for exhuming the body, and the Muslim members then resign, I shall also resign with them. But if any sect among the Muslims claims the body and has it removed for burial at some other place then troubles will be over.'[7] That was his practical solution to what had become an emotive communal issue.

The unexpected and untimely passing away of C.R. Das, a giant among men, created a vacuum in both all-India and Bengal politics.

It not only stopped a possible political settlement with the British government, but also prevented the emergence of a joint Hindu–Muslim front in Bengal. He was the only national leader whom both the Hindus and the Muslims trusted. Not only was his death mourned by stalwarts like Gandhi and Rabindranath Tagore and by political leaders like Motilal Nehru, M.A. Jinnah, Maulana Azad and Muhammad Ali, but even by common people everywhere, Hindu and Muslim alike. One has to go through the highly emotional comments of the Muslim newspapers and periodicals of Bengal to understand the depth of their feelings. A typical comment was that of *Muhamadi* (Bengali) which described Chittaranjan's death 'as God's extreme punishment to our countrymen'.[8] Also it was he who first perceived the need for the Congress to go beyond city politics and reach out to the masses in outlying areas. In doing so, he not only made a very special effort to attract the Muslims but also co-opted into the provincial Congress hierarchy district Hindu leaders like J.M. Sengupta, a barrister in Chittagong, who had successfully led labour agitations around 1917, B.N. Sasmol, a Mahishya caste leader of Contai, Midnapore, who had led an effective non-cooperation movement in Midnapore and Anil Roy, who had led a successful anti-Union Board Movement in Bankura in 1921. He made a special effort to bring the armed revolutionaries within the fold of the Congress and thus enlist their patriotic fervour and organizational skill for the Congress cause.

There were two main groups, the roughly East-Bengal-based Anushilan Samiti, and the West Bengal-based Jugantar Party. Both accepted Das' leadership under an informal agreement, though not officially. But this carried an inherent danger of driving the Muslims away by excessive dependence on Hindu religious myths, ideals and motifs. Das was eminently successful by 1921 in roping in the newly emerging Muslim leadership and building up a joint Hindu–Muslim anti-British political front. Some of the Muslim leaders who came under his banner were Abdullahal Barqui of Dinajpur, Maniruzzaman Islamabadi of Chittagong, Akram Khan of 24-Parganas, Shamsuddin Ahmed of Kushtia, Ashraffuddin Ahmad Chaudhury of Tippera, Tamizuddin Khan of Jessore and H.S. Suhrawardy of Kolkata and

Medinipore. Tamizuddin Khan, a former Congressman and subsequently a front-rank Krishak Praja Party member and Muslim League leader, has in his memoirs paid this tribute to Das's heroic effort to build a composite platform: 'The crowning achievement was the Bengal Pact of 1923 under which the Muslims in Bengal were to be given 55 per cent of the government jobs and 60 per cent of membership of local bodies in Muslim majority districts.' This was a unique effort at co-opting the educated Muslims among the bhadralok. It was opposed by some Hindu Congressmen and some Muslims. Abdullah Suhrawardy accused Das of playing into the hands of religious zealots: 'You have given so many concessions to the Muslims that tomorrow they will say that all Muslims must grow beards. I refuse to grow a beard.' Tamizuddin Khan himself bemoaned that 'Hindu–Muslim differences were of such a radical character that the influence of one single man, however strong, could only provide a temporary diversion of the natural course of history, but it could hardly lead to different destiny unless some social upheaval uprooting the causes that divided the two people intervened.'[9]

No such social upheaval occurred. Nor was generosity, the one quality that the Hindu bhadralok needed to show towards the downtrodden Muslims, shown. This fomented bitterness amongst the Muslims. After Das's death in 1925, a great blow to the development of Bengali nationalism, the Krishnanagar session of the Bengal Provincial Congress Committee (1926), under sustained pressure from a majority spearheaded by the terrorist-dominated Karmi Parishad, rejected the Bengal Pact. Das had steamrolled the Hindu terrorists and Muslim leaders into joining the Congress, but failed to integrate them into it. Inevitably, once his dominant leadership was no more, they parted company. After the abrogation of the Bengal Pact by the Kakinad session of the Indian National Congress, the Muslims in large numbers felt betrayed and deserted the Congress. Among them was the well-known Swarajya leader H.S. Suhrawardy. They found a new pasture in the Muslim League, till then viewed by Bengali Muslims as a party of the propertied classes and therefore with only marginal influence. The first sign of this estrangement was that the Muslims fought the Calcutta Corporation election in 1927 separately. Unfortunately, the one Bengali politician who could have changed the general orientation of the Congress in favour of the interests of the Hindu rentiers and urban professionals, namely, Subhas Bose was kept away during long periods of incarceration at home and abroad (Mandalay) or externment in Europe.

3

UNMAKING OF A NATION
(1927–37)

The promise of united action against foreign rule was belied during the decade 1927–37 and thereafter. After Das there was no one who could retain the general loyalty of both the communities. Muslim separatism now started asserting itself and staking its claim to political power. Both Fazlul Huq's Krishak Praja Party (KPP) and the Muslim League, already conscious of the demographic preponderance of the Muslims over Hindus, started systematically to stake claim to all institutions of patronage, power and influence hitherto the preserve of Hindus. They adopted policies and programmes to counteract Hindu bhadralok control of these institutions and all walks of life. From 3–5 April 1926, and again from 11–25 July, Kolkata exploded into communal violence on a scale unknown before, starting with the standard issue of Arya Samaj processions playing music in front of mosques. This accentuated the process of communal polarization.

It was during these riots that poet Nazrul Islam wrote his inspiring song *Durgamagiri kantara moru dustara parobara he* asking Hindus and Muslims to unite. This was sung as the opening song at the Provincial Political Conference at Dhaka (1926) as also at the annual conference of the Bangiya Muslim Sahitya Samaj. But, by and large, his message was unheeded. The much talked of composite culture of Bengal gave way to the political stance of 'Islam in danger' accepted by large sections of Bengali Muslims. There were repercussions of the Kolkata riots at Patuakhali, Barisal and elsewhere. According to official reports, between 1922 and 1927 there were 112 communal riots during which 450 died and about 5,000 were injured.

There were two standard starting points. For the immersion of Durga idols on the occasion of Durga puja, Hindu processions would insist on playing music near mosques and Muslims would object to being disturbed while praying. Or during Bakr Id, Muslims would make it a point to kill cows in the open, thereby hurting the religious sentiments of orthodox Hindus. Incidents such as these aided by agent provocateurs would lead to ugly communal disturbances negating the efforts of so many right-thinking people (among both communities) who would have liked to see them living as friends. As always happens, anti-social elements would invariably take advantage of the situation to engage in widespread looting and destruction of property. Why the Durga puja or Janamashtami processionists could not be advised to avoid routes where mosques stood, or at least agree to stop playing music while passing by mosques, and why Muslims had to perform cow slaughter in the open and not in secluded places, will never be known. The city of Dhaka for years fell victim to this almost annual ritual of communal violence following a set pattern where anti-socials of both communities would temporarily take over, and decent people on both sides would withdraw indoors for a few days. Officialdom stayed inactive, complicating matters.

As the decade of the 1930s wore on, even separatist politics became increasingly confrontationist. The politically dominant Hindus had ridden roughshod over the genuine Muslim desire for an acceptable communal adjustment in the 1920s. It was now the turn of the Muslims to do the same unto the Hindus in the late 1930s and early 1940s. The Muslims were now fully conscious of their newly acquired political power as a result of a series of constitutional changes. The growing confrontation turned the 1940s into a period of great communal divide from which there was no turning back. The communal riots in Kolkata in 1926 gave the first signal that all was not well with delicate communal relations in Bengal. Politics tended to be dominated increasingly by communal issues. It was in 1927 that the British rulers, for the first time, gave official recognition to the dominance of Muslims in Bengal and the corresponding end of bhadralok dominance. Legislative politics, hitherto the preserve of the Hindu bhadralok, slowly but surely passed under Muslim dominance. There were now five distinct groups: a Muslim upper class group of which Nazimuddin and Suhrawardy were the two main leaders, the Muslim peasantry and professional classes of which Fazlul Huq was the undisputed leader, the Congress-centred Hindu bhadralok class, dominated by the so-called 'big five' of Bengal Congress politics (Sarat Bose, Bidhan Chandra Roy, Nalini Ranjan Sarkar, Tulsi Goswami and Nirmal Chander), a powerful and vocal non-Congress Hindu zamindari class and, last, the Hindu scheduled castes led by Jogendra Nath Mandal. These five broad groups were to attempt different permutations and combinations in legislative politics during the remaining two decades before 1947, more often than not under the manipulative control of British officialdom. The Third Legislative Council (1927–30) started with Sir Abdur Rahim being appointed chief minister on condition that he would select a Hindu minister. As he was unable to select any Hindu and resigned, the Governor appointed Byomkesh Chakraborty and A.H. Ghuznavi. But they lost the confidence vote and resigned. In October 1927, Nawab Mosaraf Hossain and Pravash Chandra Mitter were appointed. Sometime later, the raja of Nasipur replaced Mitter, who had become a member of the Governor's Executive Council.

Transfer of political power to Muslims

In a way, the formal Hindu domination of the politics of Bengal ended around 1927. Since then each successive ministry was headed by a Muslim politician who received the combined support of the elected Muslim MLAs, the Scheduled Caste Federation MLAs, the European MLAs and nominated official members. Thanks to the Congress policy of systematically sending Congressmen into the legislature only for the purpose of wrecking the dyarchy constitution, Muslim leaders in Muslim majority provinces received complete support from the government and developed a vested interest in separatism. This also paved the way for partition.[1] The Communal Award of 1932 also dealt a body blow to the power of the bhadralok. This was vigorously opposed by the Hindus of Bengal. The Hindu Mahasabha accused the Congress of betraying the interests of Hindus.[2] Interestingly, some Muslim leaders like Akram Khan also opposed it and moved a resolution in the Bengal Legislative Council that reservation of seats for the majority community in Bengal was a betrayal of their own interests. But the larger body of Muslims, including Fazlul Huq, welcomed it as a 'distinct advance'.

The composition of political parties in this House was confusing. Most of the Muslim Swarajists led by H.S. Suhrawardy had parted company with their Hindu compatriots and demanded Muslim majority in the Legislative Council in proportion to their strength and also separate electorates for them. The once strong Khilafatist group was slowly disappearing. The Muslim League was as yet inconsequential in Bengal. The most influential party among the Muslims, especially the East Bengal Muslims, was Fazlul Huq's KPP, nominally secular, but with strong Muslim orientation, dedicated to protecting farmers and ryots from exploitation and ameliorating their conditions.[3]

For nearly ten years there was no-holds-barred rivalry between two broad factions in the Bengal Congress led by J.M. Sengupta and Subhas Bose respectively. With this division, and with the Swarajists boycotting the Council from 1929, the Muslim ministers carried the show of managing the 'transferred' departments with the help of official members, Muslims and scheduled caste members in general, and some upper-class Hindu members, including some liberal Congressmen. The ministers did take some concrete legislative measures in the fields of education, local self-government and settlement of the debt burden of the peasantry and safeguarding their rights. This Third Legislative Council was indeed a turning point in the history of modern Bengal. It marked the transfer of effective political power in Bengal from upper-caste Hindus to

Muslims, aided by scheduled caste Hindus and a small section of the Hindu aristocracy. Although the Pakistan slogan and Jinnah's two-nation theory were still far off, there was a gradually emerging divide between Muslim Bengal politics and the politics of the Hindu bhadralok. There was an inevitable hardening of attitudes on both sides. Nationalism in Bengal was relying more and more on developing a Hindu cultural identity in spite of its claims that its ideology was secular. In particular, the terrorist group was unashamedly Hindu. It did not take any steps to attract middle-class Muslims[4] or even the Hindu lower castes. This Hindu divide was further strengthened by the Gandhi–Irwin Pact (1931) and the Poona Pact (1932), which made sure that the Hindu bhadralok would no longer have the final say in the politics of undivided Bengal. Henceforth, a Muslim Bengali, and a Muslim Bengali alone, was likely to be the leader of the government under any constitutional pattern. With Subhas Bose's continued detention and externment abroad, factionalism reared its ugly head in the Congress once again. Some of its members, in protest against the steep reduction of the number of caste Hindu seats in the Council following Gandhi's controversial fast, formed a Bengali Nationalist Party, fought the Congress candidate in the elections to the Central Legislative Council in 1934 and even defeated them in a number of seats.

The growing Hindu–Muslim divide vitiated the proceedings in the Bengal legislature. On the one hand, there was increasing dominance of politics by Muslim politicians who carried majority control in the assembly by sheer electoral arithmetic. They could demand a larger and larger share of government jobs where Hindus had predominated so far, specially the upper and middle echelons. This antagonized a section of Hindus who resented losing their vested interest. There was also another economic basis. The Muslims were the dominant section among the peasantry and these leaders took it as their mission to improve the lot of the famished peasantry by enacting new tenancy laws. Once again this clashed with the economic interests of the Hindu zamindars and other landlords who dominated these sections. This provided a class basis to the Hindu–Muslim divide. All Muslim politicians by and large followed this pattern, whether they were Bengali-speaking leaders from East Bengal like Fazlul Huq, or whether they were West Bengal-based Urdu-speaking leaders like Suhrawardy, or whether they were scions from old nawab families like Nazimuddin.[5] Most of them had started in the Congress and drifted away from it after Chittaranjan's passing away. Interestingly, the Muslim League, despite originating in Dhaka, never had a base in East Bengal until the Second World War. Having for at least two decades been subjected to a system where the overwhelming number of new recruits in the executive services of the provincial government like the Bengal Civil Service were Muslims, and Hindu candidates, despite their educational superiority, were taken into subordinate services, educated Hindu opinion remained sullen and resentful. Instead of viewing it as an inevitable adjustment with reality, some of them viewed it as an invidious discrimination. This attitude of mind played no inconsiderable role in their unwillingness to stay with a Muslim majority in a united Bengal and in their decision to opt for a partition.

During the 1930s, the KPP and the Muslim League represented two contrasting ideologies vying for Muslim Bengali support. The KPP broadly represented tenant and peasant interests while the Muslim League represented the interests of zamindars and the business community. The first emphasized secular aspects like economic disparity and zamindari exploitation, while the second traced the root cause to the disadvantages suffered by the Muslims as a religious under-privileged community and emphasized that the only way the community could remove the state of deprivation was to act politically with a communal identity. There was a third weak stream consisting mostly of intellectually inclined middle class Muslims, who believed in establishing a common identity with a common anti-imperialist stand. But this trend was progressively weakened as the decade of the 1930s wore on.

With deteriorating Hindu–Muslim relations, communal riots unknown in the pre-British days became a recurrent feature in some towns in Bengal and continued during the 1930s. Once again there were many deep-seated causes, the most important being the tendency of anti-social *goondas* to utilize every conceivable occasion of communal friction to create general disorder that would provide them an opportunity for looting and settling score with rivals and opponents. The manipulation of religious symbols in these riots was a standard occurrence. There was growing distrust of the 'other community', which was seen as the enemy in a battle. The true meaning of slogans like *Allahu-Akbar* (God is great) and *Bande Mataram* (homage to the motherland) were simply forgotten, making them war cries underpinning the mutual separation of the two communities. Day-to-day politics inside the Bengal assembly and outside became recriminatory. The Muslims criticized the Hindus for utilizing their majority in the Calcutta Corporation to deny the Muslims elective offices like that of the mayor, deputy mayor and aldermen. The Muslims in Bengal formally stayed out of the Civil Disobedience Movement (1930–34) led by Gandhi. The Hindu bhadralok, already threatened with the loss of its power, further viewed with alarm the Muslim alliance with the Namasudras, or lower-caste Hindu peasantry. The Hindu press was bitterly critical of the Huq ministry's agrarian reforms and, later, the efforts to take away secondary education from the control of the traditionally Hindu-controlled Calcutta University by forming a Board of Secondary Education.

Two relevant administrative reports of those times give interesting insights. The *Bengal Administrative Report* of 1929–30 remarked that 'Muslims and Hindus tended to range themselves in opposite camps on any contentious question' and illustrated this by giving the case of the Primary Education Bill which was turned into a communal issue by the Hindu members in the Council. The Dhaka Disturbance Enquiry Committee gave political jealousy among the educated classes of the two communities since the inauguration of the 'first reforms' as the root cause of all troubles. Each distrusted the other. Distrust bred distrust and the Hindus, instead of giving way to Muhammadans on non-vital points, still offended the Muslims by talk of revenge and threats of economic ruin. An interesting case in point was the somewhat irrational Muslim objection to the word *Shri* (meaning prosperity) or the symbol of the lotus in the Calcutta University motif. The Muslims protested against these and wanted their removal.

End of the Bhadralok's political supremacy

The Government of India Act of 1919 had introduced partial responsible government, enlarged the electorate, but kept 13 per cent of the Council seats reserved for nominated officials. The 1935 Act enfranchised only 13.4 per cent of the adult population of Bengal over twenty years of age. Almost anyone paying any tax had the right to vote. Under dyarchy, franchise qualifications (cess of Re 1 or *chowkidari* tax of Rs 5 a year for rural areas and Rs 1.5 a year for urban areas) were such that many Muslims were left without the right to vote. The 1935 Act enfranchised about 12.6 per cent of the population for the assembly. This was enough to cover the entire Muslim intelligentsia. This Act also substantially reduced the property qualifications (six annas of chowkidari tax and eight annas for municipal tax or cess) and the educational qualifications to completion of upper primary course for men and literacy for women. This substantially increased Muslim voting power. This coupled with the decimation of the Hindu bhadralok power after the MacDonald Award (1932) and the subsequent Poona Pact between Gandhi and Ambedkar of the same year—where Gandhi gave more power to the scheduled castes than even what the MacDonald Award had given—ensured Muslim domination of politics in Bengal with backing from the Hindu scheduled castes.[6]

Another area of acrimony was the control over secondary education by creating through legislation a Secondary Education Board. This was resented by the Hindus. This became the subject matter of a running battle in the Bengal assembly throughout the period from 1937 to 1946. Despite this, general Hindu–Muslim relations until 1944 were not marked by violence or confrontation except in isolated instances. Many individual Hindus including Nalini Ranjan Sarkar and Shyama Prasad Mukherjee served in ministries led by Huq and Nazimuddin. Even many Congress leaders were socially on good personal terms with Muslim leaders. Subhas Bose had a substantial following among Muslims and had several well-known Muslim lieutenants like Ashraffudin Ahmad Chaudhury. Huq's KPP, despite being predominantly Muslim, was essentially a secular party. His personal closeness to the Hindu Mahasabha leader, Dr Shyama Prasad Mukherjee, and Dr Bidhan Chandra Roy, a non-conformist Congress leader, surpassed all barriers.

The reforms of 1935

The political deadlock created by the Ramsay MacDonald Award and the Poona Pact ended with the announcement of the Government of India Act, 1935. In many respects, the 1935 reforms envisaged a constitutional scheme applicable to an independent country in a not too distant future. This Act had a 'federal' component and a provincial component. The federal component with a federal government covering the provinces along with the princely states, the Federal Legislature, the Viceroy's Executive Council and the Supreme Court except the last two was never implemented on account of the Congress Party's strong resentment and the refusal of the majority of the princes to join the federal scheme. But the provincial autonomy that was envisaged was accepted by the Congress in spite of reservations on the veto power vested in the Governor. Other parties also followed suit. All parties, therefore, agreed to take part in the elections to the provincial assemblies as also the proposed Central Assembly.

The Government of India Act of 1935 by giving the Muslims 119 seats and the caste Hindus only 50 (30 out of 80 for general Hindu constituency being reserved for scheduled castes under the Poona Pact) in a House of 250 with twenty-five European members, once again underscored that Bengal politics would be dominated in future by Muslims aided by the so-called scheduled caste Hindus and that the caste Hindus would lose the privileged position they had enjoyed since the beginning of British rule. This was not acceptable to a section of the caste Hindus who almost believed that they had a divine right to rule and refused to cooperate with the Muslim leaders. This further intensified the communal divide. The failure of the Congress leadership in Bengal to win the Scheduled Caste Federation's political support and the latter's steady support to the Muslim League must be considered as a crucial failure of Congress policy.

There can be no doubt that before the mid-1940s, Pakistan was never considered as a serious model by Bengal Muslims. The original Pakistan scheme conceived by Chaudhury Rehmat Ali, a student in Cambridge University in the early 1930s, and blessed by poet Sir Mohamamed Iqbal, did not even include Bengal. It was a nebulous concept and was to comprise Punjab, Sind, Kashmir, Baluchistan, North West Frontier Province and even Afghanistan. The original blueprint was not even clear about the future of the Hindus and the Sikhs in Punjab, who taken together, were only a little less than the Muslims in number. Interestingly, the leadership for the Pakistan Movement did not come from the *mullahs* and the orthodox, but from western-educated, broadly secular-minded Muslim politicians like Jinnah, Liaqat Ali and Suhrawardy who saw in it an opportunity for controlling political power and economic resources for their community. Nor did the Muslim League gain much ground with the slogan before the early 1940s in those provinces where the Muslims were in the majority and controlled political power. Rather it gained unassailable positions in the provinces where the Muslims were in a minority and suffered from a fear of being swamped by the Hindu majority.

True that Fazlul Huq, under political pressure from all sides, joined the League and even moved the so-called Pakistan resolution in Lahore in 1940, but he never believed in the Pakistan concept and all along stood for a non-communal regime where the rights of the Muslims would be amply safeguarded. In fact, Pakistan meant different things to different people. To politicians like Jinnah it was a bargaining counter. To the Muslim masses it provided an escape route from Hindu domination and the possibility of realizing a meaningful separate identity. To the Islamic orthodox groups like the Khaksars, the concept of Pakistan was a misapplication and misuse of Islamic principles. For Jinnah, who was a staunch nationalist till 1930 and adopted the concept of Pakistan only in 1940, it was an instrument of political and economic power and religion had only a secondary role. For Kamruddin Ahmed, a Bengal Muslim League leader, it was essentially a movement of the Muslim middle class against the Hindu middle class.[7] The fear of being

swamped by the majority Hindu community fanned the flames of
Pakistan, especially in those provinces where they were in a minority.
Paradoxically, nearly all the provinces that were destined to form
Pakistan in 1947, namely, Punjab, Sind and North Western Frontier
Province, were outside the Muslim League's domination as late as
1940. So was Bengal till 1943. In the wake of the Pirpur Report, in
all the provinces where Muslims were in a minority they had, to
quote Jinnah, 'sampled Congress rule and were determined not to
submit to any constitution, which would install Congress domination
over the whole country'. Ispahani, an industrialist from Kolkata and
the Muslim League's main financier, noticed an 'almost fanatical
determination amongst Muslims not to be dominated by Hindus
any longer, for it was impossible to achieve economic emancipation
at the hands of the Hindus'.[8] The resignation of the Congress
ministries in seven provinces in 1939 created a vacuum which was
exploited by the Muslim League, specially in provinces like Assam
where in place of a Congress ministry the Muslim League was
allowed to form a contrived coalition by Shadullah. Major political
changes also occurred in Punjab, Sind and Bengal. The Unionists in
Punjab, a non-communal party led by Sir Sikandar Hayat Khan, and
the KPP in Bengal under Huq's leadership were 'coopted into the
Muslim league'.[9] This led to the League, confined till then only to
the towns, reaching the rural agricultural masses. Both Huq and
Sikander Hayat Khan soon got disenchanted. Huq, who never
believed in the two-nation theory, refused to resign from the National
Defence Council as directed by Jinnah in 1940 and revolted against
'Jinnah's arbitrary use of power'. He even resigned from the Muslim
League protesting against the manner in which the interests of the
Muslims in Bengal were being ignored by Muslim leaders of provinces
where the Muslims were in a minority. He also announced that the
policy pursued by the Muslim League was neither Islamic nor
patriotic and served neither the Muslims nor anybody else. He also
complained that the policies pursued by the League were really
leading even the Muslims into political ruin and disaster.

But Huq's joining the Muslim League had given the party a
respectability it never had, and it rapidly grew in strength at the

expense of both the Congress and the KPP. The mantle of Deshbandhu had passed on to Netaji Subhas Bose who was another leader in whom the Muslims had confidence. The fact that Bose had favoured the 1937 offer of Fazlul Huq for a Congress–KPP coalition and that he fought the Calcutta Corporation election under the banner of what was loosely called at that time the Bose–League Pact (1941) illustrate this. Another example was the united movement under Bose's leadership for the removal of the Holwell monument. Significantly, leaders like Ispahani and A.R. Siddique were close friends of both Mohammad Ali Jinnah and Subhas Bose. After Subhas Bose escaped from Bengal, Muslims again felt somewhat leaderless. But it was clear that with the formation of the Indian National Army by Subhas Bose in South-East Asia and their invasion of India in 1943 and by Subhas's regular radio broadcasts addressed to the Indian people, a great deal of enthusiasm was created even among the Muslims of Bengal. After Subhas Bose's disappearance in 1945 there was no turning back and most Muslims irretrievably jumped into the bandwagon of M.A. Jinnah and the demand for Pakistan. Extremism gained ground on both sides and moderates were driven to the wall. All efforts at Hindu–Muslim collaboration such as the Huq–Shyama coalition (1941–43) failed partly on account of intrigues of British officials and there was steady polarization on communal lines and a parting of ways.[10]

Crystallization of the distinct Muslim psychosis

By the 1920s there had been the clear emergence of a Muslim middle class intelligentsia in Bengal, which staked its claim to both political power and job opportunities.[11] It was not a homogeneous group, linguistically, socially or economically. It attracted followers from both the aristocratic *ashraf* and the Muslim ryots and talukdars, although it was not coterminus with either. Some of them were as critical of Islamic fundamentalism and the activities of mullahs as of domineering Hindu attitudes and action. The Bangiya Musalman Sahitya Samiti (32 College Street, Kolkata) founded by Muzaffar Ahmad was the earliest manifestation of this trend. It brought out the *Bangiya Musalman Sahitya Patrika* in 1325 BS. Other examples were *Saogat* (1326 BS) edited by Muhammad Nasiruddin, the monthly *Moslem Bharat* (1327 BS) edited by poet Mozammel Huq, the evening daily *Nabayug* (1925) of which A.K. Fazlul Huq was the proprietor and Muzaffar Ahmad and the poet Nazrul Islam the joint editors. The eternally rebellious poet Nazrul Islam was connected with nearly all these publications. By far his most famous poem *Bidrohi* (The Rebel) was published in the Kartick 1328 BS edition of the *Moslem Bharat*. Nazrul maintained close contact with the freedom fighters and on 21 November 1921, led a procession at Comilla protesting against the Prince of Wales' visit. He himself brought out the weekly *Dhumketu* in 1922, which was stridently anti-British. For a poem titled *Anandamayeer Agamane* (Arrival of the Blissful Mother) in the Puja edition of this weekly in 1922, he was charged with sedition, went underground, was arrested from Comilla and imprisoned in Hooghly Jail where he went on a hunger strike and was released on 15 December 1923. So great was his appeal that Rabindranath dedicated his play *Basanta* to him, and the novelist Sarat Chandra Chatterjee wrote to him greeting him as one of the greatest poets Bengal had produced. He carried on his patriotic activities by editing the weekly *Langol* (Plough), mouthpiece of the Shrameek-Praja-Krishak Group (1925), the *Ganabani* (1933) and *Nabayug* (revived in 1940 with him as editor) and in courting detention a second time in 1930, from which he was released on 4 March after the Gandhi–Irwin Pact.

The Muslim Sahitya Samaj founded by some Dhaka teachers and intellectuals in January 1926 was also an illustration of this secular national trend. Its organ, *Sikha*, declared significantly 'where knowledge is confined and the intellect active, emancipation is impossible'. It also declared that it wanted 'a change of direction in the social and intellectual life of the Muslim society'. Some of the leaders of this group were Kazi Abdul Wadud, Qazi Mutahar Hussain, Abdul Qadir, Kazi Nazrul Islam, Humayun Kabir, the intellectual-politician, and Sheikh Wajed Ali, the writer who joined the group. One of its meetings in 1937 was presided over by Sarat Chandra Chatterjee, the famous novelist, showing its overall non-communal approach. Along with *Sikha*, another journal that provided sustenance to the newly rising Muslim middle class for years was the monthly *Saogat* of Abdul Hussain. The *Saogat* opposed the separate educational stream of madrassas and advocated a common educational stream for both communities 'in order to establish amity in the body politic'. Abdul Hussain even went to the length of castigating Muslims for obstructing through their folly and wretchedness every good initiative of the progressive Hindus. Many of them braved prosecution and social ostracism for their views, some of them went so far as to form a 'League against Mullahism'.

A number of other periodicals published from Kolkata and Dhaka such as *Naoroz* (June 1927), *Ganabani* (August 1926) and *Jyoti* (April 1930, editor Abdul Qadir) reflected this new liberal-humanist spirit among Bengali Muslims, which, unfortunately, became a casualty of the rising crescendo of communal bitterness during the 1930s. The middle-class Muslim had placed high hopes on the Congress–League Scheme of 1916 and on Chittaranjan's Bengal Pact and thereafter on the anti-communal patch-up efforts of Subhas Bose. Bose was a rare bhadralok politician in the post-Das period to earn praise from Muslims. In 1928, in the Bengal Legislative Council, Abdul Karim from Burdwan spoke of the earnest efforts that are being made 'by my young friend Mr. Subhas Chandra Bose, and others of his way of thinking to bring about a relation of amity and cordiality between the two communities'.[12] His continued detention and externment from Bengal frustrated all such efforts. After the death of C.R. Das and the Congress rejection of the pact, the Bengali Muslims were disenchanted with both the Congress and the League. The KPP emerged as the strongest champion of peasant and middle-class rights. This party sought to improve the conditions of ryots by legislation and raise the percentage of Muslims in government jobs. Its moves invariably met with opposition from the Hindu bhadralok.[13] Even the Swarajists bitterly opposed the KPP's proposals during the discussion in the Council on the 1928 Tenancy Act. In December 1925, a KPP-sponsored Tenancy Amendment Bill giving occupancy rights to the ryots was opposed by Hindu interests even at its introduction. There were illustrations of a deep divergence of class interests.

By the mid-1930s, the KPP and the Muslim League, representing conflicting ideologies, were both vying for Muslim support in Bengal. The first reflected peasant and tenant interests, the second zamindar and business interests. The salaried and professional classes were evenly divided. The Muslim League, essentially a party of the upper-class affluent Muslims, had become virtually a defunct body after 1920, when it was overshadowed by the Khilafatists. It was literally put on the shelf on account of Jinnah's opposition to the Khilafat Movement. It was revived in 1934 by Jinnah himself, who had been its staunch opponent earlier, and took over its leadership under Liaqat Ali's persuasion. A Bengal branch was formed only in 1936 when Jinnah visited Bengal. Its main organizers were two Kolkata-based businessmen—M.A. Ispahani and A.R. Siddique. But such were the shifting sands of political loyalty in Bengal that both of them became close allies of Subhas Bose. Soon the League attracted leaders like Nazimuddin and Suhrawardy, both seeking a platform.

The KPP originated from the first All Bengal Praja Conference held at Mymensingh in 1934. It was not a Muslim party by definition, but one does not come across any caste Hindu name among its prominent members, although it had a large scheduled caste base. The leadership was exclusively Muslim, many of them high-class ashrafs. But the party was mainly concerned with improving the conditions of the Muslims and ensuring equal rights for them. The Nikhil Banga Praja Samiti, with Maulana Akram Khan as its secretary, came up in 1934 following the disappointment of many Muslims with the Bengal Tenancy Act, 1928. Soon there was a distinct cleavage along East Bengal–West Bengal lines. For electing a successor to Sir Abdur Rahim, who resigned as president, the delegates from East Bengal supported Fazlul Huq in overwhelming numbers, while the majority of the delegates from West Bengal led by Maulana Akram Khan supported Khan Bahadur Abdul Momen. Another party, the Jamait-i-Ulema-Hind, also had some peripheral influence. Paradoxically, it had elements who were also to oppose the demand for Pakistan on the ground that creating a territorial sub-nation was un-Islamic. Its leadership was largely non-Bengali.

It is difficult to accept Jatindranath De's contention that the

KPP primarily reflected the interests of *jotedars* (landlords) and *sampanna prajas* (affluent farmers) and 'did not really launch a composite movement of the lower strata of Hindus and Muslims against exploitation of the *zamindars*'.[14] His charge that the KPP served only Muslim interests is not supported by facts. There is overwhelming evidence that it espoused the causes of ryots, both Muslim and Hindu. Also, it had a substantial scheduled caste base. It was thus an inter-communal party. Fazlul Huq's election as the secretary of the Nikhil Banga Praja Samiti in 1935, the party renaming itself as the KPP and its open demand for the abolition of zamindari without compensation met with opposition from the landed upper-class Muslim leaders from Kolkata and the western districts, like Akram Khan, Abdur Rahim and H.S. Suhrawardy. They broke away in 1936 to form the United Muslim Party (UMP), which subsequently merged with the Muslim League. It criticized the KPP as not a purely Muslim organization and said it sought its identity among Muslims only in order to serve its own class interests.

As analyzed by Tazeen Murshid, 'lack of consistency, or a certain ambivalence regarding their political destiny and ideological outlook characterised ... the majority of the intelligentsia in the pre-partition period'.[15] Leaders like Fazlul Huq, Suhrawardy, Abul Hashim, Abdul Mansur Ahmad and Maulana Akram Khan were all, in varying degrees, victims of this ambivalence. It also affected their attitudes to British rule, the Congress and the Muslim League, on the concept of Pakistan and the idea of a united Bengal. Whether they came from the ashraf aristocracy—like Abdul Latif, Amir Ali, Nawab Salimullah, or Mir Musharraf Hussain—or rose to ashraf status from rural background like Munshi Maherullah and Danshil Ketabuddin—they were all local reformers with a deep concern for the education of their downtrodden community. They resented the Hindu bhadralok's contempt for the Muslims, his refusal to accept some of the typical vocabulary commonly used by Muslims (for example, *pani* for water) as part of the Bengali language and the refusal of at least some of the Hindu Bengalis to give them the status of bhadralok or even that of Bengali.[16] In a way this attitude was refuted with vengeance in Sheikh Mujibur Rahman's emphatic assertion two decades later that East Bengalis were the true Bengalis and their country the true Bangladesh. Rabindranath Tagore could pinpoint the emerging separate psyche of Muslim Bengal. In his *Ghare Baire* (Home and the World) he expressed his empathy with the Muslim cloth-seller who was bewildered and angry to see his shop full of foreign-marked cloth burnt by the *swadeshi babus*, thus creating a communal divide. The following comments are also of great relevance.

> It is difficult to wish away a real separateness that exists between Hindus and Muslims. If we ignore this separateness in the interest of short-term gains, that in turn also will not respond to our needs. Whenever we have appealed to the Muslim we have looked on him as a mere helper in getting a job done and not as one we look upon as our own. We have not treated him as a true companion, but only as an accessory. Where there is an incongruity between the two they will stay together only so long as it is necessary for them to do so in the interest of overcoming a common external danger. The moment that necessity is over they would start fooling each other in the distribution of the spoils. It is on account of this mistrust that the Muslim has not responded to our call. It is not unreasonable of him to feel that if he can prosper through his separatism that is his obvious choice. The feeling of separateness between Hindus and Muslims was not so intense a little while ago. We had united together so well that the separateness was not visible. But a time came when the Hindu started taking pride only in his being Hindu. If the Muslim had acknowledged the glory of the Hindu and removed himself to the background, the Hindu would no doubt have felt pampered. But the Muslim now raised his Islam precisely on the same token by which the Hindu's Hinduism had become aggressive. He now wanted to be the winner through his Islam form, not by uniting with the Hindus.[17]

In her excellent research work, Tazeen Murshid[18] traces the evolution of Abul Mansur Ahmad during those years from a nationalist and

Congress position to a communalist position in the 1940s through a transitory KPP phase. Initially Mansur Ahmad was not at all anti-Hindu and strongly advocated Hindu–Muslim unity on Chittaranjan's lines. Gradually he became a Muslim communalist in the sense of being exclusively concerned with protecting Muslim interests. In 1944 he joined the Muslim League as he was said to be upset with aggressive Hindu communalism, even refusing to accept the separate characteristics of Bengali Muslims. Driven to a point of extreme communalism he would not acknowledge Rabindranath, Ishwar Chandra Vidyasagar and Bankim Chandra as a part of East Bengal culture, as they neither used East Bengali languge, nor depicted East Bengal Muslim life. Even when he participated in the Bengal Muslim Sahitya Samiti, he strove to perceive it in a communalist role unlike many of the other members of the Samiti. But after Pakistan came into being, bereft of the overwhelming Hindu threat, he became less of an exclusive communalist. He even supported the language movement in East Pakistan for recognition of Bengali as the country's official language. Abdul Mansur Ahmad, in many respects, epitomized the career of many average members of the Bengali Muslim intelligentsia who, during the late 1930s and early 1940s, changed over from nationalist positions to separatist positions on the basis of religion in politics.

The MacDonald Award (1932) and the Poona Pact between Gandhi and Ambedkar ensured that in future Muslims with the help of Hindu scheduled castes would dominate Bengal's legislative politics and the bhadralok Hindus would recede to a secondary position. The newly acquired political strength further accentuated the aggressive Muslim psyche, which tended to browbeat the Hindus much in the same way as the Hindus had done in the yesteryears. The key point of the conflict was the determination of the Hindu bhadralok classes to cling to the social and economic privileges they had enjoyed for one-and-a-half centuries and the equally vocal aspiration of the emerging Muslim middle classes for a share in the privileges denied to them so long. This point was forcefully brought out by a non-politician scientist, Sir P.C. Roy, while addressing a meeting of Muslim young men at Karachi on 26 October 1932.

Hindu Muslim differences were differences only among
intellectuals for loaves and fishes of office. It was a lie to say
that Islam was spread by sword. Hindus should have been
annihilated if this doctrine was true. The real reason for the
spread of Islam was democracy and brotherhood, and
landslides in Hinduism were due to untouchability and the
caste system. For centuries Bengal was ruled by Muslims,
and yet ninety-nine percent of zamindars were Hindus.[19]

Gradually the Muslims in Bengal came to be broadly divided into
three strands—conservatives, moderate and radical. Nazimuddin
and Tamizuddin Khan represented the first, Nausher Ali, Humayun
Kabir and, to an extent, Huq and Suhrawardy, despite strong
differences between the two, represented the second, and Muzaffar
Ahmad and Kazi Nazrul Islam represented the third. Muzaffar
Ahmad, a secular progressive nationalist leader, represented a very
striking case of one who took a leading role in Congress politics, did
his best in association with Nazrul Islam to project an intellectual
approach in the politics of Muslim Bengal and eventually turned to
communism. Born in a bilingual family in Chittagong and having
learnt both Bengali and Urdu, he was attracted to the terrorist
movement, but found it difficult to accept its identification of the
motherland with Goddess Durga and turned to literary pursuits. In
1920, he decided to opt for politics. Deeply influenced by the
Russian Revolution of 1917 and the atheism of Marxism, he gradually
turned to communism and became one of the founders of the
Communist Party operating as a part of the Congress. As a
Congressman he took a leading part in the affairs of the Bengal
Congress while also working as a communist underground worker.
But he, like so many others, was politically ineffective in influencing
the generality of Bengali Muslims who turned to the Muslim League.
Muzaffar Ahmad stayed on in India as several others like Kazi Abdul
Wadud did to become a leading figure of the Communist Party of
India and after 1964 the Community Party of India (Marxist) while
maintaining a close link with the communists in East Bengal. But in
the 1930s and 1940s he was ahead of his time as far as Muslim
Bengal was concerned.

In Nazrul Islam, the secular and nationalist Bengali tradition reached its zenith. The feeling was eloquently expressed by Subhas Bose as chief guest at a reception given to Nazrul at Albert Hall Kolkata on 15 December 1929 on behalf of the 'Bengalee nation' (its chairman was Acharya Prafulla Chandra Roy and the organizers were Md Nasiruddin Abul Kalam, Shamsuddin Ahmed, Abdul Mansur Ahmad, Habibullah Bahar).

The rebel poet Nazrul through his poems has revived mass awakening and patriotism and indeed brought about the magic of revolution in the life of the nation. The influence of his writings on the people is uncommon. Even an unmusical person like me felt like singing his patriotic songs inside the prison. We shall sing Nazrul's battle songs when we go to battles. We shall also sing his songs when we go to the prison. I have had the good fortune to listen to patriotic songs in various provincial languages. But I do not recall listening to such a stirring song as *Durgama Giri*. The dream of Nazrul is not just his own dream, it is the dream of the entire Bengalee nation.[20]

Unfortunately, there were not many takers in Bengal of this dream as the 1930s and the 1940s progressed, and more and more Bengalis surrendered themselves to the galloping cavalcade of separatist and communalist forces. Also, their leaders, Muslims and Hindus, subordinated Bengal's true interests to the dictates from leaders in northern and western India. The pathetic fact remains that the Bengal Muslim Society in the late 1930s and 1940s was not yet ready for rebels like Nazrul Islam and Muzaffar Ahmad, or even the gentle and scholarly Humayun Kabir or the poet Sufia Kamal who were inspired by the best secular humanist traditions of Bengal and upheld the religion of man above all communal considerations. Their psyché opted for communalist and separatist politics at that point of time. It was only after the creation of two Bengals in 1947 that their Bengali psyché could get the upper hand with its inevitable political fallout after a quarter of a century. But in the turbulent 1940s, their mind was dead set on separation and breaking away from Hindu-dominated India.

4

PARTING OF WAYS
(1937–45)

The Government of India Act of 1935, which was brought into effect in 1937, was a very important landmark in the evolution of the Hindu–Muslim relationship. The federal component of the Act was not acceptable to either the Congress or the princes, but the Congress accepted the provincial part of the Act and provincial elections were announced. Dyarchy, which had prevailed in the provinces since 1919, came to an end. For the first time the common masses (still only a pathetic 13 per cent of the population) cast their votes in the general elections to elect legislators, who would form responsible government in the provinces. The political history of Bengal during the eventful years 1937–45 can be divided into:

a) Fazlul Huq's KPP–Muslim League coalition (1937–41);
b) the Shyama–Huq coalition (1941–43);
c) the Muslim League coalition government led by Khwaja Nazimuddin (1943–45);
d) Governor's rule under Section 93 (1945–46).

It was during these years that the uneasy coexistence between the bhadraloks and the Muslims in a political system that had marked Bengal for about ten years gave way, leading to the parting of ways. Fazlul Huq, H.S. Suhrawardy and Khwaja Nazimuddin were the three dominant Muslim leaders who played decisive roles in the last phase of undivided Bengal. Eventually they all surrendered their initiatives to leaders from northern and western India. Of them, Huq had brought a new style of mass-based politics into the picture, not depending on official patronage as Nazimuddin did, but deriving power from demonstrated contribution to the well-being of the masses. His slogan of *daal-bhat* for the people and his concern for farmers and prajas endeared him to the Muslim peasantry of East Bengal, whose language he spoke. Yet, his career was marked by many turns and twists, many ups and downs.

Starting politics as a lieutenant of Nawab Salimullah, he supported the first partition of Bengal but thereafter gravitated to the Congress. In 1916, he supported the Lucknow Pact and stood for Hindu–Muslim unity. In 1918, he had the unique distinction of being both general secretary of the Congress and president of the League. In 1920, he opposed Mahatma Gandhi and the Swarajists' call to students to leave government schools because he felt that forsaking education was not the right thing for Muslim youth. In this respect he stood side by side with Rabindranath Tagore, Ashutosh Mukherjee and, paradoxically, Muhammed Ali Jinnah. In 1920, he opposed Muslim participation in Gandhi's civil disobedience movement as this, in his opinion, would hurt the interests of the Muslims. The repudiation by the Congress of C.R. Das's Bengal Pact in 1926 and its unwillingness to take a pro-peasantry stand in the Council discussions on the 1928 Bengal Tenancy (Amendment) Act led to general disenchantment among peasants, specially Muslim peasants, with the Congress. This led to the overwhelmingly Muslim participation in the Praja Movement in Bengal. Social and cultural segregation between the two communities added to the political bitterness. In this background, during the 1930s, Huq organized the KPP as an inter-communal though overwhelmingly Muslim party. By the beginning of the 1930s, krishak samitis had been formed in almost all the districts of east and north Bengal. In 1929, they all joined together to form an all-Bengal Praja Samiti. In April 1936, at a conference in Dhaka presided over by Fazlul Huq, the Praja Samiti turned into the KPP. Huq was elected mayor of the Calcutta

Corporation in 1936. Apart from the prajas or tenants it also claimed to represent small *jotedars* (landlords) and Muslim professionals. It did not profess to be a Muslim or communal party despite the aspersions cast by researchers like De.[1]

Suhrawardy, a barrister of liberal views, whose family was from Medinipore, started politics as a lieutenant of C.R. Das, the one Bengali Hindu leader who commanded the loyalty of Muslims in general. He came from an urban ashraf background and, like Huq, was an independent-minded politician who could not be purchased by titles. On the other hand, he could not go against his class interests and support land reforms. He was a lieutenant of C.R. Das during the Swarajya days, but left the Congress platform after Das's death and gravitated to the Muslim League. The following comments from his memoirs are of great significance:

> Entering politics in 1920, I became a member of the Bengal Legislative Assembly and joined the Khilafat Organisation. In the initial stages I was loosely associated with the Congress and was the Deputy Mayor of Calcutta with Deshbandhu C.R. Das as Mayor. He was a great Bengali, I say an Indian, scarcely less in stature than Mahatma Gandhi. I have had the good fortune to know him. He was endowed with vision, he was wholly non-communal, generous to a fault, courageous and capable of unparalleled self-sacrifice. His intellectual attainments and keen insight were of the highest order. As an advocate he commanded fabulous fees which he laid at the feet of his country. Towards the end of his days he renounced his profession, devoted himself to politics and the service of his country and died a pauper overwhelmed with debts. I believe with many that had he lived he would have been able to guide the destiny of India along channels that would have eliminated the causes of conflict and bitterness, which had bedeviled the relationship between Hindus and Muslims, which for want of just solution, led to the partition of India and creation of Pakistan.[2]

In 1937, when Nazimuddin lost to Fazlul Huq in the elections, Suhrawardy rehabilitated him by giving him one of the two constituencies from which he had won. But the two never got on with each other. Again, Suhrawardy got Huq and Nazimuddin together in 1937 to form the KPP–League coalition government. He had a somewhat questionable role during the war and the Bengal famine years and was accused by many of corruption. He was also known for his close contact with the Kolkata underworld. But in fairness to him, it should be said that he was the main fund manager for the Muslim League. In the early 1940s he, along with Abul Hashim, who was general secretary of the Bengal Muslim League, did a lot to popularize the League among the Muslim masses in Bengal, and he led the League to an overwhelming victory in the 1946 elections. He is held responsible by many for the great Kolkata killings in August 1946, which, more than any single event, paved the way for Pakistan. And yet when he had to face Pakistan as an unavoidable reality, he projected the concept of a sovereign united Bengal which, in his vision, was to be a non-communal, socialistic society. His crusading role[3] in Pakistan politics in defence of the Bengali language and the rights of the Hindu minority must also be highlighted in any overall assessment of this mercurial leader.

Khwaja Nazimuddin, a well-meaning and essentially moderate political leader, was a scion of the Dhaka nawab family. A veteran Muslim Leaguer, but not fanatically communal, he was of a bureaucratic temperament. He was not a mass leader like Fazlul Huq, nor a scheming player of realpolitik like Suhrawardy. He chose to be a questioning camp follower of Jinnah and generally maintained a low profile. As home minister in Huq's first cabinet and thereafter as prime minister in the Muslim League coalition government in Bengal between 1943 and 1945, he maintained good personal relations with many Congress leaders. Even as the first chief minister of the East Bengal province of Pakistan he did his best to protect the Hindu minority, although often overruled by the anti-Hindu West Pakistan bureaucracy. He never got along with Suhrawardy and was party to Suhrawardy's expulsion from the Muslim League and from East Pakistan in 1949.

After the dramatic escape of Subhas Chandra Bose (1941), who commanded emotional loyalty from large sections of both Hindus and Muslims in Bengal, there was no Hindu leader of national stature left in Bengal. The four Hindu leaders who played key roles were Sarat Chandra Bose (Forward Block-Congress), Shyama Prasad Mukherjee (Hindu Mahasabha), Kiran Shankar Roy (Congress) and Dr B.C. Roy (Congress). Sarat Chandra Bose, who had left the Congress with his brother Subhas in 1939 and formed the Forward Block, was in detention till 1945, and returned to the Congress on his release. He was elected to the Central Assembly and became leader of the Congress in the Assembly. He also briefly became a minister in Nehru's first interim cabinet, but had to quit to accommodate Congress Muslims when the Muslim League joined. He was distrusted by the British raj and ignored by the Congress high command. He joined up with Suhrawardy in mid-1947 in projecting the concept of a sovereign, united Bengal and continued his efforts till the very end.

Shyama Prasad Mukherjee, the son of Sir Ashutosh Mukherjee, came to public life as vice-chancellor of Calcutta University. He started his political life as a Congressman and was elected to the Bengal Legislative Council as a Congress candidate in 1929. But he resigned from both the Council and the Congress when the Civil Disobedience Movement began. He resigned from the Council because Gandhi required this and from the Congress because he was opposed to this idea. He was re-elected to the Bengal Council as an independent candidate in 1937 and was elected to the Bengal Legislative Council from the Calcutta University constituency, and would have favoured a KPP–Congress coalition, but he was appalled at the Congress leadership's pathetic naivette in turning down Fazlul Huq's coalition offer. In 1939, coming out against both the Congress and the Muslim League, he joined the All India Hindu Mahasabha. He became its president and was destined to play a key role during the period. A nationalist par excellence, he was not against Muslims but against the Muslim League and its communal policies. Passionately opposed to the partition of India, he ended up proposing and working for the partition of Bengal. He was essentially not communal-minded. He believed in cooperating in politics with progressive Muslim leaders like Fazlul Huq, whom he joined in a coalition government in 1941. This was a shining example of collaboration in an age of communal polarization. Its success could have prevented the partition. But the coalition collapsed under constant attack from communalists on both sides and the intrigues of white officialdom led by Governor Herbert. Ironically, in 1947, when the partition of the subcontinent seemed inevitable, it was Shyama Prasad who first gave the call for a parallel partition of Bengal. He joined Nehru's cabinet after independence after resigning from the Hindu Mahasabha and advising the Mahasabha to disband itself.

Kiran Shankar Roy, as leader of the Congress both before his arrest in 1942 and after the 1946 elections, played a key role in the Bengal Assembly. He had considerable literary flair and was more of an intellectual than a politician. He played a role in the abortive Congress–KPP negotiations and had good personal equations with League leaders like Suhrawardy. He was, for a while, a supporter of a sovereign united Bengal along with Suhrawardy and Sarat Bose until he was overruled by the Congress leadership. He stayed in Pakistan for some time as leader of the Congress Party in the East Bengal Assembly, but came to India in 1948 when Dr Bidhan Chandra Roy, on becoming chief minister of West Bengal, appointed him as home minister. Bidhan Roy was a Congress leader who had shot into eminence as far back as the 1920s, became a member of the Congress Working Committee in 1930, but preferred his medical profession to everything else. He kept up good personal equations as a doctor with all his political opponents like Fazlul Huq, Jinnah and Suhrawardy. But he disagreed with some of the major decisions of the Congress leadership, preferred to withdraw to the ringside and did not play any active role in politics during the years 1942–47. He was opposed to the partition and kept himself aloof from all negotiations on it.

The elections of 1937

The announcement of the elections triggered off intense political activity. The Bengal Congress, somewhat weakened by internal squabbles and its growing estrangement from the Muslim masses, was still the strongest force. The KPP, founded in 1927 by Fazlul Huq and rapidly gaining support among the Muslim peasantry of East Bengal, was also a strong political party. The Muslim League, with its landlord base, had only minimal presence in Bengal. Some Muslim leaders led by the nawab of Dhaka formed the United Muslim Party (UMP), in order to take part in the elections. M.A. Jinnah, who had returned to India in 1936 after his six-year self-imposed exile in Britain and assumed the Muslim League's leadership, made serious efforts to bring both the KPP and the UMP under the League's banner and fight the elections. The UMP agreed to merge itself with the Muslim League, its top leadership including Nawab Habibullah of Dhaka. Khwaja Sir Nazimuddin, H.S. Suhrawardy, Maulana Akram Khan, Tamizuddin Khan and Khwaja Shahabuddin were co-opted to the Muslim League central committee. A prominent role was taken in these negotiations by Jinnah's close friend, M.A. Ispahani, a leading Kolkata businessman. Huq initially agreed to join forces and took part in the negotiations for a common election manifesto. He, along with Nausher Ali, Syed Badruddza, Shamsuddin Ahmed and Hasan Ali of Bogra took part in these negotiations on behalf of the KPP. But the negotiations broke down on the issue of Huq's insistence on including in the election manifesto a promise to abolish the zamindari system and another for free universal primary education.

These demands were not acceptable to the landlord-dominated Muslim League. Huq and his colleagues, therefore, left the negotiating table. Addressing the students of Dhaka University shortly thereafter, Huq complained that Jinnah was under the influence of the non-Bengali zamindars and capitalists and of Kolkata-based leaders, and announced that he would lead a struggle on behalf of the poor, the praja, the ryots and the farmers of Bengal against the businessmen and the capitalists.

In the election campaign, Huq promised *daal-bhat* (rice and pulses) to the poor, while the Muslim League enlisted the support of the Muslim fundamentalist forces. The *daal-bhat* appeal became very popular and East Bengal's Muslim peasantry sided with Huq, so much so that Fazlul Huq had a resounding victory over Nazimuddin from Patuakhali where also the Muslim peasantry sided with the popular leader in preference to their own zamindar who, as a member of the Governor's Council, also received official support. Huq had dared Nazimuddin openly and announced that he was in reality fighting Governor Sir John Anderson rather than Khwaja Nazimuddin. A straw in the wind was that poet Nazrul Islam who contested as an independent candidate lost his deposit.

The Congress high command committed a political mistake, which cost Bengal dear, when it decided that the Congress would form ministries only in those provinces where it had an absolute majority in the Assembly and would not join hands with any other party. Thus, when Governor Sir John Herbert invited Sarat Bose as the leader of the single largest party to discuss the formation of a ministry, he declined the offer. Fazlul Huq, leading the KPP, requested Kiran Shankar Roy, the leader of the Congress in the Assembly, to join him in a coalition government under his leadership. Sarat Bose was inclined to agree and he requested Abul Kalam Azad, the Congress president, for permission to join hands with Huq, taking into account the special situation in Bengal. This idea was said to have the support of Subhas Bose, who was soon to become Congress president. But the Congress high command turned it down despite repeated requests. History would have been different had the Congress agreed to Huq's offer at this juncture. Huq now turned to the Muslim League, which promptly seized the initiative when it agreed to join the coalition under Huq's leadership. Even Bidhan Chandra Roy was reported to have favoured a KPP–Congress coalition and, on being disappointed when it did not happen, stayed aloof from active Congress politics for several years.

The correspondence between Mahatma Gandhi and Subhas Bose some time later when Bose became Congress president clearly proves that, left to himself, Subhas would have liked to join up with Fazlul Huq,[4] he tried even afterwards to upturn the KPP–League coalition, but found himself powerless to defy Gandhi. As late as December 1938, Gandhi wrote to Bose, then Congress president:

A long discussion with Maulana Abul Kalam Azad, Nalini Ranjan Sarkar and Ghanasyamadas Birla has convinced me that the present ministry in Bengal [a coalition of the Muslim League and the KPP] should not be changed. Change will be of no avail. Rather, if the Congress forms a coalition ministry in Bengal with the Krishak Praja Party, it may be injurious to the province. Nalini Sarkar has told me that if the present coalition ministry takes any measure, which is against the country's interest, he will not hesitate to resign from it.

Subhas Bose's reply to Gandhi (21 December 1938) was:

Your letter came as a profound shock to me. I have had many discussions with you over the formation of a ministry in Bengal. The matter was also discussed with you some days back in Wardha. My elder brother, Sarat Chandra Bose, too has talked with you over the matter. Both of us clearly recall that you have every time supported the idea of a coalition ministry of Congress and Krishak Praja parties in Bengal. I cannot understand how you changed your views so soon after the discussion at Wardha. It is quite clear that your talks with Azad, Nalini and Birla are responsible for the change of your views. The position therefore appears to be that you prefer to give more importance to the views of the above three persons than those of persons who are responsible for running the Congress in Bengal.

There is a hint that Gandhi was unduly influenced by G.D. Birla representing Indian business interests. Birla, as the leader of the Marwari business interests, strongly felt that political unity between the Muslims and Hindus in Bengal would threaten Marwari dominance of the business landscape in Kolkata. The existing arrangement in which the Muslim League, a party of vested interests, played the dominant role with strong links with up-country business interests through non-Bengali industrialists like Ispahani would suit both Marwari and British industrialists. Subhas Bose, in the same letter to Gandhi (21 December 1938), further wrote:

In the face of the crisis brought about by your letter I would like to have some plain speaking in the matter. In the case of Assam, Maulana Azad opposed my proposal for a coalition ministry and if Sardar Patel had not come forward to support me, you could not have accepted my views in the matter in the Congress Working Committee meeting and no coalition ministry would have been formed in Assam. Maulana Saheb was against a coalition ministry in Sind too while I along with some members of the Working Committee was in its favour. In the case of Bengal too his views are against mine. According to Maulana Saheb, Muslim ministers should be accepted where Muslims are in a majority even though those ministries are blatantly communal. It is now quite clear that Maulana Saheb is unhappy over Congress support to Alla Baksh ministry in Sind.[5]

Subhas Bose advanced many other arguments in support of his views. According to Nirad Chandra Chaudhuri, who was at the time secretary to Sarat Chandra Bose and dealt with Subhas Chandra's correspondence, Subhas came to believe that not only Maulana Azad but G.D. Birla also played a part in bringing about a change in Gandhi's views in the matter. The reason was that Birla came to believe that Marwari domination over the trade and economy of Kolkata would be lost if a political pact of Hindus and Muslims lead to a KPP–Congress coalition ministry in Bengal. There is no written evidence to corroborate Nirad Chaudhuri's views on his assessment of Gandhi on this point, but the rift that occurred between Gandhi and Subhas shortly thereafter gives some credence to this view.[6] Subhas, the Congress president at Haripura Congress (1937), defied Gandhi in seeking a second term as the Congress president and won a convincing victory, but was expelled from the Congress by a series of moves by the Congress old guard.

Fazlul Huq's coalition with the Muslim League

Thus a KPP–Muslim League coalition government, with support from the scheduled castes and some independent upper-caste Hindu

MLAs came to power. Fazlul Huq was the first prime minister of Bengal, Azizul Huq, an able lawyer, was elected Speaker of the Assembly and Satyendra Chandra Mitra, a Congressman, was elected president of the Upper House of the Legislative Council with the Congress Party's permission, defeating Raja Manmothnath Chaudhury of Santosh with only one vote.

The 1937 Bengal Assembly was full of excellent orators for whom the visitor's gallery was packed. There were five Hindu and five Muslim ministers. Interestingly, Nalini Ranjan Sarkar, essentially a Congressman and one amongst the Congress's big five in Bengal, became the finance minister and the target of the Opposition from the beginning. Initially he fumbled, but soon developed into a good parliamentarian. From the Treasury benches Huq, Nazimuddin (home minister) and Suhrawardy were the main speakers. The Opposition benches also commanded many star performers, including Shyama Prasad, an independent. Another costly blunder that had a long-term impact on all-India politics was made by the Congress in the United Provinces. Here the Congress and the Muslim League had gone jointly to the electoral battle, but as soon as the Congress got an absolute majority on its own, it forgot its understanding with the Muslim League about forming a government together and dumped the latter. Nawab Ismail Khan and Chaudhury Khalequzzaman, the two Muslim League leaders who were tipped to be part of the six-member cabinet, found themselves left out after they had enthusiastically campaigned for a Congress–League front. The League leadership never forgave the Congress for what it considered a breach of faith and went on a collision course, which embittered Hindu–Muslim relations and paved the way for the 'Pakistan' slogan. Jinnah could from then on count on the full support of Muslim leaders like Khalequzzaman who were permanently alienated from the Congress with which they had till then very close ties.[7] Soon the League complained of atrocities on Muslims in Congress-led provinces and appointed on 20 March 1938 a committee headed by the Raja of Pirpur, to enquire and report on them. The Pirpur Report highlighting alleged atrocities on Muslims in Congress-led provinces was a scathing document, which the Congress did not accept but which, nonetheless, worsened communal relations.

Muslim opinion even in Bengal was influenced by the report of the Pirpur Committee. It reported that in these provinces the minorities had 'only secondary rights' and cited the Congress decision to foist *Bande Mataram*, an 'anti-Islamic and idolatrous song', as the national anthem, the imposition of Hindi as the lingua franca, the withholding of licences for cow slaughter in some provinces, the abolition of Muslim representation in debt conciliation boards among instances of 'atrocities' against Muslims. These had no relevance for Muslims in Bengal, but nonetheless helped to fan the communal flame even here, and the Muslim attitude to the Congress stiffened. An enquiry ordered by Governor-General Linlithgow found these stories of 'atrocities' highly exaggerated, but the report had done its mischief. Even public servants were infected by the communal contagion.

In retrospect, there can be no doubt that the Congress's mistake in turning down Fazlul Huq's request in Bengal, together with its blunder in the United Provinces, did pave the way for the partition of the subcontinent ten years later. The Muslim League took full advantage of its governmental authority in Bengal to extend its support base over the Muslim masses. It also befriended Huq. In fact, in his anxiety to accommodate every interest that could support the government, Huq soon became a minority within the ministry. This, as also his abandonment of the election pledges, caused rumblings in the KPP. As early as March 1938, a majority of the KPP party in the Assembly sat with the Opposition to register their protest. Shamsuddin Ahmed at the head of twenty KPP MLAs accused Fazlul Huq of abandoning the party's election promises. Huq expelled seventeen MLAs from the party. Then, Saiyad Nausher Ali led a group of dissidents out of the KPP opposing Huq's acceptance of a proposal to start certificate proceedings against ryots to realize rent arrears due to the government. Literally placed between the devil and the deep sea, that is, the Muslim League and his coalition partner, and the Congress–KPP majority Opposition, and reduced to a minority in the coalition, Huq realized that he could save his ministry only with Jinnah's support and joined the League at its annual session at Lucknow in December 1937. Between 1937 and 1940, Huq was drawn into the vortex of Muslim League politics, although he never felt comfortable in that landlord-dominated party. In 1939, he went out of his way to declare that he was a Muslim first and a Bengali afterwards. Ironically, it was Huq, never a subscriber to the two-nation theory, who was made to move the so-called Pakistan Resolution in the Lahore session of the Muslim League in 1940. This was not only Jinnah's cynical master-stroke, but a great propaganda victory for him. By bringing Huq, the undisputed leader of the Muslim peasantry of Bengal under his umbrella, he had gained for the Muslim League, till then a weak player in Bengal politics, a strong foothold in Bengal. His short-lived honeymoon with Sikandar Hayat Khan, the unionist premier of Punjab, was another feather in his cap. He skillfully used both Fazlul Huq and Sikandar Hayat Khan, neither of whom believed in the two-nation theory or in the partition of the country, to mobilize Muslim support for these concepts.

The new ministry faced uneasy times from the beginning. Huq pressed his most important agenda of abolishing the zamindari system. This met with sharp opposition from the League ministers, one of whom, Nawab Musharraf Hussain, declared that he was willing to spend all his money to get Huq removed from the cabinet. Within a year it had to resign and reconstitute itself when a minister, Nausher Ali, was asked to resign and refused to do so. In 1938, Mahatma Gandhi himself came to Kolkata in a bid to persuade scheduled caste members to leave the coalition and join the Congress. Ten separate no-confidence motions were moved in the Assembly against the ten ministers, but they failed on account of deep divisions in the Congress ranks and the twenty-five European votes going in favour of the ministers. As Huq opened up a secret line of communication with the Congress led by Subhas Bose, the Muslim Leaguers were looking for an opportunity to throw him out. The Congress members moved a no-confidence motion on 8 and 9 August 1938 against some ministers. This provided an opportunity for confrontation.

As the League declared a hartal and its supporters barricaded all
streets in order to prevent Congress and anti-government MLAs
from reaching Town Hall—venue of the Bengal Assembly those
days—many such MLAs including Tulsi Goswami, Devendralal
Khan, Tamizuddin Khan, J.C. Gupta, K.N. Barman, Abu Hussain
Sarkar, Maniruzzaman Islamabadi and Atul Chandra Kumar spent
the night in the Assembly premises. The Muslim League goons
attacked Humayun Kabir's residence and insulted him. On 8 August,
the no-confidence motion against Maharaja Srish Chandra Nandy,
a minister, was narrowly defeated (130–110) with the help of the
twenty-three European members. Thus, Huq's government came to
depend entirely on the League and the European members. Gandhi
visited Kolkata a second time and negotiated for a coalition between
Fazlul Huq's supporters and the Congress, but Huq, who had been
repeatedly spurned by the Congress, could not trust it any more.

There was inevitably a hardening of attitudes on communal
lines, the Congress openly calling the ministry a Muslim government
and Huq's supporters raising the cry of Islam in danger. The cabinet
moved a resolution before the Assembly that India should be given
dominion status after the war and the constitution should provide
safeguards based on the full consent and approval of the minority
communities. Finance minister Nalini Ranjan Sarkar refused to
support this resolution and resigned from the cabinet (1939).
Suhrawardy replaced him as finance minister. Huq's dependence on
the League increased further. But amidst all his political turmoils,
Huq never forgot the impoverished Muslim peasantry of East Bengal.
By a series of administrative and legislative measures, such as the
Bengal Tenancy (Amendment) Act of 1938, the Money Lenders Act
of 1940 and the debt settlement boards, he enhanced his popularity
among Muslim peasants, who resented every move to bring down
Huq as a betrayal of the Muslim cause. The first of these measures
was opposed by both the League members as also the Europeans,
but was passed by 110 to 27 votes.

There were several other significant developments. First, Huq
appointed a commission of enquiry (the Floud Commission) to
suggest changes in the Permanent Settlement of 1793. The

Commission recommended the replacement of the zamindari system by a ryotwari system in which ownership of the land would vest with the ryot and the land revenue payable by him could be revised from time to time; but these recommendations could not be implemented on account of deep divisions among ministers. Fazlul Huq also proceeded with piecemeal amelioratory measures such as: (i) keeping in abeyance for ten years the right of the landlords to increase the rent payable by tenants; (ii) combining the landlords' right to enforce realization of arrears of rent (1937); (iii) protecting tenants' rights with regard to mortgaging their land (1938); (iv) the Debt Relief Act of 1940 fixing a ceiling on the rate of interest that could be charged by money-lenders, banning compound interest and fixing the rate of interest on mortgages at 9 per cent and on unsecured loans at 10 per cent; (v) passing another Act creating a relief fund to meet the needs of relief during floods, famines and other natural calamities; and (vi) providing for one-and-a-half day's leave in a week and paid leave for fifteen days in a year and work hours up to 8 p.m. in all public holdings.

In 1939, separate electorates were introduced for Muslims and Anglo-Indians for election to the Calcutta Corporation. Fazlul Huq himself justified this Calcutta Municipal Amendment Act by announcing that 'we have made it certain that Congress no longer dominates the Calcutta Corporation. I do not say that we have succeeded fully. The chances are that the Congress will not have a dominant voice in the Calcutta Corporation.'[8] This provoked Hindu reaction. Two other contemplated legislations of the Huq government ran into serious controversies, namely, the Secondary Education Bill and the Communal Ratio Bill. The first aimed at shifting secondary education from the Hindu-controlled Calcutta University to a proposed Board of Secondary Education with fifty members, of whom twenty were to be nominated from amongst the Hindus and Muslims, five from amongst Europeans and five from amongst other categories; nineteen were to be directly nominated by the government. There was to be an Executive Council of fourteen of whom six were to be ex-officio government officials. This move was interpreted by the Hindu intelligentsia as a politically motivated move to communalize school education. So great was the feeling against this Bill that even a close friend of Huq, Dr Shyama Prasad Mukherjee, took a public stand against it. In his address before the annual conference of the All Bengal Teachers Association (1939) he announced: 'If the board is established we shall sever all connections with such an anti-educational board and shall, if necessary, seek affiliation for our schools with an outside university.' In the face of such vehement opposition from the press and from within and outside the Assembly, the government was compelled to put this Bill in cold storage. Needless to say, this hardened anti-Hindu feelings among Muslims.

The various efforts of the Huq ministry to ensure a higher percentage of government jobs for Muslims and the proposed Communal Ratio Act met with stiff opposition and embittered communal relations. What Huq attempted to do was not something more than what Chittaranjan Das had assured Bengal Muslims through his Bengal Pact. But Hindu opinion continued to be resentful. Other flashpoints were the Muslim demand for the removal of the lotus flower and the word 'shri' from the Calcutta University's motif on the ground that these were Hindu symbols, the demand for appointing a large number of Muslim professors and non-teaching staff in the university and a systematic policy of nominating only Muslim League supporters as nominated members in the district and local boards. After the outbreak of the war and the natural interest of officialdom in encouraging loyalists, officials were instructed to support only Muslim League followers. M.O. Martin, commissioner of Chittagong division, admitted that 'some of the European officials are more sympathetic towards Muslims and Muslim propaganda' and wrote to E.N. Blandy, chief secretary, Bengal, on 30 April 1939: 'I find the League extraordinarily useful at least in this division because their leaders are generally willing to come to the assistance of officials and to give effect to their suggestions, especially where there are any sort of disturbances.'

Thus, the policy followed by the Huq–League coalition directly led to the increasing popularity of the Muslim League among Muslims in Bengal, especially in the districts. This was reflected in the doubling of its membership in some districts. As commented by Humayun Kabir: 'Forced into the arms of the Muslim League, Fazlul Huq did perhaps more than anybody else in India to restore the prestige of the League and win for it support among the masses of the land. Thus an awakened mass consciousness contributed to the growth of the popularity of the League.'[9] Communal relations continued to deteriorate, culminating in several Hindu–Muslim riots from 1940 onwards. The most serious of them were the riots in Dhaka in 1940 and 1941 ignited on such pretexts as Hindu religious processions playing music in front of mosques, or Muharram processions making provocative noises in front of temples, or Hindus objecting to the sacrificial killing of cows in public on Bakr-Id. Agent provocateurs started the trouble and anti-social elements took advantage of the situation. In the rioting in Dhaka that started on 17 March 1941, the army had to be called in after many lives had been lost. Rioting also spread to neighbouring villages and about 10,000 Hindus had to run away from home and hearth. Hindus, being the more affluent community, became victims of looting by anti-socials of the other community. Despite a communiqué issued by the government appealing for peace, appointment of goodwill committees at various localities and the ordering of a judicial enquiry, rioting continued through June–July 1941. Fazlul Huq was accused by the Congress and the Hindu Mahasabha of partiality to the Muslims. Huq advised Jinnah to arrive at a compromise with the Congress. Jinnah's reply was that this was not possible as long as the Congress considered itself as the only representative organization in the politics of India. There was a steady erosion in Huq's popularity and an acceleration of the Muslim League's strength among Muslims.

Huq's government showed its courage in releasing a large number of terrorists and extremists detained without trial. In so doing Huq had to ignore the views of the Governor and white officialdom. By 1940 more than 2,000 terrorists had been released from jail or from internment. Many of them were by now communists and turned their attention to organizing peasants against zamindars.

Holwell Monument agitation

An important event in 1940 in which Fazlul Huq showed his courage in overruling white officialdom was the Holwell Monument agitation personally led by Subhas Bose, who asserted his political leadership through this emotional agitation and also won back the support of large sections of Bengali Muslims. For many in Bengal, Siraj-ud-Daula, the last independent nawab of Bengal, was innocent of the heinous crime of the black hole tragedy (1756) attributed to him by a section of racially prejudiced British historians. When Subhas Bose, in mid-1940, demanded removal of the Holwell monument located at Dalhousie Square in Kolkata commemorating the black hole tragedy, he found strong mass support. The Provincial Political Conference in Dhaka (25 May 1940) responded strongly in favour of the demand. Many Muslims joined in. Subhas gave an ultimatum at a public meeting held on 29 June at Albert Hall, Kolkata, that this monument must be removed from public view by 3 July, the anniversary of Siraj-ud-Daula's murder. He followed it up by threatening to personally lead a march to this monument on that day.

Subhas was arrested on 2 July, a day before his proposed direct action on the pretext of a seditious article he had published in his journal *Forward* of 15 June 1940, arguing that India could only gain from the collapse of the British. But the movement started with batches of demonstrators advancing towards the monument every day and courting arrest. On 13 July, a huge public meeting at Albert Hall presided over by Abdul Karim criticized government repression. The government issued a directive to the press prohibiting publication of any news of the movement. Students of Islamia College replied by holding a protest meeting outside the college. But Fazlul Huq seized the initiative and defied official British opposition by announcing the removal of the Holwell Monument from public view. He also ordered the release of all the detainees on account of this movement.

Beginning of World War II

The outbreak of the second world war with Hitler's invasion of Poland on 1 September 1939 brought unexpected relief for Huq. On

3 September, Great Britain declared war on Germany. This eased the
pressure on Huq. Along with the British declaring war on Germany,
Viceroy Lord Linlithgow issued a bland proclamation on the same
day that India was at war with Germany. No Indian leader had been
consulted and India was dragged into a war with a country that was
not a direct threat to it. Gandhi's initial hunch was to unconditionally
support Britain. Nehru, who was of a somewhat different emotional
bent, wanted India to play its full part and commit all its resources
to the 'struggle for a new order' by which he could have meant the
abolition of both Nazism and colonialism. Subhas, still an important
Congress leader and, therefore, invited to the meeting of the Congress
Working Committee (10 September) at Wardha, favoured India
utilizing the international situation, including the British empire's
discomfiture, to press for freedom. Jinnah was willing to promise
the full support of the Muslims, but on condition that Congress
ministries in the seven provinces which, according to his reckoning,
had followed anti-Muslim policies, were immediately thrown out
and the British agree in principle to separate Muslim majority
provinces from the rest of the country.

The Congress Working Committee, overruling the arguments
of Subhas Bose, a special invitee, preferred only to ask the British Raj
to clarify its intention about India's independence. A disappointed
Subhas returned to Kolkata from Wardha. He now agitated for the
removal of the monument to Holwell. For nationalists, this was a
calumny wrongly attributed to Siraj. This agitation attracted
emotional support from all Bengalis, Hindus and Muslims. Eventually
Premier Huq intervened, overruling the white officialdom, and
ordered the removal of this monument from public view. This along
with international and domestic developments gave the beleaguered
Huq ministry a certain reprieve.

With the advent of the war, there was pressure on both the
Congress and the League to take a stand in relation to the war, and
also the future of British rule in India. Sandwiched between Subhas
Bose's pressure for a confrontationist policy to British rule and
Nehru's passionate antipathy to the Nazi–fascist combine, the
Congress Working Committee brought out a resolution that was a

masterly combination of inconsistencies. It preached anti-Nazism and anti-imperialism at the same time, reflecting the contradictions in the Congress.

The Muslim League Working Committee met immediately after this statement and demanded that the British recognize the League as the sole voice of Muslims and revise the federal part of the 1935 Constitution so as to reflect the demands of the League. On 17 October, Linlithgow made an announcement vaguely promising dominion status after the war and also consultation on the revision of the 1935 Constitution at that time. In trying to incorporate the concerns of all parties, it satisfied none. The Congress Working Committee now asked all Congress provincial governments to resign by the end of October. They did so in all the seven Congress-ruled provinces and the Governors took over administration under Section 93 of the 1935 Act. In retrospect, this decision to resign en masse from the provinces was politically unwise. Protest against the Viceroy's unilateral declaration could have taken other forms. In resigning, the Congress played into the hands of Jinnah and left the field open for the Muslim League and white officialdom. The Muslim-led governments of Bengal, Punjab and Sind continued. In Assam, a League-led coalition soon replaced a Congress-led coalition. Jinnah called for a 'Day of Deliverance and Thanksgiving for the Muslims on Friday, 22 December 1939 as a mark of relief that the Congress regime has at least ceased to function'. But he appealed to his followers for calm and for avoiding anything that could incite communal violence. His proclamation catalogued various Muslim grievances against the Congress governments highlighted by the Pirpur Committee report and dubbed as imaginary by the Congress.

Pakistan Resolution (1940)

Jinnah followed it with the famous Pakistan Resolution at the Muslim League council meeting in Lahore (21 March 1940). This was moved by Fazlul Huq, who had by then been driven into the arms of the Muslim League. This resolution claimed that 'the Musalmans are a nation by any definition, not a minority' and asked the British to divide the subcontinent into 'autonomous national states'. The operative part of the resolution in its third paragraph was as follows:

> No constitutional plan will be workable in this country or acceptable to the Muslims unless it is designed on the following basic principles, viz. that geographically continuous units are demarcated into regions which should be so constituted, with such territorial readjustments as may be necessary, as in the north-western and eastern zones of India should form more than one independent state and the units comprised in these states should be independent and sovereign.[10]

Significantly, the word 'Pakistan' was not mentioned by Jinnah even once, nor did it find a place in the resolution, which was vague and capable of different interpretations by different interests. Fazlul Huq, the mover of the resolution, thought that there would be an eastern Muslim-dominated state and a western one. Sikander Hayat Khan, Punjab's premier, had thought of a loose federation with strong provinces and a Centre that would control minimal subjects. Jinnah clearly intended to keep all options open as to use the slogan as a bargaining counter to gain as much concession as he could. But for the moment he had succeeded in defeating the Congress claim that it spoke for all sections of India, including the Muslims. Also, he had succeeded in making the British authorities turn to him as the only dependable ally who would support them in the war efforts. Thus, the Muslim League in general stood by the empire whereas the Congress in about a year was to launch the Quit India Movement. Subhas Bose, who in a daring escape left India secretly for Germany in 1940, was to challenge the British through the Azad Hind Fauj with the help of the Japanese in 1943.

The Shyama–Huq coalition (1941–43)

Huq's honeymoon with the League was short-lived and his exit was as dramatic and sudden as his entry. Making Huq, a strong proponent of Hindu–Muslim unity, move the resolution for partition was a

great achievement of Jinnah; but the two shared a common mutual
distrust which surfaced very soon. Jinnah wanted from his associates
complete subordination. Huq, with his strong views, could not put
up with it. The Muslim League instructed its followers to observe 23
March as Pakistan Day. As the communal situation in Bengal was
getting overheated, Fazlul Huq with Suhrawardy's support, issued
instructions to League branches in Bengal in 1941 to put off this
public celebration. But the Kolkata district Muslim League held a
public meeting in open violation of this instruction.[11] Huq was
slowly coming to the realization that the Muslim League, having
made full use of his stature, was determined to leave him high and
dry. In a bid to totally dominate the Muslim League, Jinnah had a
directive issued in 1941 to the three League premiers, namely, Fazlul
Huq, Sikander Hayat Khan and Mohammad Shadullah of Assam,
whom the Viceroy had nominated to his Defence Council, that they
must resign from the Council. He resented League members being
appointed by the Viceroy without his clearance. Sikander Hayat
Khan and Mohammad Shadullah promptly resigned. But Huq, not
a man to be cowed down by Jinnah's swashbuckling attitude,
refused to resign. Jinnah gave him ten days time and threatened
disciplinary action. Huq resigned under a lot of pressure, but at the
same time he showed his anger by simultaneously resigning from
the League Working Committee and accused Jinnah of using arbitrary
powers and being 'wholly unconstitutional'. An open split now
ensued in the Muslim League between pro-Jinnah Leaguers led by
Khwaja Nazimuddin, who had not forgotten his Patuakhali
humiliation, and H.S. Suhrawardy on the one hand, and pro-Huq
former KPP elements on the other. But Huq, according to all
contemporary accounts, was never happy in the company of the
landlord-dominated Muslim League, and while in the government
all along carried on a balancing game.

He started secret negotiations with Sarat Bose, Dr Shyama
Prasad Mukherjee and scheduled caste leaders, and looked for
friends elsewhere. A new combination, namely, the Progressive
Coalition Party, which included both the KPP and the Forward
Block, was formed secretly with 110 members who unanimously

elected Huq as leader. He thus showed his great capacity for survival. The Muslim League ministers led by Nazimuddin resigned en bloc on 8 December 1941, to put pressure on Huq. Apparently the League leaders had reckoned that the Governor would invite Nazimuddin to form the new government. But once again Fazlul Huq demonstrated his skill for flexibility and manoeuvrability when he contrived a majority with the announced support of twenty-five Congress MLAs and formed a nine-member cabinet on 12 December 1941 with four Hindu ministers and the nawab of Dhaka. One of the four was Dr Shyama Prasad Mukherjee, leader of the Hindu Mahasabha but a staunch nationalist and vice-chancellor of the University of Kolkata, who became the finance minister. He responded to Huq's invitation as he felt that this way he would be able to keep Muslim League's communalism, British divisive policies and Congress' brow-beating at bay and would bring together both Muslim and Hindu nationalists on a common platform. In an interview with the Associated Press of India on the same day, Shyama Prasad stated that 'Bengal has shown today that in spite of internal differences the important elements of our national life can combine for the good of the country'.[12] Sarat Bose, a strong supporter of this coalition, was soon interned in south India. Poet Nazrul Islam also welcomed the ministry as a big step towards Hindu–Muslim unity.

During the life of this ministry there was not a single instance of communal rioting. On 16 February 1942, while presenting the budget, the finance minister provided Rs 1 lakh for the promotion of communal harmony, a unique gesture. Thereafter Huq and Mukherjee jointly travelled to several districts of Bengal preaching the message of communal harmony. In a speech at Coronation Park, Dhaka, on 21 April 1942, Shyama Prasad said that the Bengal ministry was no longer for any particular community, but for all communities. He congratulated Premier Huq for the courageous steps he had taken to eradicate communalism and regretted that Amery, Secretary of State for India, did not have a good word for Fazlul Huq's bold steps to eradicate communalism. This would not only solve the communal problem in Bengal, but would show the whole of India how to stand shoulder to shoulder in the face of common danger. He appealed for complete Hindu–Muslim unity and asked the Hindus to defend the mosques and the Muslims to defend the temples against attacks from *goondas*.[13]

Incidentally, two of the Hindu ministers were Forward Block members who showed enough flexibility to assume office under an oath to the British king while their leader, Subhas Bose, had by that time reached Germany in a bid to enlist German support for India's independence. He knew every detail of the goings-on in Bengal and was reported to have given his nod to this new arrangement. One of the Hindu ministers was a scheduled caste member. Premier Huq, who was expelled from the League on 10 December 1941, described the new government as a coalition between the two major communities in Bengal. The Muslim League called it a Hindu cabinet in effect. In actual fact this was a great experiment, one that could have turned Bengal's history in a new direction had it been allowed to function for a reasonable length of time without becoming a victim of the British policy of divide-and-rule and communal intransigence. No doubt this government was made possible by Fazlul Huq's personal charm and the willingness of a number of Bengali leaders, including Subhas Bose and Shyama Prasad Mukherjee, following contradictory politics to come together in Bengal's larger interest. In so doing they defied the Congress high command as Fazlul Huq had defied Jinnah. Both felt that the central leadership of the Congress and the League were imposing policies that were not in the interest of Bengal.

Thus, the Shyama–Huq ministry, as it was popularly called by contemporaries, though disliked by both Congressmen and Muslim Leaguers, received tremendous goodwill from the middle-of-the-road Bengalis, both Muslim and Hindu. Fazlul Huq made no secret of his belief that the leaders from Bengal, or for that matter other provinces, must have a decisive say in forming political alliances and the central leadership of political parties must accept this. Both Subhas Bose and Shyama Prasad Mukherjee were also of the same view. In fact, Subhas Bose before his great escape had made friends with a number of Muslim League leaders in Bengal, notably Abdur

Rahman Siddique, the mayor of Kolkata, M.A. Ispahani, the leader
of the League in the Kolkata Corporation and Jinnah's main financier,
and Nooruddin. The Bose–League front jointly fought the elections
to the Kolkata Corporation and won a majority. Unfortunately,
neither the Congress high command nor the Muslim League's
central leadership agreed with this approach. Both tried to impose
their political will in Bengal. The result was a disaster for Bengal.

Huq's second administration took office at a crucial point in the
history of the subcontinent. With Japan's dramatic entry in the war
on 6 December 1941, on the side of the Axis powers, the capture of
Malaya, Singapore and Burma in quick succession and the appearance
of the Japanese army on the Bengal–Burma border, the war reached
the backyard of Bengal. Thousands of Indian refugees from Burma
trekked to Bengal. On 20 December 1942, the first Japanese air raid
on Kolkata took place. There were several other air raids. The
Japanese army attacked the borders of Bengal in Chittagong on 23
March 1942. Also, all-India politics became tense with the arrival of
the Cripps Mission and with the Congress poised for launching the
Quit India Movement.

Cripps Mission

On 23 March 1942, Sir Stafford Cripps, British minister and well-
known Labour Party leader known to be a friend of India, was sent
to India by Prime Minister Winston Churchill to win over Congress
leaders with the promise of dominion status at the end of the war.
After several long rounds of discussions with Indian leaders, Cripps
outlined a scheme which would have made India independent at the
end of the war. If any province did not want to join the federation
it could have its separate constitution and have dominion status for
itself. But the proposal did not find favour with either Gandhi—who
called it a 'post-dated cheque'—nor Jinnah. Also, there was hostility
from both Churchill and Linlithgow. Cripps returned to London
empty-handed on 11 August 1942. In retrospect, the Cripps proposals
seem eminently practicable and it also seems possible that their
acceptance could have avoided many subsequent untoward

happenings. However, neither the Congress nor the League was in a mood to accept them. Thus the Cripps Mission was a failure.

Quit India Movement (1942)

With the failure of the Cripps Mission, the Congress under Gandhi was gravitating to a direct anti-British agitation, something that Subhas Bose had pleaded three years ago. The Congress Working Committee adopted a resolution at Wardha on 14 July 1942, calling upon the British to quit India forthwith and announced the resolve to start a non-violent movement if they failed to do so. It met again in Bombay on 7 August and confirmed the Quit India resolution. The 500-strong All India Congress Committee met in Bombay on 8 August 1942 and endorsed the Working Committee's Quit India resolution reiterating that 'a non-violent struggle will start all over India under Gandhiji's leadership'. An overwhelming majority voted for the resolution, barring the thirteen communist members who were in favour of supporting the government's war efforts following the Soviet line that this was a peoples' war. Soon after this, in the evening hours the government swung into action. Gandhi, all the members of the Congress Committee and, in fact, all second- and third-rung Congress leaders all over the country were arrested under the Defence of India Act. The Congress was declared illegal and its offices were closed by the police. Mahatma Gandhi, with his wife and a small retinue, was detained at the Aga Khan Palace in Poona. Nehru, Sardar Patel and all other Congress Committee members were taken to Ahmednagar Fort. This was the beginning of the August Revolution, also called the Quit India Movement. It started with strikes and processions, but in the absence of the leaders, degenerated into violent demonstrations. Incidents of violence and anti-British rioting were reported from places as far apart as Bombay and Bihar. Viceroy Linlithgow described it in a letter to Churchill as 'the most serious rebellion since that of 1857'.

So intense was the national feeling that Shyama Prasad, a minister in the Bengal government, wrote a letter to Governor-General Linlithgow on 12 August 1942 emphasizing that 'the demand of Congress virtually constituted the national demand of India as a

whole' and that 'an immediate transfer of power is essential to the
solution of the Indian deadlock and there never was a period during
the last hundred years when the feeling against the British was so
bitter as it is today'.[14] In Bengal the August Revolution took its most
pronounced and militant form in Tamluk and Contai in Medinipore
district, which had already earned a reputation as the most anti-
British or freedom-loving district in the subcontinent.

At many places, students and Congress volunteers brought
down the British Union Jack and hoisted the Congress tricolour,
which flew for days. As the Congress leaders were arrested en masse
in all towns and even at the village level, there was little guidance at
the grass-roots level. It was war-time and the administration was
busy with various tasks connected with the arrangement of military
movement. Thus, people everywhere, on their own initiative, in a
natural outburst of anger, took various steps as they thought best.
Some of them even resorted to subversive actions. In Contai and
Tamluk subdivisions of Medinipore district, a large number of
Congressmen who had all along been non-violent freedom fighters
under leaders like Birendranath Sasmol turned violent against the
British authority and their local collaborators in the winter of 1943.
The vestiges of British rule disappeared for months together and the
revolutionaries themselves established virtual national governments.
In Tamluk, the national government lasted from 17 December 1942
to 8 August 1944. The supreme leader of this government was Satish
Chandra Samanta. Other leaders were Ajoy Mukherjee and Sushil
Dhara. An official report of that period described what happened as
follows:

> In Medinipore in Bengal, the operations of the rebels
> indicated considerable care and planning. All approach
> roads to these two subdivisions were cut off from the rest of
> the district by felling trees, digging trenches and destroying
> bridges. Military and police forces from outside could
> approach these areas after many months. An effective
> warning system had been devised and elementary tactical
> principles were observed, for instance, encirclements and
> flanking movements clearly on pre-arranged signals. The

rebel groups were accompanied by doctors and nursing orderlies to attend the casualties and its intelligence system was effective.[15]

The rebels formed a national government[16] under a supreme commander. To help him in administration there were ministers in charge of justice, law and order, health, education, agriculture and publicity. A postal system was introduced. Steps were taken for using convicts who had been released from jail. A volunteer army was formed and captains were appointed under an army chief. Besides fighting men, the army had intelligence personnel, doctors, compounders and nursing orderlies; there were arrangements for removing the injured and sick soldiers. This was the general picture. The British authorities replied with ruthless suppression.

Some ministers of Fazlul Huq's government, notably Shyama Prasad Mukherjee, made local enquiries and protested against the repressive policies. Shyama Prasad raised his voice strongly against police excesses and formed a Sufferers' Relief Committee with Fazlul Huq as president and B.M. Birla, Dr B.C. Roy and himself as co-sponsors for providing relief to survivors and relatives of victims of police and military atrocities during the August uprising. These atrocities, according to Shyama Prasad 'resembled the activities of the Germans in occupied areas as propagated by the British agencies'. Medinipore district was placed under an 'iron curtain' from which no one could come out without a permit issued by the government. But officialdom was totally impervious. As there was a strong demand in the Assembly for an enquiry into police excesses, Premier Huq gave an assurance of such an enquiry. This provoked Governor Herbert to write to the premier in intemperate language on 15 February 1943:

> You have given today in the Legislature an understanding for an enquiry into the conduct of officials in the district. You are well aware that this subject attracts my special responsibilities and you are also aware of my views on the undesirability of enquiries into the matter…I shall expect an explanation from you at your interview tomorrow morning of your conduct in failing to consult me before

announcing what purports to be the decision of the Government.

Huq paid back the Governor in his own coin by replying on 16 February:

> It appears from your letter that you are not prepared to give your consent to the constitution of a committee of enquiry. If so, the only way left open to me is to make a statement in the House in which I shall endeavour to explain that my statement made yesterday should not be taken as a commitment on the part of the government to a committee of enquiry, and I propose to read out to the House your letter under reply so as to explain my position.

Even Viceroy Linlithgow expressed his reservation over the Governor's overzealousness in a letter to Amery, the minister for India in the British government.

> I am very disturbed about this business of Herbert. I am sure it is more dangerous for governors to play politics even if they are of outstanding capacity, and I fear that poor Herbert can hardly claim to be of the latter category. My confidence in him has never, as you know, been great, but this incident has administered a severe further shock to it; and I have as you will see felt obliged to send him a pretty stiff letter, though of course I accept the necessity for protecting his position and saving his face.

But the Governor-General did not make any visible move. Even when Dr Shyama Prasad Mukherjee and, after him, Fazlul Huq resigned, such acts of oppression continued. To quote from Dr Shyama Prasad Mukherjee's letter on the subject:

> The atrocities perpetrated by the government in Medinipore can be compared only with the German atrocities in the occupied countries during the Second World War. We have received information of the police having had burnt down hundreds of houses and committed rape on women.

Government officials have incited Muslims to set fire to
and to loot the houses of Hindus and they have themselves
been guilty of such acts. The local officials did not pay heed
to government directions to stop the same. When we went
to Medinipore 15 days after the cyclone that ravaged the
district on 16 October, to inspect the extent of the calamity,
arson and looting were still going on in some parts of the
district.[17]

Premier Fazlul Huq admitted that during two weeks in the month
of August, firing by the police had taken twenty lives and caused
injury to 152 persons—the casualties actually numbered much
more. Fazlul Huq also admitted that police firing on some occasions
was not justified.

Santhals and Muslims of Bolpur in the district of Birbhum
attacked the railway station and caused a good deal of damage to it.
At other places too post offices, railway stations and courts were
targets of attack and the police and the army were always prepared
to take adequate revenge. This unequal fight between the people and
the government lasted about two weeks, but by the beginning of
1943 normalcy returned everywhere except in Contai and Tamluk.

People's attention now turned to the Japanese attacks at the
borders, the broadcasts made by Subhas Bose from Singapore
announcing the formation of the Azad Hind Government in exile
and the Indian National Army and exhorting his countrymen to rise
up against the British raj, the Japanese air raids in Kolkata and
Chittagong, the cyclone and tidal waves affecting Medinipore and
the approaching Bengal famine of 1943. People used to listen to
Subhas Bose's radio broadcasts with rapt attention. Such was his
popularity with the Bengalis that Ian Stephens, the then editor of the
Statesman, Kolkata, wrote that Subhas would only have to parachute
down to the *maidan* in Kolkata and 90 per cent of the people would
rise up and follow him.

Medinipore Cyclone, 1942

An important event during this period was the Medinipore cyclone
and tidal waves of 16 October 1942. Unprecedented tidal waves

lashed the Contai coast, killed hundreds of people and cattle and destroyed scores of villages and miles of paddy land. While this natural calamity put a halt to the Quit India Movement in Contai and Tamluk, it also exposed officialdom to the charge of ignoring the relief and rehabilitation needs of the affected villagers. Their feelings of revenge got the better of their humanitarian feelings. The affected people numbered 23.5 lakh. Shyama Prasad rushed to Medinipore on 30 October and held a meeting at the circuit house. So enraged were the authorities at his outbursts that while returning he was briefly placed under arrest by white officials at Kolaghat. On his return to Kolkata, he held a meeting presided over by Premier Huq. This meeting decided to place relief operations in the cyclone-affected areas under the direct supervision of a senior Indian Civil Service (ICS) officer, B.R. Sen. Shyama Prasad stated in the Legislative Assembly (12 February 1943) that:

> Actuated by malice and disgust for the revolutionaries of Medinipore the district magistrate declined to discharge the imperative duties of a responsible officer that were called for to lessen the distress of the affected people. He informed the government that no relief operation would be undertaken by the administration as a measure of punishment for the hostility of the people to the government and no permission would be granted to non-official organisations for carrying on relief work.

The newspapers were instructed not to publish any account of the distress of the people of Medinipore. But Huq and Shyama Prasad sought to bypass the district magistrate and created a separate and parallel relief administration headed by an official with higher status.

Erosion of Huq's popularity

Meanwhile the ground was slipping fast under Fazlul Huq's feet. The true winner in the situation created by the Quit India Movement and the mass-scale incarceration of Congressmen was Jinnah, who had a clear field to himself and made the most of the government's unstinted support extended to him. He dramatically improved his standing among Muslims and was fast becoming a leader who was acknowledged as such by the overwhelming number of Muslims in undivided India. Several chance happenings like the untimely death of Sikander Hayat Khan of Punjab, the indefatigable advocate of a united Punjab with Muslims, Hindus and Sikhs sharing power, and the assassination of Premier Alla Baksh in Sind, who was not a friend of the Muslim League, helped him. In Bengal, Fazlul Huq was fast getting isolated among Muslims. The League activists systematically attended Huq's meetings, heckled him and attacked KPP workers. In the Bengal Legislative Assembly sessions, the Muslim League trio—Nazimuddin, Suhrawardy and Tamizuddin Khan— launched bitter personal attacks on him, calling him a Muslim renegade and appealing to the religious sentiments of Muslims. Thus on 24 February 1942, Suhrawardy declared in the Assembly: 'Fazlul Huq has betrayed his colleagues in his party and his community and as such Muslim society has cast him away. Muslim Bengal will avenge his conduct.' This provoked Shyama Prasad to say: 'I strongly protest against the dirty calumny made by Suhrawardy—his party having been kicked out of the cabinet has been spreading calumnies to vent its spleen.... The new path that Fazlul Huq has chalked out with courage is the only way to save not only Bengal but India as a whole.' The results of the League's propaganda war and the erosion of Huq's popularity were evident from a bye-election for a Muslim seat in the Assembly (1942) in which the League candidate trounced the KPP candidate by 10,843 votes to 840.

Huq's government also became the victim of a set of repressive policies launched by the Government of India over which the provincial government had no control. With the Japanese army lurking on Bengal's doors, the government stopped the plying of boats on rivers so as to deny transport to the invading Japanese when they came. This affected the movement of foodgrains and prices shot up. Also, the movement of people was hindered. Indiscriminate arrests and restrictions on personal freedom also built up resentment. The government in power inevitably became the target of peoples' resentment, although all these policies were ruthlessly imposed by the bureaucracy headed by the Governor with the help of the army under direct orders from New Delhi, bypassing Huq's provincial government.

Muslim League leaders also poisoned the ears of the British authorities saying that since one of the coalition partners was the Forward Block, the party of Subhas Bose who had joined the Axis powers, Fazlul Huq and his ministers inevitably had sympathy for Subhas' anti-British activities. Such a government could not truly support the war efforts. Nazimuddin openly stated: 'This ministry is sympathetic to people engaged in traitorous activities and by facilitating enemy attacks on India is setting at naught all our war efforts.'[18] Thus, a conspiracy was being hatched by the Muslim League, the Governor and the twenty-five European MLAs to replace the Shyama–Huq coalition with a Muslim League-led coalition. This was facilitated by two unexpected developments—first, Fazlul Huq's overtures to Jinnah for rapprochement and second, Shyama Prasad's abandonment of Fazlul Huq at this critical hour. On 13 November 1942, Huq wrote a secret letter to Jinnah offering to return to the Muslim League with his party and suggesting a meeting. Jinnah in his response laid down certain conditions, which Huq did not find it possible to accept. Jinnah hit Huq below the belt by publishing this correspondence, a clear breach of faith. Huq lost credibility among the Hindus as also his own party men. Meanwhile, Shyama Prasad had written to Governor Sir John Herbert on 7 March 1942, proposing the creation of a home army for the defence of Bengal from the Japanese invaders. This was stonewalled by the government.

Also, Shyama Prasad was gradually coming to the conclusion that the bureaucracy, taking advantage of the war-time conditions and with encouragement from the Governor and the white masters at New Delhi, was determined to frustrate the efforts of the ministers to do anything concrete. Under the 1935 Constitution, the Secretary of a department could approach the Governor directly and express his view, bypassing the minister. The Governor under his special powers could uphold the Secretary and overrule the minister. Sir John Herbert was taking full advantage of this provision and dealing directly with the officials, completely ignoring the ministers. There was the ridiculous incident of the district magistrate passing a

Section 144 order against Premier Huq at Feni and preventing him from addressing the victims of military atrocities (1943). Governor Herbert ordered officials to remove foodgrains from several East Bengal districts and also strictly implement the 'boat removal policy' so as to obstruct the advance of the Japanese. He did not even consider a memorandum on this submitted by the minister. As such instances multiplied, Shyama Prasad wrote a long letter to the Governor on 26 July 1942, bitterly complaining that officialdom in Writers Building was obstructing the functioning of Fazlul Huq's cabinet in every possible way and accused the Governor himself of encouraging this defiance, favouring the Muslim League in its nefarious design and not encouraging Fazlul Huq and his colleagues in their progressive efforts.

In his letter he declared forcefully:

> For the first time in British Indian history, the influential representatives of the Hindus and Muslims respectively in Bengal have been trying to work the democratic constitution given to them in spite of the numerous defects and shortcomings in it. If their efforts succeed, it will naturally falsify the plea that the political advancement of India is impeded by communal disputes. It is therefore to the interest of the autocratic bureaucracy to see that the ministerial efforts do not succeed.

He did not hesitate to criticize the conduct of the Governor himself in the following words:

> Instead of encouraging Fazlul Huq and his colleagues in their progressive efforts, you have time and again found it necessary to hold the brief for the Muslim League. Your special pleadings for the Muslim League have, to speak the truth, shown you up before your eyes as a distinguished manipulator of the manoeuvrings of the Muslim League rather than as an impartial constitutional head and your conduct has appeared to us as quite mysterious... It is a matter of deep regret that even in important matters relating to popular demands and the right of the people, you have

allowed yourself to be guided by a class of permanent
officials instead of your constitutional advisers. The special
responsibility bestowed on you by Article 52 of the
Government of India Act is capable of a wide interpretation,
particularly now during the war, and you have brought into
existence a separate administration inside the administration
in this province, with the result that real power has passed
into the hands of people who under the democratic
constitution have no responsibility for the administration
of the province. This is a weighty allegation that I am
making. You should know that willingly or unwillingly you
have created an idea in the minds of your ministers which
stands in the way of good administration in the province...
I end this letter with this assurance that what I wanted was
also that during the war you would exercise your powers in
collaboration with the elected representatives of the people.
If you are decided in your mind that this war is a conflict
between the two ideals of brute force and authoritarianism
on the one hand and humaneness and a spirit of freedom
on the other and that you are determined to uphold the
latter, you should have no difficulty in conceding what I
have asked for.

Shyama Prasad also raised the issue of the police atrocities on
Congress agitators especially in Medinipore district and suggested a
persuasive and conciliatory approach with the help of elected
ministers in dealing with the Congress' Quit India Movement. As
the Governor once again turned down his proposals, he wrote to the
Viceroy, Lord Linlithgow, on 12 August 1942, advising that India
should be granted independence without delay and that a national
government should be formed at the Centre and also in all provinces,
consisting of representatives of all political parties. All power should
be transferred to them except the actual responsibility of conducting
military operations, which could stay with the commander-in-chief.
In his opinion this was absolutely necessary 'if India was to participate
in the war with success'. Also, 'the demand of the Congress is the
national demand of India as a whole'. He suggested the formation

of national all-party governments at the Centre as well as the provinces.

Without waiting for a reply, Shyama Prasad proceeded to resign from Fazlul Huq's cabinet on 16 November 1942, calling provincial autonomy a 'colossal mockery' and accusing the Governor of allowing official advice to prevail over the minister, especially in matters concerning the rights and liberties of the people. Significantly, there was no difference of opinion with Premier Huq nor any rancour between the two. They continued to be good friends amidst adverse political circumstances till Shyama Prasad's untimely death in 1953. His resignation was entirely due to his aversion to British policies and intrigues and his sense of frustration at not being able to achieve anything positive in the face of hostilities from the government and white officialdom and their unhelpful and unsympathetic policies in relation to the Medinipore freedom fighters and cyclone victims. His letter of resignation was suppressed under the Defence of India Rules. But in his statement before the Bengal Assembly on 12 February 1943, the great nationalist leader mentioned in detail the arrogance of the permanent British officers, how they put up obstacles in the path of ministers with the connivance of the Governor and stated that under these circumstances it was not possible for any self-respecting person to continue as minister. He repeated in the statement the same arguments that he had advanced in his letters to the Viceroy and the Governor in support of his proposal for granting independence to India immediately and of entrusting the defence of the country to the Indian Army.

He also referred to the reign of terror let loose by the bureaucracy with the support of the Governor in Medinipore and other places for suppressing the movement of 1942 and described how the people of cyclone-devastated Medinipore were denied relief as a punishment for their seditious activities and were thus pushed into the jaws of death. He expressed his deep regret that the ministers were totally powerless to render any help to the afflicted people. According to him, the wily bureaucracy with the help of arrogant officials and the ready support of the Governor set at naught all the efforts of the ministers in that regard.

Referring to the arrogance of the British officials he said:

> The insolence of a British civilian officer reached a height
> that he went the length of recording in a note that the
> unfortunate displaced persons from East Bengal did not
> deserve the amount of monetary help that was being given
> to them and that as an officer of the Imperial service he was
> not bound to carry out the orders of the provincial
> government in that regard. That officer is still smug as a
> trusted official in a responsible post.[19]

He bitterly complained how in the name of suppressing a political
movement relief was being denied by a heartless administration to
genuinely distressed people after the Medinipore cyclone. After this
devastating catastrophe of 16 October, it had been hoped that
political disputes would end and the people and the government
would cooperate in taking relief to the distressed victims of the
cyclone. But far from relieving the distress of the people, the officials
did not even allow the news of this catastrophe to be published for
a fortnight with the object of preventing non-government relief
from reaching the suffering people. The district magistrate refused
permission to any non-official organization to start relief work in
the areas. The Governor himself remained impervious to any
suggestions. No attempts were made to improve the political situation
by calling for cooperation in the relief operations from persons
inside and out of jail in connection with the movement. Rather, the
government followed a sinister policy of carrying on relief work
during the day and looting and harassment during the night.

> In the presence of local officers, people have made numerous
> complaints of oppression on them but we have not been
> able to give them any protection. Before I finish this account
> of my experience concerning Medinipore, I would point
> out that the information about an attack on a village about
> a month back that has reached us, reveals many shameful
> incidents of systematic rape on women by those who are
> responsible for maintenance of law and order. I have with
> me the statements of the women who were violated and

these have smeared the administration with an indelible black stain.

Fall of Fazlul Huq's second government

After Shyama Prasad's resignation, the fall of Fazlul Huq's ministry was only a question of time. The Muslim League made overtures to Hindu legislators as no government could be formed without the support of some of them. On 27 March 1943, both Nazimuddin and Suhrawardy appealed to Hindus to discard Fazlul Huq and join up with the League in forming a new government. Suhrawardy announced that 'I give this understanding on behalf of the Muslim League that if Fazlul Huq stands aside, we Hindus and Muslims jointly should be able to carry on the administration peacefully.' But Fazlul Huq still demonstrated his majority by winning on a cut motion on 27 March 1943. In a memorable emotion-paced speech he pleaded for a national government, which alone could alleviate Bengal's distress.

But the very next day he was tricked into resigning by the wily Governor, Sir John Herbert. The Governor sent for him in the evening and from 7.30 p.m. to 9.30 p.m. discussed the possibility of the formation of a national cabinet. Then he requested Huq to resign to facilitate the formation of such a cabinet and even placed a typed letter of resignation before him for his signature, giving him the impression that he would invite Huq again to form such an all-party national government. Huq naively signed the letter,[20] which was as follows:

My dear John,
Understanding that there is a probability of the formation of a ministry representative of most of the parties in the event of my resignation, I hereby tender my resignation of my office as minister in the sincere hope that this will prove to be in the best interest of the people of Bengal.

Yours sincerely
A.K. Fazlul Huq

Huq went home, only to be informed at 10 p.m. that the Governor
had accepted his resignation. The expected invitation to form a new
government never came. Clearly, the Governor reneged on the
understanding he gave Huq. According to another version, Huq was
not willing to resign, but was forced to sign a letter of resignation,
already prepared, under threat of dismissal. Fazlul Huq himself
never told the full story of what transpired in Government House,
but only stated in the Assembly on 5 July 1943 that he was forced
to resign as a result of a deep conspiracy to which the Governor was
party. He still asserted that he commanded the majority in the
Bengal Assembly. The manner in which Fazlul Huq was made to
resign perfidiously in March 1942, by an intriguing double-faced
British Governor, will always remain a blot on British rule in Bengal.
Fazlul Huq's coalition with Shyama Prasad (1941–43) was a shining
example of right-thinking politicians shedding their political labels
and coming together in the province's larger interest to save Bengal
from its journey to political disaster. Also, it gave a good example of
communal harmony in the enveloping communal darkness. But fate
decreed otherwise.

Nazimuddin's Muslim League coalition (1943–45)

Governor's rule was proclaimed under Article 93 of the Constitution
but only as an interregnum for about a month. On 24 April 1943,
Khwaja Nazimuddin, the leader of the Muslim League in the
Assembly, was invited to form a cabinet. Evidently, this was what
Governor Herbert and officialdom had intended. This cabinet
included some breakaway Congressmen like Tulsi Goswami and
Barada Pyne as also some scheduled caste leaders. But it was
essentially a Muslim League government, not a national government.[21]
The duplicity with which Fazlul Huq's cabinet was bundled off and
a Muslim League-led government was installed came in for a lot of
criticism. Both Huq and Shamsuddin Ahmed, the KPP parliamentary
party leader, wired the Viceroy demanding the installation of a
national government in Bengal. A public meeting held in the Town
Hall on the same day (24 April 1943) under the chairmanship of
Abdul Halim Ghuznavi, bitterly criticized the action of a partisan

Governor. Shyama Prasad said that the Governor and the British
trading community of Kolkata could not accept Fazlul Huq's
independent attitude and had, therefore, entered into a heinous
conspiracy to oust him. Huq himself complained that he was made
to sign on a false assurance and accused the Governor of breach of
faith and of bringing through the backdoor the Nazimuddin ministry,
which was not 'national' but communal. The meeting adopted a
resolution condemning the Governor's action and demanding a
national government. Needless to say, the British raj remained
unmoved. What must have weighed with the British authorities in
removing Fazlul Huq and bringing in a government[22] led by the
loyalist and pliable Nazimuddin was the fact that in the context of
the deteriorating war situation for the British, the spectacular Japanese
occupation of South-East Asia, the formation of the Azad Hind
government led by Subhas Bose and their joint advance to Bengal's
borders, they could not tolerate an independent-minded premier in
Bengal and wanted a 'yes man' like Nazimuddin who would not
oppose their 'denial' policies or repressive steps on grounds of
public suffering. Thus Governor Sir John Herbert was given a free
hand in engineering the political coup.

The great famine of 1943

The single biggest happening of these two years, apart from the
raging world war—the one that overshadowed everything else—was
the great Bengal famine of 1943 (1350 BS). Occurring towards the
end of British rule, this famine popularly called *panchasher
manwantar* (the great famine of 1350 BS) is comparable in its
magnitude with the great famine of 1770 (1176 BS)—*chhiattarer
manwanter*—that had ravaged Bengal at the commencement of
British rule. Almost as many people died in this famine as those who
were killed in the second world war raging—a slow lingering death
by starvation. The official Enquiry Commission headed by Sir John
Woodhead put the death toll at 15 lakh. Unofficial estimates spoke
of figures as high as 50 lakh. Applying the Commission's own
method of calculation, Amartya Sen has estimated a figure of
around 30 lakh deaths.[23] The importance of this great catastrophe,

almost wholly man-made, also lay in the fact that it severely damaged Bengal's rural economy and rural life, and also played havoc with the 'social value system'. The principal causes were the following:

a) The Japanese occupation of Burma had cut off the supply of rice from that country. Bengal had traditionally depended to a significant extent on rice from Burma.

b) The widespread confiscation of boats and other means of transport such as bullock carts by the government all over the province in pursuance of the so-called 'denial' policy to Japanese invaders affected normal trade channels and caused acute scarcity in a large number of pockets. The ruthless manner in which this policy was implemented with the backing of the army created serious dislocation. Not only were the boats and carts destroyed or confiscated, the police even forcibly removed or destroyed stocks of paddy from the godowns of the rice merchants or often the peasants. Such destruction and seizure of paddy on a large scale took place in the districts of Medinipore, 24-Parganas, Khulna, Bakharganj and Noakhali and several other districts. The seized rice was generally passed on to the hands of government agents who hoarded it and brought it out later as ration rice. In his memoirs of the famine, Ashok Mitra graphically described how Munshiganj subdivision, that is, Bikramapur Pargana, was rendered completely devoid of rice and paddy in 1942–43 and countless people died as a result of severe scarcity.[24] In this area, the price of rice, which was Rs 3-4 per maund in February 1942, became Rs 90-100 per maund by December 1943. As this was a riverine area, there was not enough flow of rice from the normal trade channels to this area. Nor was the government prepared for a contingency of this type. What was happening in Munshiganj by and large happened in many pockets all over Bengal. Along with the destruction of trade and commerce through the 'denial' policy, the forcible removal of the inhabitants of a large number of villages in the coastal areas (speech by K.C. Neogy in the Central Legislative

Assembly on 17 September 1942) also aggravated the conditions.

c) Large-scale procurement of foodgrain from the market for feeding the huge military personnel of the allied powers.

d) Restrictions imposed by the government on movement of goods including foodgrains by railways and roadways also hindered the movement of foodgrains from other provinces to Bengal. This was further worsened by the choking of the available railway capacity by military movement.

e) Influx of several lakhs of refugees from Burma to Bengal and the need to feed so many additional mouths.

f) There was wide-scale hoarding of paddy and rice by dishonest businessmen with a view to black marketeering and profiteering. It was rumoured that this was often assisted by dishonest ministers and government officials who had links with those traders. Appointing Ispahani's company as the sole buying agent for the government without calling for tenders and giving it an advance of Rs 2 crore came in for much criticism. The anti-hoarding drives conducted by the government agencies were more cosmetic than serious. In a radio speech, the acting Governor, Ratherford, admitted that on account of the administration's laxity the ration shop owners could sell essential articles to dishonest black marketeers at high prices and that a section of dishonest officials obstructed the policy of government distribution at fair prices.

g) Farmers were removed from several parts of Bengal for war needs and the lands remained fallow.

The disastrous cyclone of 1942 that ravaged Medinipore, 24-Paraganas and other coastal areas reduced large sections of marginal farmers and landless labourers to poverty and left them without any purchasing power. It also killed a huge number of menfolk, thereby reducing their womenfolk and children to penury. This was responsible for the presence of a very large number of famished women among the beggars that one saw in Kolkata streets and other urban areas crying for food.

There was a certain spirit of revenge in Governor Herbert and a section of the white officialdom against Bengal after Subhas Bose's escape from custody on 27 January 1941, which subjected the entire administration and the security arrangements to ridicule, and the August Movement, especially in Medinipore, which had for all practical purposes freed large areas from the colonial administration and turned them into liberated zones.

The situation was aggravated by the government's inability to start relief work in a timely fashion, set up adequate organization for food procurement and distribution and declare famine in Bengal under the Famine Code. As early as 24 April 1943, in a meeting at the Kolkata Town Hall, Shyama Prasad announced that the new ministry had done the greatest disservice to the people of Bengal by emphasizing that there was no shortage of food supplies in Bengal. Again, on 14 July 1943, he thundered in the Bengal Assembly, 'The government was fiddling while the villagers in Bengal were crying for a morsel' and blamed the British administration in India fairly and squarely. But all these warnings were simply ignored by the government in both Kolkata and New Delhi.

It is possible to get at the truth of this phenomenal happening from the proceedings of the Bengal Assembly, in particular from the speech of Dr Shyama Prasad Mukherjee on 29 February 1943, from the speeches of Fazlul Huq on 29 March and 5 July, and the proceedings of both the British Parliament and the Indian Central Assembly. It was a clear case of the Governor's administration enforcing certain high-handed policies in the interest of the war, but totally unmindful of their disastrous effect on the life of the common people, while the so-called provincial government only played a very secondary role in a highly inept manner. This famine also received considerable academic attention even at that time from scholars like P.C. Mahalanobis, who did not have access to any data, and subsequently from Amartya Sen in his seminal work Poverty and Famine: An Essay on Entitlement and Deprivation, 1981[25] after nearly four decades. What is a matter of great surprise is that this famine, unlike its predecessors, did not affect the bhadralok class, but only the poorer sections of society, especially the rural poor who found themselves without anything to sustain themselves in their villages and were forced into cities and towns in the quest for food, which was available in significant quantities in shops in the towns for those who had the purchasing power. These famished poor had none. They had neither the money to buy food nor the courage to defy the police and the army and start food riots. They simply starved and died in thousands in silence. Subhas Bose offered, in his radio broadcasts from Saigon, to send two shiploads of rice for the dying people of his beloved Bengal and asked the British authorities to accept these ships and get them unloaded. But this was rebuffed both by the Allied supreme commander, Mountbatten, and the minister for India, Amery, who said that this would amount to appeasement of the nationalists.

There were ominous signs even in 1942. The price of rice jumped up in three months from Rs 10 a maund to Rs 45 per maund. But these were ignored by Fazlul Huq's government, which was rendered ineffectual by its internal weaknesses, by a callous Governor busy with his intrigues and a heartless Viceroy in Delhi, who never found time even once to visit Bengal even when the famine was raging in its full fury. In fact, the entire government machinery showed utmost callousness and indifference. The Congress leadership, almost in its entirety, was behind bars. The Muslim League leaders were busy playing power games. Officialdom was demoralized and incompetent. Part of it, especially white officials, were too busy enforcing war-time restrictions. Strict censorship kept the public in the dark, and suppressed all the warning signals. It was only when hundreds had died of starvation in the countryside, and thousands of famished villagers made their way to the metropolis of Kolkata and district towns, many of them dying in full view of the public, that the full magnitude of the raging disaster dawned on the authorities and the world outside. Apathy in Delhi and incompetence and corruption in Kolkata combined together to bring about by far the worst famine in recent history, a largely man-made disaster. The whole of Bengal was rent with anguished cries of the hungry seeking *bhat* (rice) or even *fan* (the water drained out after boiling rice). The streets of Kolkata were littered with dead bodies and dying men and women. The majority of those who used to beg for *fan* day in and day out on the streets of Kolkata were women from the Medinipore and 24-Parganas districts who had lost their men during the cyclone of 16 October 1942. The *New Statesman* of London in its issue of 24 September 1943 under the headline 'Black Death in Calcutta' said: 'The description of life in Calcutta reads like extracts from medieval chronicle of black death.'

But even when faced with this grim reality, Nazimuddin's government proved hopelessly incompetent. It came in for severe criticism in the Assembly from Fazlul Huq, Shyama Prasad Mukherjee and many others. There were dark hints that some of the ministers were party to the hoarding of foodgrains, racketeering and black marketeering. It was during this time that a new expression 'black market' entered the Indian English vocabulary. The Civil Supply Department, of which Suhrawardy was minister, came in for criticism. All efforts by distinguished observers like Hridaynath Kunzru, who visited Bengal early in 1943, failed to make the government in Delhi sit up to take steps to rush supplies to Bengal. But Jinnah acquitted Nazimuddin's government by describing it as 'a fire brigade called too late to put out the raging flame'.[26] There were, however, large-scale private relief efforts spearheaded by Shyama Prasad's Bengal Relief Committee in which prominent non-officials like B.C. Roy, G.D. Birla, Fazlul Huq, Saraogi and Anandilal Poddar participated.

It was only the departure of Linlithgow and the arrival of Field Marshal Lord Wavell as the new Viceroy on 17 October 1943 which for the first time imparted a sense of urgency to famine control measures. Within a week after being sworn in as Viceroy, Wavell with his instinct as a soldier flew to Kolkata to study the Bengal famine for himself. He spent three days in discussions with Bengal ministers and officials. At night he went round the streets to see piled up dead bodies and sleeping destitutes. He spent one day in the Contai area of Medinipore, which had been ravaged thrice, first by the Quit India Movement, next by the unprecedented cyclone and tidal waves and now by the famine. He made the director general of the Indian Medical Services cancel all his programmes in Shimla and rush to Kolkata to arrange for medicines to deal with starvation-related diseases which were stalking Bengal. He badgered both Churchill's government in London and his own administration in Delhi for shipment of foodgrains and other aid to Bengal, and at one point even threatened to resign if London did not arrange immediate shipments.

Wavell also instructed the Bengal government to take the following steps immediately:

a) Construction of shelters outside Kolkata for the countless famine-stricken people who were staying on the streets or in the open and arranging to shift them there and providing them food.

b) Dispatch of foodgrains to the scarcity-affected village areas with the help of the army.

c) Introduction of full statutory rationing in Kolkata.

After this, the civil supply department under Suhrawardy showed some signs of activity. But the famine had already taken a heavy toll. According to official records, 15 lakh people died in this famine. Unofficial estimates placed the number around 30 lakh between July 1943 and June 1944. In Dr Shyama Prasad Mukherjee's reckoning, around 50 lakh people died. The relief efforts launched by Shyama Prasad in, among other things, setting up the Bengal Relief Committee, opening around 250 relief centres covering 24 districts, feeding starving people in these centres with collected foodgrains and appealing to all legislators in India to donate Rs 10 out of their daily allowance of Rs 40 provided a shining example of what the private efforts of a visionary nationalist free from communal considerations could achieve in the face of a hostile government environment. He received commendation even in the secret reports of the Central intelligence branch. Wavell himself blamed the Bengal ministry for this man-made famine and after his personal visit was said 'to have recommended the dismissal of this ministry and Governor's rule under Section 93. But the home government did not agree. Thus, Bengal was ravaged by a severe famine at the close of British rule as it had been by another even at its advent.[27] It took long to recover from the ravages.

The famine coincided with another man-made scarcity—that of cotton textiles in 1944–45. Cotton simply disappeared from the market. Once again, there were complaints of large-scale hoarding by Marwari black marketeers, and dark hints of the complicity of the civil supply minister, Suhrawardy, and the officials of his department. Day in and day out there was mud-slinging between the Treasury and the Opposition in the Assembly. Even the leader of the European group in the Assembly, H.R. Norton commented openly: 'As a businessman of 36 years experience in Calcutta I have never known such a dearth of cloth as there has been during the last 12 months.' 10 March 1944 was observed as the 'textile crisis day' and a public meeting in Wellington Square presided over by the Assembly Speaker, Nausher Ali, lambasted the government for creating this artificial scarcity.

Fall of Nazimuddin's government and Governor's Rule (1945)

Nazimuddin's government tried unsuccessfully to get a modified version of the KPP–League government's 1940 Bill on Secondary Education passed by the Assembly, but once again the Hindu members were adamant and moved about 3,000 amendments to the bill. Even a parliamentary secretary to the government, Atul Chandra Kumar, resigned in protest. The passage of the bill was deadlocked as before.

But all this added to the League's popularity among the Muslim masses, further helped by the mass contact programme launched by Abul Hashim after he was elected secretary of the Bengal Muslim League. The Pakistan slogan was also steadily gaining ground. A straw in the wind was the Muslim League's unprecedented success in the 1944 elections to the Calcutta Corporation, ending the balance that had continued since Subhas Bose's pact with the League. Securing seventeen seats in the 1944 elections when the Congress was divided between Subhasists and non-Subhasists and with the Hindu Mahasabha further splitting Hindu votes, the League captured power in the Calcutta Corporation and got its nominees elected to all the aldermen's seats.

But the Nazimuddin ministry, which had lost popularity, was also fast losing its legislative strength. On 28 March 1945, during the budget session, it was defeated on the floor by 106 votes to ninety-seven on the grant for the agriculture department. In a historic ruling, the Speaker, Nausher Ali, declared Nazimuddin's government as invalid after its defeat on the floor. There were accusations that the Marwari businessmen played some role with their money power to induce some members to leave the Treasury benches and vote against the government. Suhrawardy openly made accusations on the floor of the House: 'If the voting goes against us and we have to resign, the only reason for that would be that members would be casting their votes against us out of greed for money offered to them by hoarders, profiteers and black marketers. If we had not moved for de-hoarding illegally hoarded stocks, we would not have to face this predicament.'[28]

In a desperate move, Nazimuddin asked for Jinnah's permission to form a coalition with the Congress and Jinnah gave his nod so long as the coalition was on honourable terms. But in a swift move, Governor Sir Richard Casey, who had joined on 22 January 1944, after Sir John Herbert's death, dismissed the Nazimuddin government and took over administration under Section 93. In his memoirs, Casey, who later on became Australia's foreign minister, made the following observations on his experience in Bengal: 'It is a matter of great regret that a certain proportion of Muslim and scheduled caste politicians are seduced to defect from the party and do not hesitate to join another.'[29] To set the record straight, we should also mention that the defection of Nawab Habibullah of Dhaka with ten followers reportedly because of his not being given the supply portfolio that he wanted played a major role in the government's defeat. In a statement issued on 19 April 1945, Nawab Habibullah and his ten followers accused the Nazimuddin ministry of ruining Bengal through their corruption and incompetence. They also accused the government of openly favouring Marwari businessmen and said that there was only one Muslim among the twenty agents appointed by the government for importing textiles from outside the province; all others being Hindus, mostly Marwaris. Thus, paradoxically, both

Suhrawardy and Nawab Habibullah of Dhaka blamed the Marwari businessmen, the former for the fall of the Nazimuddin ministry, and the latter for being hand in glove with that ministry. Perhaps both were partially right.

True, that no tears were shed for the fall of an inept government, but in fairness it must be said that on account of the prevailing war-time conditions and of the Defence of India Rules, the provincial government did not sometimes have the powers to set things right. Much of the administration took orders directly from the Government of India through the Governor. And their priority lay in meeting the supply needs of the Allied army fighting in Assam, Manipur and Chittagong, in facilitating military movements and in organizing activities such as air raid precautions. Unfortunately, the rising communal divide also had a role to play. The more the Hindu press attacked the government and some of its ministers personally, the more would a section of Muslims treat it as an unfair attack on Muslims and would more often than not impart a communal colour to it. This served as a shield for the government.

In retrospect, it should be highlighted that during these years from 1937 to 1945, the Muslim League, till then a small upper-class marginal party in Bengal, was transformed from an elitist to a mass-based party on account of a variety of circumstances. Entry to the League was made easier by reducing the annual membership fee from Re 1 to 2 annas. Old pro-zamindar policies were replaced by pro-tenant policies. In this process, Suhrawardy, who was popular among students, and Abul Hashim with his leftist leanings, played a major role. On his election as general secretary to the Bengal Provincial League in November 1943, Abul Hashim criticized the League's inability to meet people's needs. The League, according to him, had pawned itself thrice.[30] It had pawned its political leadership to the nawabs of Ahsan Manzil since the time of Salimullah; it had pawned its publicity rights to the owner of daily *Azad*, Maulana Akram Khan, and its finances to the business tycoon Ispahani. He promised to free the League from these shackles and let the Bengali Muslim middle class find its rightful place. He, as also Suhrawardy, toured the districts of Bengal extensively to build up grassroots support for the League. Students were extensively used to move from village to village and propagate the League. Workers of the KPP joined the League in large numbers. The Bengal famine of 1943 was seized as an opportunity to make mass contact in the name of relief. In 1944, the League leftists invited some KPP and Congress old guards to join the League. While Humayun Kabir and Ashraffuddin Chaudhury preferred to join the Congress, others like Maulana Abdullah-il-Baqi, Abul Mansur Ahmad, Shamsuddin Ahmed and Nawabzada Syed Hassan Ali joined the League. So great was the pull that a liberal lawyer and old follower of Gandhi and C.R. Das like Ali Ahmed Khan (1900–66) felt emotionally compelled to join the League and was elected to the Bengal Assembly in 1946 on its ticket.

By 1944 in his annual report Abul Hashim, as general secretary of the Bengal Provincial League, could announce that the Muslim League had become a revolutionary 'mass' movement and had penetrated rural Bengal. He claimed that in 1944 about 5,50,000 new members had been enrolled in Bengal. By abandoning its traditional pro-landlord stand in the United Provinces for the demand for the abolition of zamindari in Bengal, the League had drastically transformed itself. Dhaka University, by no means a League stronghold till the mid-1930s, became one in the 1940s. Its students offered themselves as volunteers to the League for the 1946 elections. Huq faced black flag demonstrations from students almost in every town of East Bengal after he left the League in 1941. Thus by 1945, the Muslim League had replaced all others as the overwhelmingly dominant party among Bengali Muslims. The rising tide of Bengali Muslim aspirations had no time for secular Muslims like Muzaffar Ahmad or Humayun Kabir, scholars like Saiyad Mujtaba Ali and nationalist politicians like Saiyad Nausher Ali and Ashraffuddin Ahmad Chaudhury. With extreme communalism rearing its head on both sides, all moderate sections were simply pushed to the wall.

Unfortunately, Hashim's efforts to propagate some sort of Islamic socialism and turn the League into a leftist organization came a cropper. His experiment in setting up a party house in Dhaka with a weekly paper *Hushiar* to carry on within the League a left-oriented movement that would eventually take over leadership from the khwajas and ashrafs also failed in the prevailing atmosphere of Muslim solidarity caused by the explosive slogan of 'Islam in Danger'. It had to wait until after partition when, faced with the rising tide of Bengali nationalism, the Muslim League disappeared from East Bengal almost as rapidly and as dramatically as it had made its advent ten years ago. In this process, leadership came not only from new leaders like Sheikh Mujibur Rahman and Maulana Bhashani but also, paradoxically, from veterans like Fazlul Huq and Suhrawardy.

5

UNITED BENGAL: LAST HOUR

Bengal was in a sullen mood under a spell of Governor's rule when the second world war ended in 1945 with the surrender of Germany (8 May) and Japan (8 August) after the Americans dropped the atom bomb on Hiroshima and Nagasaki. Politics in India had reached a virtual deadlock after the en masse arrest of Congress leaders and the petering out of the Quit India movement. The only gainer was the Muslim League under Jinnah. Gandhi went on a fast in protest against cruelties on *satyagrahis* from 9 February to 2 March 1943. But he failed to move an impervious colonial regime. The British authorities now released Gandhi for talks with Jinnah, which took place at Poona on 9–27 September 1944. These talks broke down because Gandhi was not willing to accept Jinnah's two-nation theory, although he gave his nod to the concept of an autonomous Muslim majority Pakistan. In a way, Gandhi, by his tacit acceptance of the idea of a partition and by calling Jinnah Qaid-e-Azam, strengthened Jinnah's position among Muslims. Also Jinnah, sensing victory, raised the stakes. He retorted to Gandhi's non-acceptance of the two-nation theory with his famous statement:

> Muslims and Hindus are two major nations by any definition or test of a nation. We are a nation of a hundred million, and what is more, we are a nation with an even distinctive culture and civilization, language and literature, art and

architecture, names and nomenclature, sense of values and proportions, legal laws and moral codes, customs, calendar, history and traditions, aptitudes and ambitions. In short, we have our own distinctive outlook on life and of life. By all canons of international law we are a nation.

What a long way to travel for one who was once hailed as an angel of Hindu–Muslim unity and one who till 1930 described himself as a nationalist Muslim and steadfastly opposed all forms of Muslim fundamentalism like the Khilafat agitation![1] Even those opposed to him now started flocking under his banner. A significant section of the Hindus remained resentful of Gandhi's meek surrender.

Shimla Conference—Labour Party in power in Britain

Even before the British elections on 26 July 1945, and the surrender of Japan in August, Governor-General Wavell called leaders of all political parties to a conference at Shimla. The main proposition that Wavell put before the Indian leaders was a fully Indian Executive Council with near full powers. But the Shimla Conference lasting from 25 June to 14 July 1945 ended in a fiasco, as the Muslim League and the Scheduled Caste Federation demanded that the Muslim and scheduled caste members in the Governor-General's Executive Council must be their respective nominees and the Congress rejected these demands, claiming the right to represent all sections of Indians, including the Muslims. Meanwhile, in the British elections in July 1945, Churchill's Conservative Party was defeated and the Labour Party formed the new government with Clement Attlee as Prime Minister. India's independence was one of the election pledges of the Labour Party. On 21 August, Attlee announced that elections to the central and provincial legislatures would be held immediately and thereafter a conference would be arranged for drafting a constitution for independent India.

The Indian National Army trials

At this time, the trial of the Indian National Army (INA) officials who had deserted the British Indian Army and joined Subhas Bose's

Azad Hind Fauj and fought the British, galvanized the whole country in 1945. They were accused of treachery against the king emperor and court-martialled. Not only did it spark off countrywide protests, but also brought about a temporary Hindu–Muslim unity. Thus the INA, when it was no more, proved much more trouble for the British raj than when it existed. The trial of the captured officers of Bose's Azad Hind Fauj by the authorities in 1945 on charges of treason and waging war against the king shook the whole subcontinent. Viceroy Wavell and Commander-in-Chief Auchinleck must have regretted subsequently their decision to publicly try the INA officers.

The first in a series of 15 court-martials were held in the Red Fort of Delhi, from 5 November 1945. The accused were Lt Col Shah Nawaz Khan, Captain Sehgal and Major Gurbax Singh Dhillon, the first a Muslim, the second a Hindu and the third a Sikh. The result was an emotional union of all the three communities in protesting against the trial. Public outcry compelled the Congress and the Muslim League leaders, initially hostile to the INA, to join up together on this issue. Congress leaders like Bhulabhai Desai, Tej Bahadur Sapru and even Nehru appeared before the military tribunal at the Red Fort to defend these officers. By this action they made up for their earlier lack of enthusiasm for Netaji and his INA. There was a frenzied public feeling against these trials, which also focused the spotlight on Subhas and the INA. In Kolkata there was widespread popular disturbance leading to police firing, in which forty were killed, and there was burning of trams, buses and police vans. The military tribunal sentenced the three officers to transportation for life. But on Gandhi's personal request and in response to popular feelings, the government commuted these sentences to dismissal from military service. No punishment was given to any officer or men of the INA who were tried in the next few months in 1945–46. On 21 November, a joint demonstration of the Congress, the Muslim League, the Forward Block and the Communists in Kolkata led to pitched battle conditions in which thirty-five people including students were killed in police firing. Many were arrested and subjected to sentences of up to seven years of rigorous imprisonment. Even the members of the Indian armed forces made no secret of their sympathy with the INA prisoners. Auchinleck commented in a report that every Indian commissioned officer is a nationalist.[2] The British were confused to see the intensity of Indian reaction and realized what a big political mistake they had made.

On 1 December, Auchinleck announced that the charge against the INA, accused of waging war against the king, would be dropped, and that further trials would be only for murder or brutality against other prisoners of war (POWs). But this failed to satisfy public opinion.

The trial of Captain Rashid Ali, one of the last in the series, on 11 February created a great deal of public hysteria. There were pitched battles between the police and the demonstrators in Kolkata leading to fatal casualties. Hindus and Muslims faced police bullets and lathi-charge shoulder to shoulder in this near-revolution, and eighty-four people were killed and 300 injured, including British and US soldiers. The Muslim League, the Congress and the Communists jointly took part in the movement. The army and the police took two days to restore normalcy. The Hindu–Muslim togetherness seen in Kolkata on that occasion was unbelievable. None could anticipate that in a few months, they would actually fight each other on the same streets in Kolkata during the Muslim League's Direct Action Day on 16 August 1946.

Naval mutiny, 1946

If the INA trials focused on the widespread anti-British feelings among the armed forces, another happening, namely, the mutiny in the Royal Indian Navy (18 February 1946) also highlighted this widespread phenomenon of wavering of loyalty in the armed forces. On that day, a number of Royal Indian Navy ships in the Bombay and Karachi naval bases openly revolted against the British, starting with protests against the court-martial of a Bengali naval rating, P.C. Dutt, for scribbling Jai Hind—the INA slogan—on walls. The mutiny spread like wildfire to seventy-eight ships and twenty shore establishments. Some of these ships opened fire against British naval ships. As the news of this revolt in the harbour reached Bombay there was widespread anti-government rising in the city. The police was unable to control the violence and the army had to be called in, leading to the killing of about 200 men. The Congress leadership did not encourage these anti-government disturbances at a time when it was about to assume power. Vallabhbhai Patel intervened and persuaded the mutineers to surrender on 23 February 1946. Jinnah also advised the Muslim seamen to return to their ships and lay down their arms. The naval mutiny did play a role in unsettling the psychology of the British rulers. In a way, it revived for many of them the memories of the 1857 mutiny. Also, the low morale of the British soldiers in India, anxious to return home, unnerved them. There were several cases of near revolt (for example, the revolt by British soldiers and airmen of the RAF units at Dum Dum, who had to be detained by Indian soldiers). Slowly the realization was dawning that the sooner they left India, the better.

On 19 February 1946, that is, one day after the naval mutiny, Prime Minister Attlee announced that a cabinet mission consisting of Lord Pathick Lawrence (leader), Sir Stafford Cripps and A.V. Alexander would be visiting India in a few days to negotiate with the Indian leaders a time frame for the British to leave India and the future Constitution for free India. Clearly, the British had realized that they could no longer count on the loyalty of Indian soldiers to hold India and should, therefore, hand over power to Indians. The memory of Subhas Bose and his Azad Hind Fauj loomed large on their mental horizon.

Central Assembly elections, December 1945

The elections held in December 1945 (for the Central Assembly) and March 1946 (for the provincial assemblies) returned the Congress in majority in the Central Assembly and in most of the provinces, the Muslim League to majority in Bengal and Sind and to the largest party position in Punjab. The Congress won 91.3 per cent of the votes in the general (all except Muslim) constituencies, nearly eliminating all other parties including the Hindu Mahasabha. Similarly, the Muslim League secured 88.6 per cent of the votes in the Muslim constituencies and bagged all the Muslim seats, thereby reinforcing its claim that it alone could, for the time being, speak on behalf of the Indian Muslim community. The new Central Assembly which had limited legislative powers under the 1935 Government of India Act, was composed of the following (figures in parentheses show the strength in the previous Assembly): Indian National Congress—fifty-seven (thirty-six), Muslim League—thirty (twenty-five), Nationalist Party—zero (ten), Akalis—two (zero) and Europeans—eight (eight). Sarat Chandra Bose, who had been welcomed back to the Congress on his release in 1945 and was elected to the Central Assembly as a Congress candidate, was elected leader of the Congress Party in the Assembly. But there are reasons to believe that the British were never happy to have dealings with Sarat Bose, a brother and close ally of that arch enemy of the British, Subhas Bose, and the Congress leadership soon realized this.[3]

Thus, in the entire negotiations for the transfer of power in 1946, the leader of the Congress in the Central Assembly was bypassed completely against normal constitutional practice. Nehru, Patel and Azad negotiated on behalf of the Congress, leaving Sarat Bose severely alone.

Bengal Assembly elections (March 1946)
Suhrawardy in power

In the campaign for Assembly elections in Bengal, the Muslim League made Pakistan the single issue and asked Muslims to vote only for Muslim League candidates to show that the League alone represented the Muslims. Jinnah had declared that this election was 'a plebiscite of Muslims of India on Pakistan'. Abul Hashim brought out a pamphlet titled 'Let us Go to War' in which he made the following appeal:

> The general election is the beginning of our struggle. Immediately after recording our votes in favour of Pakistan at the polling centres, immediately after winning our plebiscite liquidating the false claims of the Congress to represent the Muslims, we shall direct our attention towards British imperialism and demand immediate transference of power to the people of India on the basis of Pakistan.

The Muslim League enlisted the support of both Muslim student organizations and the mullahs in its campaign, and also launched a terror campaign on all non-League nationalists and Muslim KPP candidates. There were a number of complaints of assault on such candidates, their kidnapping in some cases or forcibly detaining some of them in their own houses. Even such well-known persons as the Speaker of the Assembly, Nausher Ali, and KPP leaders like Syed Jalaluddin Hashemi and Azahar Ali were attacked. Some of the mullahs put the fear of divine punishment on illiterate Muslims, warning them to vote only for League candidates.[4]

The result was a resounding success for the League. It got 115 seats out of 250 and the Congress 87. The KPP and the Communists got only four and three seats respectively. The only exception to the general tide was Fazlul Huq's convincing victory in the two seats that he contested. The Europeans had twenty-five seats. The Assembly election results showed that the anti-British unity seen during the INA trials had as good as disappeared. In the elections, the Muslim League was led by H.S. Suhrawardy, who had intrigued to scuttle Nazimuddin's nomination as a Muslim League candidate. Complaints of widespread rigging, manipulation and open partiality by government officials in the elections came from politicians as far apart as Abul Kalam Azad and Fazlul Huq. Others like Nausher Ali and Syed Badruddoza proposed in the Assembly that a commission be appointed to enquire into the allegations of complicity by British officials in favour of League candidates. Suhrawardy denied these allegations and pointed to the narrow margin with which League candidates won in many seats. He was elected leader of the League in the Assembly and was invited on 2 April 1946 by Governor Frederick John Burrows to form a ministry. The Bengal Muslim League, like the Bengal Congress, was rife with factionalism. Suhrawardy was apparently not even sure that the diehard followers of Nazimuddin or Tamizuddin Khan would not ditch him on the floor of the house. He was reported to have even secretly proposed an alliance with the Congress through Kiran Shankar Roy, the leader of the Congress Party in the Assembly. Roy referred this to Maulana Azad, who was Congress president. Suhrawardy discussed this proposal with Azad in Delhi, where he had gone to attend the Muslim League Convention.[5] But nothing came of it.

Suhrawardy now formed his League ministry with only Muslim Leaguers. The only exception in his ministry was Jogendra Nath Mandal, who represented the Scheduled Caste Federation. The formation of a cabinet with only Muslims save one (J.N. Mandal) and the omission of any caste Hindus among ministers hardened the Bengali caste Hindus and sent a strong message to them that the government was determined to rule Bengal without associating the caste Hindus with the governance of the province. For them this was a foretaste of what was likely to happen to them if the whole of Bengal went to Pakistan. Till then the League had always associated some breakaway caste Hindu leaders with the government. Now it was out and out a Muslim League ministry.

The fact that the Muslim League ministry could count on the unfailing support of the European members for its continuance in power illustrated the extent of the British raj's support to the League. But at the all-India level, the provincial elections did not on the whole record as overwhelming a success for Jinnah as in the Central Assembly elections. In sharp contrast to the Congress forming governments in eight provinces, including the overwhelmingly Muslim North West Frontier Province, and a coalition government in Punjab with the Unionists and the Akalis, the League could form governments only in Bengal and Sind, and that too with the support of the European members. But two impressions were clear. First, by winning 442 out of 509 Muslim seats in these assemblies and nearly 87 per cent of the Muslim votes, Jinnah had demonstrated his overwhelming hold over Muslims. Second, and interestingly, his success was total in those provinces which would never be part of Pakistan, if formed, but much less so in provinces like Punjab and North West Frontier Province which were envisaged as parts of the proposed Pakistan. In the face of such overwhelming evidence, Congress leadership should perhaps have accepted his claim to be the representative of the Muslim community. That might have made negotiations easier.

The Cabinet Mission, 1946

The Cabinet Mission reached New Delhi on 24 March 1946. It had prolonged and tortuous meetings and negotiations for seven weeks with not only Congress leaders, including Gandhi, officially not even a member of the Congress, but really still the supremo, Nehru, Azad and Patel and the Muslim League leaders (Jinnah and Liaqat Ali), but leaders of all other political shades like the Scheduled Caste Federation (Ambedkar and J.N. Mandal), the Akalis (Master Tara Singh and Baldev Singh). It interviewed 472 people in 181 formal meetings. In general, nearly every political party agreed to disagree with others. Even among some of the political parties there were sharp disagreements, such as the Akalis who pressed for Sikhistan, but each leader had his own concept, or the scheduled castes, where the followers of Ambedkar sharply clashed with those of Jagjivan Ram.

Eventually, the Cabinet Mission announced and broadcast its plan on 16 May 1946. It rejected the concept of a sovereign Pakistan as unworkable and impractical, as with the two wings being separated by 700 miles, the communication between them in war and peace would be dependent on the goodwill of Hindustan. It also ruled out any partition of the two provinces of Bengal and Punjab. On the whole it tried to maintain a facade of united India with complete self-government for the provinces. It was somewhat influenced by a three-tier scheme suggested by Azad. In a nutshell, the Cabinet Mission proposals were as follows:

a) India would constitute a federal union with both the British Indian provinces and the princely states as constituents. The union would be in charge of foreign affairs, defence and communications (railways, posts and telegraphs etc.) and all other subjects would be under the charge of the provinces and the princely states.

b) The provincial assemblies and the princely states would elect 296 members to form a Constituent Assembly to frame a constitution for the Union. These members were to be elected on the basis of separate electorates.

c) The British Indian provinces would be grouped into three: (i) a group comprising Punjab, North West Frontier Province, Sind and Baluchistan, all Muslim majority provinces; (ii) Bengal and Assam; and (iii) the rest of the provinces, all of them with a Hindu majority.

d) There would also be a loose regional government for each of these groups and the representatives of each separate group would draw up the constitution for the provinces in the group concerned.

e) The new Constitutions, both provincial and national, would continue for ten years after which every province would have the option to consider the matter and leave the Union and form a separate state.

f) Until the new Constitution was in place, the country would be run by the Executive Council to be designated as an interim government consisting of Indian leaders. This would also include a war member, the position the British were unwilling to part with in 1942 and one the Indian leaders were determined to have.

g) The paramountcy of the British Crown over the princely states would lapse. The precise status of the states would have to be negotiated during the building up of the new constitutional structure.

The proposals met with a mixed reaction. The two main parties, that is, the Congress and the Muslim League were initially silent. The Sikhs and the scheduled castes expressed their vehement opposition. On 6 June, the Muslim League accepted the Cabinet Mission's three-tier formula. A few days later, the Congress agreed to participate in the Constituent Assembly but not to join the interim Executive Council. Any agreement on the issue of interim government was not possible on account of the Congress' known position that it also represented the Indian Muslims and, therefore, had the right to nominate Muslim members in the interim government while the Muslim League was absolutely adamant on the point that it alone represented the Muslims. After three weeks of debate, the Congress Working Committee was persuaded by Nehru and Azad on 25 June to accept the Cabinet Mission Plan subject to a few reservations such as the proposed grouping of Assam with Muslim-majority Bengal and the grouping of the Congress-ruled North West Frontier Province in the north-west group of states which would be dominated by the Muslim League. When the Cabinet Mission members flew back to Britain on 29 June, they had thought that the mission was by and large successful. The All India Congress Committee accepted the plan by a massive majority on 6 July 1946. There was a certain euphoria, which was, however, short-lived.

Nehru's faux pas

In the same All India Congress Committee session on 6 July 1946, at the end of Azad's term as Congress president, Jawaharlal Nehru took over as the new president. He was imposed by Gandhi and not chosen by a majority of the provincial committees who had a clear preference for Vallabhbhai Patel. Apart from Gandhi's personal fondness for Nehru, he felt that Nehru understood the English language and English mind better than Patel. This, he felt, would be an advantage in the negotiations ahead. But Gandhi's judgement was a serious error in several respects. First, the replacement of the captain of the boat in the middle of the negotiations was in itself unfortunate, all the more so because a gentle, affable and scholarly Muslim was replaced as Congress president by a doctrinaire and highly temperamental Hindu Brahmin. Nehru did not share Azad's commitment to the Cabinet Mission scheme. Second, there was a basic incompatibility between him and Jinnah. No two persons could be as intolerant of each other as Nehru and Jinnah. One has only to read their speeches and writings to know how they hated each other. History might have been different if these two did not face each other at the negotiation table.

Nehru was in the habit of thinking aloud, and it was in one of his spells of loud thinking at a press meeting at Bombay on 10 July 1946 that he put a spanner on the whole issue. At a juncture in history 'when circumspection should have been the order of the day and there was much to be gained by silence',[6] Nehru decided to make, to quote Michael Brecher, his biographer, 'one of the most fiery and provocative statements in his forty years of public life'. Asked whether the Congress had accepted the Cabinet Mission Plan in toto, he answered that his party was 'completely unfettered by any agreements and free to meet all situations as they arise'. As regards the formation of three groups of provinces as envisaged by the Cabinet Mission, he more or less ruled it out on the ground that Group A would decide against it and so would NWFP in Group B and Assam in Group C. Notwithstanding the fact that the Congress had accepted the three-tier formula, Nehru said, 'we are not bound by a single thing except that we have decided to go into the Constituent Assembly'. In his opinion the Constituent Assembly would be a sovereign body free to do whatever it chose and the Central government would also be much more powerful than what the Cabinet Mission scheme had envisaged and free to modify the scheme as it pleased.

Nehru did not realize that after both the Congress and the League had accepted this compromise formula, which did not fully satisfy anyone, he was once again reopening the issue and thus sabotaging the cause of Indian unity. He was bitterly criticized by his colleague Maulana Azad in his memoirs *India Wins Freedom*: 'I have to say with regrets that he is at times apt to be carried away by his feelings. Not only so, but sometimes he is so impressed by theatrical considerations that he is apt to underestimate the realities of a situation... The mistake of 1946 proved costly.' This was, to quote Brecher again, 'a serious tactical error.' Nehru played into the hands of Jinnah and gave him the excuse that he needed to repudiate the agreement. 'Mr. Jinnah reacted to Nehru's statement like an army leader who had come in for armistice discussion under a flag of truce and finds himself looking down the barrel of a cocked revolver. He dived for cover screaming treachery as he did so.'[7]

All hopes of a united India were shattered and the idea of an independent Pakistan, which Jinnah had compromised in accepting the Cabinet Mission's Plan, was revived. In Jinnah's reckoning the Congress had given a foretaste of how exactly the Hindus would behave towards the Muslim minority after the British had departed.

This was too much of an affront to him after he had climbed down from his declared aim of Pakistan to persuade the League to accept an arrangement minus a 'sovereign Pakistan'. Also, he was somewhat disillusioned by what he had thought was reneging by Wavell on his promise to ask the League, which had first accepted the Cabinet Mission Plan, to form an interim government after the Congress refused to take part. On 22 July, Wavell had written to both Nehru and Jinnah proposing an interim government of fourteen ministers: six from the Congress (including one representative from the scheduled castes), five from the Muslim League and three representing the other minorities. Jinnah was aghast at what he considered a breach of faith. On 27 July, the League council met to withdraw its acceptance of the Cabinet Mission Plan. Jinnah accused the Congress, the Cabinet Mission and the viceroy of repeatedly going back on their commitments over the interim government. Feelings ran very high and the Muslim League council prompted by Jinnah adopted a resolution to the following effect:

> Whereas it has become abundantly clear that the Muslims of India would not rest contented with any thing less than immediate establishment of an independent and fully sovereign State of Pakistan, the time has now come for the Muslims to resort to Direct Action to achieve Pakistan, to assert their just right, to vindicate their honour and to get rid of the present slavery and the contemplated caste Hindu domination.

In other words, the Muslim League now decided to repudiate the Cabinet Mission's three-tier formula and opt for Pakistan. It instructed its followers to prepare for a 'programme of Direct Action to organise the Muslims for the coming struggle to be launched as and when necessary'. It also called upon Muslims to protest against the British Raj and, as a token of their deep resentment of the attitude of the British, to renounce all titles conferred upon them by the alien government. The Working Committee gave a call for the declaration of 16 August as a 'Direct Action Day', which was to be a 'universal Muslim hartal'. Jinnah also gave a provocative speech in the course of which he announced:

Never have we in the whole history of the League done anything except by constitutional methods and by constitutionalism. But now we are obliged and forced into this position. This day we bid goodbye to constitutional methods. Today we have also forged a pistol and are in a position to use it.

Direct Action and the Great Calcutta Killings, 1946

This directly triggered off the communal holocaust in Kolkata, then India's largest city with a population of 25 lakh. The violence that erupted on 16–19 August sparked off a chain of communal violence that led to the partition of the country within a year. Suhrawardy's government declared 16 August, the Direct Action Day, as a public holiday for both Muslims and Hindus. By contrast, neither in Sind nor in Punjab, the two other Muslim-dominated provinces, was this day declared a holiday. Whether or not Suhrawardy had a sinister design in mind is difficult to say. But many contemporaries believed that the clear object of calling a hartal on that day was to enable the murderous gangs to identify for attack those shops and establishments that opened their shutters in defiance of the hartal and were, by implication, not Muslim-owned. In fact, these attacks started in the Muslim localities in a pre-planned manner. In these localities there were murderous assaults on unsuspecting Bihari rickshaw-pullers and milk-vendors from early morning. Also, at Shyambazar and Hatibagan, violence started when Muslim League supporters tried to compel Hindu shopkeepers to close their shops.[8] Further, the crossing of the river early in the morning, from the Howrah side, of a substantial number of Muslim toughs on a string of boats with the clear intention of violence could not have been unpremeditated. What happened during those four days can best be described in the words of Leonard Mosley, an objective non-partisan British researcher.[9]

The British governor of Bengal was Sir Frederick Burrows, an ex-railwayman and union official, who had been appointed by the Labour Government in February 1946 to succeed R.G. Casey. He was an able and amiable administrator who got on well with Hindus and Muslims alike, and was popular with the local British Army Command; but he was not exactly a man of great strength or quickness of mind. As a personality he was certainly no match for the Chief Minister of Bengal, Shaheed Suhrawardy, an Oriental politician of considerable shrewdness, deviousness of mind, and great natural charm. Suhrawardy was a member of the Working Committee of the Muslim League, and therefore might have been expected to jump at the crack of Jinnah's whip with the same alacrity as the other Muslim satraps. In fact, he exercised considerable independence and made it clear to Jinnah that he would brook no interference in his administration. Jinnah did not like him, particularly since he suspected that Suhrawardy—though he was always careful to pay lip-service to the idea of Pakistan—secretly cherished an ambition of his own: to carve an independent Bengal out of free India and run it as a separate state, outside Jinnah's control. To this outwardly affable but inwardly ruthless politico, the decision of Jinnah to declare 16 August 1946 as 'Direct Action Day' seemed a golden opportunity to demonstrate his power over Bengal's Muslims and his enthusiasm for Pakistan. He announced that 16 August would be a general holiday in Kolkata for Muslims and Hindus alike; and when Hindu members of the provincial legislature protested that they had no wish to share in a Muslim political *hartal*, he ordered his party machine to vote them down. On 5 August, under the *nom de plume* of 'Shaheed', he wrote an article in *The Statesman*, Calcutta, in which he said, somewhat cryptically, 'Bloodshed and disorder are not necessarily evil in themselves, if resorted to for a noble cause. Among Muslims today, no cause is dearer or nobler than Pakistan.' In a speech in Delhi on 10 August, he threatened to turn Bengal into a separate government if Congress went ahead and formed an interim government on its own. 'We will see that no revenue is derived from Bengal for such a Central Government, and will consider ourselves as a separate government having no connection with the Centre,' he declared. And in a declaration on the eve of 'Direct Action Day', one of his aides called upon the Muslims to adopt the slogan of *Lar ke lenge Pakistan*, which could be translated as 'Pakistan by Force'. The stage was set for the demonstration that was to split India in two.

One cannot ignore Bengal's contribution to the cause of India's freedom, or to India's intellectual and cultural life. Rabindranath Tagore, the great poet, was a Bengali, as were Michael Madhusudan Dutt, the father of modern Indian poetry, Rammohun Roy, Swami Vivekananda and Bankim Chandra Chatterjee, the founders of Hindu nationalism. But the Bengalis who counted on 16 August were the mobs from the slums.[10]

They crossed the Hooghly River from Howrah into Kolkata soon after dawn. They were armed with lathis (long sticks), knives, bottles and automobile cranks and other kinds of iron bars. Most of them at this time were Muslims. They waited in doorways and alleyways until it was time for shops to open, and they watched to see which shops did open (in the circumstances, they were bound to be non-Muslims). The doorkeeper who opened the shop was swiftly clubbed down, or kicked, or stabbed; then the contents of the shops were smashed or looted.

It began quietly at first and scarcely anyone realized what terrible things were taking place. A Briton cycling across Chowringhee Square on his way to a hospital where he worked saw a sweeper running towards him, pursued by a mob. At the moment he dismounted, one of the mob reached the sweeper and whacked him so hard across the legs that the sound of his bones breaking could be clearly heard. The moment he touched the ground, another member of the mob leaned down and cut the man's throat and then sliced off his ear. Then the rest of the mob came up, nodded and smiled and touched their hearts and foreheads to the Englishman, saying: 'Good day to you, sir' before turning to make off across the square. It all happened so swiftly that the Englishman found it hard to believe it had happened at all.

In the beginning there were isolated incidents. By noon, however, the small, evil spurts of violence had begun to develop into flames and fires. It was catching. At first, it had only been groups of goondas who killed and battered, while small scatterings of wary onlookers followed them and looted and smashed shops or helped to overturn cars. But, gradually, the onlookers became participators in the killings. From many parts of Kolkata, the noise of human voices began to be heard; voices raised in anger or in pain, a steadily increasing keen sound that rose and fell, like the voice of hell, for the next four days to come.

At two o'clock on the afternoon of 16 August 1946, H.S Suhrawardy addressed a mass meeting in the Maidan, Kolkata's main square. He was in an ebullient mood and thanked his listeners for turning out in large numbers, their enthusiasm and their active work for Pakistan. While he spoke, men were being killed a couple of streets away. The smoke from fires started by the mob (who had broken into petrol stations by now and were spraying nearby shops with fuel) could be plainly seen from the square. But neither Suhrawardy nor his considerable retinue of police bodyguards seemed to be aware of them.

In truth, the Kolkata police were finding the job of putting down the riots almost insuperable. There was the psychological difficulty at first (when the acts of murder were being mostly committed by Muslims) that the killers and violators were of their own religion, for most of the Kolkata police were Muslims. By afternoon, the bellows of artificial fury had done the work and the Hindus and Sikhs came out on the streets too, red hot for revenge and reprisal. They came out not to meet the Muslim goondas in head-on clashes, nor even to protect their own people and put down the rioting. That is not the way Kolkata mobs work. While Muslim gangs went on hunting helpless Hindus and looting Hindu shops, Hindus and Sikhs went out on a hunt for helpless Muslims. It was always old men, children and women that they were after. The only pitched battle that took place between Muslims and Hindus happened at Ripon College, when the Muslims hoisted a Muslim League flag on the pole. A Hindu climbed up and replaced it with the Congress banner, while below the mobs fought briefly and then swiftly retired. They were not there to get hurt themselves but to kill and maim the unarmed among their enemies. And though the police managed to clear the main streets by firing tear-gas on the mob, they reappeared as soon as the patrols had passed; there is always an alleyway in Kolkata down which you can disappear until the police has gone away.

Jinnah had called the 'Direct Action Day' a demonstration against the British for their refusal to recognize Pakistan, but of all the communities in Kolkata once the rioting began, the British were the only ones who were safe. 'I have a stomach made strong by experiences of a war hospital, but was never like this', wrote Kim Christen.[11]

I made my way on a cycle, up Chittaranjan Avenue, to the Medical College. There I hoped to use my wartime experience in hospitals to do whatever I could do to help. There had been a mob killing two hundred yards south of the Medical College, and bodies lay about in the roads among the wreckage of burning cars. I waited awhile until the mob moved towards a side street and then continued to the hospital, where I first realised the enormity of the situation. Ambulances, service units, police trucks emptied themselves of bleeding, shattered and wounded, while open carts were piled with those who had not survived the journey back. I approached a Red Cross truck and joined a group of young medical students. They pinned a paper cross to my shirt and then drove to the Mirzapur area, dismounted when the bodies grew thick, and searched among them for any flicker of life in the pulse. They were few, and they were lifted on to stretchers, already red and sodden, to be taken to a hospital already overcrowded. This search for survivors continued throughout the day and night. We went North and East, over the canal, gathering broken heads and stricken bodies, and took them to whatever hospital was nearest. Weapons of every shape and size had been gathered by the mobs—heavy tools, iron bars, spikes tied to lathis, while barrel loads of bricks were wheeled to the edge of the encounters. One man whose back was streaming with blood, having been hurled through a plate glass window behind him, squatted on the kerb. I saw him, while still bleeding, tear strips of cloth from his shirt and tie a piece of glass to the split of a stick so as to use it as an axe. All the hospitals had hung 'Full' notices outside. Doctors and nurses operated continuously, and medical students whose medical books were still clean were called up to exercise their knowledge in the most practical of schools. The ambulances were told to refuse all pleas for refuge and confine their loads to those not yet dead.

At the end of the first forty-eight hours, an air of death and desolation hung over Kolkata.[12] It was hot, muggy and raining slightly. The smoke from the fires hung heavy in the air. Only an occasional cycle (usually ridden by an Englishman) or a military jeep, canopied in wire netting, rushed by. The city had come to a standstill. No more trains were coming to Howrah or Sealdah from the country. The sewers overflowed; and in the fetid gutters the bodies of dead men and women and dead cows lay side by side, being picked at by vultures.

There were already 4,000 dead and countless numbers wounded, but it was not over yet. The military (that is the army under British command) had been called in by now and more troops were being rushed in from the up-country garrisons. The sight of British or Gurkha troops was always a signal for the mob to stop their depredations and often they received a cheer; they moved about the city, calmly moving barricades, breaking up demonstrations, stopping to investigate and rescue whenever they heard a cry from a house. But they had been called in too late to have the great psychological impact, which might have put an end to the rioting right at the start. From now on, they would be able to stop the big riots and keep the gangs off the main streets, but there was little they could do to prevent the knifings and batterings that still went on in the alleyways.

Sir Frederick Burrows had made his own tour of the riot-stricken areas on the first day, but the mobs squeezed back into the woodwork whenever he passed, and the chief minister, Suhrawardy, had been able to persuade him that all was under control. It was only when the Hindus and Sikhs had come out in retaliation that the chief minister had called for military aid, afraid for the first time of the enormity of the tragic events that had been set in motion.

On the third day the general Hindu retaliation was spearheaded by the Sikhs from the Bhawanipur area branching out across the city in their vehicles with guns and swords and attacking the Muslims wherever they could be found all over the city. The whole metropolis was now literally on fire. There was a pitched battle near the Howrah Bridge as Muslim mobs from Howrah tried to advance into Burra Bazaar, the central business district of Kolkata. The Sikhs, Kolkata's motor mechanics and drivers, jumped into the fray from the third day and charged through Muslim localities like a motorized cavalry, killing anyone they could lay hands on without mercy. It is established that the army was not called by the government till the third day although several battalions of British forces were ready in Fort William. It was only when the whole metropolis was involved in the worst form of communal violence that the army was called in following a conversation between the viceroy, Lord Wavell, and the Governor of Bengal, Frederick Burrows. Suhrawardy himself was visibly panicky by the third day and was spending most of his time in the conference room of the Kolkata police. Hounded by the question of his direct complicity with the initial happenings, he clearly saw that what had happened had gone far beyond what he had initially conceived of on a limited scale. His detractors cite his presence in the control room as yet another proof that he was masterminding the whole thing.[13] His apologists, on the other hand, point out that he was truly trying to control the situation with his personal presence and personal supervision.[14] A pro-government newspaper, the *Statesman*, declared:

> We wrote two days ago that conditions in Calcutta were horrifying. They have gone beyond since. Whatever the appropriate adjective is, they were nothing in comparison with what we have subsequently seen. The last estimate of dead is 3,000, who have lain thick about the streets. The injured number many thousand and it is impossible to say how many business houses and private dwellings have been destroyed. This is not a riot. It needs a word found in medieval history, a fury. Yet fury sounds spontaneous, and there must have been some deliberation and organisation to set this fury on its way. The horde who ran about battering and killing with lathis may have found them lying about or brought them out of their pockets, but that is not to be believed. We have already commented on the bands who found it easy to get petrol and vehicles when no others were permitted on the streets. It is not mere supposition that men were brought into Calcutta to make an impression. Thousands have been brutally hurt, smashed eyes, smashed jaws, smashed limbs of men, women and children—these are the kind of political argument the twentieth century does not expect.

Fazlul Huq, the veteran leader, narrated in the Assembly instances where the police either connived with the mob that looted or remained mere spectators, for example, during the looting of the Mahishadal Palace, around 100 traffic policemen were in a barrack in the neighbourhood, but did not stir out. He commented in anguish: 'I have felt that the greatest disturbances did not arise in a moment, but seem to be a well-planned action—maybe on one side or maybe on both sides.'[15] There were innumerable reports in the first two days where the police, on being told of violent incidents, either did not pay heed, or said they had no instructions to take action.

Amrita Bazar Patrika, a Hindu nationalist paper, wrote: 'Hindus and Muslims must hang down their heads in shame that exhibitions of such unmitigated beastliness should have been allowed to occur in our modern city. The tallest among us must look small in the eyes of the outside world.'

Suhrawardy made no statement defending himself. It seems certain from his subsequent behaviour and his actions, that even he was bewildered by the great massacre. Both Nehru and Jinnah were quick in their condemnation. The Muslim League leader issued a statement saying:

> I unreservedly condemn the acts of violence and deeply sympathise with those who have suffered. At present I do not know who are responsible for the resultant loss of life and property, which has been reported in the Press. Those who are guilty of resorting to indefensible conduct must be dealt with according to the law, as their actions, as far as the Muslim League is concerned, are contrary to instructions. They play into the hands of the enemy. They may be the actions of agent provocateurs.[16]

But in his heart of hearts Jinnah no doubt noted with satisfaction that if there was one lesson that the Kolkata riots had proved it was that when India became independent, Hindus and Muslims could no longer live together and civil war would be the inevitable result.

But there were still signs of sanity and humanity as shown by many stories of how in the midst of the carnage, when some Muslims were killing Hindus, and some Hindus killing Muslims, others tried to save innocent victims from their co-religionists. There was still a gleam of light in the midst of the gloom. All over the city, examples of Hindus who had died trying to save Muslims, of Muslims who had sheltered Hindus at the risk of their own lives and, towards the end, bands of young Muslims and Hindus marching through the streets, dispersing mobs, crying *Hindu-Muslim ek ho* (Hindus and Muslims unite), with the flags of the Congress and the League tied together, came to light. In her memoirs *From Purdah to Parliament*, Begum Ikramullah records a moving account of how a Hindu doctor risked his life to provide medical help to her critically ill father in a Muslim locality. There is also the well-known story of how some Hindu neighbours saved Dr Qudrat-i-Khuda, principal, Presidency College, who was attacked in his home at Bhawanipur and escorted him and his family to the safety of a Muslim locality, endangering their own lives. There were many such events to demonstrate that there was still some civilization left in the ugly city of Kolkata and that there were still some secular people who could work and fight together in spite of their religious differences and uphold a common humanity. These shining examples sharply contrasted with the venomous hatred that marked other sections of Muslims, Hindus and Sikhs in Kolkata of that time.

Meanwhile, the British and Gurkha troops started pouring in from the third day of rioting. By the end of 19 August, there were 45,000 British soldiers in the city. On that day a peace committee was formed and, on its behalf, Muhammad Ali of Bogra made a public broadcast on All India Radio appealing for peace. A peace procession, including prominent leaders like Nazimuddin, Kiran Shankar Roy and Muhammad Ali of Bogra went round the streets of the disturbed localities. Slowly life in the metropolis was returning to normalcy.

The question of the degree of Premier Suhrawardy's involvement in the unfortunate and regrettable killings in Kolkata from 16 to 19 August 1946 has remained a mystery ever since and perhaps will always remain so. Many contemporaries sincerely believed that he was the main schemer behind this tragedy. His apologists have felt that he had been more sinned against than sinning. A typical observation of the first school of thought quoting contemporary sources is from R.C. Majumdar:

It is beyond doubt that the communal riots that rocked Calcutta for four days were an offshoot of conspiracy by the Muslim League. The misuse of power by the Muslim League ministry of Bengal is unique in the civilised world and the British administration is also guilty of indifference and partiality.

Quoting from the accounts given by the then director of publicity of Bengal, P.S. Mathur, Majumdar also speaks of an attitude of indifference on the part of the European officialdom. According to him, the British police commissioner retorted when asked to take strong action that 'when both Hindus and Muslims are asking us to leave the country, why should I interfere? Better inform the Congress office.' This typifies the attitude of the white officialdom. According to Mathur, Suhrawardy himself requested the Governor to agree to the summoning of the army on the third day, but the Governor did not take any action.

The *Statesman*, edited at the time by a known pro-Leaguer, Ian Stephen, wrote:

> What befell India's largest city last week was no mere communal riot, as we have hitherto understood the sanguinary term. For three days, the city concentrated on unrestrained civil war. Upon whom the main guilt for it rests is manifest. There has been criticism of the Governor [Sir Frederick Burrows]. We do not think he has emerged particularly well. But none except a very great man holding his traditionally constitutional office during a swift crisis could have done so. Where the primary blame lies is where we have squarely put it – upon the provincial Muslim League Cabinet which carries responsibility for law and order in Bengal, and particularly upon the one able man of large administrative experience there, the Chief Minister [Suhrawardy]. That in the whole of India the only province where carnage occurred, on the League's professed peaceful Direct Action Day, should have been in Bengal, where a League ministry holds office, astounds us.

The following observations by two recent researchers[17] also have relevance. 'In Bengal, however, and particularly in Kolkata, things quickly got out of hand, thanks largely to the Chief Minister and Leader of the League in Bengal, Hussain Shaheed Suhrawardy.' Shortly before Direct Action Day, Suhrawardy threatened to declare Bengal an independent state, withholding all revenues, if Nehru was allowed to form a Central government.

On Tuesday, 13 August, Suhrawardy announced a three-day

public holiday starting on Friday, Direct Action Day itself. Why he did this is not clear. One explanation is that, fearing communal violence, he hoped to direct the wrath of the mob away from public offices and departments. Whatever its purpose, the result was to release Muslims to take part in meetings and marches—and mischief. On Friday, Suhrawardy had planned to address a mass meeting at the *maidan*.

Intelligence reports reaching Lt-General Sir Francis Tucker, general officer commanding-in-chief Eastern Command, said that Suhrawardy himself had told the huge Muslim crowd at the Ochterlony monument that 'Direct Action Day would prove to be the first step towards the Muslim struggle for emancipation.' He had urged the crowds to return home early and said that he had arranged with the police and military not to interfere with them. Whether this promise of immunity was meant as an invitation to loot and kill is hard to say—but a number of well-known Muslim *goondas* were among the crowd, and they needed no second bidding. When the meeting ended, they set off into the narrow streets of the city and soon Hindu shops, easily identifiable as they were not closed in response to the hartal, and houses were looted and burnt. Hindu *goondas* soon retaliated. At 4.15 p.m, Fortress Headquarters sent out the code-word 'Red' to indicate that there were incidents all over Kolkata.

Suhrawardy's apologists, on the other hand,[18] point to his association with C.R. Das and the Swarajists, his secret parleys with some Congress leaders even after the 1946 elections to form a coalition government, his joint call for a sovereign united Bengal with Sarat Bose, his association with Mahatma Gandhi in 1946 and 1947 when he often risked his own life for the sake of preventing communal violence and his subsequent role in Pakistan politics in favour of the Hindu minority and Bengali language to disprove his alleged complicity with the riots in Kolkata in 1946. Suhrawardy himself stated in the Bengal Assembly that miscalculation on his part of the explosive effect of Jinnah's call for Direct Action, rather than mischievous intent, was the real culprit.

As against these contradictory views, the following balanced observations from a scholar, on the whole unbiased, but in sympathy with Suhrawardy are also relevant.[19]

> Suhrawardy has been accused not only of being responsible for the Calcutta killings in 1946 but also of having organised them. Though as Chief Minister, Suhrawardy was responsible for law and order in Bengal, it must be remembered that 16 August was declared Direct Action Day by Jinnah, not Suhrawardy.

Abul Hashim's statement to the press issued on 13 August declared that the Muslim League would observe Direct Action Day to demonstrate its grievances against British imperialism. Khwaja Nazimuddin and Raja Ghaznafar Ali Khan of Lahore saw their struggle as being 'against the Congress and the Hindus'. It has, in fact, been suggested that the target of Direct Action were the Hindus as the British and the Christians were left unmolested. According to S.A. Masud, who defended Suhrawardy on behalf of the Muslim League along with B.A. Siddiqui, an inquiry into the killings revealed that the riots had begun even before Direct Action was defined. He places the blame squarely on the 'Mahasabha and Hindu communalism'. Masud recalls that the earliest incidents of rioting occurred at 8 a.m. that day. Others have suggested that it began at 6 a.m. It started with the looting and burning of an entire Muslim area in Bow Bazaar Street in central Kolkata. Suhrawardy drove alone to the spot to try and bring the incident under control. A strike had been called on that day and several meetings were scheduled to be held, such as the one at Islamia College at 4 p.m. and another at the Maidan at 3 p.m. Muslims were totally unaware of the trouble brewing. S.A. Masud, Abul Hashim and others went to the Maidan with their little children. Muslim women students from Munnujan Hall, a post-graduate hostel for women, headed for Islamia College on foot and waited there for several hours before being warned that a communal riot had started. In the meantime, the hostel had been attacked, the valuables looted and furniture burnt. The women had to take shelter in the office of the weekly *Millat*. At 3 p.m., Suhrawardy requested the Muslim public to return to their homes; for while the men had assembled at the Maidan leaving their homes unguarded, Muslim pockets and *bustees* (slums) had been attacked. To quote M.A. Masud:

> Hindus planned to make Direct Action Day unsuccessful so that the British Government would think that the people of Bengal did not want Pakistan...while the Muslims were coming to the Maidan and returning back to their homes they were attacked by gunfire from rooftops and with bricks which were collected in Hindu houses along the main roads.

To quote Abul Hashim:

> The Muslim League had no knowledge, no apprehension or anticipation as to the unprecedented violence that started...the Muslims were unarmed and unprepared to meet the situation...if we had apprehended any danger we would not have taken our sons and grandsons to the Maidan.

The accusations against Suhrawardy seem implausible on two counts. As chief minister, he would be held responsible for any breakdown in law and order, which would also discredit his ministry. He could not want a riot on his hands while he was in government. If he was responsible for organizing the riots he would certainly not have wanted a united Bengal, but a divided one. Nor would public meetings be organized in such a way as to encourage Leaguers to attend them with their children; and women would not have been encouraged to participate in these public meetings if rioting on such a scale was anticipated. Abul Hashim writes in his memoirs that when Suhrawardy realized that the Kolkata police force was not strong enough to tackle the situation, he requested Burrows, the Governor of the province, to call out the army, but the army did not come. Finally, after five days of rioting, the situation was brought under control with the help of a big contingent of armed constables sent on request by the Punjab government. In the meantime, Suhrawardy himself took charge of the control room at Lal Bazaar police headquarters and directed the police operations at grave risk to his life. He could not rely on the commissioner of police who was a European, but received help from his Hindu friend, Hiren Sarkar, who was an inspector of police. Another factor which helped quell the riots was a peace procession on 21 August, led by all party leaders including Suhrawardy, Sarat Bose, Khwaja Nazimuddin, Kiran Shankar Roy, M.A. Ispahani, J.C. Gupta, Shamsuddin Ahmed, Abul Hashim, etc.

The accusations against Suhrawardy came primarily from the Congress, the Hindu Mahasabha, British officials and other non-Muslim scholars. It is not the intention here to discuss the merits and demerits of these charges except to point out that Muslims had a totally different perspective on the issue. Apportioning blame for the riots instead of attempting to understand why they happened is an exercise in futility. The evidence cited is generally unreliable and faulty, as the witnesses were inevitably partisan. Impartiality could not be expected of British officials, including Governor Burrows, whose inaction or belated action contributed to the spread of the carnage. Few are willing to talk about those horrific and shameful events today, let alone admit to participating in them, although many are still alive. The Hindu Mahasabha had made clear in no uncertain terms that it would prevent the observance of a hartal on Direct Action Day. Along with the Congress, it resented the declaration of a public holiday on this day by the government and resolved to foil it. The police force was guilty of inaction. The Congress had exhibited total disregard and contempt for Muslim aspirations by refusing to come to any understanding with the Muslim League on the formation of an interim government. The Muslim League ministry obviously wanted Direct Action Day to be successful in terms of the observance of the hartal and had built up a sense of fervour in order to 'win Pakistan' by force if necessary. The League ministry, though in charge of law and order, had to rely for help on senior European and Hindu officials, which was not forthcoming. The scene was, therefore, set for accusations and counter-accusations.

Speculation has continued since these charges were not investigated exhaustively and the results were not published.

Suhrawardy's connections with the *goondas* (underworld hooligans) of Kolkata was often cited as proof of his role in the Kolkata killings, although other politicians from the Congress and the Mahasabha also had similar connections. The fact that Suhrawardy took charge of the police control room set up by the European commissioner to monitor developments in the city was seen as a sinister act of mischief by some investigators. Little notice was taken of the fact that he did so at grave risk to his own life only when the European commissioner and the police force controlled by him failed to act to restore order. His alleged release of eight Muslim rioters was highlighted, though the number is paltry considering that 10,000 people, most of them Muslim, were killed in the carnage. Although he was chief minister, his use of official vehicles to patrol the streets and offer protection and shelter to those caught in the crossfire was misrepresented as an example of his misuse of the state machinery to incite rioters and show them 'sympathy'. The anomaly in the evidence cited has not always been explained. For example, Das[20] states that 65 per cent of property destroyed belonged to Hindus and 25 per cent to Muslims. However, a larger number of *goondas* arrested were Hindus, who numbered 1,704 as against 1,192 Muslims, and the proportion of Muslims killed in the massacre far exceeded that of Hindus. Such facts raise doubts about his claim that Muslims had 'organized' the riots, nor lend credence to his silence on the extent of Hindu preparation which went into the massacre.

While blind and unreasoned communalism may have played a part in the Kolkata killings, the riots could not all have been totally 'organized'. If Muslims had planned the event they would have taken care to protect themselves, particularly their women and children, and stayed indoors. The responsibility for the killings must be shared by all parties and active politicians of the time. The nightmare was created by politicians, both Hindu and Muslim, who had successfully whipped up the emotions of their co-religionists and created an atmosphere of fear, intimidation and expectation of violence. It became a wish-fulfilling prophecy. Hatred and suspicion was generated by the distribution of provocative leaflets, threats and speeches. The breakdown of negotiations over the interim government also contributed to the exacerbation of communal tension to an unprecedented degree. The highly charged atmosphere set the scene for mindless and frenzied killings. The guilt must be shared by all concerned. Although Suhrawardy's main concern before partition was the welfare of the community, after partition he became a champion of minority rights. He cannot be bracketed with the extreme communalists of his time who were responsible for killing in the name of religion.

On an impartial assessment of the available evidence it seems plausible that Suhrawardy had planned violence on some scale, maybe modest, but he failed to take adequate precautionary steps to prevent communal violence on a large scale which was not anticipated by him. Possibly he wanted to demonstrate how serious the Muslims were in their demand for Pakistan and also that the League and he himself represented Muslim Bengal. If the League could organize such demonstrative violence in a city where Muslims were very much in a minority, there was every case for the whole of Bengal, including Kolkata, going to Pakistan. But the extent of the violence that actually occurred surpassed his own calculations. He was struck by remorse, which drove him to Gandhi's umbrella. He tried his best to atone for his sins of omission and commission in his subsequent politics in India and Pakistan.

The scars of those four maddening days of the holocaust in Kolkata took long to heal. For quite some time after this the city continued to be divided into Hindu zones and Muslim zones with little cross movement, especially at night. Even the public buses and tram cars would ply through notoriously riot-disturbed localities with armed sentries. Hindus would not get off in Muslim localities and Muslims would not get off in Hindu localities. There was universal fear of the unknown assassin's knife lurking somewhere and striking at an innocent passerby. The Great Calcutta Killings, as they came to be known, had indeed changed the course of Bengal's history by making partition certain. There is a fairly objective description of the rioting in Kolkata between 16 and 19 August 1946 in Bangabandhu Sheikh Mujibur Rehman's *Unfinished Memoirs* (Penguin Viking 2012, pp. 65–72).

Politics in Delhi: the Interim Government

Neither Nehru nor any of the top Congress leaders nor Jinnah found the time to visit riot-ravaged Kolkata, India's premier city. They were politicking for or against the formation of the interim government. Only Wavell, the viceroy, felt compelled to visit the city. He had written to both Nehru and Jinnah on 22 July 1946 and requested them to join the interim government. He had expressed the British leadership's firm decision to install an Indian interim government in Delhi as quickly as possible, making use of the Viceroy's Executive Council. The Congress rejected the offer straightaway. The Muslim League also rejected it, while at the same time giving a call for direct action. After the riots of Kolkata, Wavell could persuade Nehru and the Congress to join the interim government without any more delay. On 24 August, only a few days after the Kolkata riots, Wavell announced the names of the members of the interim government which was to take office. Nehru had wanted to have nationalist Muslims in two of the five Muslim seats, but the Viceroy announced the names of three of them hoping that Jinnah could still be persuaded to make an announcement for the two remaining Muslim vacancies. Between his announcement and swearing-in of the interim government on 2 September, Wavell visited Kolkata for eighteen hours to see the situation for himself and to share the sorrows and sufferings of the citizens. The visit convinced him that the Congress and the League must make a show of unity if further catastrophes were to be avoided. On 27 August, Wavell summoned both Nehru and Gandhi, narrated to them his experience in Kolkata and requested them to agree on a formula under which the Congress would formally announce that it accepted the intentions behind the Cabinet Mission's formula.

The author of the idea was said to be Nazimuddin, who was seldom known to take an initiative, but took a very significant one at this stage.[21] He had suggested to Wavell during his visit to Kolkata that as Nehru's thoughtless repudiation of the concept of three groups of provinces under the Cabinet Mission Plan of a federal India had been the reason for the Muslim League's rejection of the plan, the only way by which the League could be persuaded to retrace its steps back to the earlier agreement was for the Congress to make an announcement that it accepted the Cabinet Mission Plan as intended by the Mission and not as the Congress interpreted it. There should be another guarantee that no minority province in the three groups would be allowed to opt out of its group before the ten-year period specified by the Mission. Nazimuddin was a member of the League Working Committee and was known to be close to Jinnah. Wavell, therefore, put this proposition to Gandhi and Nehru in his meeting with them on 27 August 1946. He also told them what he had seen in Kolkata and appealed to them to accept this as the last chance for a peaceful transfer of power. Its acceptance by them could perhaps have still saved the subcontinent's unity, but it was not destined to be. Both Gandhi and Nehru refused point blank to sign a draft announcement that Wavell proposed. Their ground was that this would amount to surrendering to the Muslim League's blackmail. They also raised the old argument that the Congress was not pro-Hindu or pro-Muslim and would never legislate against the interests of the Muslims. Also, they would not accept the Muslim League as the only representative body of Indian Muslims. Thus, the Nizamuddin formula was stillborn, and Wavell's meeting with Gandhi and Nehru ended on an acrimonious note.

In a way, this interview was also the end of Wavell's viceroyalty, for immediately thereafter Gandhi cabled to Attlee that the Viceroy had become 'unnerved owing to the Bengal tragedy and needed to be bolstered by an even mind'.[22] Nehru was also reported to have written private letters to a number of friends in the Labour Party like Cripps accusing Wavell of being unfriendly to the Congress and being pro-Muslim League and appeasing Jinnah. He also used his friend Krishna Menon and Sudhir Ghosh to influence Labour Party leaders in Britain to the idea that Wavell was not the right man for the hour and that India needed a new Viceroy with a fresh mind to pilot her to independence.

Wavell, under considerable pressure from Attlee, could persuade the Congress to join the interim cabinet and went ahead with the swearing in of the cabinet on 2 September 1946, minus the Muslim League. The new government consisted of the following: Nehru, designated as deputy chairman of the Viceroy's Executive Council, Vallabhbhai Patel, Rajendra Prasad, Rajagopalachari, Asaf Ali, Sarat Chandra Bose,[23] John Matthai, Baldev Singh and C.H. Bhabha. Shafat Ahmed Khan and Sayid Ali Zaheer would join after a little while.

The Muslim League still stood away protesting against the Congress nominating two Congress Muslim leaders to the cabinet. Jinnah had demanded an exclusive right to nominate Muslims—a claim that seemed quite convincing in the light of the League's demonstrated hold over the Muslims of the subcontinent as shown in the 1946 elections, and yet was not acceptable to the Congress. Wavell went on patiently negotiating with Jinnah. Eventually he succeeded in persuading Jinnah to let the Muslim League join the interim government. This was indeed a great diplomatic achievement on his part. But when five members of the Muslim League joined the interim cabinet on 26 October 1946, Jinnah, like a master chess player, disputed the right of the Congress to speak for the scheduled caste Hindus and nominated Jogendra Nath Mandal, a scheduled caste leader from Bengal, as a Muslim League nominee. This was his quid pro quo to the Congress claim of representing Muslims. If the Congress put itself up as representing some sections of Muslims, Jinnah wanted to show that it did not enjoy the support of all sections of Hindus and that the Hindu scheduled castes looked for support to the Muslim League rather than the Congress. Also, he himself did not join the interim cabinet, as that would mean accepting Nehru's superior status as deputy chairman. He left it to Liaquat Ali to lead the Muslim League contingent. But interestingly, apart from Liaquat, Jinnah did not nominate any heavyweight Muslim League leader like Nazimuddin.

Significantly, there was no Muslim League nominee from Bengal. As the Congress could nominate only five ministers, and was keen to nominate a Muslim, Sarat Chandra Bose was excluded at the last minute. Thus his tenure as Central minister was barely for two months. Apart from being a persona non grata with the British raj, Sarat Bose's opposition to the 'partition' plan already under serious consideration was also said to have been a cause of his estrangement with the Congress leadership. In January 1947 he resigned from the

Congress Working Committee in protest against the decision to partition Punjab.

The Noakhali Riots

The Great Calcutta Killings had triggered off the Noakhali anti-Hindu riots in October 1946 and the Bihar anti-Muslim riots shortly thereafter, both vitiating the communal situation in Bengal to a point of no return. In Noakhali district, which was predominantly Muslim (82 per cent), and some adjoining areas of Tripura district violence started on 10 October 1946—the day dedicated to the worship of Lakshmi, the Hindu goddess of prosperity. Organised gangs of Muslim League miscreants attacked Hindu villagers, a helpless minority, killing them, burning their houses, looting their possessions, dishonouring their women, abducting and forcibly marrying many of them, forcibly converting people to Islam and desecrating Hindu temples in order to spread terror and force them to emigrate from their hearths and homes. The police force was by and large inactive. One of the most sensational cases was the open attack on the village home of Rajendralal Roychowdhury, a respectable zamindar, in broad daylight and the killing of the whole family of twenty-three. Such incidents were pre-planned to create terror among the Hindus systematically. Wavell himself commented in a letter to Pathick Lawrence that the riots were deliberately planned by the worst political elements 'those in East Bengal by a discarded supporter of the Muslim League'.[24] The news of what was happening in Noakhali countryside was not allowed to be published in the press for a week under orders of the Bengal government. Strangely enough, the leader of the murderous gang was a former Congressman, Gholam Sarwar, an ex-MLA who had joined the Muslim League. Sarwar was not apprehended by the administration despite a warrant of arrest against him. As news started slowly trickling out to the outside world from 17 October onwards and the magnitude of the disaster came to be known, there was an outcry all over the subcontinent. The press reported that around 5,000 Hindus had been killed and about 1.5 lakh lost their homes and all possessions. Premier Suhrawardy flew over Noakhali to see the extent of destruction and simply commented that the newspapers reports were grossly exaggerated.

True, official sources invariably described the newspaper reports as highly exaggerated, but even if we had to discount them, there is no doubt that what happened was itself of huge proportions. General Butcher of the Eastern Command himself admitted that the Hindus had sufficient cause for running away. The news of the happenings in Noakhali caused much consternation all over the country. Mahatma Gandhi felt extremely disturbed and decided to proceed to Noakhali. The government of Bengal deputed Simpson, a high-ranking official, to Noakhali and Tripura for an on-the-spot study of the situation and for a report on what happened and remedial steps needed to be taken. This report was not released, but according to newspaper reports, it had supported the story of widespread killing, looting, and raping and abduction of women. The gist of the report was leaked out in the *Statesman* of 13 November 1946. It brought out that no substantial structure was found standing in most of the Hindu localities. It also supported reports of forcible mass conversion of Hindus to Islam, confining Hindu womenfolk in large numbers to force them to change their religion and marry Muslims. Inquiring pointedly, Judge Simpson tried to ascertain if the rioters who attacked the villages were local people or hired goondas imported from outside. He was told definitely that most of the rioters came from the neighbouring villages. On the same day when Simpson's report was published, Gandhi visited Ramganj village and found telltale evidence of destruction all around. J.B. Kripalani, who was the president of the Congress, also visited some of the areas. He met the Governor of Bengal and recorded that the Governor was totally indifferent to the happenings in Noakhali.

Mahatma Gandhi started from Sodepur near Kolkata on 6 November 1946 and reached Noakhali the following day. He stayed there for about four months and left Noakhali on 2 March 1947. He toured the disturbed areas on foot, lived in Muslim villages, held numerous meetings trying to re-establish communal amity, appealing to both the communities to live peacefully and amicably as before. His Noakhali tour was not only a high watermark in his own life, but was also a major event in the chronicle of happenings before independence. However, it produced different reactions among different sections of the people. It obviously had a considerable effect on Suhrawardy.

Noakhali and Tripura continued to be in the grip of fear for many months. The following portion from a 'confidential, top secret' report sent by the commissioner of the Chittagong division to the government on 13 May 1947[25] illustrates this:

> Though outwardly Noakhali is quiet, the Hindus there are still panicky; the reason for the panic is the petty oppression of the Hindus by the Muslims in the countryside away from the towns and the abuses they are subjected to. The Hindus comprise four lakhs out of a total population of eighteen lakhs and, remembering the October atrocities, they, particularly the upper class among them, are passing their days in fear and terror. They do not dare to report to the police station the harassment and oppression they are subjected to. If they do so, they apprehend greater harassment when the Muslims come to know of it. If again any such information is given, the informant denies it at the inquiry but, in spite of that, the complaint on many occasions is found to be true. The Muslims can be categorised into four classes. First, though their number is small, are those who want to live peacefully with the Hindus and they gave shelter to many Hindus during the riots. The second category, and this comprises the largest number of them, are supporters of the Muslim League and they want the Hindus to leave the district. They do not want to kill the Hindus outright but oppress them in various ways; they would turn their face when the Hindus face violence and at times would also join in it. Many members of the Union Boards belong to this category. The third category comprises of those who really hate the Hindus in the name of religion or out of greed for personal reasons and they are prepared to exterminate them by all means. The recent events have

swelled their ranks and a large number of *goondas* have joined this class in the hope of profiting by looting Hindu property. Many of this class are good speakers and they incite others against the Hindus. Abul Kashim and Ali Akbar are two of the prominent men of this category. There are complaints against them and they have absconded and are evading arrest by the police. The fourth category comprises the *goondas*. About 56,000 men of this district used to earn a good salary during the war and they do not let go any opportunity for looting. They are adept in theft, dacoity, arson, murder and other crimes and the Hindus mostly are their target.

The Hindus are subjected to other forms of oppression and humiliation too. Since the last killings, the Muslims have started to address the Hindus publicly as 'kafirs', 'malwun', etc. and to snatch cash from them. Forcible snatching of articles purchased from the market, forcible plucking of fruits from the trees of the Hindus, forcible removal of timber, tin and cattle, destroying paddy standing on the lands of the Hindus, setting fire to the houses of the Hindus who might have made complaints at police stations, are matters of daily occurrence. Attempts are being made to stop the shows in cinema houses belonging to Hindus. Though most of the weavers are Hindus, the Muslims are demanding 50 per cent of licences for working looms for themselves. Attempts are being made for ejecting Hindu shopkeepers from the markets. A big wholesale dealer has stated that he and many others have received anonymous letters threatening them with dire consequences if they did not close their business. Many old shopkeepers have been ejected and Muslims have opened shops in the premises. The Hindus who have constructed new structures after the late killings and arson are being threatened with evil consequences if they persisted in continuing to stay. Those who filed cases in court after the disturbances in October last are being forced under threat to withdraw their cases.

The houses of 7,700 families were destroyed by arson during the disturbances and over 22,000 farmers and weavers were driven away from their villages. Arrangements for their rehabilitation with government help have been made.

The Gandhi Camps and other volunteers did not succeed in affording much relief to the distressed people. The volunteers have no contact with the local Muslims; they regard each other with suspicion.

The main reason for the moral and psychological weakness of the Hindus is the partisan attitude of the government for the miscreants in the October disturbances leading to an increase in the latter's surge for oppressing and harassing the Hindus. After the disturbances, 1,529 criminal cases involving over 13,000 persons were instituted but cases against 164 accused persons only are now going on. Of the 677 persons arrested by the police only 50 are in detention. The Hindus know that the police do not want to arrest the miscreants and the miscreants know full well that they will not have to suffer punishment. The police cannot trace out the two master criminals, Abul Kashim and Ali Akbar, though they are freely moving about and are addressing public meetings saying that it was a mistake not to have done away with all the Hindus on the last occasion and that this mistake would not be committed at the clash to come. In spite of all this, the police do not arrest them and this has resulted in adding to the apprehensions of the Hindus and also in increasing the boldness and spite of the Muslims. Magistrates, under pressure from the authorities, are being forced to release accused persons on bail and these miscreants are threatening witnesses and forcing them to give false evidence. Correct information of the indifference, partisanship and oppression of the police is not forthcoming and the government is giving out that the trouble is at an end. It is this conduct and attitude of the police that made the terrible killing of October last possible and very likely there is going to be a repetition of the same.

There is no doubt that the Noakhali atrocities served to harden the attitude of the Bengali Hindus in favour of the partition of Bengal.

Holocaust in Bihar, 1947

If Noakhali hardened the Hindu attitude, the Bihar riots had the same effect for the Muslims. In Bihar it was the turn of the Muslims to suffer at the hands of armed murderous bands of Hindus who had been inflamed by reports from Kolkata of mass killings of many Bihari rickshaw-pullers and milk-vendors by Muslim *goondas* in August. As the news of the atrocities had spread to the villages in Bihar, invariably there was retaliatory action on a scale that surpassed the Kolkata killings. Armed mobs went round the countryside attacking Muslim villages in a planned manner. It was a replay of Noakhali, the only difference being that there was no forced conversion or dishonouring of women. Village after village was burnt, the inhabitants killed or injured and movable property looted. While the Bengal government was accused of inaction in the early days of the violence in Noakhali, in Bihar the army was deployed in the very first instance to check widespread rioting and arson. The prime minister of the interim government, Jawaharlal Nehru, and some of his Hindu colleagues who had not thought it necessary to visit the riot-torn Kolkata and Noakhali, rushed to Bihar. Nehru even threatened aerial bombing unless the rioting stopped. As Noakhali had hardened Bengali Hindu opinion in favour of partition, the happenings in Bihar hardened the attitude of Muslim Bengalis in favour of not staying in Hindu India.

British plan for withdrawal: arrival of Mountbatten

Continued communal violence in Noakhali and Bihar had further worsened the problem of finding a constitutional framework for India after British withdrawal. The British authorities were now working on a plan to completely leave India by June 1948. Wavell came to the conclusion that the British simply would not be able to govern India for more than eighteen months or so. He kept two contingency plans ready from April 1946. One was for the emergency evacuation of British civilians. The other was for the withdrawal of the British army and administrators province by province (called Operation Ebb-Tide) after making conditions reasonably safe in each province and their eventual convergence in Bombay and Karachi from which ports they could sail home. Meanwhile, things were moving fast in London. On 20 February 1947, Prime Minister Clement Attlee made the following historic announcement in the British Parliament. 'His Majesty's government wishes to make it clear that it is their definite intention to take the necessary steps to effect the transfer of power into responsible Indian hands by a date not later than June 1948.' In spite of determined opposition from Winston Churchill who had for nearly four decades opposed every move towards India's independence, the House of Commons overwhelmingly endorsed Clement Attlee's decision to end British raj in India by June 1948. The same speech also made another important announcement, namely, the replacement of Field Marhshal Wavell by Admiral Lord Louis Mountbatten as Governor-General and Viceroy. It was rumoured, as already stated, that Nehru through his associate in London, Krishna Menon, who had close contacts with the British Labour Party, had canvassed with the British government leaders in favour of replacing Wavell with Mountbatten with whom he had struck up a friendship during his visit to Singapore where Mountbatten, the supreme commander of the Allied forces in South-East Asia, had treated him like a head of government. Nehru had never got on with the matter-of-fact Wavell during the negotiations. Incidentally, general mistrust rather than confidence was the order of the day, the last thing needed at the negotiating table. Nehru did not trust Jinnah. Jinnah also had total mistrust for Nehru. Nehru did not fully trust his colleague, Patel, just as Jinnah did not trust Suhrawardy. Also, Nehru mistrusted Wavell and the Governor-General fully reciprocated this feeling. There was mistrust between Wavell and British Prime Minister Clement Attlee, who overruled Wavell's decision to postpone the swearing-in of the interim government until the Muslim League would agree to join, and enforced its swearing-in only with Congress ministers. Thus, Attlee had shown his no-confidence in Viceroy

Wavell even before the latter was sacked.

In retrospect, the replacement of Wavell by Mountbatten as Britain's last Governor-General in India was somewhat unfortunate for the ongoing negotiations on transfer of power. Wavell had tried to prevent the partition of the country as best as he could and, therefore, continued his seemingly endless negotiations. In that process he had even become unpopular with Indian leaders, who often lost patience with him. But Mountbatten, who arrived on 19 March 1947, saw his role as a military commander who had to accomplish a task, namely, British withdrawal from India, as fast as possible. His announcement to bring forward the date of transfer of power from June 1948 to August 1947 produced a lot of unforeseen and unfortunate effects, directly paving the way for the communal holocaust in Punjab.

The Punjab civil war

In Punjab, many people felt that their immediate future was uncertain and took recourse to arms to ensure things in their own ways. Muslims in West Punjab straightaway thought of driving out the Hindus and the Sikhs and grabbing their land and property. The result was disastrous and the government was simply not prepared to face the situation that emerged in Punjab. While Bengal during these months remained relatively quiet, except for Kolkata, the storm centre moved to Punjab where the situation deteriorated very fast. At that time Punjab was under the administration of a coalition government of the Congress, the Akalis and the Unionists under Khizar Hyat Khan who was the premier. The Muslim League, although returned as the largest party in the Assembly after decimating the once formidable Unionist Party, was in the Opposition because three other parties chose to form a coalition.

With Pakistan in sight, the Muslim League entered an armed confrontation with the coalition government in power through a no-holds-barred civil disobedience movement. The League's National Guards and the Hindu Rashtriya Swayamsewak Sangh clashed everywhere and, for all practical purposes, created civil war conditions. The militant Sikhs scattered all over Punjab in innumerable pockets felt insecure and tried to protect these pockets with arms or migrate to safer areas in what was likely to be a part of the Indian Union, using force ruthlessly. Their leader, Master Tara Singh, issued an open appeal to the Sikhs to draw their swords out and fight the Muslims. Militant Muslims all over western Punjab started an orgy of violence in trying to drive out Hindus and Sikhs from their hearths and homes. Hindus and Sikhs in eastern Punjab in retaliation started a similar process of ethnic cleansing. The administration in Punjab found itself thoroughly unprepared to deal with this kind of civil war, which it had never anticipated.

Faced with civil war conditions and unable to control the situation, Premier Khizar Hyat Khan resigned on 2 March 1947. The Governor of Punjab, Sir Evan Jenkins, invited the Khan of Mamdot, leader of the Muslim League in the Punjab Assembly, to form a government. But such was the electoral arithmetic in the Punjab Assembly that the League could not have a majority of its own, and both the Congress and the Akali Party refused to extend support to it. Unavoidably, Governor's rule under Section 93 followed. But the Muslim League, determined to seize political power by force, and carry into effect the slogan of 'Ladke lenge Pakistan' started widespread rioting. This started in Lahore and engulfed the whole of Punjab like wildfire. It also spread to neighbouring NWFP where armed Muslim League supporters tried with brute force to overthrow the Congress government elected only the year before, led by Dr Khan Sahib, the brother of Khan Abdul Ghaffar Khan, the legendary Frontier Gandhi. So strong was the communal contagion that Jawaharlal Nehru, on a special visit to the province which he had thought all along was a Congress-friendly one, was heckled and almost manhandled and had to return so disappointed that he never took a strong stand on the issue of asking the NWFP to go through a referendum to decide whether to join India or Pakistan. The Congress could have taken a strong stand against referendum in a province that had voted for it only eighteen months ago.

With all these developments, in particular the experience of a deadlocked administration in the interim government caused by Liaquat Ali, who was in charge of the finance portfolio, blocking all proposals from Congress ministers, Nehru and the Congress leadership were slowly getting reconciled to the inevitability of partition. In a conversation with Leonard Mosley several years later Nehru confided: 'We were tired men. We were not prepared to go to jail again.' V.P. Menon, who had by then become reforms commissioner and constitutional adviser to Governor-General Mountbatten, played a leading role in persuading them that a united India was virtually impossible and that it was inevitable that the British would transfer power to two Central governments, one representing the Muslim majority in Pakistan and the other representing the Hindu majority in India on the basis of dominion status. Once Nehru and Patel accepted that the partition was inevitable, V.P. Menon quickly formulated an outline plan, got Wavell's approval and sent it to the India Office in London.[26]

The idea of the partition of Bengal

But just when Pakistan had become a certainty as also the inclusion of the whole of Bengal in it, a totally unforeseen development took place, namely, the idea of a partition of Bengal, which, paradoxically, Bengal had rejected half a century ago. Taking the cue from Punjab where a decision was taken to divide Punjab on religious lines in early March, a proposal was mooted for the partition of Bengal under which all Hindu majority districts were to be given the option to remain in India. This proposal, first suggested in the Tarakeshwar Conference of the Bengal Provincial Hindu Mahasabha (4–6 April 1947) rapidly gathered support like a rolling snowball. In his presidential address, N.C. Chatterjee said: 'Let us declare today that as the Muslim League persists in its fantastic idea of establishing Pakistan in Bengal, the Hindus of Bengal must constitute a separate province under a strong national government. This is not a question of partition. This is a question of life and death for us, the Bengalee Hindus.' One of the principal protagonists was Shyama Prasad Mukherjee who declared: 'I conceive of no other solution of the communal problem in Bengal than to divide the province and to let the two major communities residing here to live in peace and

freedom.' The conference authorized Mukherjee to take all steps for
the establishment of a separate homeland for the Hindus of Bengal
in collaboration with all the nationalist elements. The West Bengal
Congress accepted this idea almost immediately and passed the
following resolution:

> If His Majesty's Government contemplate handing over its
> power to the existing Government of Bengal which is
> determined to the formation of Bengal into a sovereign
> state and which by its composition is a communal party
> Government, such portions of Bengal as are desirous of
> remaining within the Union of India should be allowed to
> remain so and be formed in a separate province within the
> Union of India.

Thus the cycle had made a full turn since 1905. Bengali Hindus who
in 1905 launched a full-scale political movement to protect the unity
of Bengal and their destiny as its essential part now started a political
movement for Bengal's partition in order to protect their Hindu
identity. There was a hartal in Kolkata in support of the partition of
Bengal. Fifty jurists of the Calcutta High Court, in a statement,
pressed for the partition of Bengal on the ground that by going to
Pakistan the Bengali Hindus would only exchange one form of
slavery for another, and that they needed a homeland of their own.
On 1 April 1947, eleven members of the Constituent Assembly from
Bengal submitted a memorandum to the viceroy supporting the
partition of the province. On 24 April 1947, the *Statesman*, Kolkata,
commented that the minds of the middle-class Bengali Hindus had
been so embittered that nothing except a partition of the province
would satisfy them. The Marwari business interests of Kolkata led by
G.D. Birla also lent their solid support to the proposed partition of
Bengal. On 30 April 1947, a meeting of the Chambers of Commerce
held in Kolkata supported the partition of Bengal. According to
G.D. Birla, this was not only unavoidable, but an excellent way out
of the problem. On 1 June, addressing the Bengali community in
Delhi, Shyama Prasad Mukherjee called for a division of Bengal on
'linguistic, cultural and economic considerations if India had to be

divided'. Even the Muslim business interests wanted the partition, which would free them from unequal competition with the Tatas and Birlas. Thus when the decision to partition Bengal was announced in Mountbatten's broadcast on 3 June 1947, this was relayed through microphones on street crossings of Kolkata by jubilant crowds who saw in this proposal a liberation from the dark days of Muslim League rule. For many of them, tired of a winter of discontent (1946–47) caused by communal riots and economic misery through scarcity and rising prices of essential commodities and an economic slump that followed the end of the war, this mirage of early independence (for Hindus of West Bengal an independent India, and for Bengali Muslims the promised homeland) seemed to be the light at the end of the tunnel. For average Muslim middle-class Bengalis who had been seeking a separate identity since the 1920s, the quest appeared to seek fulfilment in Pakistan.[27]

The countervailing idea of a sovereign united Bengal

Suhrawardy was totally unprepared for such a move for partition of Bengal. At a press conference in New Delhi on 27 April 1946, he described it as a suicidal move and pleaded for 'an independent sovereign undivided Bengal in a divided India'.[28] He even expressed his willingness to accept a joint electorate to allay the suspicions of the Hindus. He appealed to the Hindus to accept his proposal and said that the future of independent and undivided Bengal was very bright. 'I promise', he said, 'that the future will be unlike the present. Bengal's wealth, peace and happiness will befit a great nation. If the Hindus can forget the past and accept the proposal, I promise to fulfil their hopes and aspirations to the full.' He also announced: 'Independent Bengal will frame its own constitution and its Legislative Assembly will take the final decision in the matter. We Bengalees have a common mother tongue, and common economic interests.'

For him a Pakistan without the city of Kolkata was simply not acceptable. Also, his relations with Jinnah were already under strain. He got in touch with several other kindred souls like Sarat Chandra Bose and Kiran Shankar Roy who were also opposed to the prospect

of a divided Bengal. Their response now was an independent sovereign
Bengal as a third succession state after the withdrawal of the British,
along with India and Pakistan. For a while this idea also caught the
imagination of some people. Many Bengali Muslims supported this
idea. Abul Hashim, who had emerged as the spokesman of the
progressive sections of the Muslim League, made the following
statement:

> Let the Hindus and Muslims agree to C.R. Das's formula of
> 50:50 enjoyment of political power and economic privileges.
> I appeal to the youths of Bengal in the name of her past
> traditions and glorious future to unite, to make a determined
> effort to dismiss all reactionary thinking and save Bengal
> from the impending calamity.

But the concept of a united sovereign Bengal was stillborn. Its
success largely depended on the support of the Hindu Bengalis in
general, which was not forthcoming. Suhrawardy, according to P.S.
Mathur, at that time his press secretary, had envisaged that the
proposed undivided independent Bengal would include the districts
of Manbhum, Singbhum and Purnea from Bihar and the Surma
Valley of Assam, with the result that there would not be a substantial
difference in the numerical strength of the Hindus and the Muslims.[30]
In fact, the two communities would be evenly balanced in an
independent enlarged Bengal. This was Suhrawardy's way of removing
the misgivings of the Hindus. Whether Bihar or Assam would have
agreed to readily part with their territory is a different issue. Also,
apart from Suhrawardy, some of his trusted followers like Abul
Hashim and Muhammad Ali, and only two Hindu leaders, namely,
Sarat Chandra Bose and Kiran Shankar Roy, there were very few
takers for this proposal. Both the Congress leadership and the
Muslim League leadership cold-shouldered the idea of an
independent Bengal. Kiran Shankar Roy soon backed out under
pressure from Congress leaders.

Above all, the Hindus of West Bengal were in 1947 not convinced
of a united Bengal and in no mood to settle for continued Muslim
domination in the politics of undivided Bengal, after experiencing

for nearly two decades so many irritants like the reservation of an overwhelming majority of government jobs for Muslims. Many of them had suspicion that this was Suhrawardy's camouflage to lure them into an eastern Muslim-dominated sovereign state. Even the Muslim business interests opposed this as yet another Hindu conspiracy to keep Muslims in bondage. There were reports of meetings both in Kolkata and in the districts to protest against Bengal's division. In Rangpur and Mymensingh, where the communist-led Tebhagha Movement was at its height, slogan-shouting peasants were reportedly saying: 'We will not divide Bengal. We will not kill each other.' The Communist Party of India also raised its voice against the partition of Bengal, although it supported the proposal of Pakistan with Bengal as a part of the new state.

The joint proposal formulated by Suhrawardy and Sarat Chandra Bose envisaged the following arrangement:

a) Bengal would constitute an independent state, which would determine the relationship it would establish with the other states of India, but without a two-third majority vote in the Legislative Assembly it would not join either India or Pakistan.

b) Election to the Legislative Assembly would be on the basis of adult suffrage. The number of seats for the two communities in the Legislative Assembly would be determined by the numerical strength of the communities, respectively, but the electorate would be a joint one.

Gandhi made a statement that he would support the proposal if each and every Bengali Hindu could certify openly that he would be able to live without fear in any part of Bengal. Sarat Bose kept Gandhi fully informed of his efforts to preserve Bengal's unity even in a divided India and secured his support in principle.

Five days after the publication of the Cabinet Mission proposal of 3 June, Gandhi said at the end of his prayer meeting at Gurgaon:

It is rumoured that the proposal for an integrated Bengal is getting support from many quarters as it had got my support; I have also heard that large sums of money are being spent on securing votes in support of the proposal. I admit the value of unity but I am not in favour of establishing its value by dishonest means. I have been criticised by many for having supported Sarat Bose's proposal. Sarat Bose is my friend; there is no doubt about it; it is also true that there had been an exchange of letters between us over the proposal. I do not approve of undesirable means to achieve a desirable end and I am against any act which cannot be done openly and by fair means.

In a speech at Himayetpur in the district of Pabna, which appeared in the journal *Parbasi* (Chaitra 1353 BS) Sarat Bose stated:

A partition of Bengal is desired by some. Netaji's objective was a greater India and a greater Bengal. I am personally in favour of inclusion in Bengal of the Bengali speaking districts of Sylhet, Singbhum and Purnea. If there is any move to partition Bengal—this beautiful land—another strong movement will start to resist it and all classes of people will join the agitation. We are all Bengalees. Let people of both West and East Bengal live together in amity. We do not want either Bengal or India to be divided.

Much has been said for Gandhi's support for a united independent Bengal. Gandhi did at one stage lend his half-hearted support, but not the full-throated support that it needed. Sarat Chandra Bose met Gandhi on several occasions with the proposal for an undivided Bengal. On some of these visits he was accompanied by Suhrawardy and Abul Hashim. Hashim told Gandhi 'Language, tradition and history have created an unshakable bond of unity between the Hindus and Muslims of Bengal. We are after all Bengalees in spite of the difference in religion. It is a matter of shame that Pakistan would rule us from a distance of thousand miles.' Gandhi advised Suhrawardy and Hashim to gain the trust of the Hindus first. Suhrawardy and Sarat Chandra Bose did not give up their hope for an undivided Bengal and fought a valiant rear-guard action till the end. In May 1947, at a meeting held in his house for a discussion of the proposal, Suhrawardy, Abul Hashim, Fazlur Rahman of Dhaka,

Muhammad Ali of Bogra, Kiran Shankar Roy and Satyaranjan Bakshi unanimously favoured this. Their proposal was forwarded to Gandhi at Patna under the signature of Sarat Bose and Abul Hashim (23 May 1947). While Gandhi was at Sodepur before this, he had told Sarat Bose and some Muslim leaders who had met him that the foundation of an undivided independent Bengal would be that no government proposal would be effective unless it was agreed to by a two-thirds majority of the cabinet and of the Legislative Assembly. Referring to this, he wrote to Sarat Bose:

> The new proposal makes no mention of the above condition, nor does it contain any admission of the unity of culture of the Hindus and Muslims of Bengal. Besides that, it is necessary to ascertain that the Central Muslim League was in favour of the proposal. I shall however move it before the Congress Working Committee.

But the Congress leadership made its position clear in no uncertain terms. So did the strident Hindu Mahasabha led by Shyama Prasad. At a meeting on 23 May, when Mountbatten raised Suhrawardy's proposal, Nehru made his task simpler by saying that the Congress could accept a united Bengal if it stayed in India. Both the Congress and the Muslim League accepted the partition of Bengal and Punjab in terms of the viceroy's declaration of 3 June. Still Sarat Bose did not abandon hope. He met Gandhi in Delhi on 6 June. On 1 June, Gandhi wrote to Sarat Bose:

> I have discussed your proposal of an undivided independent Bengal with Sardar Patel and Pandit Nehru both of whom are very much opposed to it. According to them, it is just a device to drive a wedge between the caste and the depressed-class Hindus and this is not their doubt only. They say they are convinced of it.

Sarat Bose still persisted in his efforts. He met Jinnah at Delhi and on 9 June wrote to him from Kolkata requesting him to direct the Muslim League members of the Bengal Legislative Assembly to vote against joining Pakistan. Needless to say, nothing came out of it. The

fact is that, in the face of strong opposition from both the Congress
and the Muslim League leadership and strong reservations among
the majority of the Hindus of West Bengal, the concept of a united
sovereign Bengal was simply stillborn.

The Mountbatten Plan

Mountbatten took over as Viceroy and Governor-General on 24
March 1947 with a clear mandate to arrange transfer of power to a
unitary government, if possible, but in any case to two governments
by 1 June 1948. He was given time till 10 October 1947 to persuade
the Indian parties. But, in any case, with communal violence at its
crescendo and with the Muslim League's persistent refusal to join
the Constituent Assembly, partition seemed inevitable. On 2 June
1947, a little less than three months after he had assumed charge,
Mountbatten announced the following proposals in a meeting with
seven leaders: Jawaharlal Nehru, Sardar Vallabhbhai Patel, J.B.
Kripalani (representing the Congress), M.A. Jinnah, Liaquat Ali
Khan and Abdur Rab Nishtar (representing the Muslim League)
and Baldev Singh (representing the Sikhs).

a) A separate independent state would be constituted with
    Muslim majority provinces, but before that representatives
    of the Hindu majority areas in Bengal and Punjab would be
    at liberty to opt for a partition of these two provinces.
b) A plebiscite in NWFP would decide whether that province
    would form a part of Pakistan.
c) The people of the Bengali-speaking district of Sylhet in
    Assam would also decide through a plebiscite whether that
    district would form part of Pakistan.
d) A Boundary Commission would be appointed for
    demarcating the boundary of the Hindu majority and
    Muslim majority areas in Bengal and Punjab, which would
    go to India and Pakistan respectively.
e) No immediate change was envisaged for the princely states,
    but they were advised to join either of the two dominions
    on the lapse of British paramountcy.

Significantly, there was not a single representative in this meeting from Bengal, the province that along with Punjab had the most at stake. It is a measure of the extent to which Bengal politicians— Hindu and Muslim—had abdicated their authority and surrendered it to political leaders from other parts of the subcontinent. It also demonstrated that, whether in the Congress or in the Muslim League, Bengali leaders were no longer counted as front rankers. All the parties concerned gave their consent formally or informally. Mountbatten literally steamrolled all 'ifs' and 'buts' to which Wavell would perhaps have lent a patient ear and tried his negotiating skills. He summarily dismissed Nehru's feeble plea for independence as a third option in the NWFP referendum, stating that the Congress could not ask for it when it had denied the same option to Bengal.

True to his proverbial speed, Mountbatten met Gandhi immediately after his meeting, secured his approval and announced this scheme that same evening (3 June 1947) in a broadcast over the All-India Radio. He was followed in that radio programme by Nehru, Jinnah and Baldev Singh, each of them announcing the acceptance of the partition scheme and praising Viceroy Mountbatten. The British House of Commons also approved on the same evening what came to be known as the Third June Plan. Next morning Mountbatten, in a press conference, casually announced that the transfer of power would take place not in June 1948, but on 15 August 1947, that is, in just about two months time. If there was any single event that contributed most to the communal holocaust in Punjab, it was this advancing of the date of partition and independence.

The NWFP referendum passed off peacefully on 6–17 July 1947 with the Congress and Red Shirts, with total lack of logic, abstaining from it to register their protest. The result in favour of Pakistan was, therefore, a foregone conclusion. Also, the referendum in Sylhet, of more concern to Bengal, passed off peacefully. The people of the district decided to join East Pakistan by a clear majority. But in Punjab the situation deteriorated very fast, the whole province becoming a vast killing field.

6

BENGAL DECIDES ON PARTITION

The last nail in the coffin of united Bengal was struck on 20 June 1946. The Bengal Legislative Assembly voted for Pakistan. Thereafter, in a separate session, the MLAs from notional Hindu majority districts voted in favour of partitioning the province and staying in India. The Muslim League MLAs of both East and West Bengal voted against partition. H.S. Suhrawardy announced in anguish that the idea of a sovereign undivided Bengal had been stabbed in the back and that the partition of Bengal was inevitable. On 3 July, 1947 a shadow cabinet was formed for the province of West Bengal with Dr P.C. Ghosh—member of the Congress Working Committee and Gandhian—as chief minister. The idea was that although the Suhrawardy cabinet would continue for the whole of Bengal till 15 August, all matters concerning the notional territory of West Bengal would need the concurrence of the shadow cabinet.

Later on the Muslim League members from East Bengal districts elected as their leader Khwaja Nazimuddin, who was to take over as the first chief minister of the province of East Bengal in the new dominion of Pakistan. Suhrawardy was elected leader of the Muslim League in the West Bengal Assembly.

Thus Pakistan under Jinnah had no use for the man, who, next to Jinnah, perhaps contributed most to the creation of Pakistan. In fact, he was destined to be expelled from the Pakistan Constituent

Assembly and later on from the province of East Bengal in 1948 by his own Muslim League colleagues for his strong support for the Bengali language and the rights of the Hindu minority and was dubbed as anti-Pakistan and even anti-Muslim. He stayed in India till 1949 but returned to Pakistan in 1949 to build up the Awami League brick by brick and, in association with his old rival Huq and Maulana Bhashani, stormed the citadel of the Muslim League in Bengal in 1954 which he had personally done so much to build a decade ago.

Several other proposals, essentially in the nature of trial balloons, need to be mentioned. In a bid to protect the interests of the 20,000-strong foreign community of Kolkata city, its trade and industry and its character as an international city, Governor Burrows proposed that Kolkata be turned into a free city and free port serving both India and Pakistan, but not becoming a part of either. For the present the British government was to nominate a Governor to be assisted by a council of advisers consisting of an equal number of Hindu and Muslim members and two nominated members, one representing the British community and the other the elite. A year after independence, the citizens of Kolkata were to decide by a majority vote whether they would like to join India or Pakistan, or prefer to continue as a free international city. Needless to say, the proposal did not receive support from either the Congress or the League and died a natural death instantaneously. With the advantage of hindsight, one can say that had this proposal been accepted, Kolkata might have developed like Hong Kong or Singapore well before these two cities developed in the 1950s and 1960s.

The other proposal, a stray thought from Jinnah, was for an 800-mile long corridor connecting West Pakistan and East Pakistan. It was impracticable even on the face of it, like Jinnah's other proposal for the exchange of Hindu and Muslim populations between India and Pakistan. It was rejected straightaway by Nehru and Patel.

Meanwhile, with the future of Kolkata still uncertain (whether in Pakistan or in sovereign united Bengal or an international city) there was a relapse of communal violence in the city from 29 May till the end of July. Between 29 May and 24 June, forty-five persons were killed. In July, 163 persons received injuries, 113 were hit by bullets and forty-seven received acid burns. On 28 May, Governor Burrows informed Viceroy Mountbatten that the situation in the city was explosive with both the rioting sides having stored huge quantities of explosives and arms. On 18 July he further wrote to the viceroy that any announcement about Kolkata remaining in India could be followed by large-scale rioting, with the city being divided into two armed camps. All kinds of panicky rumours were circulating adding to tension. Peace appeals jointly from Gandhi and Jinnah were being distributed from aeroplanes flying over the city. In this phase of rioting the Muslim *bustees* were mainly at the receiving end. The removal of Muslim police officers by the shadow cabinet of P.C. Ghosh at one stroke not only removed a protective umbrella but exposed them to attacks from Hindu anti-socials. Several bustees were burnt at Beliaghata, Kashipur and Entally in the first half of August. The en masse departure of Muslim officials and businessmen for Dhaka in the beginning of August left many of the Muslim localities vulnerable. Suhrawardy, who had gone to Karachi, cut short his programme there on hearing of the fresh outbreak of violence and returned to Kolkata on 10 August. He appealed to Gandhi not to proceed to Punjab and to return back to Kolkata.

The British House of Commons passed the Indian Independence Act on 14 July 1947 and the House of Lords did it a day later. The Act announced that the province of Bengal Presidency as under the Government of India Act, 1935, would cease to exist. With the decks cleared for the inevitable partition, all attention was focussed on the division of government personnel, including the army, and assets of undivided Government of India and of a provincial government of Bengal which itself was going to be partitioned. In the Bengal Secretariat in Kolkata and the headquarters of many of the districts there was feverish activity. Nothing like this had happened in all history. The date for independence or transfer of power was advanced to the night of 14 August 1947. Mountbatten wanted to be the common Governor-General for the dominions. Nehru and the Congress readily accepted him, but not Jinnah who himself wanted to be Pakistan's first Governor-General, with Liaquat Ali as the first prime minister. Jogendra Nath Mandal was nominated as the law and education minister in Pakistan in the first Central cabinet. Jinnah flew to Karachi from Delhi on 9 August 1947 after selling his house in Delhi. At the airport he was reported to have confided to a British ADC that he found it difficult to believe that he was after all getting his Pakistan.[1] Writers Building in Kolkata witnessed an unprecedented spectacle of division of files, furniture and staff. Train-loads of government personnel left Kolkata for Dhaka where they were accommodated in make-shift offices after turning a college building into the provincial secretariat. Government officials were asked whether they would want to serve India or Pakistan. As expected, the Hindu officials with a few exceptions exercised their option for India, while the Muslim officials, once again only with a few exceptions, opted for Pakistan. The British ICS officers, by and large, decided to quit except some who opted for Pakistan. All the Hindu ICS officers opted for India and all the Muslim ICS officers, except one, opted for Pakistan. Sir Frederick Bourne was appointed Governor of the East Bengal province of Pakistan and C. Rajagopalachari, a front-ranking Congress leader, became the Governor of West Bengal. A joint statement was issued by Premier Suhrawardy, chief minister-designate for West Bengal Dr P.C. Ghosh, and chief minister-designate for East Bengal Khwaja Nazimuddin on August 9.

> We...appeal to the people not to take the law into their own hands, but work in a peaceful and orderly manner. We want to give a fair deal to minorities in both parts of Bengal. But the minorities also must cooperate with the majority in making the states happy and prosperous.
>
> About a week from now, transfer of power from British to Indian hands will take place. Undoubtedly, it is an event of great historical importance. By agreement between the Congress and the Muslim League, power will be transferred to two dominions on 15 August. The boundaries of the two dominions are not yet fixed. The matter will be decided by the Boundary Commission.

Both the Congress and the Muslim League have agreed to abide by the decision of the Boundary Commission. We do appeal to all sections of people in Bengal to accept the decision of the Boundary Commission, however unpalatable it may be to one community or to the other. We have no doubt that the vast majority of the people with allegiance to the Congress and the League will respond to the wishes of these organisations.

But during the transitional period, some undesirable elements may try to create trouble for their own interests. If they do so, the government would deal with them sternly.

The flag of the Dominion of India has been accepted by the Constituent Assembly. We do hope that the flag will be hoisted by all sections of the people in West Bengal and, in the same way, whatever flag is accepted by the Pakistan Constituent Assembly it will be hoisted by all sections of people of East Bengal.

We are going to be masters of our destiny. Let us hope God will give us courage and wisdom to shape it in the interest of the toiling and starving masses.

History was to show that these lofty wishes were followed more in the breach than in the observance.

Radcliffe Boundary Commission

Meanwhile two boundary commissions had been appointed, one for Bengal and one for Punjab, both presided over by Sir Cyril Radcliffe, a British jurist. For Bengal the two Muslim members were Justice A.M. Akram and Justice S.A. Rahman and the two Hindu members were Justice Bijon Mukherjee and Justice C.C. Biswas. Radcliffe arrived from England on 8 July 1947. He realized within a few days after briefly visiting Kolkata and Lahore and meeting members of the two boundary commissions that the Hindu and Muslim members could not agree on any point. He thereupon decided not to sit physically with either of the two commissions and stayed in New Delhi only, going through the records of the proceedings every day and the voluminous materials submitted by the counsels representing various parties, flown to him in Delhi every evening. Eventually he took upon himself, for all practical purposes, the entire responsibility of drafting the report on all contentious points. He overruled both the sub-reports and gave his own award. The award on Bengal was submitted to Mountbatten on 9 August 1947 and the one on Punjab after a few days. Radcliffe sailed for home on 15 August, having accomplished his task in less than five weeks, for which he did not accept any fee. Mountbatten chose not to publish the reports until after Independence Day on 15 August. Thus on the midnight of 14 August 1947, undivided Bengal disappeared from the map of the world and in its place the new provinces of West Bengal (in India) and East Bengal (in Pakistan) came into being. On the day of independence there was a sort of notional division. All the Hindu majority districts hoisted the Indian tricolour to celebrate India's independence and all the Muslim majority districts hoisted the Pakistani flag. On 17 August 1947, the Radcliffe report consisting of sixteen pages was released, of which nine pages were devoted to Bengal. This award was as follows:

Sir Cyril Radcliffe's Award
TO HIS EXCELLENCY THE GOVERNOR-GENERAL

1. I have the honour to present the decision and award of the Bengal Boundary Commission, which, by virtue of section 3 of the Indian Independence Act, 1947, is represented by my decision as Chairman of the commission. This award relates to the division of the Province of Bengal and the Commission's award in respect of District of Sylhet and areas adjoining thereto will be recorded in a separate report.

2. The Bengal Boundary Commission was constituted by the announcement of the Governor-General, dated the 30th of June 1947, Reference No. D50/7/47R. The members of the Commission thereby appointed were:

Mr Justice Bijon Kumar Mukherjee,
Mr Justice C.C. Biswas,
Mr Justice Abusaleh Mohammed Akram, and
Mr Justice S.A. Rahman.
I was subsequently appointed Chairman of this Commission.

3. The terms of reference of the Commission, as set out in the announcement were as follows:

'The Boundary Commission is instructed to demarcate the boundaries of the two parts of Bengal on the basis of ascertaining the continuous area of Muslims and non-Muslims. In doing so, it will also take into account other factors.'

We were desired to arrive at a decision as soon as possible before the 15th of August.

4. After preliminary meetings, the commission invited the submission of memoranda and representations by interested parties. A very large number of memoranda and representations was received.

5. The public sittings of the Commission took place at Kolkata, and extended from Wednesday, the 16th of July, 1947, to Thursday, the 24th of July, 1947, inclusive, with the exception of Sunday, the 20th of July. Arguments were presented to the Commission by numerous parties on both sides, but the main cases were presented by counsel on behalf of the Indian National Congress, the Bengal Provincial Hindu Mahasabha and the New Bengal Association on the one hand, and on behalf of the Muslim League on the other. In view of the fact that I was acting also as chairman of the Punjab Boundary Commission, whose proceedings were taking place simultaneously with the proceedings of the Bengal Boundary Commission. I did not attend the public sittings in person, but made arrangements to study daily the record of the proceedings and all material submitted for our consideration.

6. After the close of the public sittings, the remainder of the time of the commission was devoted to clarification and discussion of the issues involved. Our discussions took place at Calcutta.

7. The question of drawing a satisfactory boundary line under our terms of reference between East and West Bengal was one to which the parties concerned propounded the most development has been on lines that do not well accord with a division by continuous majority areas of Muslim and non-Muslim majorities.

8. In my view, the demarcation of a boundary line between East and West Bengal depended on the answers to be given to certain basic questions which may be stated as follows:

(i) To which state was the City of Calcutta to be assigned, or was it possible to adopt any method of dividing the City between the two States?

(ii) If the City of Calcutta must be assigned as a whole to one or other of the States, what were its indispensable claims to the control of territory, such as all or part of the Nadia river system or the Kulti rivers, upon which the life of Calcutta as a city and port depended?

(iii) Could the attractions of the Ganges-Padma-Madhumati river line displace the strong claims of the heavy concentration of Muslim majorities in the districts of Jessore and Nadia without doing too great a violence to the principle of our terms of reference?

(iv) Could the district of Khulna usefully be held by a state different from that which held the district of Jessore?

(v) Was it right to assign to Eastern Bengal the considerable block of non-Muslim majorities in the districts of Malda and Dinajpur?

(vi)   Which State's claim ought to prevail in respect of the districts of Darjeeling and Jalpaiguri, in which the Muslim population amounted to 2.42 per cent of the whole in the case of Darjeeling, and to 23.08 per cent in the whole in the case of Jalpaiguri, but which constituted an area not in any natural sense contiguous to another non-Muslim area of Bengal?

(vii)   To which state should the Chittagong Hill Tracts be assigned, an area in which the Muslim population was only 3 per cent of the whole, but which it was difficult to assign to a State different from that which controlled the district of Chittagong itself?

9. After much discussion, my colleagues found that they were unable to arrive at an agreed view on any of these major issues. There were of course considerable areas of the Province in the south-west and north-east and east, which provoked no controversy on either side; but, in the absence of any reconciliation on all main questions affecting the drawing of the boundary itself, my colleagues assented to the view at the close of our discussions that I had no alternative but to proceed to give my own decision.

10. This I now proceed to do: but I should like at the same time to express my gratitude to my colleagues for their indispensable assistance in clarifying and discussing the difficult questions involved. The demarcation of the boundary line is described in detail in the schedule which forms Annexure A to this award, and in the map attached thereto, Annexure B. The map is annexed for purposes of illustration, and if there should be any divergence between the boundary as described in Annexure A and as delineated on the map in Annexure B, the description in Annexure A is to prevail.

11. I have done what I can in drawing the line to eliminate any avoidable cutting of railway communications and of

river systems, which are of importance to the life of the Province: but it is quite impossible to draw a boundary under our terms of reference without causing some interruption of this sort, and I can only express the hope that arrangements can be made and maintained between the two States that will minimize the consequences of this interruption as far as possible.

New Delhi   CYRIL RADCLIFFE
The 12th August, 1947

There were many surprises. Khulna and Chittagong Hill districts, which had hoisted the Indian national flag two days ago, became parts of Pakistan, while Murshidabad and Malda districts which had hoisted the Pakistani flag were made parts of India. The districts of Jalpaiguri, Malda and Nadia remained in India while losing substantial territory from the districts to Pakistan. On the other hand, although Jessore and Dinajpur were allotted to Pakistan, a subdivision each from both the districts (Bongaon sub-division in Jessore and Balurghat sub-division in Dinajpur) were allotted to India. The state of West Bengal as it emerged from Radcliffe's scissors was also moth-eaten. The districts of Darjeeling and Jalpaiguri were physically separated from the West Bengal mainland. The Muslims were sad to see that Kolkata had gone to West Bengal, as also the Muslim majority district of Murshidabad.

What weighed with Radcliffe in giving Murshidabad to India while, as a compensatory measure, giving Khulna to Pakistan was that the entire length of the Hooghly River from the point where it branches off from the Ganges should be with India in order to maintain the navigability of the Kolkata port. The Hindus were sorry that the predominantly Buddhist district of the Chittagong Hill Tract had been given to Pakistan. All its normal communication routes to the outside world lay through the Chittagong district and apparently that had influenced Radcliffe's judgement, although he failed to notice in his haste that the hill tracts of Chittagong had a long border with the Lushai Hills district of the Indian province of Assam. It was somewhat immoral to award the Chittagong Hill

Tract to Pakistan. As all the parties had given a guarantee that they would accept Radcliffe Award without any question, they had to keep quiet and accept whatever had been decreed by Radcliffe in what was by far the strangest, most illogical and arbitrarily drawn boundary line in history between two countries.

Partition: the extinction of One Bengal

On 15 August 1947, the Indian subcontinent won freedom for two countries from British rule. It was not the kind of freedom for which two generations of people in India had willingly fought and sacrificed. In that process Bengal was also partitioned, two-thirds of it joining Pakistan and one-third remaining in India. No Bengali wanted the partition of Bengal and yet the partition happened because the Hindu Bengalis, especially those from West Bengal, did not want to leave India and go into a predominantly Muslim state whereas the Muslims of East Bengal did not want to merge themselves into a predominantly Hindu India. The fact that despite much provocation and tension there was communal peace in all the districts of Bengal except Kolkata and Noakhali-Tripura was ignored by the politicians.[4] Even when communal violence was rampant in Kolkata and Noakhali, the Muslim and Hindu peasants of the Tebhagha Movement in predominantly Muslim Rangpur and Dinajpur were fighting under the charismatic leadership of Ila Mitra and opposed partition. Such examples were ignored. The Congress leadership sans Mahatma Gandhi was as responsible as Jinnah and Mountbatten for accelerating the movement of events that made partition inevitable. Gandhi, on the other hand, opposed the division till the very end and even in his last meeting with Mountbatten requested the British not to partition the country, but to demit power either to the Muslim League or to the Congress to run India as a whole. If there was to be chaos, let that chaos be faced by Indians. On 31 March he announced that the Congress could agree to the country's partition only over his dead body. He was conspicuous by his absence from the festivities at New Delhi and preferred to stay at a dilapidated Muslim house in riot-torn Calcutta—the Hyder Manzil—at Belighata. His companion was Suhrawardy, the man the Hindus of Kolkata at that time hated the most, whom he had invited to live in the same house with him. In his daily prayer meetings, in meeting countless groups and in the course of journeying through the disturbed localities of Calcutta driven by Suhrawardy himself, Gandhi preached communal harmony and unity of religions and brought about a miracle. What the 50,000-strong boundary force in Punjab, led by General Rees, could not do was accomplished in Bengal, to quote Mountbatten, by this 'one-man boundary force'. Bengal remained trouble-free and there were unprecedented scenes of Hindus and Muslims rejoicing and celebrating together on Independence Day, 15 August 1947. This was Gandhi's great achievement.

In any case, an undivided Bengal disappeared from the atlas on 15 August 1947, thanks to the sins of omission and commission by two generations of its leaders. In spite of a common language of which every Bengali is proud, a shared culture and lifestyle and a common history for at least one thousand years, Bengal was irretrievably partitioned between two sovereign countries. Only the Bay of Bengal remained as a mute witness to what had been old Bengal, by far the most prosperous tract of the whole region. It was only the emergence of an independent Bangladesh in 1971 which partially restored the old historical pattern.

The question remains whether the 1947 partition of Bengal which, to quote the poet Akhtar-uz-Zaman Elias, was 'so catastrophic, so deplorable, so heart-rending and meaningless that we are realising it more every day, could have been avoided'. There can never be a unanimous answer to the question. Fazlul Huq, as chief minister of East Bengal in 1954, announced in public that he did not understand the political boundary separating the two Bengals. Suhrawardy chose to live in Kolkata until 1949. Annada Sankar Roy, the writer and former civil servant, chided the political leaders for breaking Bengal as little children break glass pots. Nirad C. Chaudhuri never accepted the partition and never got reconciled to a West Bengal without the mighty rivers of East Bengal. For Ritwick Ghatak, the film-maker, the indivisible Bengal was an article of faith and the cruelty of dividing this unity was shown in his series of memorable films. For Kayes Ahmad, the novelist, the partition was only 'the freedom to be a refugee'.

PART II

TWO BENGALS
A Split Family

7

BENGALI OR URDU
(1947–54)

From 14 August 1947, East Bengal and West Bengal stopped sharing a common political history. On that day, the new state of Pakistan was formed with East Bengal as one of its provinces. The province now included the Sylhet district of Assam (minus Cachar and Karimganj), which had decided to join Pakistan through a referendum. A Muslim League government headed by Khwaja Sir Nazimuddin took charge in Dhaka, the capital of the province of East Bengal. The Congress constituted the main opposition both in the East Bengal Assembly and the National Assembly. Kiran Shankar Roy stayed on in Dhaka as the leader of the Congress opposition. In a speech to the Pakistan Constituent Assembly on 11 August, Muhammad Ali Jinnah, the Governor-General of the new country, assured the people:

> You are free, you are free to go to your temples, you are free to go to your mosques or to any other place of worship in this state of Pakistan. You may belong to any religion or caste or creed. That has nothing to do with the business of the state. We are starting in the days when there is no discrimination, no distinction between one community and another, no discrimination between one caste or creed and

another. We are starting with this fundamental principle
that we are all citizens and equal citizens of one state...'.

He continued, 'I think we should keep this in front of us as our ideal
and you will find that in course of time Hindus would cease to be
Hindus and Muslims would cease to be Muslims, not in the religious
sense, because that is the personal faith of each individual, but in the
political sense as citizens of one state'. However, he emphasized, 'let
me make it clear to you that the state language of Pakistan is going
to be Urdu and no other language.' Two things became clear. First,
Jinnah would not, left to himself, have developed Pakistan into a
theocratic state. Second, he showed his political misjudgement when
he ignored the sensitive issue of language with regard to East Bengal.

From the very beginning of the new state, the issue of giving
Bengali, the language of the majority of the population in Pakistan,
the status of a state language became important and was soon to
unite all sections of the people. As early as 15 September 1947,
Tamuddun Majlis, a cultural organization among Muslim
intellectuals, brought out a book titled *State Language of Pakistan:
Bengali or Urdu?* demanding that Bengali be made one of the state
languages of Pakistan. Professor Abul Kashim, secretary of the
Majlis and professor of physics at Dhaka University, convened a
literary meeting in the Fazlul Huq Muslim Hall of Dhaka University
to discuss this issue. Very soon a political party was formed called
the 'Khilafat-e-Rabbani Party' with Professor Abul Kashim as the
chairman, to focus on the claim of Bengali to be Pakistan's official
language.

On 23 February 1948, Dhirendra Nath Dutta, a member of the
Congress opposition in the Pakistan Constituent Assembly, moved
a resolution in the very first session of the Assembly for recognizing
Bengali as a state language along with Urdu and English. Both Prime
Minister Liaquat Ali Khan and, regrettably, Khwaja Nazimuddin
and other non-Bengali members in the Assembly opposed this
move. Even when Dhirendra Nath Dutta came up with a few
amendments in the original resolution, these were opposed by the
West Pakistanis and their Bengali stooges. On 25 February 1948,
Begum Ikramullah stated in the Constituent Assembly that, 'A

feeling is growing among the East Pakistanis that Eastern Pakistan is being neglected and treated as a "colony" of West Pakistan'. This shows that along with the Bengali language, the alleged discrimination against East Bengal and her economic exploitation was also becoming a major issue. On 2 March 1948, Nazimuddin, chief minister of East Bengal, told the members of Parliament that, 'we must have a fair and proper share in the Armed Forces'.

On 6 March 1948, H.S. Suhrawardy,[1] who till 1949 remained in India dividing his time between the two countries, stated in a memorable speech in the Pakistan Constituent Assembly: 'If this State (Pakistan) is not founded on the cooperative goodwill of all the nationals, a time will come when this State will destroy itself. I am reminded of one of the statements of Mahatma Gandhi that if the Indian Union eliminates Muslims within its fold and forms a Hindu state, Hindism will be destroyed in the Indian Union, and if Pakistan eliminates non-Muslims from within its fold and forms a Muslim state, Islam will be destroyed in Pakistan. We have to think it out very carefully.' In the same month of March 1948 the 'objective' resolution of the Pakistan Constituent Assembly recognized the legitimacy of the demand for provincial autonomy by proposing a federation wherein the units would be autonomous, with such boundaries and limitations on their powers and authority as may be prescribed.'

But the demand for Bengali as a state language equal in status to Urdu gathered momentum among all sections of the people of East Bengal. This got the spontaneous support of the Bengali civil servants, academics, students and various groups of the middle class. Several members of the Provincial Assembly, including some ministers, were reportedly active in supporting the movement. The East Pakistan Students League, founded in the first week of January by Sheikh Mujibur Rahman, then a university student, was in the forefront of the agitation. By the end of February 1948, the controversy had spilled over to the streets. A committee of the students of Dhaka University representing all shades of opinion— artists, leftists and centrists—was formed to carry on the objective of achieving national status for the Bengali language. This was known as the Students' Committee of Action. On 11 March 1948, students demonstrating for Bengali as the official language were lathi-charged and many of them arrested in Dhaka. The situation was gradually worsening and shortly before 19 March 1948, when Jinnah was to visit Dhaka, the then chief minister, Nazimuddin, under great public pressure, entered into negotiations with the help of Muhammad Ali of Bogra with the Committee of Action. An agreement was signed between the government and the Committee which provided: (i) the Provincial Assembly shall adopt a resolution for making Bengali the language of East Pakistan and the medium of instruction at all stages of education in the province; and (ii) the Assembly will pass another resolution recommending to the Central government that Bengali should be made one of the official languages of Pakistan.

The whole thing reached a climax on 24 March 1948, when Jinnah, on the occasion of Dhaka University's convocation, held in Curzon Hall, announced that while the language of East Bengal could be Bengali, 'the state language of Pakistan is going to be Urdu and no other language and any one who tries to mislead you is an enemy of Pakistan'. He viewed the language controversy as really one aspect of a bigger problem—that of provincialism. The remark evoked immediate vocal protest from the students who took it as an affront to a language that was spoken by 54 per cent of the population of Pakistan. The protest was led by Sheikh Mujibur Rahman, who was taken into custody. Jinnah met the representatives of the Students' Committee of Action to persuade them to have only one national language, but he failed to convince them. The government then resorted to repressive policies in order to crush the movement for Bengali to be made a state language. Prime Minister Liaquat Ali announced, 'we must kill this provincialism for all time'.

Jinnah died in 1949. Khwaja Nazimuddin succeeded him as Governor-General. Nurul Amin became East Bengal's chief minister.

In 1950, serious anti-Hindu riots, encouraged by West Pakistan officials, broke out in Dhaka and several other districts such as Khulna, Rajshahi and Sylhet. These led to the large-scale exodus of minorities to West Bengal and Assam on an unprecedented scale.

This led to the Nehru–Liaquat Pact (1950) providing for safeguards against communal violence in both East Bengal and West Bengal. But the proposed measures failed to check the spread of communal riots. Even J.N. Mandal, Pakistan's law and labour minister and Jinnah's favourite, left Karachi on hearing about the disturbances and proceeded to Dhaka. He stayed in Dhaka for eight months at a stretch trying to stop the anti-Hindu riots and then went to Kolkata seeking asylum in India. He sent his resignation dated 9 October 1950 to Prime Minister Liaquat Ali Khan, claiming that the Hindu minority was not safe in Pakistan and accused West Pakistani officialdom of inciting the communal violence in a bid to throw out the minority from East Pakistan with the object of neutralizing East Pakistan's demographic advantage over West Pakistan. Extracts from this letter are given in the Appendix to this chapter. Interestingly, he accused Liaquat Ali Khan of personally masterminding the 1950 communal rioting. Also Fazlul Huq in his meeting with Liaquat Ali Khan at the Barisal Circuit House accused the Muslim League of anti-Hindu rioting. Inevitably, the 1950 communal riots in East Bengal provoked anti-Muslim rioting in some areas of West Bengal leading to the influx of largely non-Bengali Muslim refugees to East Bengal, especially from the factory areas around Kolkata.

On 28 September 1950, the Basic Principles Committee (BPC) of the Constituent Assembly of Pakistan submitted its first interim report. Its recommendations included the creation of a federal legislature, which would consist of House of Units and House of People. The House of Units would be elected by the provincial legislatures, each of which would have equal representatives. The House of People would be directly elected. The two Houses would have equal powers. The official language of the state would be Urdu. The proposal for giving equal powers to the House of Units and the House of the People was attacked by the Dhaka Bar Association as 'definitely framed to cripple East Pakistan'. There were widespread protest demonstrations in which even officials of the Muslim League, the government party, took a prominent part. Also, East Bengal strongly objected to the choice of Urdu as the only official language to the exclusion of Bengali. Other events were the hartal by students against the BPC's decision, protest meetings and demonstrations and demand for setting up of a university committee on the national language.

The distribution of various language groups in Pakistan was tabulated during the decennial census conducted in 1951.

Distribution of various language groups in Pakistan (1951)

Language Groups	Percentage of the Total Population
Bengali	54.6
Punjabi	28.4
Pushto	7.1
Urdu	7.2
Sindhi	5.8
English	1.8

On 17 October 1951, Nazimuddin became Prime Minister after the assassination of Liaquat Ali Khan by unknown assailants. But he failed to be a true champion of East Bengal's interests and continued to sing the tune of the West Pakistan leaders. Nurul Amin, the chief minister of East Bengal, took the same line, ignoring the true interests of East Bengal.

During 1952 the requirement of passport and visa was made compulsory for travel between the two Bengals. This further impelled sections of the minority to migrate to India. It was rumoured that the East Bengal politicians were not in favour of it and that West Pakistan officials serving in East Pakistan imposed it after steamrolling opposition from the ministers.

There was simmering discontent on the language issue for several years until it reached a crisis in early 1952. On 26 January 1952, the Basic Principles Committee of the Constituent Assembly of Pakistan recommended, riding roughshod over popular Bengali opinion, that Urdu should be the only state language. This was echoed by the then Prime Minister, Nazimuddin, in a public meeting at Paltan Maidan in Dhaka. On 28 January 1952, the students of Dhaka University held a protest meeting calling both Prime Minister Nazimuddin and the provincial ministers 'stooges' of West Pakistan, and asking them to resign. On 30 January 1952, an All-Party State Language Committee was set up at a meeting held in the Bar Library Hall, Dhaka. On the same day the Awami League of Hussain Shaheed Suhrawardy held a secret meeting, which was attended by leftists, including Communists. The meeting expressed the opinion that the language agitation was no longer merely a students' movement and it was necessary to mobilize full public support. It was decided that Maulana Bhashani would assume leadership of the language movement. The next day, Maulana Bhashani presided over a party convention in Dhaka, which was attended by prominent leaders like Abul Hashim and Hamidul Haq Chaudhury, who had resigned from the government and the Muslim League on the language issue.

In a public meeting, Maulana Bhashani reiterated East Bengal's determination to continue the struggle until Bengali was accepted as one of the state languages. In the meanwhile, an All-Parties Language Committee was set up on 30 January and there were strikes and demonstrations all over East Bengal. An All-Party Committee of Action (APCA) was constituted on 3 February 1952, to coincide with the commencement of the budget session of the East Bengal State Assembly with Maulana Bhashani as chairman and with two representatives each from the Awami League, Students League, Youth League, Khilafat Rabbani Party and the Dhaka University State Language Committee of Action. The government followed it up by proclaiming on 20 February 1952, a prohibitory order under Section 144 of the Code of Criminal Procedure prohibiting processions and meetings in Dhaka city.

On 21 February 1952, the whole of East Bengal was in a state of complete general strike. At noon, at a meeting held on the Dhaka University campus, students decided to defy the official ban imposed by Nurul Amin's administration and to take out a procession in the direction of the Provincial Assembly. Inevitably, there was teargas shelling by the police and retaliation through brickbats by the students. The riot spread to all the nearby campuses including the

medical and engineering colleges. At 4 p.m., the police opened fire
in front of the medical college hostel killing five students—
Mohammad Salauddin, Abdul Jabbar, Abdul Barkat, Rafiquddin
Ahmed and Abdul Salam. Bangladesh has observed the day as
Martyrs' Day ever since. The United Nations marks this day as the
'Universal Mother Language Day'. The news of this killing sparked
off the gunpowder of discontent all around, and there was complete
lawlessness. Inside the Provincial Assembly, six opposition members
pressed for adjournment of the House and demanded a judicial
inquiry into the incidents.

When chief minister Nurul Amin proposed to proceed with the
planned agenda for the day, the opposition members staged a
walkout in protest. On 22 February 1952, Dhaka city was literally
taken over by the people. Thousands of men and women roamed
the streets offering prayers for the victims of the police firing. The
police once again opened fire on an angry mob, killing four persons.
The government had to call in the military to bring the situation
under control. Eventually, Nurul Amin, the chief minister, decided
to bow down to public pressure and moved a motion recommending
to the Constituent Assembly that Bengali should be one of the state
languages of Pakistan. The motion was passed unanimously. For the
first time, Muslim League members broke their party rank to vote
in favour of the amendments moved by the opposition, till then
consisting mostly of Hindu Congress members. The split in the
Muslim League became formalized when some of its members
demanded a separate block from the Speaker.

But East Bengal had been deeply hurt and on 23 February 1952,
despite the Provisional Assembly's resolution, the whole of East
Bengal continued the general strike. The government's repressive
measures further complicated the situation. An all-party Committee
of Action gave another call for a general strike on 25 February 1952
to protest against the government's action. The students of the
medical college erected a 'Shahid Minar' overnight at the spot where
one of their students, Barkat, was shot dead. This monument was to
become the rallying symbol for Bengali nationalism. On 24 February
1952, the government gave full authority to the military to bring the
situation in Dhaka to normal within forty-eight hours and arrested

almost all the students and political leaders. The next day Dhaka University was closed sine die. This only meant that the movement, although it had temporarily lost its momentum in Dhaka, spread into the districts. Apart from demanding the recognition of Bengali as one of the state languages of Pakistan, students now began to call for the resignation of the 'bloody Nurul Amin cabinet'. Nurul Amin claimed that his government had saved the province from disaster and chaos by its repressive measures. This was ridiculed by the students who claimed that they had already 'written with their blood the success story of the movement on the streets'. There can be no doubt that the language movement played a leading role in weakening the Muslim League and in building up a secular/linguistic Bengali nationalism in East Pakistan which was to swamp the Muslim League out of power in the 1954 elections by the united front of opposition political parties led by the troika—Fazlul Huq, H.S. Suhrawardy and Maulana Bhashani. Suhrawardy, who during the years 1943–46 had transformed the Muslim League in Bengal from a small, rich men's party to a mass-based party, now took the lead in demolishing brick by brick the edifice that he had created a few years ago.

The language movement added a new dimension to politics in East Bengal. Eventually, on 7 May 1954, the Pakistan government was compelled to recognize Bengali as a state language followed by an appropriate resolution by the Constituent Assembly.

In retrospect, whatever the merits of government and student actions, it is clear that the movement did sow the seeds of a secular-linguistic Bengali nationalism in East Bengal. Its immediate impact was to prepare the ground for the complete routing of the Muslim League in the 1954 elections by the United Front of opposition political parties, on a nationalistic plank of cultural, political and economic autonomy for East Bengal. The language movement in East Bengal brought about a sea change in politics in Pakistan. It left deep impression on the minds of the younger generation of Bengalees and imbued them with the spirit of Bengali nationalism. The passion of Bengali nationalism, which was aroused by the Language Movement, shall kindle in the hearts of the Bengalees forever. Perhaps very few people realised then that with the bloodshed in 1952 the new born state of Pakistan had in fact started to bleed to death.[3]

Meanwhile, on 17 April 1953, Governor-General Ghulam Muhammad dismissed Nazimuddin and his cabinet and appointed Muhammad Ali of Bogra as the new Prime Minister of Pakistan. On 29 July 1953, the Krishak Sramik Party (KSP), a revival of the Krishak Praja Party (KPP) of Fazlul Haq a decade ago, announced its twenty-one-point programme. Its major demands were full regional autonomy for East Pakistan on the basis of the Lahore Resolution of 1940, recognition of Bengali as a state language, separation of the executive from the judiciary and the release of all political prisoners. On 7 October 1953, Prime Minister Mohammad Ali (Bogra) moved the Constituent Assembly for consideration of the report of the Basic Principles Committee in an amended form. The new proposal was that the two Houses should be constituted on the basis of the equality of units in the Upper House and population in the Lower House. The report was debated for thirteen days. After the exit of Nazimuddin, the non-Muslim League political parties became active in East Pakistan in their demand for elections. A sense of common danger from the establishment forged the United Front. It was composed of the Suhrawardy-led Awami Muslim League (soon renamed the Awami League), the Huq-led KSP and the Nizam-i-Islam. It was supported by the leftists and the 'minority' parties. Its twenty-one-point charter demanded inter alia recognition of Bengali as the official language along with Urdu, rejection of the draft Constitution, complete autonomy for East Pakistan in all matters except defence, foreign policy and currency, complete freedom from the Centre with regard to export of jute, consultation between the Centre and East Pakistan on the allocation of foreign exchange, abolition of Indo-Pakistan passport and visa system and all the existing restrictions on trade between East and West Bengal. On 16 November 1953, the East Pakistan Awami League issued its manifesto. It demanded complete regional autonomy and the declaration of Bengali as a state language.

On 11 March 1954, in the provincial elections in East Bengal the United Front (comprising the Awami League, KSP, the Nizam-i-Islam and the minority parties) won a sweeping victory with 223 members in a House of 310. Of the 237 Muslim seats, the breakdown among different parties was as follows: United Front 223; Muslim League 10; Independents 3; Khilafat-i-Rabani 1. Huq, Suhrawardy and Maulana Bhashani were the three main architects of the United Front's overwhelming victory and the Muslim League's decimation within six years of Pakistan coming into existence.

Appendix

Extracts of J.N. Mandal's letter of resignation to Prime Minister Liaquat Ali Khan:

> It is with a heavy heart and a sense of utter frustration at the failure of my life long mission to uplift the backward Hindu masses of East Bengal that I feel compelled to tender resignation of my membership of your Cabinet. It is proper that I should set forth in details the reasons, which have prompted me to take this decision at this important juncture of the history of Indo-Pakistan subcontinent...
>
> After the establishment of Pakistan on August 14, 1947 you formed the Pakistan Cabinet, in which I was included and Khwaja Nazimuddin formed a provisional Cabinet for East Bengal. On August 10 I had spoken to Khwaja Nazimudin at Karachi and requested him to take 2 scheduled castes Ministers in the East Bengal Cabinet. He promised to do the same sometime later.
>
> What happened subsequently in this regard was a record of unpleasant and disappointing negotiations with you, Khwaja Nazimuddin and Mr Nurul Amin, the present Chief Minister of East Bengal. When I realised that Khwaja Nazimuddin was avoiding the issue on this or that excuse, I became almost impatient and exasperated. I further discussed the matter with the Presidents of Pakistan Muslim League and its East Bengal branch. Ultimately I brought the matter to your notice. You were pleased to discuss the

subject with Khwaja Nazimuddin in my presence at your residence. Khwaja Nazimuddin agreed to take one scheduled caste Minister on his return to Dacca. As I had already become sceptic about the assurance of Khwaja Nazimuddin, I wanted to be definite about the time limit. I insisted that he must act in this regard within a month, failing which I should be at liberty to resign. Both you and Khwaja Nazimuddin agreed to the condition. But alas! You did not perhaps mean what you said. Khwaja Nazimuddin did not keep his promise. After Mr Nurul Amin had become Chief Minister of East Bengal, I again took up the matter with him. He also followed the same old familiar tactics of evasion. When I again called your attention to this matter prior to your visit to Dacca in 1949, you were pleased to assure me that a Minority Minister would be appointed in East Bengal, and asked 2/3 names from me for consideration. In deference of your wish, I sent you a note stating the strength of the Federation Group in the East Bengal Assembly and suggesting three names. When I made enquiries as to what had happened on your return from Dacca, you appeared to be very cold and only remarked: 'Let Nurul Amin return from Delhi'. After a few days I again pressed the matter. But you avoided the issue. I was then forced to come to the conclusion that neither you nor Nurul Amin had any intention to take any Scheduled Castes Minister in the East Bengal Cabinet. Apart from this, I am noticing that Mr Nurul Amin and some League leaders of East Bengal were trying to create disruption among the Members of the Scheduled Caste Federation.

When the question of partition of Bengal arose the scheduled caste people were alarmed at the anticipated dangerous result of partition. Representations on their behalf were made to Mr Suhrawardy, the then Chief Minister of Bengal who was pleased to issue a statement to the Press declaring that none of the rights and privileges hitherto enjoyed by the scheduled caste people would be curtailed after partition and that they would not only continue to enjoy the existing rights and privileges but also receive additional advantages. This assurance was given by Mr Suhrawardy not only in his personal capacity but also in his capacity as the chief Minister of the League ministry. To my utter regret it is to be stated that after partition, particularly after [the] death of Qaid-e-Azam, the scheduled castes have not received a fair deal in any matter. You will recollect that from time to time I brought the grievances of the scheduled castes to your notice. I explained to you on several occasions the nature of inefficient administration in East Bengal. I made serious charges against the police administration. I brought to your notice incidents of barbarous atrocities perpetrated by the police on frivolous grounds. I did not hesitate to bring to your notice the anti Hindu policy pursued by the East Bengal Government, especially the police administration and a section of Muslim League leaders.

The first incident that shocked me took place at a village called Digharkul near Gopalgunj where on the false complaint of a Muslim brutal atrocities were committed on the local Namasudras. The fact was that a Muslim who was going in a boat attempted to throw his net to catch fish. A Namasudra who was already there for the same purpose opposed to throwing of the net in his front. This was followed by some altercation and the Muslim got annoyed who went to the near-by Muslim village and made a false complaint that he and a woman in his boat had been assaulted by the Namasudras. At that time, the S.D.O of Gopalganj was passing in a boat through the canal who without making any enquiry accepted the complaint as true and sent armed police to the spot to punish the Namasudras. The armed police came and the local Muslims also joined them. They not only raided some houses of Namasudras but mercilessly beat both men and women, destroyed their properties and took away valuables. The merciless beating of a pregnant woman resulted in abortion on the spot. This brutal action on the part of the local authority created panic over a large area.

The second incident of police oppression took place in early part of 1949 under P.S. Gournadi in the district of Barisal. Here a quarrel took place between 2 groups of members of a Union Board. One group, which was in the good books of the police conspired to punish the opponents on the plea of their being communists. On the false information of a threat of attack on the Police Station, the O.C. Gournadi requisitioned armed forces from Head Quarters. The police helped by the armed forces then raided a large number of houses in the area, took away valuable properties, even from the houses of absentee-owners who were never in politics, far less in the Communist Party. A large number of persons over a wide area were arrested. Teachers and students of many English high schools were Communist suspects and unnecessarily harassed. This area being very near to my native village I was informed of the incident. I wrote to the District Magistrate and the SP for an enquiry. A section of the local people also prayed for an enquiry to the SDO. But no enquiry was held. Even my letters to the District authorities were not acknowledged. I then brought this matter to the notice of the highest authority in Pakistan, including yourself but to no avail.

The atrocities perpetrated by the police and the military on the innocent Hindus, especially the Scheduled Castes of Habibganj in the District of Sylhet beggar description. Innocent men and women were brutally tortured, several women ravished, their houses raided and properties looted by the police and the local Muslim Military pickets were posted in the area. The military not only oppressed these people and took away foodstuffs forcibly from Hindu houses, but forced Hindus to send their women folk at night to the camp to satisfy the carnal desire of the military. This fact also I brought to your notice. You assured me a report on the matter, but unfortunately no report was forthcoming.

Then occurred the incident at Nachole in the district of Rajshahi where in the name of suppression of Communists not only the Police but also the local Muslims, in collaboration with the police, oppressed the Hindus and looted their properties. The Santhals there crossed the border and came over to West Bengal. They narrated the stories of atrocities wantonly committed by the Muslims and the police.

An instance of callous and cold-blooded brutality is furnished by the incident that took place on December 20, 1949 in Kalshira under P.S. Mollahat in the District of Khulna. What happened was that late at night four constables raided the house of one Joydev Brahma in village Kalshira in search of some alleged Communists. At the scent of the police, half a dozen young men, some of them might have been communists, escaped from the house. The police constables entered the house and assaulted the wife of Joydev Brahma whose cry attracted her husband and a few companions who escaped from the house. They became desperate, re-entered the house, found 4 constables with one gun only. That perhaps might have encouraged the young men who struck a blow on an armed constable who died on the spot. The young men then attacked another constable when the other two ran away and raised an alarm, which attracted some neighbouring people who come to their rescue. As the incident took place before sunrise when it was dark, the assailants fled with the dead body before the villagers could come. The S.P of Khulna with a contingent of military and armed police appeared on the scene in the afternoon of the following day. In the meantime, the assailants fled and the intelligent neighbours also fled away. But the bulk of the villagers remained in their houses, as they were absolutely innocent and failed to realise the consequences of the happenings. Subsequently the SP, the military and the armed police began to beat mercilessly the

innocent inhabitants of the entire village, encouraged the
neighbouring Muslims to take away their properties. A
number of persons were killed and men and women were
forcibly converted. Household deities were broken and places
of worship desecrated and destroyed. Several women were
raped by the police, military and local Muslims. Thus a
veritable hell was let loose not only in the village of Kalshira
which has a large population, but also in a number of
neighbouring Namasudra villages. The village Kalshira was
never suspected by the authority to be a place of Communist
activities. Another village called Jhalardanga, which was at a
distance of 3 miles from Kalshira was known to be a centre
of Communist activities. This village was raided by a large
contingent of police on that day for hunt of the alleged
Communists, a number of whom fled away and took shelter
in the aforesaid village of Kalshira which was considered to
be a safe place for them.

I visited Kalshira and one or two neighbouring villages
on 28th February 1950. The SP, Khulna and some of the
prominent League leaders of the district were with me.
When I came to the village Kalshira, I found the place
desolate and in ruins. I was told in the presence of SP that
there were 350 homesteads in this village, of these only
three had been spared and the rest had been demolished.
Country boats, and heads of cattle belonging to the
Namasudras had been all taken away. I reported these facts
to the Chief Minister, Chief Secretary and Inspector General
of Police of East Bengal and you.

It may be mentioned in this connection that the news
of this incident was published in West Bengal Press and this
created some unrest among the Hindus there. A number of
sufferers of Kalshira, both men and women, homeless and
destitute, had also gone to Kolkata and narrated the stories
of their sufferings, which resulted in some communal
disturbance in West Bengal in the last part of January.

It must be noted that stories of a few incidents of

communal disturbance that took place in West Bengal as a sort of repercussion of the incident of Kalshira were published in exaggerated form in the East Bengal press. In the second week of February 1950 when the Budget session of the East Bengal Assembly commenced, the Congress Members sought permission to move two adjournment motions to discuss the situation created at Kalshira and Nachone. But the motions were disallowed. The Congress members walked out of the Assembly in protest. This action of the Hindu members of the Assembly annoyed and enraged not only the Minister but the Muslim leaders and officials of the Province. This was perhaps one of the principal reasons for Dacca and East Bengal riots of February 1950.

It is significant that on February 10, 1950 at about 11 o'clock in the morning a woman was painted with red to show that her breast was cut off in Calcutta riot, and was taken round the East Bengal Secretariat at Dacca. Immediately the government servants of the Secretariat struck work and came out in procession raising slogans of revenge against the Hindus. The procession began to swell as it passed over a distance of more than a mile. It ended in a meeting at Victoria Park at about 1 o'clock in the noon where violent speeches against the Hindus were delivered by several speakers, including officials. The fun of the whole show was that while the employees of the Secretariat went out in procession, the Chief Secretary of the East Bengal Government was holding a conference with his West Bengal opposite number in the same building, to find out ways and means to stop communal disturbances in the two Bengals.

The riot started at about 1 p.m. Simultaneously all over the city arson, looting of Hindu shops and houses, and killing of Hindus wherever they were found, commenced in full swing in all parts of the city. I got evidence even from the Muslims that arson and looting were committed even in the presence of high police officials. Jewellery shops belonging to Hindus were looted in the presence of police officers. They not only did not attempt to stop [the] loot, but also helped the looters with advice and direction. Unfortunately for me I reached Dacca at 5 o'clock in the afternoon on the same day, that is, February 10, 1950. To my utter dismay I had occasion to see and know things from close quarters. What I saw and learnt from first hand information was simply staggering and heart-rending.

The reasons for the Dacca riot were mainly five:

(1) To punish the Hindus for the daring action of their representatives in the Assembly in their expression of protest by walking out of the Assembly when two adjournment motions on Kalshira and Nachole affairs were disallowed. (2) Discussions and differences between the Suhrawardy Group and the Nazimuddin Group in the League Parliamentary Party were becoming acute. (3) Apprehension of launching of a movement for re-union of East and West Bengal by both Hindu and Muslim leaders made the East Bengal Ministry and the Muslim League nervous. They wanted to prevent such a move. They thought that any large-scale communal riot in East Bengal was sure to produce reactions in West Bengal where Muslims might be killed. The result of such riots in both East and West Bengal, it was believed, would prevent any move for re-union of [the] Bengals. (4) Feeling of antagonism between the Bengalee Muslims and non-Bengalee Muslims was gaining ground. This could only be prevented by creating hatred between Hindus and Muslims in East Bengal. The language question was also connected with it. (5) The consequences of non-devaluation and the Indo-Pakistan trade deadlock to the economy of East Bengal were being felt most acutely first in urban and rural areas and the Muslim League members and officials wanted to divert the attention of the Muslim masses from the impending economic breakdown by some sort of jehad against Hindus.

During my nine days' stay at Dacca I visited some of the riot-affected areas of the city and suburbs. I visited

Mirpur also under PS Tejgaon. The news of the killing of hundreds of innocent Hindus in trains, on railway lines between Dacca and Narayanganj, and Dacca and Chittagong gave me the rudest shock. On the second day of Dacca riot I saw the Chief Minister of East Bengal and requested him to issue immediate instructions to the District authorities to take all precautionary measures to prevent spreading of the riot in district towns and rural areas. On the 20th February 1950 I reached Barisal town, and was astounded to know of the happenings in Barisal. In the district town a number of Hindu houses were burnt and a large number of Hindus killed. I visited almost all riot-affected areas in the district. I was simply puzzled to find the havoc wrought by the Muslim rioters even at places like Kasipur, Madhabpasha and Lakutia, which was within a radius of six miles from the District town and were connected with motorable roads. At the Madhabpasha zamindar's house about 200 people were killed and 40 injured. A place, called Muladi, witnessed a dreadful hell. At Muladi Bandar alone the number killed would total more than three hundred, as was reported to me by the local Muslims including some officers. I visited Muladi village also, where I found skeletons of dead bodies at some places. I found dogs and vultures eating corpses on the riverside. I got the information there that after the wholesale killing of all adult males, all the young girls were distributed among the ringleaders of the miscreants. At a place called Kaibartakhali under P.S. Rajapur, 63 persons were killed. Hindu houses within a stone's throw from the said Thana Officer were looted, burnt and inmates killed. All Hindu shops of Babuganj Bazaar were looted and then burnt and a large number of Hindus were killed. From detailed information received, the conservative estimate of casualties was placed at 2,500 killed in the district of Barisal alone. Total casualties of Dacca and East Bengal riot were estimated to be in the neighbourhood of 10,000 killed. I was really overwhelmed with grief. The lamentation of women and children who had lost their all including near and dear ones melted my heart. I only asked myself 'what was coming to Pakistan in the name of Islam'.

The large scale of exodus of Hindus from East Bengal commenced in the latter part of March. It appeared that within a short time all the Hindus would migrate to India. A war cry was raised in India. The situation became extremely critical. A national calamity appeared to be inevitable. The apprehended disaster, however, was avoided by the Delhi Agreement on April 8. With a view to revive the already lost morale of the panicky Hindus, I undertook an extensive tour of East Bengal. I visited a number of places in the districts of Dacca, Barisal, Faridpur, Khulna and Jessore. I addressed dozens of largely attended meetings and asked the Hindus to take courage and not to leave their ancestral hearths and homes. I had this expectation that the East Bengal Government and Muslim League leaders would implement the terms of the Delhi Agreement. But with the lapse of time I began to realise that neither the East Bengal Government nor the Muslim League leaders were really earnest in the matter of implementation of the Delhi Agreement. The East Bengal Government was not only much too slow to set up a machinery as envisaged in the Delhi Government, but also was not willing to take effective steps for the purpose. A number of Hindus who returned to their native villages immediately after the Delhi Agreement were not given possession of their homes and lands, which were occupied in the meantime by Muslims...

In one of my public statements I expressed the view that the appointment of D.N. Barari as a Minister representing the minorities not only did not help restore any confidence, but on the contrary destroyed all expectation or illusion, if there were any in the minds of the minorities, about the sincerity of Mr Nurul Amin's Government...

I would like to reiterate in this connection my firm conviction that the East Bengal Government is still following the well-planned policy of squeezing Hindus out of the Province. In my discussion with you on more than one occasion I gave expression to this view of mine. I must say that this policy of driving out Hindus from Pakistan has succeeded completely in West Pakistan and is nearing completion in East Pakistan too...

I have failed to understand why the question of electorate has not yet been decided. It is now three years that the Minority Sub-Committee has been appointed. It sat on three occasions. The question of having joint or separate electorate came up for consideration at a meeting of the Committee held in December last when all the representatives of recognised minorities in Pakistan expressed their view in support of joint Electorate with reservation of seats for backward minorities. We on behalf of the scheduled castes demanded joint electorate with reservation of seats for the scheduled castes. This matter again came up for consideration at a meeting held in August last. But without any discussion whatsoever on this point, the meeting was adjourned sine die. It is not difficult to understand what the motive is behind this kind of evasive tactics in regard to such a vital matter on the part of Pakistan's rulers.

Coming now to the present condition and the future of Hindus in East Bengal as a result of the Delhi Agreement, I should say that the present condition is not only unsatisfactory but absolutely hopeless and the future completely dark and dismal. Confidence of Hindus in East Bengal has not been restored in the least. The Agreement is treated as a mere scrap of paper alike by the East Bengal Government and the Muslim League. That a pretty large number of Hindu migrants mostly scheduled caste cultivators are returning to East Bengal is no indication that confidence has been restored. It only indicates that their stay and rehabilitation in West Bengal, or elsewhere in the Indian Union, have not been possible. The sufferings of refugee life are compelling them to go back to their homes.

Besides many of them are going back to bring moveable articles and settle or dispose of immovable properties. That no serious communal disturbance has recently taken place in East Bengal is not to be attributed to the Delhi Agreement. It could not simply continue if there were no Agreement or Pact...

What is today the condition in East Bengal? About fifty lakhs of Hindus have left since the partition of the country. Apart from the East Bengal riot of last February, the reasons for such large-scale exodus of Hindus are many. The boycott by the Muslims of Hindu lawyers, medical practitioners, shopkeepers, traders and merchants has compelled Hindus to migrate to West Bengal in search of their means of livelihood. Wholesale requisition of Hindu houses even without following due process of law in many cases, and non-payment of any rent whatsoever to the owners have compelled them to seek for Indian shelter. Payments of rent to Hindu landlords were stopped long before. Besides the Ansars, against whom I received complaints all over, are a standing menace to the safety and security of Hindus. Interference in matters educational and methods adopted by the Educational Authority for Islamisation frightened the teaching staff of secondary schools and colleges out of their old familiar moorings. They have left East Bengal. As a result, most of the educational institutions have been closed. I have received information that sometime ago the Educational Authority issued a circular to Secondary Schools enjoining compulsory participation of teachers and students of all communities in recitation from the Holy Koran before the schoolwork commenced. Another circular requires Headmasters of schools to name the different blocs of the school premises after 12 distinguished Muslims, such as Jinnah, Iqbal, Liaquat Ali, Nazimuddin etc. Only very recently, in an educational conference held at Dacca, the president disclosed that out of 1,500 High English Schools in East Bengal only 500 were working. Owing to the migration of medical practitioners there is hardly any means of proper treatment of patients. Almost all the priests who used to worship the household deities at Hindu houses have left. Important places of worship have been abandoned. The result is that the Hindus of East Bengal have got now hardly any means to follow religious pursuits and perform social ceremonies like marriage where the services of a priest are essential. Artisans who made images of gods and goddesses have also left. Hindu Presidents of Union Boards have been replaced by Muslims by coercive measures with the active help and connivance of the police and Circle Officers. Hindu Headmasters and Secretaries of schools have been replaced by Muslims. The life of the few Hindu government servants has been made extremely miserable as many of them have either been superseded by junior Muslims or dismissed without sufficient or any cause. Only very recently a Hindu Public Prosecutor of Chittagong was arbitrarily removed from service as has been made clear in a statement by Srijukta Nellie Sengupta against whom at least no charge of anti-Muslim bias, prejudice or malice can be levelled.

Commission of thefts and dacoities even with murder is going on as merrily as before. Thana officers seldom record half the complaints made by Hindus. That the abduction and rape of Hindu girls has been reduced to a certain extent is due only to the fact that there is no caste Hindu girl between the ages of 12 and 30 living in East Bengal at present. The few depressed class girls who live in rural areas with their parents are not even spared by Muslims goondas. I have received information about a number of incidents of rape of scheduled caste girls by Muslims. Full payment is seldom made by Muslim buyers for the price of jute and other agricultural commodities sold by Hindus in market places. As a matter of fact, there is no operation of law, justice or fair play in Pakistan so far as Hindus are concerned.

Now this being in brief the overall picture of Pakistan so far as Hindus are concerned, I shall not be unjustified in stating that Hindus of Pakistan have to all intents and purposes been rendered 'stateless' in their own houses. They have no other fault than that they profess Hindu religion. Declarations are being repeatedly made by Muslim League leaders that Pakistan is and shall be an Islamic State. Islam is being offered as the sovereign remedy for all earthly evils. In the matchless dialectics of capitalism and socialism you present the exhilarating democratic synthesis of Islamic equality and fraternity. In that grand setting of the Shariat Muslims alone are rulers while Hindus and other minorities are jimmies who are entitled to protection at a price, and you know more than any body else, Mr Prime Minister, what the price is. After anxious and prolonged struggle I have come to the conclusion that Pakistan is no place for Hindus to live in and their future is darkened by the ominous shadow of conversion or liquidation. The bulk of the upper class Hindus and politically conscious scheduled castes have left East Bengal. Those Hindus who will continue to stay accursed promise and for that matter in Pakistan will, I am afraid, by gradual stages and in a planned manner be either converted to Islam or completely exterminated. It is really amazing that a man of your education, culture and experience should be an exponent of a doctrine fraught with so great a danger to humanity and subversive of all principles of equality and good sense. I may tell you and your fellow workers that Hindus will never allow themselves whatever the threat or temptation, to be treated as jimmies in the land of their birth. Today they may, as indeed many of them have already done, abandon their hearths and homes in sorrow and in panic. Tomorrow they will strive for their rightful place in the economy of life. Who knows what is in the womb of the future? When I am convinced that my continuance in office in the Pakistan Central Government is not of any help to Hindus I should not, with

a clear conscience, create the false impression in the minds
of the Hindus of Pakistan and peoples abroad that Hindus
can live there with honour and with a sense of security in
respect of their life, property and religion. This is about
Hindus. And what about the Muslims who are outside the
charmed circle of the League rulers and their corrupt and
inefficient bureaucracy? There is hardly any thing called
civil liberty in Pakistan. Witness for example the fact of
Khan Abdul Ghaffar Khan than whom a more devout
Muslim had not walked this earth for many many years and
of his gallant, patriotic brother Dr Khan Sahib. A large
number of erstwhile League leaders of the Northwest and
also of the Eastern belt of Pakistan are in detention without
trial. Mr Suhrawardy, to whom is due in a large measure
the League's triumph in Bengal, is for practical purposes a
Pakistani prisoner who has to move under permit and open
his lips under orders. Mr Fazlul Huq, that dearly loved
Grand Old Man of Bengal who was the author of now
famous Lahore resolution, is ploughing his lonely furrow in
the precincts of the Dacca High Court of Judicature, and
the so-called Islamic planning is as ruthless as it is complete.
About the East Bengal Muslims generally the less said the
better. They were promised at Lahore of an independent
State. They were promised autonomous and sovereign units
of the independent State. What have they got instead? East
Bengal has been transformed into a colony of the western
belt of Pakistan, although it contains a population which is
larger than that of all the units of Pakistan put together. It
is a pale ineffective adjunct of Karachi doing the latter's
bidding and carrying out its orders. East Bengal Muslims in
their enthusiasm wanted bread and they have, by the
mysterious working of the Islamic State and the Shariat, got
stone instead from the arid deserts of Sind and the Punjab.
I can no longer afford to carry this load of false pretensions
and untruth on my conscience and I have decided to offer
my resignation as your Minister, which I am hereby placing

in your hands and which, I hope, you will accept without delay. You are of course at liberty to dispense with that office or dispose it of in such manner as may suit adequately and effectively the objectives of your Islamic State.

8

TOWARDS AYUB'S MARTIAL LAW

On 3 April 1954, A.K. Fazlul Huq formed the United Front government. He affirmed cooperation to the Centre provided his demands on language, the Constitution and provincial autonomy were met. A few days later, Abdul Ghaffar Khan, the veteran Pakistani leader, stated in the Constituent Assembly that the 'official languages of the Republic should be Urdu and Bengali and such other provincial languages as may be declared to be such by the Head of the State on the recommendation of the provincial legislature concerned'. On 20 April, the Muslim League party in the Constituent Assembly decided that Urdu and Bengali should be the state languages of Pakistan and that English should continue as an official language for another twenty years. But there were clear signs of a serious rift between the Centre and the new government in East Bengal.

On 17 May, there were riots and disturbances in the country, notably the unrest and violence in Adamji jute mills, Dhaka, and Karnapuli paper mill in Chittagong. Prime Minister Muhammad Ali (Bogra) saw the hand of the communists and subversive elements 'within and from outside the country'. He denounced them as a 'foul conspiracy' against the industrial progress of Pakistan. Fazlul Huq rejected these allegations as 'fantastic'. He along with some cabinet colleagues flew to Karachi to clear up the misunderstanding with the Central leadership.

197

On 29 May, failing in his talks with the leaders of the Central government in Karachi, Fazlul Huq and his cabinet colleagues issued a joint statement saying that, 'there had been a great deal of misunderstanding created against the United Front Ministry of East Bengal in the West Pakistan press and publications'. The statement added, 'we are for the autonomy of provinces and not for their independence or for separation. We stand for our election manifesto of leaving only defence, foreign affairs and currency to the centre but nowhere in our election manifesto or speeches have we ever advocated the separation of Eastern and Western Pakistan.' The Central government persisted in its strong criticism of Huq's leadership and also took exception to Fazlul Huq's emotional outburst in Kolkata while in transit between Karachi and Dhaka about the cultural unity of the two Bengals despite the political boundary between them. On the very next day, following a series of violent incidents in East Bengal, Fazlul Huq's ministry was dismissed and Governor's rule was proclaimed on the ground of emergency threatening the security of East Bengal. Major General Iskander Mirza was sworn in as Governor. Prime Minister Muhammad Ali (Bogra) called Huq a 'traitor'. He added further that, 'Huq's pronouncements regarding the independence of East Bengal, viewed against his previous statements on this subject in Calcutta, convinced my colleagues and myself that in Fazlul Huq we are dealing with a Provincial Chief Minister whose government would not take the administrative measures that any responsible government would take and with a political leader who was fundamentally not loyal to Pakistan.'

On 31 May, Huq was placed under house arrest and Sheikh Mujibur Rahman, minister for cooperation in his government, was arrested. Maulana Bhashani, who happened to be on a visit to Kolkata, could not be arrested and continued to stay there till April 1955. On 24 September 1954, the Governor-General dissolved the Constituent Assembly and proclaimed a state of emergency.

On 10 April the next year, a public meeting was held under the auspices of the Krishak Sramik Party (KSP) and Nizam-i-Islam. At this meeting, Fazlul Huq appealed to the people to express themselves against the unrepresentative government and launched a province-wide campaign against it. He demanded that Bhashani be allowed to return and declared that the country would not accept a constitution promulgated by an ordinance framed by a body of nominated persons. On 15 April, the Awami League organized a 'protest day'. The party demanded the withdrawal of restrictions on Bhashani's entry, release of political prisoners and restoration of parliamentary government. On 25 April, Maulana Bhashani returned to Dhaka and was given a great ovation. In a few days, he called upon the people to observe a 21-point programme week from that day. Fazlul Huq declared 30 May 1955 as United Front Day and announced that meetings would be held on that day to appeal to people to preserve the unity and solidarity of the United Front and resolutions were to be adopted, emphasizing the necessity of implementing the 21-point programme of accord.

Unfortunately, there was a simmering rivalry between the followers of H.S. Suhrawardy and the followers of Fazlul Huq, and the West Pakistan leadership took full advantage of it. It also turned to a new strategy to reduce the political importance of the majority province. All the provinces in West Pakistan were to be grouped into one unit, namely, West Pakistan, which was to be given the same political weightage as East Pakistan, thereby denying the latter its numerical advantage. In June 1955, elections were held for the new Constituent Assembly. Both the west wing and the east wing were given forty members. The East Pakistani contingent contained many new members. The concept of one unit was envisaged in the west wing as an effective counterpoise to East Bengal. To East Pakistan, it was a threat which sought to efface its standing as a majority province.

On 3 June 1955, Prime Minister Muhammad Ali (Bogra), taking advantage of the absence of the Governor-General and Suhrawardy in the country, started talks between his party and Fazlul Huq and the United Front. It was designed to weaken Suhrawardy's position. On 5 June, a proclamation revoked Governor's rule and Abu Hussain Sarkar, an associate of Fazlul Huq, headed a KSP–Nizam-i-Islam coalition to form a new government. It was a manoeuvre by Mirza–Muhammad Ali (Bogra). On 14 June, the United Front Government took the decision to join the Constituent Assembly. On 5 August, Major General Iskander Mirza took over as Acting Governor-General. Two days later, Chaudhuri Mohammad Ali was elected leader of the Muslim League parliamentary party, which was dominated by the Punjabis. Muhammad Ali (Bogra) resigned on 16 September. The Awami League demonstrated throughout the province demanding the disbanding of the two-unit structure and the formation of a new Constitutional system that would give East Pakistan its rightful place. Mujibur Rahman, speaking at a public meeting, reiterated his party's adherence to the 21-point programme and demanded the withdrawal of the One-Unit Bill and substituting it with a Constitution Bill for East Pakistan.

On 19 October, a convention of the workers of the Awami League was held at Joypurhat in Bogra. The convention marked the re-emergence of Maulana Bhashani as the leader of the Awami League. The convention took four major decisions: (i) full realization of the 21-point programme; (ii) throwing open the Awami League to non-Muslims; (iii) condemnation of the Pak–US military pact; and (iv) stand for joint electorate. On 25 November, the United Front parliamentary party had a three-day session presided over by Fazlul Huq. Most of the members present were reported to have expressed themselves very strongly on the question of provincial autonomy. They wanted East Bengal to have a very high degree of autonomy.

On 23 March 1956, the Constitution of Pakistan was promulgated. Article 214 (1) of the Constitution stated: 'The state language of Pakistan shall be Urdu and Bengali; provided that for the period of twenty years from the Constitution Day, English shall continue to be used for all official purposes for which it was used in Pakistan immediately before the Constitution Day.' Thus the people of East Bengal through a hard struggle and a remarkable show of solidarity had won for the Bengali language its rightful status. But the story of neglect and exploitation of the province by West Pakistan continued.

The Abu Hussain Sarkar ministry in East Pakistan lost its majority on 20 May 1956; Suhrawardy's Awami League attracted the 'minority' parties. There was, for a short while, a musical chairs type of situation, with the United Front's Abu Hussain Sarkar and the Awami League's Ataur Rahman alternatively serving as chief minister several times. Governor's rule was now imposed in East Pakistan. On 1 June, Governor's rule was revoked and the Sarkar ministry was reinstated. On 3 September, in the midst of a food problem, food marchers defied prohibitory orders in Dhaka and the police opened fire. Ataur Rahman was sworn in as chief minister of an Awami League ministry. Meanwhile, at the Centre, Suhrawardy took over as prime minister from Chaudhury Muhammad Ali with the backing of the newly formed Republican Party of Dr Khan Saheb. On 8 October, it was decided that the sitting of the National Assembly would be held in East Pakistan and the first such session began in Dhaka. Three days later, the National Assembly passed the Electorate Bill under which the principle of joint electorate was accepted for East Pakistan.

From 6–8 February 1957, the Awami League council met at Kagmari and adopted forty resolutions. The podium was decorated with portraits of pre-partition leaders, in particular Chittaranjan Das. Among the resolutions passed were the holding of general elections, both at the Centre and in the provinces early in 1958, full regional autonomy for East Bengal on the basis of the 21-point programme, implementation of the principles operative between East and West Pakistan in all spheres. At the council, Maulana Bhashani, speaking with regard to regional autonomy, said that if the demand was not considered, a time might come when East Pakistan may have to split from the country. There was opposition to Maulana Bhashani and a chorus of protests. There was also a difference of views regarding foreign policy between Suhrawardy and Maulana Bhashani.

On 5 March 1957, President Iskander Mirza, addressing the Chambers of Commerce and Industry, sternly warned that he could not tolerate any attempt to break the unity of Pakistan. He said, 'I shall not hesitate to take extreme measures to put down any effort to subvert the unity and integrity of Pakistan.' Maulana Bhashani's reaction was quick and he immediately came out with the statement 'that the demand of regional autonomy is no longer the demand of any particular party. On the other hand it has to take the united demand of inhabitants of East Pakistan and no political party can exist in East Pakistan which ignores this demand'. On 21 March, Maulana Bhashani announced that he had resigned as president of the Awami League. On 3 April, the Provincial Assembly adopted the resolution on regional autonomy and it was passed with acclaim with only two negative votes. The resolution recommended regional autonomy for East Pakistan giving three subjects to the Centre, namely, defence, foreign affairs and currency. The resolution was proposed and seconded by members of the pro-Bhashani group within the League. Mujibur Rahman spoke strongly in favour of the motion but laid more emphasis on the economic needs of the province. On 5 April, Maulana Bhashani expressed anger at the reported statement made by Prime Minister Suhrawardy that the regional autonomy resolution was a 'stunt' and that people need not attach too much importance to it. Maulana said, 'I could not even dream that Mr Suhrawardy would so blatantly fall back on his own stand on the question of regional autonomy as enumerated in 21-point.'

Awami League minister Mujibur Rahman resigned from office to work for the party organization on 30 May 1957. Within a fortnight, the Awami League council met at Dhaka for two days. In the council, it was evident that the group led by Suhrawardy was numerically superior to that led by Maulana Bhashani. The council passed a vote of confidence on Suhrawardy's foreign policy with very little opposition. One of his resolutions debarred the Youth League, a leftist pro-Bhashani organization, from membership of the Awami League. Thus the Awami League moved towards a formal split between the followers of Suhrawardy and those of Bhashani. On 30 June 1957, Muzaffar Ahmad, a lieutenant of Maulana Bhashani, gave a call to the pro-Bhashani elements to rally round the Maulana.

The Democratic Convention called by Maulana Bhashani met at Dhaka on 5–26 July 1957. As a result, a new political party with the name of National Awami Party came into being consisting of the dissidents from the Awami League. The party adopted its constitution, its aims and objectives with an emphasis on an independent foreign policy, provincial autonomy and agrarian reform very similar to the 21-point programme of the Awami League. Meanwhile, on 11 October 1957, Suhrawardy was forced to resign as prime minister of Pakistan as he lost majority through manipulative power politics in the Pakistan National Assembly. On 18 October 1957, I.I. Chundrigar became Prime Minister of Pakistan, but his was a short-lived government, as in a few days Chundrigar quit on the electoral issue. The Muslim League reopened the issue and insisted on separate electorates. Mujibur Rahman threatened to undo the parity formula. The proposals and counter-proposals wrecked the Constitution. On 16 December 1957, Chundrigar was succeeded by Firoz Khan Noon, now a Republican, who headed a six-party coalition, including the Republicans, the Awami League, the Scheduled Castes Federation, the Pakistan National Congress, and the Hamidul Haq Chaudhury group of the KSP.

On 3 January 1958, Awami League leaders broke the party discipline in the coalition government by not supporting a government Bill. On 31 March 1958, pandemonium broke out in the East Pakistan Assembly and the Finance Bill could not be introduced. The House adjourned. The musical chairs continued when Ataur Rahman and Abu Hussain Sarkar alternated as chief minister. On 1 April 1958, Chief Minister Ataur Rahman advised the Governor, Fazlul Huq, to prorogue the Assembly, but the Governor asked him to resign. On his refusal, he was dismissed. Abu Hussain Sarkar was invited by the Governor to become the chief minister. Now, President Mirza dismissed Governor Fazlul Huq for acting unconstitutionally. Ataur Rahman was reinstated. On 19 June 1958, the Ataur Rahman ministry fell on a cut motion. Nine Awami League members had crossed the floor and ten members of the Pakistan National Congress voted against the Ataur Rahman's ministry. Abu Hussain Sarkar returned as chief minister. On 20 June 1958, this ministry lost on a motion of no-confidence and Governor's rule was imposed for two months.

On 24 August 1958, Ataur Rahman's ministry came back to office. The East Pakistan Provisional Assembly met on 20 September 1958. The Opposition protested against the presence of six government supporters disqualified by the Election Commission for holding an office of profit. There was physical fighting between the Awami League and the Treasury benches. Clearly the political situation was becoming near anarchical. This was a prelude to the martial law that was to follow in a few days.

In his memoirs Bangabandhu Mujib has vividly described how Ghulam Muhammad, an official, was appointed first as finance minister and then as the president of the country, and similarly how another Punjabi official, Choudhury Muhammad Ali, was appointed the finance minister and then the prime minister. This showed that the West Pakistan officialdom had effectively captured political power. With the help of non-Bengali officials like Aziz Ahmed and later N.M. Khan as Chief Secretary, they wielded power in the province of East Bengal and Chief Ministers like Nurul Amin did not dare take any significant step without their approval. They also had links with the top guns of the Pakistan Army. This was to lead to the army takeover in 1958, formalizing the de facto situation where East Bengal was kept out of power.

9

CRYSTALLIZATION OF THE
BANGLADESH CONCEPT

With the parliamentary system virtually coming to a standstill on 7 October 1958, President Iskander Mirza abrogated the Constitution and declared martial law. General Ayub Khan was made the chief martial law administrator. Slowly but surely, power was gravitating to the armed forces. On 25 October, in his last bid to remain in power, President Mirza constituted a twelve-man cabinet to replace the advisory council set up under martial law administration. The East Bengal contingent comprised inconsequential puppets. On 27 October 1958, President Mirza was eased out by General Ayub, who assumed the presidency. The next day, President Ayub proclaimed an American-type cabinet with no prime minister. East Pakistan was ominously silent on the changeover.

In the year that followed, a series of authoritarian measures were promulgated by President Ayub, for example, the Public Conduct Scrutiny Ordinance of 1959, the Public Offices (Disqualification) Order, 1959, the Elective Bodies (Disqualification) Ordinance, 1959, an order amending the Legislative Powers Order, 1959, which had the effect of giving the Centre and the provinces concurrent powers of legislation in all fields outside those specifically reserved for the Centre under the Constitution of 1956, and, finally, the Basic Democracy Order of 27 October 1959. They also aimed at decimation of the political classes.

President Ayub visited East Pakistan from 21–28 January 1960. Speaking at the Dhaka University convocation, he talked of oneness and 'common ideology'. On 14 February, in the first elections to the presidency held under the new basic democracy order, President Ayub received a near-unanimous vote of confidence from 80,000 electors, 96.62 per cent of them voting confidence in the President. Three days later, Ayub took over as the first elected President under the new dispensation. He appointed an eleven-man commission to frame the Constitution. Representation was given to both the wings. A questionnaire was circulated fairly widely seeking representative views.

Two months later, Lt-General Azam Khan was sworn in as Governor of East Pakistan. By 25 July, President Ayub was warning the people of East Pakistan of the dangers emanating from the communists, with their political stronghold in Kolkata. On 6 August, his apprehensions were echoed by the Governor of East Pakistan, who said that he was concerned about communism attacking the country on a very vulnerable front—the economic front. He was referring to the food shortage in East Pakistan.

On 6 May 1961, the Constitution commission submitted its report to the President. But contrary to Ayub's wishes, it did not recommend a presidential system as hinted by the President. The President now appointed a sub-committee to study the issue further. In October 1961, the sub-committee concluded its work. It favoured the presidential system of government. The law minister (who belonged to East Pakistan) supported parliamentary reforms.

The Ayub Khan government's prohibition in 1961 of the celebration of the birth centenary of Rabindranath Tagore and the ban imposed on singing of Rabindra Sangeet were bitterly resented by the public in East Bengal, which defied these orders. Dhaka held a grand function on the occasion, which was attended by judges of the high court and many other functionaries.

On 20 January 1962, President Ayub said that he would use American arms supplied under the US Mutual Security Act in the event of any threat to Pakistan. Ten days later, H.S. Suhrawardy was arrested under the Security Act for acting 'in a manner prejudicial to the security and safety of Pakistan'. On 6 February 1962, more than 200 university students rioted in Dhaka and called for an end to martial law in Pakistan. The next day, a large number of members of the Awami League were arrested in Dhaka. President Ayub, who had left for Karachi, had warned the people against 'irresponsible action'. Officials in Dhaka said the students had been 'unruly' since 1 February 1962, when President Ayub called a 'high level' conference in Dhaka to 'review conditions in the country'. On 8 February, 128 persons were arrested in Dhaka for 'having defied a ban on public meetings, processions and demonstrations and for having attacked policemen'. Those arrested included Mujibur Rahman, general secretary of the Awami League. On 1 March that year, President Ayub announced a new Constitution of Pakistan. It envisaged a presidential form of government, an independent judiciary, indirect election of the President and members of the Central and provincial legislatures. East Pakistan kept up a mood of 'sullen silence'.

Pakistan's Constitution for Basic Democracy also accorded recognition to Bengali as the state language of Pakistan at par with Urdu. Article 215 of the Basic Democratic Constitution was a faithful replica of Article 214 of the 1956 Constitution. On 31 March 1962, President Ayub inaugurated the Karnaphuli Hydroelectric Dam in East Pakistan built at a cost of $100 million. On 28 April 1962, elections for the National Assembly were held. Only 80,000 electors called the 'Basic Democrats' participated. The results indicated 'an overwhelming endorsement of Ayub's Government'. On 8 June, martial law formally ended in Pakistan. The new Constitution went into effect and the new National Assembly was sworn in. On 14 July 1962, the National Assembly approved a government Bill to allow the revival of political parties. Opposition members failed to bring about the deletion of the clause that excluded from party office membership all those politicians (officially estimated at 100) who had been disqualified from public office under the Electoral Bodies Disqualification Order. On 22 September 1962, the police opened fire on students who were observing 'Protest Day'—a nationwide expression of disapproval of electoral reforms in Misraj, East Pakistan. On 25 September 1962, leaders of the defunct United Front, the National Awami Party, Jamat, Nizam-i-Islam and a faction of the

Muslim League resolved in Lahore to go ahead with the formation of the National Democratic Front under the leadership of Suhrawardy. On 29 September 1962, President Ayub denounced Pakistan politicians who announced the organization of the National Democratic Front. He called them 'opponents of the Constitution' who were 'trying to exploit the ignorance of the people for their own personal ends as they have always done in the past'. He also bitterly criticized Suhrawardy, calling him an enemy of Pakistan.

On 7 October the same year, in Dhaka, Suhrawardy called for a 'grassroots' campaign to bring pressure on Ayub to permit a 'democratic Constitution'. He was exiled from the country shortly thereafter and breathed his last some time later as an exile in Beirut, Lebanon—a sad end for a politician who contributed to the birth of Pakistan and was also a strong proponent of a united sovereign Bengal. On 18 October, President Ayub summoned the National Assembly to meet in Dhaka on 10 December 1962. But even before that, on 25 October, Abdul Monaim Khan, President Ayub's stooge and a known opponent of Bengal's autonomy, was appointed Governor of East Pakistan in place of Ghulam Faruq, who had earned the people's goodwill. This sent out the wrong message.

On 3 September 1963, the government of East Pakistan issued an ordinance similar to the one issued in West Pakistan restricting the press 'to ensure correct reporting of proceedings in the National Assembly, Provisional Assembly and different courts of justice'. Five days later, newspapermen threatened to strike in protest against the verdict requiring newspapers to publish complete text of all government news releases. On 25 November 1963, the National Assembly began its session in Dhaka. It was reported that both the government parties, the Muslim League (Conventionalist) and the opposition party Muslim League (councillors) were expected to advocate issues of franchise and fundamental rights. On 25 December 1963, the National Assembly approved the Fundamental Rights Bill, which amended the 1962 Constitution making civil rights enforceable in the courts.

Meanwhile, East Pakistan continued to resent its economic backwardness. The economic disparity between the two wings of Pakistan at the end of the first five years of Ayub's presidency (1958–63) could be seen clearly (see tables 1, 2 and 3).

Table 1: Trade between East and West Pakistan

Period	Imports into East Wing from West Wing (in Rs crore)	Exports into West Wing from East Wing (in Rs crore)
1958–59	660.7	277.6
1959–60	542.6	361.0
1960–61	798.7	361.0
1961–62	829.7	392.5
1962–63	917.6	446.0

Table 2: Regional Distribution of Investment by Semi-Public Institutions

Institution	Share of investment in East Pakistan	Share of investment in West Pakistan
Industrial Development Bank	20	80
House-Building Corporation	12	88
Pakistan Industrial Credit Investment Corporation	24	76
Pakistan Industrial Development Corporation	45	35

Table 3: Monetary Aid Given to Various Regions of Pakistan

		(in Rupees million)
Monetary Aid	East Pakistan	West Pakistan
Financial Assistance	1,260	10,000
Defence Expenditure	100	4,650
Capital Expenditure	620	2,100
Educational Grants	240	1,530
Share from Foreign Aid	150	720

Source: Records of the ministry of external affairs

This disparity became a key issue in the minds of the people of East Pakistan together with the suppression of their democratic rights. On 19 March 1964, at a demonstration held in Dhaka, people demanded direct elections for the country's presidency and legislative assemblies. On 18 September, police in Dhaka fired on students parading in memory of two colleagues killed on 17 September 1960. On 20 September 1964, the supporters of Fatima Jinnah, who was emerging as the Opposition's candidate for President, held a nationwide 'day of protest' against the government, disrupted traffic and closed shops in Dhaka. On 30 September, opening her election campaign, Fatima Jinnah charged that the government had created 'an atmosphere laden with fear and reeking with corruption' and the issues were essentially moral and political. On 21 October 1964, the president of the East Pakistan Federation of Labour charged that nearly 400 jute workers had been killed since the province-wide strike on 12 October. He attributed the killings to 'hooligans' hired by employers and asked for a governmental enquiry. Fatima Jinnah supported the demand. On 7 November, Mujibur Rahman, leader of the combined opposition parties, was arrested in Dhaka on 'unspecified charges of sedition', but was released on bail. On 9 November, balloting for 40,000 electors began in Dhaka.

On 2 January 1965, Ayub defeated Fatima Jinnah in the presidential election. In March, he was sworn in for a second term. He appointed an 'inner cabinet' composed of Z.A. Bhutto, Mohammad Shoiab, Khan A. Sabur Khan and Khwaja Shahabuddin. On 8 June 1965, the second National Assembly was sworn in. Next month, the government announced a twelve-month moratorium on press laws, leaving the press free for self-regulation through a code of ethics. In September 1965, a six-day undeclared war broke out between Pakistan and India on the issue of disputes over the Rann of Kutch. It was fought entirely along the West Pakistan–India border. But East Pakistan was scrupulously left free from any military action by India. The fact that the Pakistan army virtually left East Pakistan undefended was noted by the people of East Pakistan, including the so-called pro-Pakistan elements.

On 10 January 1966, India and Pakistan signed the Tashkent

Declaration. Whereas West Pakistan's reaction to the Tashkent Declaration was violently hostile, the political scene in East Pakistan was placid. By mid-February 1966, while the West Pakistan opposition still tried to hammer out a common line against the Tashkent Declaration, Sheikh Mujibur Rahman came out with his own far more 'practical' six-point programme. The essence of his six demands was a federal constitution that would give the federal government control over nothing but foreign affairs, defence and currency. On 16 March 1960, speaking at Rajshahi, President Ayub warned the nation that the six-point programme of the Opposition was aimed at achieving their dream of 'greater sovereign Bengal' and added that the 'fulfillment of this horrid dream would spell disaster for the country and turn the people of East Pakistan into slaves'. On 20 March 1966, at the closing session of the pro-Ayub Muslim League council, President Ayub said, 'they should be prepared to face a civil war, if forced upon them to protect the sovereignty and integrity of the country.... If the nation faced disruption, it [the civil war] had to be accepted'. On 31 March 1966, in reply, the *Pakistan Observer* said, 'stability cannot be ensured by calling in question the patriotism of a large section of our people belonging to a particular region'.

On 18 April 1966, Sheikh Mujibur Rahman was arrested. He was released on 9 May 1966, but immediately re-arrested under the Emergency Regulations. On 7 June 1966, violent mass demonstrations took place in East Pakistan in support of regional autonomy. There were clashes between the demonstrators and the police in Dhaka and Narayanganj.

But the Pakistan government now took official note of secessionist trends in East Bengal. On 6 January 1968, twenty-eight people including a naval officer were arrested on charges of being part of a conspiracy to bring about the secession of East Pakistan. Those arrested included a number of non-commissioned officers, senior civil servants, seamen and civilians. It was alleged that some of the conspirators were in touch with the First Secretary of the Indian Deputy High Commission in Dhaka and had discussed their plans with him. On 19 June 1968, the trial of twenty-five persons including Sheikh Mujibur Rahman opened in Dhaka in what came to be designated the 'Agartala conspiracy case'. They were accused of 'plotting to deprive Pakistan of its sovereignty over a part of its territory by an armed revolt with weapons, ammunition and fund provided by India'. On 7 December 1968, anti-Ayub demonstrations spread to East Pakistan when the National Awami Party called a general strike in Dhaka. On 13 December, the opposition parties called a general strike throughout East Pakistan. Police opened fire at Chittagong on unruly crowds. In many respects the Agartala conspiracy case was a forerunner to East Bengal's secessionist movement against Pakistan.

On 8 January 1969, the leaders of eight opposition parties formed the Democratic Action Committee. The demands of the Committee included: (i) restoration of democracy and direct elections on the basis of universal adult franchise; (ii) full autonomy for East Pakistan; transfer of all the powers of the Central government except defence, foreign affairs and foreign exchange to the provinces; introduction of a separate currency for East Pakistan; introduction of separate armed forces or paramilitary forces and ordnance factory and naval headquarters in East Pakistan; (iii) establishment of sub-federal units in West Pakistan giving full autonomy to Baluchistan, NWFP and Sind; (iv) release of all political prisoners; and (v) abandonment of the Agartala conspiracy case. On 17 January 1969, the Democratic Action Committee observed a Protest Day and demonstrations were held throughout the country.

Serious disturbances occurred in Dhaka where many students were injured in clashes with the police. On 24 January 1969, a central strike paralysed East Pakistan. In Dhaka 10,000 students and workers stormed the government secretariat. There were also clashes in Chittagong, Mymensingh, Narayanganj and Khulna. On 30 January 1969, Maulana Bhashani, leader of the National Awami Party and over 1,000 persons of the party were arrested. On 1 February 1969, President Ayub announced in a broadcast that he was prepared to discuss changes in the Constitution with representatives of 'responsible opposition parties'. On 5 February 1969, President Ayub abandoned the stipulation that talks must be confined to the responsible parties and expressed his willingness to invite anyone who would be prepared to attend the discussion. On 7 February 1969, the Awami League stated that it would not take part in the talks unless it was represented by Sheikh Mujibur Rahman. On 16 February 1969, President Ayub conceded that Rahman should be allowed to attend the talks.

There was serious disorder in East Pakistan at the funeral of one of the accused in the Agartala conspiracy case, shot dead while allegedly trying to escape. Maulana Bhashani told a huge crowd that the 'time has come to achieve democracy through violence. The days of constitutional struggle were over.' On 21 February 1969, during disturbances in Khulna, eight people were shot dead by the police. The same day, the crowd surrounded the home of the chairman of the local council of Basic Democrats in Kushtia demanding his resignation. He opened fire wounding two students, and was subsequently beaten to death.

President Ayub now announced his decision not to seek re-election as President. In a speech, he said, 'I am fully conscious of the dissatisfaction that exists in the country with the present system of elections. People want direct elections on the basis of adult franchise. I realise also that the intelligentsia feels left out and wants a greater say in the affairs of the State. People in East Pakistan feel that in the present system they are not equal partners and also that they do not have full control over the affairs of their Province.'

Meanwhile, on 22 February 1969, a rally of 100,000 students called for the National Assembly members and the Basic Democrats to resign by 3 March or 'face the consequences'. The government withdrew all charges against Sheikh Mujibur Rahman and the thirty-three other accused in the Agartala conspiracy case, who were released on the same day. Four days later, the conference between President Ayub and the opposition leaders opened at Rawalpindi and, after a brief preliminary session, was adjourned till 10 March 1969. The Round Table Conference between the government and the opposition leaders was resumed. The eight parties constituting the Democratic Action Committee agreed on two points, that is, a federal parliamentary system of government with regional autonomy and the election of the national and provincial assemblies by direct adult franchise. They were, however, divided in their other demands.

Sheikh Mujibur Rahman, president of the Awami League, put before the conference the six-point programme for general autonomy for East Pakistan, which he had sponsored in 1966. He also suggested that the federal capital be transferred from Islamabad, in West Pakistan, to Dhaka, the capital of East Pakistan, and that representation in the National Assembly should be based on population rather than on parity between East and West Pakistan, giving East Pakistan 56 per cent of the seats. He also stressed the rising disparity in real per capita income between the two wings to the detriment of East Bengal. He said, 'underlying such disparity, is the disparity in general economic structure and infrastructure of the two regions, in the rates of employment, in facilities for education, in medical and welfare services'. He cited many figures. During 1961–66, power generation in West Pakistan became five to six times higher than in East Pakistan. As against 36,200 hospital beds for West Pakistan there were only 6,900 in East Pakistan. Whereas there were forty-eight polytechnics in West Pakistan, there were only eighteen in the eastern wing. 'More than 80 per cent of all foreign aid has been utilised in West Pakistan in addition to the transfer of East Pakistan's foreign exchange earnings to West Pakistan. This made it possible for West Pakistan over 20 years to import Rs 3,109 crore worth of goods against the total export earnings of Rs 1,337 crore, while during the same period East Pakistan imported Rs 1,210 crore worth of goods as against its total export export earnings of Rs 1,650 crore. This was "gross economic injustice" to East Pakistan.' This line of political propaganda made a deep impact on the psyche of the people of East Bengal and slowly but surely the concept of an independent Bangladesh free from Pakistan control was getting crystallized.

This was to be symbolized in Bangabandhu's utterances 'I am a Bengali', 'My language is Bengali' and 'My home is Bangladesh'.

10

FROM MARTIAL LAW TO
INDEPENDENCE

The simmering discontent in East Bengal was slowly reaching a crisis point. On 10 March 1969, President Ayub Khan stated that rifles and other weapons were being smuggled into East Pakistan from an unknown source and distributed to villages. This was denied by Sheikh Mujibur Rahman, who questioned the credibility of the intelligence reports quoted by the President. By 25 March, faced with uncontrollable agitation in East Bengal, President Ayub Khan resigned. Before that, martial law was proclaimed once again and General Yahya Khan (commander-in-chief) was appointed chief martial law administrator. The Constitution was abrogated and the national and provincial assemblies were dissolved.

General Yahya Khan announced that he had no political ambitions other than 'the creation of conditions conducive to the establishment of a constitutional government'. The military government immediately cracked down on 'violators' of the martial law administration. Sheikh Mujibur Rahman now announced a plan for a true federal set-up. On 30 March 1969, Maulana Bhashani demanded a national government. He was interned in his village home at Kagmari. The very next day, the Government of Pakistan banned all political activities and in a rapid series of developments,

General Yahya Khan assumed presidency and a Council of Administration consisting of three people was appointed.

On 10 April, at a press conference, General Yahya Khan said that 'after a sound, clean and honest administration' had been established, a Constituent Assembly would be elected on the basis of adult franchise. When asked for his views on regional autonomy for East Pakistan, he replied, 'My personal views are of no consequence. It is entirely for the elected representatives of the people to decide what they want.' On 24 April, continuing his series of talks with political leaders, General Yahya Khan flew to Dhaka for a four-day visit. He met Sheikh Mujibur Rahman, Hamidul Haq Chaudhury and Sheikh Mashiur Rahman representing Maulana Bhashani, who then was ill. He seemed to take cognizance of the sentiments expressed during these meetings. On 6 May, Shafiul Azam, a Bengali was appointed as Chief Secretary, Government of East Pakistan. In a bid to further satisfy Bengali aspirations, five other Bengalis were appointed as secretaries to the Central ministries of home affairs, agriculture, information and commerce, labour and health. Prior to this, only one Central ministry was headed by a Bengali and only on one occasion had a Bengali served as Chief Secretary of the province.

In July 1969, the Government of Pakistan came out with a proposal to replace English with Bengali and Urdu as the official languages. In a broadcast, General Yahya Khan announced the appointment of a chief election commissioner to prepare for elections to be held within twelve–eighteen months. In his broadcast, General Yahya Khan said, 'one of the reasons for dissatisfaction on the part of the people belonging to East Pakistan was a feeling that they were not being allowed to play their full part in the decision-making process at the national level, and in certain important spheres of national activity. In my view they were fully justified in being dissatisfied with this state of affairs. My administration has taken certain steps to correct this situation in certain spheres including civil administration.' On 11 August 1969, seven civilians were sworn in as ministers and three more were added between August and October. Five of the ministers came from East Pakistan. General

Yahya Khan kept the portfolios of foreign affairs, defence and planning with himself.

On 1 September 1969, Admiral S.M. Ahsan was appointed Governor of East Pakistan. On his arrival in Dhaka, Admiral Ahsan said that he was 'pretty sure' that by 1971 a new government of elected representatives would replace the present interim government. In November, in a broadcast, General Yahya Khan outlined the legal framework for the restoration of a federal parliamentary system and promised the holding of elections on 5 October 1970 on the basis of 'one man one vote'. The constitution-making task of the newly elected National Assembly would have to be completed within 120 days, failing which the National Assembly would be dissolved and a new National Assembly elected. He also announced conferment of maximum authority on the province consistent with the maintenance of a strong federation; and permission for the resumption of unrestricted political activity from 1 January 1970: 'Maximum autonomy to the two wings of Pakistan as long as this does not impair the national integrity and solidarity of the country....' 'People of both East and West Pakistan are almost unanimous on demanding the break-up of one unit. My decision is, therefore, based on a popular wish.' 'People of the two regions of Pakistan should have control over their economic resources and development as long as it does not adversely affect the working of a national government at the Centre.'

On 1 January 1970, the ban imposed on political parties was lifted. In March, General Yahya Khan announced the Legal Framework Order, 1970, that was to be published on 29 March. It was announced that a comprehensive flood control project would be undertaken in East Pakistan and that a team from the World Bank was studying the project at the government's request. When it came as promised, the Legal Framework Order laid down the fundamental principles to be incorporated into the new Constitution. Pakistan would be a federal Islamic republic. The National Assembly would consist of 313 members, of whom 300 would be elected to fill general seats and thirteen seats were reserved for women. East Pakistan was allotted 162 general seats and seven seats were reserved for women. West Pakistan was to be divided into four provinces and Centrally-administered tribal areas that would have the rest of the seats. In the provincial assemblies, East Pakistan had 300 general and ten reserved (women) seats. On 1 April 1970, General Yahya Khan ordered the dissolution of the one-unit West Pakistan. This was in response to East Bengal's long-standing demand for restoring its status as the province with more than half of Pakistan's population, instead of being equated as East Pakistan with one-unit West Pakistan.

On 15 July 1970, published electoral rolls showed the number of registered voters as a little over 56,400,000 of whom 31,200,000 were in East Pakistan and 25,200,000 in West Pakistan. On 15 August 1970, because of floods in East Pakistan, election to the National Assembly was postponed to 7 December 1970. The decision was criticized by both Sheikh Mujibur Rahman and Zulfikar Ali Bhutto. In October 1970, nomination of national and provincial assembly seats were finalized. In a broadcast, Sheikh Mujibur Rahman advocated equality of all citizens and particularly equal rights for the minority community. While rejecting the thesis of Islam being in danger due to the six-point formula, he reiterated that 'anything which permits prejudice between region and region and man and man can be opposed to Islam'. He urged General Yahya Khan once again to repeal the restrictive provisions of the Legal Framework Order to allow the elected representatives of the people to function as a sovereign Assembly in the task of formulating the Constitution. In the field of foreign policy he stated that normalization of relations with neighbours would be to the best advantage of Pakistan. He stated there should be 'a just settlement of the Kashmir dispute in accordance with the UN resolutions' and the Farakka problem which threatened to do 'grave and permanent damage to the economy of Bengal'.

In November 1970, a severe cyclone devastated the coastal areas in East Bengal. About 1 million people were reportedly killed. Bitter general criticism was voiced in East Pakistan about West Pakistan's delayed response and apathy. Maulana Bhashani and Sheikh Mujibur Rahman were the first to make an extensive tour and criticized the Central government for its slow response and ineptitude. General

Yahya Khan paid a belated visit to the affected areas to supervise relief measures. He said he could not be blamed for the past omissions towards East Pakistan and that, unlike the leaders of the past, he had recognized the realities of the situation and felt that East Pakistan should have maximum political autonomy within the overall framework of Pakistan. Following the cyclone disaster, there was a demand from several prominent East Pakistan leaders like Maulana Bhashani, Nurul Amin and Ataur Rahman that elections be postponed. But the Awami League stood firm on holding the elections on schedule. The Election Commission stated that the elections would be held on schedule except in eight or nine constituencies of East Pakistan directly affected by the cyclone. The natural calamity heightened the political disaffection in the eastern wing, adding weight to the popular demand for autonomy.

Significantly, in his election-eve speeches, Zulfikar Ali Bhutto abstained from comments on the burning topics between East and West Pakistan. He said nothing about the six-point programme of the Awami League. On 4 December 1970, General Yahya Khan warned all political parties that martial law would remain supreme until after power was transferred to the elected representatives in the wake of the framing of a constitution. General elections were held on 7 December 1970. The Awami League obtained a decisive victory for the National Assembly from East Pakistan. It won 151 seats out of 153 results declared. On 9 December 1970, Maulana Bhashani said that he would launch a movement for the separation of East Bengal. He described the success of the Awami League as positive proof of the Bengalis wanting a free, independent and sovereign East Pakistan. On 10 December 1970, Mujibur Rahman said that there could be no Constitution except on the basis of the six-point programme.

On 17 December, elections to the provincial assemblies were held in Pakistan. In East Pakistan, the Awami League secured an absolute majority (268 seats out of the 279 results declared), while in West Pakistan, Zulfikar Ali Bhutto's People's Party secured the same in Punjab and Sind. On 20 December, Z.A. Bhutto, referring to Mujibur Rahman's majority in the National Assembly, made an uncharitable remark that 'majority alone did not count in national politics'. In yet another affront to Bengali sentiments he added that the People's Party had won a majority in Punjab and Sind where 'lay the real centre of power' and no government could run at the centre without the cooperation of this party. That the dominant political group in West Pakistan was not willing to hand over political power at the national level to the Bengalis became clear from Bhutto's statement. The next day, Tajuddin Ahmed, secretary of the East Pakistan Awami League, said that the Awami League with the clear mandate of the electorate was quite competent to frame a constitution and form the Central government. He added that Punjab and Sind could no longer aspire to be 'bastions of power'. Z.A. Bhutto made a statement that there were good chances for the establishment of a coalition government of the Awami League and the Peoples Party. He ruled out the possibility of Mujibur Rahman going it alone as that would ignore the geographical peculiarity of Pakistan where both the wings must share power.

On 27 December 1970, Bhutto said that his party was the only party that supported the cause of the people of East Pakistan and hoped that he would be able to reach some understanding with East Pakistan on the making of the Constitution. He felt that the Constitution should reflect the consensus of all provinces of Pakistan. If a majority party insisted on making a Constitution of its own liking, he would step aside 'and his party would not be responsible for the consequences'. On 29 December, General Yahya Khan conceded to Mujibur Rahman's demand for holding the National Assembly session in Dhaka.

As the year 1971 started, the relationship took a turn for the worse. On 3 January, Mujibur Rahman reiterated at a public rally that the Constitution would have to be on the six-point programme, for which he would seek the cooperation of the western wing. He warned the people that they should not be complacent and be prepared for any sacrifice that might be needed to achieve their rights. The next day, Mujibur Rahman said that the six-point programme would provide an equal quantum of autonomy to the people of the west wing also. On 8 January, he announced at a press conference that an attempt had been made on his life. He warned that conspiracies were being hatched to frustrate the verdict of the people and that he would start a mass movement if the anti-people elements persisted in such activities.

On 9 January 1971, newspapers reported that Maulana Bhashani, Mashiur Rahman, general secretary of the East Pakistan National Awami Party, Ataur Rahman Khan (PNL) and Commander Moazzam Hussaina, a leader of the Lahore Resolution Implementation Committee, had met at Santosh in Tangail District to discuss the implementation of a five-point programme. The programme envisaged: (i) the establishment of a sovereign East Pakistan on the basis of the 1940 Lahore resolution; (ii) boycotting of imported goods including those from the western wing; (iii) a gradual socialization of the means of production; (iv) adherence to the principles of anti-imperialism and anti-fascism; and (v) launching of a mass movement to press for a referendum on these issues.

Three days later, General Yahya Khan had talks with Mujibur Rahman and five other Awami League leaders at Dhaka. He described the talks as satisfactory and referred to Mujibur Rahman as the future prime minister of Pakistan and expressed the hope that the conditions in the country would improve after the government was installed. On 13 January 1971, Bhutto said that he favoured the idea of a genuine federation in Pakistan with all provinces having equal powers. On 17 January, President Yahya Khan met Bhutto. He said that the two parties should come to an understanding and if it became necessary another meeting between himself, Bhutto and Mujibur Rahman could be held. On 27 January, Bhutto arrived in Dhaka for talks with Mujibur Rahman. After the talks, Bhutto said at a press conference that the talks had neither failed nor had they reached a deadlock. He said he had agreed to two points of the Awami League pertaining to the question of federation and the right of the provinces to maintain paramilitary forces and that, for the remaining points, he would have to consult his colleagues.

At this crucial moment, an unexpected incident indirectly influenced the course of events. On 30 January 1971, an Indian Airlines plane was hijacked by some pro-Pakistan Kashmiri militants to Lahore and blown up after two days. In retaliation, India banned Pakistani planes from flying over Indian air space. This created great difficulty in communication between Rawalpindi and Dhaka. On 3 February, Mujibur Rahman condemned the blowing up of the Indian plane and called for a thorough probe. Bhutto said Pakistan was not responsible for the act since the hijackers were Kashmiris.

On 13 February, General Yahya Khan fixed 3 March for the start of the National Assembly session. Mujibur Rahman, addressing a meeting of the members of the Awami League elected to the national and provincial assemblies and the working committee of the party, reiterated that the constitution should be based on the six-point programme. On 16 February, Z.A. Bhutto, at a press conference, expressed his party's inability to attend the National Assembly unless it was given an understanding that there was scope for adjustment and compromise on the six-point programme.

On 17 February, Mujibur Rahman stated that the people of 'Bangla Desh' could no longer be suppressed. Simultaneously, he started referring to 'Bangla Desh' vis-à-vis 'Pakistan' in his statements. On 21 February, Mujibur Rahman told newsmen that his party was firmly committed to framing a constitution on the basis of its six-point programme. On 26 February, Mujibur Rahman warned the Governor, Vice-Admiral S.M. Ahsan, that the postponement of the National Assembly session would create a tragic and dangerous situation. On 28 February, Z.A. Bhutto announced that his party would attend the Assembly session if it were postponed to allow his party time to hold talks with the Awami League, or if the time limit of 120 days for framing the constitution was lifted. He threatened a mass movement 'from Khyber to Karachi' if the National Assembly was held without the participation of the Pakistan Peoples Party.

On 1 March, General Yahya Khan postponed the National Assembly session. The President said that the Pakistan Peoples Party, the majority party of West Pakistan and certain other political parties, had declared their intention of not attending the Assembly session on 3 March. He said that the general situation of tension created by India had further complicated the situation. The same day the President reinstated full martial law, removed the more liberal Vice-Admiral Ahsan as Governor of East Pakistan and appointed the hawkish General Tikka Khan in his place. On 3 March, Mujibur Rahman launched a civil disobedience campaign and called upon the people to stop all communication systems and directed that nobody should pay any rent/taxes or cooperate with the anti-people government. He asked the people to resort to non-cooperation. He called upon the troops to return to their barracks and asked the martial law administrator to hand over power to the elected representatives of the people before 7 March.

On 6 March 1971, President Yahya Khan announced that the National Assembly would meet on 25 March. He warned the politicians that he and the armed forces would ensure at all costs the solidarity, integrity and security of Pakistan. On 7 March, Mujibur Rahman said at a public meeting that he would not attend the National Assembly unless martial law was lifted, the troops had returned to their barracks, an enquiry held into the current firings and power was handed over to the civil authorities. He announced that the 'hartal' would be continued till 25 March.

On 8 March, a civil disobedience movement was launched in a remarkable show of solidarity by all sections in East Bengal. The next day, judges in East Pakistan refused to swear in Lt-General Tikka Khan as Governor. This illustrated how the Bengalis were determined to rebel against West Pakistan's swashbuckling attitude. On 14 March, the Central government issued an ultimatum asking workers to return to work by 15 March. On the same day, Mujibur Rahman announced a sort of unilateral declaration of autonomy and issued thirty-five directives to the people of East Bengal. General Yahya Khan now arrived in Dhaka and talks between him and Mujibur Rahman began the next day. On 17 March, General Tikka Khan announced an inquiry into the army killings, but Mujibur Rahman rejected this offer for an inquiry. On 21 March, Z.A. Bhutto arrived in Dhaka and conferred with Yahya Khan. Mujibur Rahman had an unscheduled meeting with Yahya Khan. On 22 March, General Yahya Khan postponed the inauguration of the National Assembly indefinitely. On 25 March, the Awami League announced that constitutional talks were deadlocked. More killings were reported.

Then all of a sudden General Yahya Khan left for Karachi on the evening of 25 March, leaving the army a free hand to eradicate the Awami League. The Pakistan Army launched a full-scale attack on East Pakistan Police barracks and the EPR Rifle bases. This was the signal for the Pakistan Army to virtually declare a war on the entire population of East Bengal. There were en masse dishonouring of Bengali women, murder of Bengali nationalist activists and destruction of property. Sheikh Mujibur Rahman was arrested by the army on the night of 25 March and moved to an unknown destination in West Pakistan. There was no official announcement. On 26 March 1971, before his incarceration, Sheikh Mujibur Rahman proclaimed East Pakistan as a sovereign independent People's Republic of Bangladesh. A clandestine radio station identified as Swadhin Bangla Betar Kendra announced: 'The Sheikh has declared the 75 million people of East Pakistan as citizens of the sovereign independent Bangla Desh.'

On the same night, Major Ziaur Rahman, the future President, seized the Chittagong radio station and announced that he had formed an independent government in the name of Sheikh Mujibur Rahman and asked Pakistani forces to surrender to the Bangladesh Army. President Yahya Khan, in a broadcast, charged Sheikh Mujibur Rahman with treason and with insulting the Pakistan national flag and called him and his followers 'enemies of Pakistan'. The Awami League was completely banned as a political party. Large-scale arrests of Awami League leaders and workers followed. Many of them went underground or crossed over to India. The Swadhin Bangla Betar Kendra announced the formal proclamation of the Government of Bangladesh. Sheikh Mujibur Rahman was named President of a six-member government and Syed Nurul Islam was named Vice-President. The council of ministers consisted of Tajuddin Ahmed (Prime Minister), Khondkar Mushtaq Ahmed, A.H.M. Kamruzzaman and Mansur Ali.

On 17 April 1971, at a public function at Mujibnagar (in Kushtia), Bangladesh was proclaimed a sovereign democratic republic.

A National Assembly member, Professor Yusuf Ali, read out the proclamation in Bengali which stated 'we ratify the Declaration of Independence by Banga-bandhu Sheikh Mujibur Rahman [on 26 March]'. The function began with the singing of Rabindranath Tagore's *Amar sonar Bangla ami tomay bhalobashi*, which became the national anthem of free Bangladesh. The new government appealed to foreign countries to accord recognition to Bangladesh. On 18 April 1971, the Pakistan deputy high commissioner in Kolkata, Hussain Ali, declaring his allegiance to Bangladesh, took over charge of the office and hoisted the flag of Bangladesh. The next day, the Bangladesh Mission, formerly the Pakistan Deputy High Commission in Kolkata, started functioning.

On 1 May 1971, the Bangladesh government appointed Justice Abu Syed Choudhury, vice-chancellor of Dhaka University, as its representative to the United Nations (*Statesman*, 2 May 1971). On 3 May 1971, a former Pakistani diplomat in New Delhi, Shahabuddin, who had defected from Pakistan, was appointed chief of the Bangladesh Information Bureau in Delhi, a spokesman of the Bangladesh Mission announced in Kolkata.

Meanwhile, with military repression let loose all around, there was a tidal wave of refugee movement across the border to India, the number of refugees reaching the figure of 90 lakhs. This gave India a good reason, both to assist the freedom fighters and also to appeal to the international community to put pressure on the military government of Pakistan to stop repression in East Bengal and to hand over power to the elected representatives of the people. From the beginning, India drew the world's attention to this gigantic refugee problem and the Pakistan government's inability to create conditions where masses of people did not feel compelled to leave their homes and cross the border to seek safety and shelter. India complained of the tremendous economic burden the country had to bear in providing food and shelter to this vast multitude of refugees spread over the states of West Bengal, Tripura and Assam. Indian Prime Minister Indira Gandhi travelled to the leading western countries requesting them to put pressure on the military rulers of Pakistan to accept the democratic right of the people of the eastern wing, to take the refugees back and to rehabilitate them. The west's apathy was in fact one of the main reasons for India's subsequent military intervention.

From April to May 1971, civil war conditions prevailed in Bangladesh with the Mukti Fauj, backed by the Indian Army from across the border, carrying on a relentless guerilla war against the Pakistan Army units. For the people of Bangladesh it was nine months of misery. The Mukti Fauj became the Mukti Bahini under the command of General Osmani. One of its sector commanders was Major (then Colonel) Ziaur Rahman who was destined to become the President of Bangladesh. The people assisted them everywhere and opposed the Pakistan Army. The Mukti Bahini also received logistic support from the Indian Army. Also the people of West Bengal and the city of Kolkata stood by their East Bengal brethren in every possible way. On 6 December 1971, the Indian Army crossed the border in support of the Bangladesh Mukti Bahini and launched frontal attacks on the Pakistan armed forces in Bangladesh on three fronts. Backed effectively by the Indian Air Force, which eliminated the Pakistan Air Force in 24 hours, and the Indian Navy, it overpowered the Pakistan forces in three to four days. It also received overwhelming popular support and was welcomed everywhere as the liberator. It liberated Jessore, Khulna, Mymensingh, Jamalpur, Rangpur, Dinajpur and all major towns in a three-pronged attack, encircled Dhaka and asked the Pakistan forces to surrender.

Bangladesh's war of independence had its international repercussions. Both the US and China supported Pakistan in the UN Security Council, while the Soviet Union stood solidly behind India and Bangladesh in their efforts to secure Bangladesh's independence. The situation reached a critical point when the US Seventh Fleet advanced to the Bay of Bengal in a clear gesture of support to Pakistan forces in Bangladesh. This coincided with General Niazi, the commander of the Pakistan forces in Bangladesh, appealing for ceasefire. Had the Indo-Bangladesh joint military command agreed to the ceasefire, Bangladesh's independence would have been delayed considerably, as Pakistan forces would still have been in possession of Dhaka and Chittagong. But the united command of Bangladesh and India simply ignored this development and redoubled their efforts to capture Dhaka.

On 15 December 1971, the Pakistan-appointed Governor, Dr A. M. Malik, resigned, creating a vacuum, as the Indian forces and the Mukti Bahini reached the outskirts of Dhaka from three sides. On 16 December 1971, Dhaka was liberated. General Niazi, the commander of the 93,000-strong Pakistan force, surrendered to General Jagjit Singh Aurora, the commander-in-chief of the joint forces of the Indian Army and the Mukti Bahini. Dhaka was now firmly established as the capital of the independent People's Republic of Bangladesh. But even in the hour of their defeat the Pakistan Razakars and Ansars, backed by the Pakistan Army, committed a dastardly crime against humanity by slaughtering hundreds of intellectuals and professionals after arresting them at several locations around Dhaka.

On 11 January 1972, Sheikh Mujibur Rahman, on his release from detention in Pakistan, returned to Dhaka via London to a hero's welcome. A new dawn came after the eight-month-long war of liberation when an independent Bangladesh started its existence as a free member of the comity of nations. This was also a great victory for Bangladeshi nationalism that had smarted for a quarter of a century since the withdrawal of British rule in 1947 under conditions of exploitation, oppression and discrimination by Pakistan's ruling class. It was a long struggle, the last nine months of which were marked by frontal warfare.

11

THE WEST BENGAL STORY
(1947–77)

West Bengal celebrated Independence Day with Mahatma Gandhi staying in Kolkata amidst unprecedented scenes of Hindu–Muslim friendship after a year of nightmares. The Congress government led by Dr P.C. Ghosh was sworn in. Also, C. Rajagopalachari, a veteran Congress leader, replaced Sir Frederick Burrows as Governor. Mahatma Gandhi, at the request of H.S. Suhrawardy, who returned from Karachi on hearing of the relapse of communal violence in Kolkata, stayed on in Kolkata to work for communal peace and harmony. Gandhi stayed at a dilapidated house at Belighata called Hyder Manzil and travelled to various trouble spots of the city accompanied by Suhrawardy. There was a miraculous show of communal harmony on 15 August.

But the euphoria was short-lived as communalism, largely triggered by anti-social elements, once again raised its ugly head by 31 August. This led to Gandhi's fast unto death, which he said he would break only when all parties responsible for the violence openly repudiated it. It had a magical effect once again, and on 4 September 1947, peace returned and Gandhi broke his fast. He announced that he would now travel through trouble-torn Punjab. He left for Delhi on October 9, 1947 and stayed there until his assassination on January 30, 1948 by a fanatic Hindu who wanted to punish him for his appeasement of Pakistan and Muslims.

Meanwhile, the Radcliffe Boundary Award had been announced on 17 August, creating a strange situation where Murshidabad and Malda, which had celebrated Pakistan's independence two days ago, had now to hoist the Indian tricolour while Khulna and Rangamati (Chittagong Hill Tract), which had hoisted the Indian tricolour two days ago now became part of Pakistan. Inevitably there was tension in all these districts. But Dr Prafulla Chandra Ghosh, the West Bengal premier, and Khwaja Nazimuddin, his East Bengal counterpart, issued a joint appeal to the people of the two Bengals asking them to accept the Radcliffe Award peacefully.

The Congress government, led by Dr Prafulla Chandra Ghosh as chief minister was short-lived. It was in power for only five months. In January 1948, Congress MLAs chose Dr Bidhan Chandra Roy as their leader. Dr Ghosh, essentially without experience in either legislative work or party structure, had an uneasy time from the beginning. With the vast Congress organizational network left behind in East Bengal (now Bangladesh) and with the West Bengal Congress coming under the complete control of the close-knit Hooghly-Medinipore group, P.C. Ghosh found himself without any support base. His uncompromising nature and acid tongue set many against him, including powerful business interests. His handling of the West Bengal Security Bill and the resultant agitation, including police firing killing one student, led to further troubles, and he had to make way in less than six months. Dr Roy formed his government on 23 January 1948. Kiran Shankar Roy, the Congress veteran, who had willingly stayed on in East Bengal, became home minister at Dr Roy's request. His departure from East Bengal left the Hindus there leaderless. Another veteran, Nalini Ranjan Sarkar, became finance minister. One of the first acts of the new administration was to ban the Communist Party of India in West Bengal, defying the Central leadership on the ground that this party was seeking to overthrow the government by armed rebellion. This party stayed banned till 1950 when, taking advantage of the newly proclaimed Constitution, it moved the Kolkata High Court invoking Fundamental Rights and got this ban rescinded.

Also, Dr Roy had to face a grave threat within his own party when a large number of Congress dissidents, including some ministers, tried to unseat him. Dr B.C. Roy showed great determination in taking up this challenge. He showed a killer's instinct in this power game. He dismissed the dissident ministers and re-established his hold over the party by calling an emergency meeting of the Congress MLAs who reaffirmed his leadership by an overwhelming majority.

Bidhan Chandra Roy was destined to dominate West Bengal politics and also play a leading role in national politics for nearly two decades. Meanwhile, a drastic change came about in the West Bengal Congress Party with the so-called Hooghly-Medinipore group led by Atulya Ghosh assuming dominant position, by and large replacing the East Bengal-based leaders. Atulya Ghosh became the president of the provincial Congress Party and gave solid support to Dr B.C. Roy during his entire regime. Very soon the Gandhian group in the Congress, under the leadership of Dr P.C. Ghosh, left the Congress to found the Krishak Praja Party, which was to merge into the Kisan Mazdoor Praja Party of J.B. Kripalani at the all-India level. Dr B.C. Roy could now turn his attention to restoring law and order and also start the process of rebuilding the shattered economy of West Bengal. The years 1948–52 were the years of reconstruction, rehabilitation and stabilization. He had to spend much time and energy in undoing the adverse effects of partition, for example, emphasizing on the cultivation of jute in West Bengal and in selected stretches of Orissa and Bihar to feed the Kolkata jute mills that were traditionally dependent on jute crop from East Bengal, providing relief and rehabilitation benefits to refugees from East Bengal, restoring vital communication links and taking steps towards West Bengal's industrial recovery.

In 1949, the princely state of Cooch Behar acceded to the Indian Union and was put under a chief commissioner temporarily. It was thereafter merged in West Bengal as one of the districts. Also, the French possession of Chandannagar (Chandernagore) became part of West Bengal as a subdivision in Hooghly District after the merger of the French territories with the Indian Union through negotiations between France and India.

The Constitution of India came into effect on 26 January 1950 and West Bengal became a state of the Union of India. Serious communal riots in East Bengal triggered off a large-scale movement of Hindu refugees to West Bengal and Assam. Retaliatory communal riots broke out in some parts of West Bengal. The refugee problem seriously affected West Bengal's economy. The government had also to contend with the problem of communist insurgency and the economic problems of partition, like promoting jute cultivation replacing paddy to feed the jute mills in the Kolkata industrial belt that no longer had access to it as the traditional jute-growing areas were now part of East Pakistan. The princely state of Cooch Behar merged with West Bengal and became a new district of the state.

The Nehru–Liaqat Pact, signed between the prime ministers of India and Pakistan, concerned the borders and the Hindu minority in East Bengal. It reiterated that the minority population in Bengal should generally stay on in their respective homes instead of migrating to the other country, as had happened in the case of the two Punjabs. Dr Shyama Prasad Mukherjee and K.C. Neogy resigned from the Union cabinet in protest against the pact, which in their opinion failed to address itself to the problem of insecurity and discrimination faced by the minority in East Bengal. Shyama Prasad formed a new political party, the Bharatiya Jana Sangh. Shortly thereafter, Jogendra Nath Mandal, the law and labour minister of Pakistan since 1947, resigned and sought political asylum in India after his arrival in Kolkata, announcing that Pakistan was no place for Hindus to live with safety and dignity. West Bengal now faced an unprecedented refugee problem. Refugee colonies sprang up along the border districts and all around Kolkata. In many instances, refugees simply squatted on the sprawling estates of rich people around Kolkata or on government land, with the authorities looking away, and shanty towns with inadequate housing and unsanitary conditions came up. Often families were separated. Giving displaced persons title to the land they squatted upon and providing them other rehabilitation benefits took many years. Unlike the refugees from West Punjab, the Bengali refugees never got any evacuee property as very few houses or plots of land left by migrating Muslims were available in West Bengal. There was no exchange of population as between the two Punjabs.[1] West Bengal always had to face migration, sometimes in trickles, and sometimes like tidal waves.

Shortly thereafter came India's first general elections in 1951. It returned the Congress to power in the West Bengal Assembly with the Communist Party of India, whose legality had been restored by the high court, as the main opposition. Jyoti Basu led the CPI. Shyama Prasad Mukherjee was elected to the Lok Sabha from south Kolkata and made a great mark as an opposition leader in the Indian Parliament but he died an untimely death in 1953, while in detention in Kashmir for entering that state without permission and courting arrest in protest against the requirement of Indian nationals to secure a special permit to enter Jammu and Kashmir. West Bengal was grief-struck.

The question of incorporating the Bengali-speaking areas from Bihar and Assam into West Bengal occupied the forefront of attention for a while. In 1956, the Government of India set up a States Reorganization Commission. West Bengal had demanded the inclusion of Manbhum and Singhbhum districts and a portion of Purnea district of Bihar, which were Bengali-speaking districts. West Bengal also wanted the district of Goalpara in Assam. There was opposition from both Bihar and Assam. In the meantime, B.C. Roy along with Chief Minister Srikrishna Sinha pressed for a merger between West Bengal and Bihar in the interest of economic and administrative stability. However, public opinion in West Bengal did not approve of this suggestion. Following a by-election to the north Kolkata parliamentary constituency when the Congress candidate was defeated by the opposition with merger being the main issue, Dr B.C. Roy withdrew that proposal. Finally, as a result of the reorganization of the states, Purulia sub-division of Manbhum district and Islampur sub-division of Purnea district in Bihar were added to West Bengal. Islampur's addition provided a connecting link to Darjeeling, Jalpaiguri and Cooch Behar district, with the rest of West Bengal, thereby ending the enclave status of these three districts.

India's First Five-Year Plan (1951-56) started under Dr B.C. Roy's leadership. West Bengal's economy, after undoing the damages of partition, grew at a fast pace. It once again became India's number one industrial state.

During the years 1952-59, there was a steady ascent of West Bengal's economy to the high noon of prosperity. With his great vision and penchant for innovative ideas, Dr B.C. Roy initiated and implemented a large number of schemes like the Damodar Valley Corporation, Chittaranjan Locomotives, Durgapur Steel Project, Digha Sea Beach Project, Kalyani Township, Salt Lake Reclamation Project in Kolkata, Himalayan Mountaineering Institute in Darjeeling, Indian Institute of Technology, Kharagpur, Indian Institute of Social Welfare and Business Management, Kolkata, Indian Institute of Mangement, Kolkata, abolition of the zamindari system, the new land reform measures in West Bengal, the Bandel Thermal Plant, proposal for a subsidiary port at Haldia, several new universities like Burdwan, Kalyani, North Bengal and Rabindra Bharati and countless other schemes. His aim, to quote him, was 'a prosperous Bengal in a prosperous India'. As West Bengal did not have enough land surface, he tried to settle successive waves of migrants from East Bengal in the Andaman Islands, in the Terai region of Uttar Pradesh and lastly in the Dandakaranya Forest region covering portions of Orissa and Madhya Pradesh. Unfortunately these schemes were opposed by the leftists, who for their own political compulsions wanted rehabilitation only in West Bengal.

On 1 July 1962, Dr B.C. Roy's long rule ended when he died on his eighty-first birthday. Indeed, West Bengal's history from 1948 to 1962 can truly be called the Bidhan Roy age. Prafulla Chandra Sen succeeded him as chief minister. In October and November 1962, following border disputes along the north-eastern Himalayas, a militarily unprepared India was humbled by the Chinese in several border skirmishes. Due to these military clashes in the North East Frontier Agency areas and India's military unpreparedness, her defence spending increased manifold with adverse effects on the economy.

The three northern districts, namely, Darjeeling, Jalpaiguri and

Cooch Behar became the centres of military concentration for defence preparedness in relation to the Chinese threats to the northern border. Vigorous construction activities in these districts to strengthen road and rail links with Assam and the north-east were started.

In 1964, serious communal riots broke out in several parts of East Bengal as a reprisal to the reported theft of a sacred relic of Hazrat Mohammad, the prophet of Islam, from a mosque in Srinagar (Kashmir). There were also retaliatory communal incidents in some parts of West Bengal. This led to large-scale migration of Hindu refugees to West Bengal who were mostly taken to the distant Dandakaranya Forest covering Orissa, Madhya Pradesh and the foothills of Uttar Pradesh (which is now part of Uttaranchal). Communal disturbances were put down in both Bengals in a short time. Prime Minister Jawaharlal Nehru died in May 1964. Lal Bahadur Shastri succeeded him as prime minister.

During March–May 1965, some border skirmishes took place between India and Pakistan over the Cooch Behar enclaves. In September 1965, there was a short war between these two countries along the Jammu and Kashmir and Punjab borders. A ceasefire was followed by the Tashkent Peace Agreement brokered by the Soviet Union. But the East Pakistan–West Bengal border was free from any military clashes, thanks to the decision of Prime Minister Lal Bahadur Shastri not to extend military activities to East Pakistan. This was to pay a rich dividend in a few years.

1966 was a year of intense political unrest. The leftist parties spearheaded by the Communist Party of India (Marxist), which had broken away from the undivided CPI, launched a succession of civil disobedience movements against the government on issues like non-availability of foodgrains and general price rise. These movements would at times lead to serious law and order problems. As the general elections drew nearer political rivalry sharpened. There was a partial split in the West Bengal Congress with two top leaders, Ajoy Mukherjee and Humayun Kabir, quitting the party and establishing the Bangla Congress. But the opposition failed to unite. Two political formations fought the Congress in the 1967 elections— the Peoples United Left Front (PULF) consisting of the Bangla

Congress, CPI, Forward Block and the Bolshevik Party and the United Left Front (ULF) consisting of the CPI (M), Revolutionary Socialist Party, Forward Block (Marxist) and others.

But in spite of the division in the opposition ranks, the Congress failed to secure a majority in the Assembly. Thus the long rule of the Congress Party in West Bengal ended. Both P.C. Sen and Atulya Ghosh, president of the West Bengal Provincial Congress Committee, lost in their respective assembly and parliamentary constituencies. Internal squabbles leading to a split in the party and the formation of a breakaway new party, the Bangla Congress led by Ajoy Mukherjee and Humayun Kabir, were mainly responsible for the debacle. The Congress, though the largest party, refused to stake a claim for forming the government. Now faced with the prospect of securing power, the People's United Left Front and the United Left Front agreed to combine.

A United Front government consisting of the Bangla Congress, CPI, CPI (M), the Forward Block and other smaller parties, in a way a combination of the PULF and ULF, took over power under Ajoy Mukherjee as the chief minister and Jyoti Basu as finance minister. Soon it was to face its biggest challenge, not from the Congress, but from a section of its own extremist followers, namely, the Naxalbari agitation.

The Naxalbari agitation of share-croppers started in Naxalbari police station of Darjeeling district led by CPM extremists, who broke away from their party. It spread to a few other pockets, but its violent activities forced the United Front government to suppress this movement by police action. In November 1967, the United Front broke up and a breakaway group, the People's Democratic Front (PDF), with the support of the Congress, was sworn in with Dr Prafulla Ghosh as chief minister. This was the second time that Dr Ghosh became the chief minister. But soon the coalition government was under strain on account of internal bickerings. Dr Ghosh's refusal to accept certain demands from a powerful Congress Party manager led to the wavering of support from a large section of the Congress Party. An abortive attempt was made by those sections under the leadership of a Congress leader, Sankardas

Banerjee, to stake a claim to power. Besides, a piquant situation was created by the Speaker of the Assembly, Bijoy Banerjee, who refused to recognize the Governor's action in dismissing Ajoy Mukherjee's government and installing Dr P.C. Ghosh's government and adjourned the Assembly indefinitely. As the Assembly could not meet there was a constitutional crisis.

By February 1968, the PDF government, reduced to a minority as a result of Congress' withdrawal of support, was dismissed by the President under Article 356 of the Indian Constitution and Governor Dharma Vira took over administration. The Assembly was now dissolved.

The elections were held and a second United Front government came to power with Ajoy Mukherjee as the chief minister and Jyoti Basu as the deputy chief minister and home minister. Once again Naxalite violence continued unabated, this time joined by some idealist but misguided students who left their studies to join the Naxalite ranks. Also, the gherao movement unleashed by the leftist parties, under which industrial workers were given the freedom to physically surround industrialists and managers in industrial disputes without the intervention of the police, seriously disturbed industrial relations. Flight of capital started and continued unabated for a long time. West Bengal started losing her industrial supremacy. This was the beginning of the long process of West Bengal's industrial downward slide caused by Naxalite violence, chronic labour troubles, flight of capital and investment, strikes and sharp deterioration of work culture and productivity. West Bengal lost her industrial primacy to other states like Gujarat, Maharashtra, Karnataka, Tamil Nadu and Orissa.

In 1969, the Congress also split between the Indira Gandhi-led Congress in power at the Centre and the Congress (Organization) led by the old guard leadership. The 1971 mid-term elections to Parliament returned Indira Gandhi to power at the Centre on her *Garibi Hatao* slogan. The Congress (O) was seriously decimated.

Meanwhile, serious disagreement between Ajoy Mukherjee and the Communists led to the dismissal of the second United Front government and the proclamation of President's rule again in 1970.

In the general elections to the West Bengal Assembly, a new combination with Ajoy Mukherjee as chief minister and Bejoy Singh Nahar as deputy chief minister, the Congress as a constituent party came to power (this was popularly called the Ajoy-Bejoy[2] coalition) with a precarious majority. But events were moving very fast across the border. On March 23, 1971, Pakistan's military crackdown on East Bengal was followed by the declaration of independence by Bangladesh led by Sheikh Mujibur Rahman. India expressed total support for East Bengal's freedom. West Bengal faced a massive refugee problem with around 90 lakh refugees pouring in. The fragile coalition government was not equipped to cope with the growing problems of the state and resigned, leading to yet another spell of President's rule. There were also military movements along the borders. A short war between India and Pakistan took place during 6–16 December 1971, when Indian forces intervened on the side of the Bangladesh freedom fighters (Mukti Bahini). On 16 December, Dhaka fell to the joint Indo-Bangladesh forces, signalling Pakistan's total military defeat. The surrender of the Pakistan Army in Dhaka on 16 December 1971 led to the emergence of Bangladesh as a free country, no longer East Pakistan, as East Bengal was officially known in 1947–71. From now on, in terms of international law, West Bengal could no longer lay claim to the title 'Bangladesh' in the political sense.

In the elections to the State Assembly held in 1972, the Congress, led by Siddhartha Shankar Ray, returned to power after winning the election amidst vociferous complaints of widespread rigging by the leftists. The Naxalite movement was put down with unprecedented ruthlessness. This led to the return of industrial confidence to some degree. However, large-scale factionalism prevailed in the Congress during the entire five-year Congress rule.

On 11 June 1975, a judgement by Allahabad High Court declared Prime Minister Indira Gandhi's election to Parliament in 1971 as invalid on grounds of electoral malpractices. Political uncertainty set in thereafter. On 25 June, Prime Minister Indira Gandhi declared a state of emergency with S.S. Ray as one of her principal advisers. The government clamped down on the press and censorship was introduced. This was followed by arrest of political opponents and dissident journalists. The Congress party steadily lost its popularity during the two years of the emergency.

On 12 January 1977 Prime Minister Indira Gandhi declared an end to the state of emergency and announced dates for new general elections. In March 1977, the Indira Gandhi Congress was defeated in the elections and the Janata Party government, a combine of anti-emergency right and left forces, came to power in Delhi with Morarji Desai as the Prime Minister. Congress candidates were defeated in all but two of the Lok Sabha seats from West Bengal indicating that the public had not approved the emergency of 1975-76. On 30 April 1977 the Central Government dismissed the Siddhartha Shankar Ray cabinet in West Bengal on the ground that the recent Lok Sabha elections had demonstrated that the Congress had lost the people's confidence and brought West Bengal under President's rule. Elections were held within two months time, that is, by June 1977. The Janata Party, led by P.C. Sen and the CPI (M)-led Left Front, failed to arrive at an electoral understanding and fought each other. The Left Front, backed by its grassroot organisation, gained an absolute majority and formed the first Left Front government with Jyoti Basu as chief minister. This combine ruled West Bengal for over three decades. Jyoti Basu was chief minister for twenty-three years, that is, till 2000 when he stepped down on grounds of old age. Basu was succeeded by Buddhadeb Bhattacharjee. But there was growing opposition to the Left Front rule and eventually the Trinamool Congress led by Mamata Banerjee inflicted a crushing defeat on the leftists in 2011.

EPILOGUE

The creator of Bangladesh, Bangabandhu Mujibur Rahman's government lasted till 1975 when he, along with all his family members except two daughters who were abroad at the time, was assassinated by a coterie of middle-level army officers due to personal vendetta. The conspiracy, no doubt backed by pro-Pakistan elements, led to Khondkar Mushtaq Ahmed, a minister in Sheikh's government, becoming President. This lasted for a few days, when civil war conditions prevailed, with army groups fighting one another. Eventually, troops loyal to Major General Ziaur Rahman, who had no hand in Mujib's killing, seized power and started a military dictatorship. Ziaur Rahman consolidated power and eventually transformed military rule to a democracy, starting his own political party, the Bangladesh National Party (BNP), which had a substantial number of freedom fighters. Zia was also assassinated by a group of fellow army officers whose motives were not clear. History repeated itself when the army chief, General Ershad, seized power. After a short spell of army rule, parliamentary democracy was restored, with Ershad leading his own Jatiya Dal. He had soon to contend with united opposition from two confederate groups, one led by Mujib's daughter Hasina, and the other led by Ziaur Rahman's widow Begum Khaleda Zia, both wanting free elections and the restoration of parliamentary democracy. Faced with this strong opposition, Ershad gave in and ordered elections to be held. But the tactical unity between Hasina Wajid and Khaleda Zia ended and a bitter confrontation ensued.

Since then, Bangladesh has been ruled alternately by the two coalitions led by Hasina Wajid and Khaleda Zia respectively. In 2002, Hasina's five-year rule ended when a BNP-led coalition defeated the Awami League-led coalition in the elections. This coalition included a small component of fundamentalist Muslim parties which also found their place in the coalition government. This has become somewhat controversial. There is a view that, thanks to their overt and covert role, Muslim fundamentalism has been strengthened in Bangladesh and is threatening the national forces. Bangladesh has made great progress in economic development during the last ten years. In spite of the many political changes and violence, democracy in a broad sense appears to have been established in Bangladesh. Efforts to establish military rule from time to time have not been successful in the face of strong popular feeling in favour of electoral politics and parliamentary democracy. The main issues facing the nation are: (i) whether the ruling BNP, which has a nationalist past, can keep the fundamentalistic forces under control and (ii) whether Bangladesh can evolve as a Muslim majority but non-theocratic nationalist state like Egypt, Indonesia and Turkey.

Turning to West Bengal, during the long period of Left Front rule, despite the government's achievements of land reforms, cultural development and Panchayat Raj leading to the empowerment of the lower classes and have-nots in the villages, West Bengal's general economy has steadily declined. West Bengal's position has slipped from among the top states as has Kolkata's position as the foremost industrial city. The Left Front government has now completed nearly three decades of being in power and has won yet another general election in 2006. There have been some winds of change in recent years when Buddhadeb Bhattacharjee, influenced no doubt by the examples of Chinese and the Vietnamese communists, has taken some initiatives to break away from dogmatism and encourage private sector initiative, foreign direct investment and market economy. But the militant trade unions are still not reconciled to it. History will decide whether these initiatives will succeed.

But the Left Front government faced opposition from the farming community spearheaded by Mamata Banerjee's Trinamool Congress on the issue of the Tatas setting up an automobile plant on land taken over from the farmers at Singur, which led to the cancellation of the Tata Motors plant. Thereafter, at Nandigram in Midnapore district the farmers rose in rebellion against the move to take over their farmland for the setting up of new industries. All these led to a series of mass movements and eventually the Trinamool Congress combined with the Indian National Congress defeated the Left Front in both the Lok Sabha elections on 2009 and the state assembly elections of 2011. This was indeed a turning point in West Bengal's history.

There is no doubt that people from both the Bengals cherish their commonality of cultural outlook and shared attitudes over other factors. In the case of Bangladesh, while they are proud of their own language and cultural identity, they have to guard against two powerful 'pulls': first, pan-Islamic Wahabi Islamic fundamentalism and jehadi fanaticism and second, the powerful pan-Indian cultural and social system. Naturally, they have to strike a balance in the face of these strong pulls. While they are proud of their Bengali cultural identity, they are also proud of their Islamic heritage, but would not like to see their Bengali identity being swamped by either of these two. Similarly, Bengalis in India have to balance their trans-national Bengali cultural identity with the very powerful force of pan-Indian identity of which they are also partners. The fact is, in a world where Bengali-speaking people today constitute the fifth largest language group, Bangladesh willy-nilly has assumed the driver's seat of championing Bengali cultural identity and values and West Bengal has necessarily to play the second fiddle. But this is an unavoidable cultural situation which all Bengalis, whether belonging to Indian Bengal or to Bangladesh, will have to contend with.

Considering that there are several leading examples in history like the union of Poland after three partitions, the union of the two Germanys and of the two Vietnams, one can envisage that the two Bengals, even though politically separate, can have much commonality in terms of their common culture, their shared history and geography and economic complementarity. In a larger context one can also envisage a loose confederation between Bangladesh, India and Pakistan, which can create by far the strongest entity in the comity of nations. After all, history moves on and there can always be hope for the best.

REFERENCES

1. Genesis of Separatism

1. See Nitish Sengupta, *History of the Bengali-Speaking People*, Chapter 9, UBSPD, New Delhi, 2001.
2. Ibid., p. 76.
3. W.W. Hunter, *Indian Mussalman*, London, 1870 and Lahore 1964.
4. Sufia Ahmed, *Muslim Community in Bengal*, Oxford University Press, Dhaka, 1884, p. 92.
5. Ibid., p. 2.
6. Ibid., p. 8.
7. Ibid., p. 14.
8. Tamizuddin Khan, *Memoirs*, Dhaka, p. 37
9. Ibid., p. 39.
10. Sufia Ahmed, *Muslim Community in Bengal*, p. 131.
11. Ibid., p. 10.
12. Ibid., p. 164.
13. Mohammed Noman, *Muslim India*, Allahabad, 1942, pp. 74–75.
14. Nitish Sengupta, *History of the Bengali-Speaking People*, op. cit., pp. 302-303.
15. D.N. Banerjee, *East Pakistan: A Study in Muslim Politics*, Vikas, New Delhi, 1969, p.14.
16. Ibid., pp. 16–17. Also see Tazeen Murshid, *The Sacred and the Secular*, University Press, Dhaka, 1996.

2. From Camaraderie to Conflict

1. Durga Das, *India From Curzon to Nehru and After*, Collins, London, 1969, p. 44.

2. Ibid., p. 6.
3. Ibid., p. 117.
4. H.N. Dasgupta, *Chittaranjan Das*, Government of India, Publications Division, New Delhi.
5. Aparna Devi, *Manush Chittaranjan* (in Bengali), pp. 287–95.
6. Ibid., p. 290–91.
7. Ibid., pp. 290–91.
8. Sankari Prasad Basu, *Samakalain Bharati Subhas* (in Bengali)
9. Bidyut Chakravorty, *Subhas Chandra Bose and Middle Class Radicalism, 1928–40*, Oxford University Press, Delhi 1990, pp. 10, 13, 51–52. Also pp. 184–85.

3. Unmaking of a Nation (1927–37)

1. P. Acharya, Educational and Communal Politics in Bengal, IIM Kolkata, Working Paper Series, Kolkata, September 1998.
2. B. Chakraborty, 'The Communal Award of 1932, its Implications in Bengal', in Lowe, D.A. (ed) *Soundings in Modern South Asian History*, 12, 3, pp. 493–523, Weidenfeld, London, 1968.
3. Jatindra Nath De, History of the Krishak Praja Party (MS) (1929–47), University of Delhi, 1977. Also see Tazeen Murshid, The House Divided: The Muslim Intelligentsia of Bengal in D.A. Lowe (ed.), *The Political Inheritance of Pakistan*, Macmillan, London.
4. Sumit Sarkar, *Swadeshi Movement in Bengal*, People's Publishing House, New Delhi, 1973. Also see his *Modern India*, Macmillan, New Delhi, 1983.
5. Tazeen Murshid, The House Divided: The Muslim Intelligentsia of Bengal, *Modern India*, Macmillan & Co., New Delhi.
6. B. Chakraborty, 'The Communal Award of 1932, its Implications in Bengal'.
7. See Tazeen Murshid, op. cit.
8. Ibid.
9. See Ayesha Jalal, *Jinnah, Muslim League and the Demand for Pakistan*, Cambridge, 1985. Also see Bimal Prasad, *Foundation of Muslim Nationalism*, Manohar, New Delhi; Anisuzaman, *Muslim Manesar Bangla Sahitya* and Rajat Kanta Ray, *Social Conflict and Political Unrest in Bengal—1875–1927*, Oxford University Press, New Delhi, 1984.

10. Jatindra Nath De, History of the Krishak Praja Party. Op. cit.
11. Tazeen Murshid, op. cit.
12. Rabindranath Tagore, *Rabindra Rachnavali* (in Bengali), Vol. 9, p. 605.
13. Tazeen Murshid, op. cit.
14. Quoted in Bhola Chatterjee, *Aspects of Bengal Politics in the Early 1930s*, World Press, Kolkata, 1969, p. 62.
15. Tazeen Murshid, op. cit.
16. Tamizuddin Khan, *Memoirs*.
17. Quoted in R.C. Majumdar, *History of Bengal.*
18. Tazeen Murshid, op. cit.
19. R.C. Majumdar, *History of Bengal.*

4. Parting of Ways (1937–45)

1. Jatindra Nath De, op. cit.
2. *Memoirs of Hussain Shaheed Suhrawardy* (ed) Mohammed H. R. Talukdar, Dhaka, page 102. Also see Begum Ikramullah, *Hussain Shaheed Suhrawardy: A Biography*, Oxford University Press, Karachi, 1991.
3. R.C. Majumdar, *History of Bengal*, Vol. 4. Also see Gordon Leonard, *Bengal: The Nationalist Movement 1876-1940*, Oxford University Press, New York, pp 283-85, and Biswas Kalipada, *Yukta Bangar Sesh Adhyaya* (in Bengali), Orient Book Co., Kolkata, 1966.
4. Ibid.
5. Ibid.
6. Ibid.
7. Chaudhury Khalequzzaman: *Pathways to Pakistan*, Longman, Lahore, 1961.
8. Bengal Assembly Proceedings 1937–47, West Bengal Legislative Assembly.
9. Humayun Kabir, *Muslim Politics and other Essays 1906-1942*, p. 32
10. R.C. Majumdar, ibid. pp. 141-142.
11. Bandyopadhyaya S—Abibhakta Banglar Sesh Adhaya 1937–47 (in Bengali) published in *Chaturanga* of 5 Sept and 6 October, 1990.
12. S.C. Das, *Biography of Dr Shyama Prasad Mukherjee*, Abhinav Publications, New Delhi, 2000, p. 52.

13. Majumdar, op. cit.
14. Ibid. pp. 54-55
15. Ibid.
16. Ibid.
17. Ibid .
18. Proceedings of the Bengal Assembly. Vol LXXXI, 1946. West Bengal Assembly.
19. Majumdar op. cit.
20. Ibid.
21. Ibid.
22. Ibid.
23. Amartya Sen, *Poverty and Famine—An Essay on Entitlement and Deprivation*, Oxford 1981, pp, 52-53.
24. Ashok Mitra, *Teenkuri Dash* Vol II pp 113–117, also his two articles in *Chaturangaa* 11 March 1992 and 12 April 1992
25. Op. cit.
26. R.C. Majumdar, op. cit. p. 364
27. Amartya Sen, *Hunger and Public Action*, 1989. Also see Tarak Chandra Das, *Bengal Famine*, Calcutta University Press, Kolkata, 1943, Dr S.P. Mukherjee, *Panchasher Mannantar*, a collection of essays, Kolkata, 1946.
28. Bengal Assembly Proceedings, op. cit.
29. Quoted in R.C. Majumdar op. cit. p. 370.
30. Murshid Tazeen, op. cit. pp. 207–08.

5. United Bengal: Last Hour

1. Jamalauddin Ahmad, *Speeches of Jinnah*, Vol. II, Ashraf, Lahore, pp. 179–84
2. Read Anthony and David Fisher. *The Proudest Day—India's Long Road to Independence*, London, 1997, p. 367.
3. Article by Sisir Kumar Bose and Krishna Bose in the *Telegraph*, Kolkata, Nehru Centenary edition.
4. Humayun Kabir, 'Bengal Elections 1946—A Mockery', *Amrita Bazar Patrika*, 14 April 1946. Also Maulana Abul Kalam Azad's 'Report on Bengal Elections', *Amrita Bazar Patrika*, 5 April 1946.

5. R.C. Majumdar, *History of Bengal*, Vol. IV, p. 382. This is not corroborated by any other source, but there are allusions to it in Begum Ikramullah's biography of her cousin, *Hussain Shaheed Suhrawardy: A Biography*.

6. Leonard Mosley, *Last Days of the British Raj*, Weidenfield and Nicolson, London, 1961, pp. 21, 23.

7. Michael Brecher, *Nehru*, Oxford, 1959.

8. Report of the Police Commissioner quoted in V.N. Bandyopadhyaya, *Bangla Samayika Patra*, Vol. II, Kolkata, 1952, p. 460.

9. Leonard Mosley, *The Last Days of the British Raj*, pp. 26–36.

10. Those who attacked the physicist Qudrat-i-Khuda, the distinguished principal of Presidency College, or those who butchered Haren Ghosh, the impresario, had no concept of education or culture. For them the only thing that mattered was whether he was a Muslim or a Hindu.

11. There was no transport, of course. Tramcars and buses had stopped, since they are the first things that Kolkata mobs overturn and burn when angry.

12. The exact number of casualties during those four days will never be known. According to the government's *Fortnightly Report* for the second half of August, 4,000 people were killed and 10,000 injured.

13. Even Wavell wrote in his diary: 'The chief points to my mind were Suhrawardy's continued presence in the Control Room on the first day with many Muslim friends and his obvious communal bias.' Wavell, *Field Marshal Sarl–The Viceroy's Journal*, Oxford University Press, 1973.

14. Begum Ikramullah, op. cit.

15. Bengal Legislative Assembly Proceedings, Vol. LXXI, No. 3, 1946, p. III.

16. See Leonard Mosley, *The Glorious Fault*, Harcourt Brace and Co, New York, 1960, p. 36.

17. Read Anthony and David Fischer, *The Proudest Day—India's Long Road to Independence*, Jonathan Cape, London, 1997. pp. 394–95.

18. Begum Ikramullah, op. cit.

19. Tazeen M. Murshid, *The Sacred and the Secular*, Dhaka, 1975, pp. 177–81.

20. Suranjan Das, *Communal Riots in Bengal: 1905–1947*, Oxford University Press, New Delhi, 1991, pp. 172–95.

21. Begum Ikramullah, op. cit.

22. Pyarelal, *Mahatma Gandhi: The Last Phase*, Navjeevan, Ahmedabad.

23. It was rumoured that Wavell was opposed to the inclusion of Sarat Bose, but yielded on Nehru's insistence on observing the constitutional propriety of recognizing the leader of the Congress in the Central Assembly.

24. Quoted in S. Bandyopadhyaya, *Abibhakta Banglar Sesh Adhaya 1937–47*, pp. 401–402.

25. Quoted in R.C. Majumdar, *History of Bengal*, Vol. IV, pp. 401–402.

26. V.P. Menon, *The Transfer of Power in India*, Longman, Greens, 1957.

27. Dhurjati Prasad Dey, *Bengal Muslims in Search of Social Identity*, The University Press, Dhaka.

28. *Amrita Bazar Patrika*, 28 April 1947.

6. Bengal Decides on Partition

1. Leonard Mosley, *Last Days of the British Raj*, pp. 21–23.

7. Bengali or Urdu (1947–54)

1. Quoted in R.C. Majumdar, op. cit. pp. 224–225.

2. Mosley, Leonard, op. cit.

3. There was one marked territorial difference with the 1905 partition. While in 1905 the Presidency Division had not gone to East Bengal, in the 1947 notional scheme this had gone to East Bengal except the districts of 24-Parganas, Nadia and Khulna.

11. The West Bengal Story (1947–77)

1. For a true-to-life picture see Ashoka Gupta, *In the Path of Service, Memoirs of a Changing Century*, Stree, Kolkata, 2005.

2. Bejoy Singh Nahar from the Congress was the deputy chief minister.

SELECT BIBLIOGRAPHY

Ahmad, Abdul Mansur, *Amar Dekha Rajniti Panchas Bachahar* (in Bengali), Kitabistan, Dhaka, 1968.

Ahmed, Sufia, *Muslim Community in Bengal 1884-1912*, Oxford University Press, Dhaka, 1974.

Aiyar, S.A., *Selected Speeches of Netaji Subhas Chandra Bose*, Publications Division, Government of India, 1974.

Andrew, C.F. and Mukherjee, G., *The Rise and Growth of the Congress in India*, London, 1938.

Azad, Maulana Abul Kalam, *India Wins Freedom*, Orient Longman, Mumbai, 1988.

Bandopadhyaya, B.N., *Bangla Samayik Patra Vols I & II*, (in Bengali), Bangla Academy, Dhaka, 1952.

Banerjee, D.N., *East Pakistan: A Case Study in Muslim Politics*, Vikas Publishing House, N. Delhi, 1969.

Banerjee, Rakhal Das, *Banglar Itihas* (in Bengali), 2 volumes, Dey's Publishing, Kolkata, 1997.

Banerjee S.N., *A Nation in Making*, Kolkata, 1925.

Basham, A.L, *The Wonder That Was India*, Picador, India, N. Delhi, 1967.

Bhuiyan, Md Abdul Wadud, *Emergence of Bangladesh and Role of Awami League*, Vikas Publishing House, Delhi, 1982.

Bose, Subhas Chandra, *The Indian Struggle, 1920-34*, Thacker Spink, Kolkata, 1948.

Bose, Sugata, *Agrarian Society and Politics in Bengal, 1919-47*, University of Cambridge, Cambridge, 1983.

Bromfield, J.H., *Elite Conflict in a Plural Society: Twentieth Century Bengal*, University of California Press, Berkeley, 1968.

Chakraborty, Bidyut, *Subhas Chandra Bose and Middle Class Radicalism, 1928-40*, Oxford University Press, Delhi, 1990.

Chatterjee, Anjali, *Bengal in the Reign of Aurangzeb 1658-1707*, Progressive Publishers, Kolkata, 1967.

Chatterjee, Bhola, *Aspects of Bengal Politics in the Early 1930s*, World Press, Kolkata, 1969.

Chatterji, Suniti Kumar, *The Origin and Development of Bengali Language*, Rupa, Kolkata, 1985.

Chaudhuri, S.B., *Civil Disturbances during the British Rule in India, 1765-1857*, World Press Ltd, Kolkata, 1955.

Chaudhury, Sukanta (ed), *Calcutta the Living City Port*, Oxford University Press, Kolkata, 1990.

Crosim, Rich and Paul, *British Policy and Administration in Bengal 1905-1912*, Firma K.L. Mukhopadhyaya, Kolkata, 1977.

Dani, Ahmad Hassan, *Bibliography of the Muslim Inscriptions of Bengal Down to 1538*, Dhaka, 1957.

Das, Suranjan, *Communal Riots in Bengal: 1905-1947*, Delhi, Oxford University Press, 1991.

De, Amalendu, *Roots of Separatism in Nineteenth Century Bengal*, Jadavpur University/Ratna Prakashan, Kolkata, 1974.

De, Dhurjati Prasad, *Bengal Muslims in Search of Social Identity*, University Press, Dhaka.

Dodwell, H.H. (ed.), *The Cambridge History of India*.

Dutt, R.C., *The Economic History of India in the Victorian Age*, Vol. I, Morrison and Gibb, London, 1950.

Eaton Richard., *Essays on Islamic and Indian History*, Oxford University Press, June 2003.

Edwards, Michael, *Asia in the European Age: 1498-1955*, Asia Publishing House, London, 1961.

——, *A History of India*, Cassel, London, 1961.

——, *Last Days of British India*, Cassel, London, 1963.

Ghose, Sudhir, *Gandhi's Emissary—A Non-Conformist Inside Story of India's Past Twenty Years*, Houghton Miffin Co., Boston, 1967.

Ghosh, N. and Mukhopadhyaya, Ashoke, *Partition of Bengal, 1905-1911*, Sahitya Sansad, Kolkata, 2005.

Gopal, S., *The Permanent Settlement in Bengal and its Results*, Allen & Unwin, London, 1949.

Gordon, Leonard A., *Bengal: The Nationalist Movement 1876-1940*, Columbia University Press, New York, 1974.

Griffiths, Percival, *The British Impact on India*, Macdonald, London, 1952.

Gupta, Atul (ed.) *Studies in Bengal Renaissance*, Bipin Pal Centenary, National Council of Education, Kolkata, 1961.

Habibullah, A.B.M., *Foundation of Muslim Rule in India*, Central Book Depot, Lahore, 1945.

Hunter, W.W., *Annals of Rural Bengal*, 3rd edition, Longmans, Green & Co., London, 1908.

Hussain, Abdul, *Bangali Musalmaner Siksha Samasya* (in Bengali), Kolkata, 1925.

Ikramullah, Shaista, *From Purdah to Parliament*, Oxford University Press, Pakistan, 1963.

Islam, Mustafa Nurul, *Bengali Muslim Public Opinion as Reflected in the Bengali Press (1901-1930)*, Bangla Academy, Dhaka, 1973.

Islam, Rafiqul, *A Tale of Millions*, Ananna, Dhaka, 3rd edition, 1986.

Jalal, Ayesha, *The Sole Spokesman: Jinnah, the Muslim League and the Demand for Pakistan*, Cambridge University Press, 1985.

Kabir, Humayun, 'Muslim Politics 1942-47' in C.H. Phillips and M.D. Wainwright (eds.) *The Partition of India, Policies and Perspectives*, George Allen and Unwin, London, 1970.

Low, David (ed.), *Soundings in Modern South Asian History*, Weidenfield, London, 1969.

——(ed.), *Congress and the Raj, Facts of the Indian Struggle (1917-47)*, Heinemann, London, 1977.

Karim, A. Muhammadan, *Education in Bengal*, Kolkata, 1900.

Kling, B.B., *The Blue Mutiny*, University of Pennsylvania Press, Philadelphia, 1966.

Maitra, Jayanti, *Muslim Politics in Bengal, 1855-1906: Collaboration and Confrontation*, KP Bagchi and Co., Kolkata, 1984.

Majumdar, R.C., (general editor) *History of India* (10 volumes), Bhartiya Vidya Bhawan, Mumbai, 1960.

——*History of Bengal:* Vol. 1, *History of Ancient Bengal;* Vol. 2, *History of Medieval Bengal* (ed) J.N. Sircar; Vol. 3, Part 1, *History of Modern Bengal;* Vol. 3, Part 2, *Freedom Movement,* General Printers and Publishers, Kolkata.

——(ed.), *Bangla Desher Itihas* (4 volumes in Bengali).

Mallick, A.R., *British Policy and the Muslims in Bengal 1757–1856: A Study of the Development of the Muslims in Bengal with Special Reference to their Education,* Asiatic Society of Pakistan, Dhaka, 1961.

Manserg, N., Lumby, K.W.R. and Moon, Penderel (eds), *Constitutional Relations between Britain and India: The Transfer of Power, 1942-47,* 12 volumes, London, Her Majesty's Stationery Office, 1970.

Menon, V.P., *The Transfer of Power in India,* Princeton University Press, Princeton, 1957.

Moreland, T., *Agrarian Systems of Muslim India,* Heffer, Cambridge, 1929.

Mosley, Leonard, *The Last Days of the British Raj,* Weidenfeld and Nicolson, London, 1961.

Mukherjee, Jadugopal, *Biplabi Jibaner Smriti* (Bengali) Academic Publishers, Kolkata, 1982.

Murshid, Tazeen, *The Sacred and the Secular,* Dhaka University Press, Dhaka, 1976.

Nevinson, H.W., *The New Spirit of India,* Harper & Bros, London, 1957.

Pal, Pratapaditya, *Sites and Sights of Bengal,* Marg Publications, Mumbai, 2003.

Panikkar, K.M., *Geographical Factors in Indian History,* Mumbai, 1959.

Rahman, Sheikh Mujibur, *The Unfinished Memoirs,* Penguin Books India, New Delhi, 2012.

Rashid, Harun, *The Bengal Provincial Muslim League, 1906-47,* University of London, 1983.

Ray, Jayanta Kumar, *Democracy and Nationalism on Trial—A Study of East Pakistan,* Indian Institute of Advanced Studies, Shimla, 1968.

Ray, Rajat Kanta, *Social Conflict and Political Unrest in Bengal, 1857-1927,* Oxford University Press, Delhi, 1984.

Ray, Nihar Ranjan, *Bangalir Itihas* (in Bengali)

Salik, Siddiq, *Witness to Surrender*, Oxford University Press, Karachi, Pakistan, 1977.

Sarkar, Tanika, *National Movement and Popular Protest in Bengal, 1928-34*, University of Delhi, 1980.

Sarkar, Sumit, *Modern India*, Macmillan, New Delhi, 1973.

Sarkar, Sushobhan, *Notes on the Bengal Renaissance*, Papyrus, Kolkata, 1979.

Sastri, Sivnath, *Ramtenu Lahiri & Tatkalin Bangasamaj* (in Bengali).

Sen, Shila, *Muslim Politics in Bengal, 1937-47*, Impex Press, New Delhi, 1976.

Sen, Sukumar, *Bangla Sahityar Itihas*, 2 volumes (in Bengali).

Sengupta, Nitish, *Dr Bidhan Chandra Roy*, Publications Division, Ministry of Information and Broadcasting, New Delhi.

Sengupta, Sukhoranjan, *Bangasamher Ebang*, Naya Udyog, Kolkata, 2002.

Sinha, N. (ed), *Freedom Movement in Bengal*, Who's Who, Kolkata, 1968.

Sinha, N.K., *Economic History of Bengal*.

Sinha, Pradip, *Nineteenth Century Bengal: Aspects of Social History*, Kolkata, 1965.

Smith, V., *Oxford History of India*, Clarendon Press, Oxford, 1920.

Smith, W.C., *Modern Islam in India*, Princeton University Press, Princeton, 1957.

Som, Reba, *Differences Within Consensus*, Orient Longman, Delhi, 1998.

Spear, Percival, *History of India*, Vol. II, Viking, New Delhi, 1995.

Talukdar, Manairuzzaman, *The Bangladesh Revolution and its Aftermath*, Bangladesh Books International Ltd, Dhaka, 1980.

Tarachand, *Influence of Islam on Indian Culture*, Indian Press, 1936.

Thomas, K.P., *Dr. Bidhan Chandra Roy*, West Bengal Congress Committee, 1955,

Tinker, Hugh, *South Asia: A Short History*, Oxford University Press, London, 1966.

Zaheer, Hasan, *The Separation of East Pakistan—The Rise and Realisation of Bengali Muslim Nationalism*, Oxford University Press, Karachi, Pakistan 1994.

INDEX

HORNSEY 1968

HORNSEY 1968
THE ART SCHOOL REVOLUTION

LISA TICKNER

F

FRANCES LINCOLN LIMITED
PUBLISHERS

For friends and colleagues, Hornsey and after

Frances Lincoln Ltd
4 Torriano Mews
Torriano Avenue
London NW5 2RZ
www.franceslincoln.com

A catalogue record for this book is available from
the British Library.

ISBN 13: 978-0-7112-2874-0

Printed and bound in Singapore

9 8 7 6 5 4 3 2 1

CONTENTS

PREFACE & ACKNOWLEDGMENTS

Opening his book on art education in the American university, Howard Singerman explains that he is doubly implicated in the object of his research. First, he is subject to 'the blindnesses of ideology and interest, the entanglements of identification and transference, and the traps of textuality' that lie in wait for any historian. But second, and more specifically, he is a product of the system he sets out to describe: 'even before I begin, and in ways I cannot tell, I am captured by and folded inside the object of my research.'[1] I, too, am 'folded inside' the history of Hornsey College of Art. I enrolled in 1961, when I was sixteen, beginning as a student on the intermediate course (the first two years of the four-year National Diploma in Design), and switching in 1962 to the pre-diploma course (the foundation year for the new Diploma in Art and Design). In 1966 I graduated with the first cohort of DipAD students and in 1967, after a post-diploma year in sculpture, I embarked on a Ph.D. at Reading University. In the autumn of 1968 I was invited back to teach art history part-time. Hornsey, and its successor institutions, have been at the centre of my professional life.

Only in retrospect, sifting through the archives, have I come to grasp how this unfolding sequence was shaped and enabled by wider forces: by the Ministry's decision (political, pedagogic and pragmatic) to reform art education at the end of the 1950s; by the appointment of the 'Coldstream Council' (1959) and the 'Summerson Council' (1961), and through them the introduction of the DipAD in 1963; by disaffection and escalating student unrest, culminating at Hornsey in the 'sit-in' of 1968 (whose grievances included the irrelevance of obligatory, academic art history); by the shortage of qualified art historians required for the new diploma (let alone historians with studio experience or historians of design); and by a desire on the part of accrediting authorities to see the diploma's 'degree-equivalence' tested and confirmed (for example as a legitimate basis for postgraduate work in the university sector).[2] We make our own history, as Marx put it, but not in conditions of our own choosing.[3]

Officially, I missed the sit-in, which erupted months after I left in 1967 and was over, bar the after-shocks, by the autumn of 1968.[4] In fact I still had friends at Hornsey and was an intermittent visitor to the college and to 14 Hanley Road where the rump of the sit-in adjourned in July.[5] Coming clean about this, I should like to think it places me closer to a 'participant observer' (in terms of anthropology) than a contaminated witness (in terms of law).[6] I know that one of the difficulties of oral history is that the historian is 'especially vulnerable to the very forces that constituted the group and set it in motion', and must resist seduction; that an uprising finds its waiting rhetoric and has a better, if bitter, story to tell; and that history is not always written by the victors, so that *The Hornsey Affair*, compiled by participants and published in 1969, is still the only source in the field.[7]

This avowedly 'partisan and provocative' record of the summer's events is necessarily incomplete. The Parliamentary Select Committee did not report until 1969, after it had gone to press, and private and public archives, including those of the Principal, the local authority, and the Coldstream and Summerson Councils, had yet to emerge in the public domain. Forty years on, the occupation emerges not only as a rather extraordinary event in its own right, but as a powerful lens through which to focus a turbulent period in art education, as a 'social drama' revealing latent conflict (over the rights of students, the politics of design, the needs of capital and the social role of art), and as a particular instance of the 'microphysics of power', of power in its 'capillary forms', surging and ebbing through the charged relations of 1968.[8]

I am grateful to a number of people who have lent papers and photographs, shared memories of Hornsey, or otherwise smoothed my path. These include Sue Adams, Prue Bramwell-Davis, Stuart Brisley, the late Britt-Marie Darracot, Trevor Frankland, John Goldschmidt, Peter Green, Kim Howells, Anne Hulland, Michael Kustow, Jonathan Miller, John Mitchell, Fred Orton, David Warren Piper, David Poston, John Rae, the late David Robins, Fred Scott, Jim Singh-Sandhu, Phil Shaw, Denis Short, Eirian Short and Nick Wright. I owe particular thanks to David Page for correspondence and the generous loan of an extensive archive; to Richard Robbins who lent his manuscript memoir; to John Field for extracts from letters to his parents in 1968; to Alex Roberts and also to John Rae, for papers and contact prints; to David Warren Piper for letting me rifle through his filing-cabinet; and to Paul Wood, both for copies of the *Politics of Art Education* and other semi-samizdat publications of the 1970s and 1980s, and for the typescript of his essay on art education for Tate's forthcoming *History of British Art*. I can guess at, and sympathize with, the reservations of those who chose not to respond to my inquiries. Others are no longer traceable and many of those in authority at the time, being older, are, like Coldstream, Summerson, Pevsner and Shelton, beyond the reach of interviews now.

This is not to presume, of course, anyone's likely agreement with everything that follows. A revolution, even a local and relatively domesticated one, is by definition a site of conflict – within positions as well as between them – and this runs on in subsequent narratives. Memories are fallible but archives, too, are shaped by investments, lapses and repressions. If this is in the end only one possible account of the 'sit-in' it is still, I hope, a rigorous and usable one.

Among those responsible for public collections I should like to thank Eva White of the Victoria and Albert Museum Art and Design Archives at Blythe Road (Harold Shelton Papers); Judy

Vaknin, Archivist in Learning Resources at Middlesex University (Hornsey College of Art Papers); Jeff Gerhardt of the Haringey Libraries, Archives and Museums Service, Bruce Castle Museum (Haringey Council Papers); Simon Fenwick, Archivist at the Bankside Gallery (Hornsey papers donated by Trevor Frankland); James King in the Modern Records Centre at the University of Warwick and staff in the National Archives (NACAE or 'Coldstream' and NCDAD or 'Summerson' Papers). I am indebted to Penny Dade and all those in Learning Resources at Middlesex University, and to staff at the British Library, the London Library, the National Art Library and the Hyman Kreitman Research Centre at Tate Britain.

I collected David Page's archive from Frederika Adam, who used it before me for work on her Oxford University D.Phil. I am grateful to Dr Adam for conversation and for sharing bibliographic material with me, but I have not sought to read her thesis in which Hornsey figures among other art college disturbances in 1968. I revised the final draft at the Sterling and Francine Clark Institute in Williamstown, Massachusetts. There could be no more congenial or convivial setting and I am grateful for the interest of Michael Ann Holly (Director of Research) and Valérie Bajou, Faya Causey, Philip Conisbee, Sandy Nairne, Timothy Standring and Michael Taylor (my fellow Fellows).

Thanks are due to Michael Brunström, who designed the book, to Tim Cawkwell, my copy-editor and – especially – to John Nicoll who took a risk. As a research project this has proved altogether more curious and uncomfortable than anticipated, due, presumably, to my 'enfolding' in it, and to the somewhat poignant experience of looking back – towards the end of my teaching career – at a student-self embarking on it. My thanks, as ever, to Sandy Nairne, for his encouragement, and for understanding this.

EPIGRAPH

Dear Sirs,

The students of Hornsey College of Art have taken over direct control of the college, its buildings and facilities for the purpose of implementing a 'new' educational structure. . . .We are demonstrating that it is entirely possible [to] . . . organize in co-operation with our tutors a curriculum in which individual needs are no longer subordinated to a predetermined system of training requiring a degree of specialization which precludes the broad development of the students' artistic and intellectual capacities. . . . We aim to prove that the reputation of the college and the quality of the work students produce can only advance further in an atmosphere of democratic co-operation and mutual respect. . . . The student action committee calls upon all colleges of higher education, universities and student bodies to support us in the effort to establish a real and genuine system of education in this country.

Document 3a, 31 May 1968[1]

A bunch of crackpots, here in Haringey, or in Grosvenor Square, or Paris, or Berlin, or Mexico, can never overthrow an established system. . . . The system is ours. We the ordinary people, the nine-to-five, Monday-to-Friday, semi-detached, suburban wage-earners, we are the system. We are not victims of it. We are not slaves to it. We are it, and we like it. Does any bunch of twopenny-halfpenny kids think they can turn us upside down? They'll learn.

Editorial, the Wood Green, Southgate and Palmers Green Weekly Herald, *27 September 1968*[2]

BACK STORY: NDD TO DIPAD
1957-64

In Tom Stoppard's *Rock 'n' Roll*, Max complains that the impetus for political change in the 1960s was wasted on sex, drugs and rock 'n' roll. This leads to the following interchange:

> LENKA [protests loudly] Excuse me, we changed the world.
> CANDIDA Yes – what about 1968?
> MAX What happened in 1968?
> CANDIDA Revolution!
> MAX I'm sorry, I've got that disease where you can't
>   remember the name of it – you'll have to help me.
> LENKA Candida means the cultural revolution.
> CANDIDA No, I don't, I mean the occupations – Paris, the
>   LSE, or in my case Hornsey College of Art.[1]

If '1968' conjures Paris, Prague, the London School of Economics, civil rights and the Vietnam solidarity campaign, it is Hornsey – described in its earlier incarnation as 'a mouldering suburban hutment teaching pottery and basketmaking' – that has dropped off the revolutionary map.[2] And it *was* a revolution, according to Tom Nairn at the time, in which 'a few North London crackpots achieved more than the working class of this overwhelmingly proletarian country'.[3]

On 28 May 1968, students occupied Hornsey College of Art, initially for twenty-four hours, in a dispute triggered over control of the Student Union funds. A planned programme of films and speakers expanded rapidly into a critique of all aspects of art education. It led to six weeks of intense debate, the production of more than seventy documents, a short-lived Movement for Rethinking Art and Design Education (MORADE), a three-day conference at the Roundhouse in Camden Town, an exhibition at the Institute of Contemporary Arts, prolonged confrontation with the local authority, and extensive representations to the Parliamentary Select Committee on Student Relations (1969). The Hornsey sit-in merits a mention in accounts of the period, if at all, as a further instance of student unrest and, since art students were widely perceived as apolitical, as evidence of its reach.[4] In fact it was more particular than this. Caught up as it was in the radical politics of 1968, the sit-in needs to be understood in terms of the interaction between local conditions (factors and forces peculiar to Hornsey) and sweeping changes in national art education (initiated in 1957 and established in 1961). These underpinned the Principal's ambitions for the college in the 1960s and, as fault-lines appeared, the students' rebellion of 1968, in which broader disputes as to the function and future of art and design were refracted and developed. It is therefore in 1957 that we have to begin.

Harold Shelton was appointed Principal of Hornsey College of Art and Crafts in March 1957, the governors already having in mind the development of the college in the context of forthcoming changes to the structure of art education.[5] Since 1946 the principal art-school qualification had been the National Diploma in Design.[6] Most students embarked on the NDD after leaving school at sixteen and took the Intermediate Examination after their first two years. This was intended to give them a grounding in a wide range of technical competences – there were tests in Life Drawing, Costume Life Drawing, Anatomy, Architecture, Creative Design for Craft, Drawing and Painting from Memory, Modelling and General Knowledge – before two years of specialization leading to the NDD. For this students chose a major and a minor subject, or a combination of two from an approved list of craft and design options ranging from book-binding to wrought iron work.

Papers were set and examined centrally, and it was a considerable labour and inconvenience to transport quantities of art and craft work across the country for assessment. There was a high failure rate, sometimes among the best students, and widespread dissatisfaction. By 1960, according to Robert Medley, the NDD 'had long been regarded with something approaching contempt'.[7] Staff chafed at examinations still conducted by the Ministry, the Ministry wished to be rid of them, students found the requirements restrictive, and professionals complained that the system produced 'neither good industrial designers nor satisfactory art teachers'.[8] For politicians, this was the nub of the problem. Despite its title the NDD had been about handicraft rather than design, and mechanization threatened the vocational viability of courses in bookbinding, marquetry, mosaic work, tapestry or lace. The lack of industrial designers was hindering the impetus to improve trade products, modernize production and increase exports in a period of intensified international competition. In this sense the reform of art and design education, the consequence of liberal pedagogy and ministerial pragmatism, was one aspect of a broader strategy to modernize higher education in the context of the Cold War.[9]

In April 1957 the Minister of Education published the Report of the National Advisory Committee on Art Examinations. This proposed a gradual winding-up of the external assessment system and a move towards college autonomy.[10] Recognition for advanced courses of study would now be granted only to a limited number of selected colleges, in a pattern 'reflecting recent policy relating to the development of technological education and the raising of the status of certain institutions to Colleges of Advanced Technology'.[11] In July 1958, Circular 340 reported that the Committee's main recommendations had been accepted by the Minister. A new three-year, degree-level course would take the place of the old NDD. Entry would be at eighteen-plus, and students would be expected to have reached 'a satisfactory standard in general education'. Responsibility for developing the system would be vested in a new body to include 'progressive' representatives from commercial and industrial design as well as the fine arts.[12] The National Advisory Council on Art Education (NACAE), known informally as the Coldstream Council after its chairman, Sir William Coldstream, was appointed in 1959.[13] The 'First Coldstream Report', published in October 1960, proposed a complete restructuring of art education, phasing out the NDD in favour of the new Diploma in Art and Design.[14]

Hornsey's prospects here were mixed.[15] Successful validation could lead to an increase in applications, particularly since students would no longer be tied to their localities by the terms of their grants.[16] But a number of regional colleges had improved their resources and Hornsey's London competitors – Chelsea, Central, and St Martin's Colleges of Art – could between them offer broader courses and better facilities. The college was well situated, in a residential area close to commercial contacts. Its Teacher Training Department, linked to London University's Institute of Education, gave it status and maturity. On the other hand, it was desperately short of space, which meant boxing and coxing in studios and workshops. And its courses were chiefly directed to fine and commercial art, with 'only spasmodic and limited numbers' available for 'one or two industrial design courses' (the focus of Shelton's ambitions for the future).[17]

The introduction of the DipAD reduced the number of diploma courses and students and was, indeed, designed to do so. This raised the question of those students, hitherto accommodated by the NDD, who 'would not be suitable for training of this [new] type or might not require it for the employment they have in mind'. The development of the DipAD as a degree-level course thus conjured in the same move a second-class field of vocational students, courses and institutions. Coldstream suggested that colleges that failed to gain diploma accreditation or were unsuited for it might run the new full- and part-time vocational courses that would now be necessary, or part-time day-release courses for young people, or courses in design appreciation for the distributive trades or the general public.[18]

This echoed an old distinction, already evident in the nineteenth-century Schools of Design, between 'trade' students developing a career in art, design or teaching, and those who found in art colleges a liberal education in art and crafts.[19] Many of these were women, and most of them were middle class. Hornsey had not been unusual in continuing to hold separate classes for Ladies, Gentlemen, Teachers and Artisans after the first World War, and it was a matter of status for John Platt, Shelton's predecessor as Principal from 1947 to 1957, to stress the educational rather than vocational orientation of the School: 'The School is in no sense a Trade School' but in aspiration at least 'the cultural centre of the district'.[20]

Hornsey was also not unusual in the large number of its part-time students. The First Coldstream Report had been chiefly concerned with full-time advanced art education but, as Circular 340 noted, 'the main volume of work for the great majority of art schools has consisted, and will continue to consist, of work of other kinds.'[21] In the run-up to DipAD accreditation the emphasis began to be placed on advanced-level, full-time courses at the expense of lower-level, vocational or part-time work. This had implications for the relations between art schools and their local communities, as we shall see, but it was not entirely misplaced. Colleges would indeed be questioned as to whether diploma courses could be realistically combined with junior, vocational or part-time work.[22]

The Coldstream Report had recommended that a separate executive body be set up to implement its proposals. This became the National Council for Diplomas in Art and Design (NCDAD), appointed by the Minister of Education in May 1961. Known as the Summerson Council after its chairman, Sir John Summerson, it was responsible for the maintenance of standards, the validation of courses and the approval and supervision of examination procedures.[23] It was advised by five Area Panels, composed of specialists in each of the four DipAD study areas – Fine Art, Graphic Design, Three-Dimensional Design and Fashion & Textiles – together with History of Art and Complementary Studies.[24]

There was nothing completely new in the general concept and terms of reference of the Summerson Council. As Robert Strand points out, it followed a pattern established for the National Council for Technological Awards, which administered the Diploma in Technology (DipTech). But in the art and design sector it marked 'the final emancipation' of art education from central government control of its examinations (and, by extension, its curricula).[25] The DipAD was to be a nationally recognized qualification that nevertheless allowed a measure of local autonomy and diversity (the Summerson Council stressed in the strongest terms its concern 'not to impose any pre-determined pattern but to test the ability of colleges to evolve their own personal standards').[26]

The *First Report of the National Council for Diplomas in Art and Design*, known as the Summerson Report, was published in 1964. Schools and colleges of art had been invited to submit course proposals for DipAD recognition in July 1961, and the Report was almost entirely concerned with the Council's review of these submissions.[27] A course review consisted of an initial scrutiny of the application forms, a team visit of two or three specialists drawn from the five Area Panels, and the submission of a detailed report to the Council itself. The process was fast, and draconian. One panel member referred to his colleagues as the 'Dr Beechings' of the art-school system.[28] The NCDAD considered applications for 201 courses from 87 colleges. Seventy-two colleges were visited, most of them between February 1962 and March 1963. Sixty-one courses were eventually recognized – less than a third – at twenty-nine colleges.[29] This left swathes of the country including East Anglia and much of Wales with no diploma places at all, but ten recognized colleges in and around London (including Hornsey, which received approval in Fine Art and Graphic Design).[30] The effect was traumatic for the majority of colleges, left without nationally recognized courses in any area and obliged to diversify with part-time and lower-level vocational work. There were national protests over individual judgements and the Council's decision to privilege 'academic merit' – measured after a one- or two-day visit – over other criteria (institutional scale, local authority provision, regional distribution) led to national protests and questions in Parliament.[31] That said, Strand credits the reforms with establishing 'the status of art and design alongside the other disciplines in higher education', with conferring 'a large measure of academic freedom' on participating colleges, and with stimulating 'a flow of resources' to these colleges on an unprecedented scale. That they 'also sowed some dragon's teeth did not become apparent until some time later'.[32]

THE POLYTECHNIC QUESTION
1966-7

> We feel that the demands of polytechnic organization are
> at odds with the Diploma of Art and Design and that
> they jeopardize the tremendous advances brought about
> in art education by [its] establishment.
>
> > *Bryan Robertson, Kenneth Armitage, Ralph Brown,*
> > *Lynn Chadwick, Prunella Clough, Terry Frost,*
> > *Bridget Riley and William Scott.*[1]

Before the first cohort of DipAD students had even graduated, Hornsey was threatened with merger in a new
polytechnic. The Robbins Report (1963) had called for the
expansion of higher education (pointing out that 20 per cent
of school leavers went on to university in the United States,
8 per cent in France, 6 per cent in the USSR and only 4.6 per
cent in Britain).[2] It recommended that the Colleges of
Advanced Technology become self-governing universities
awarding their own degrees (rather than the Dip.Tech.); and
it envisioned an expanded, unitary system of higher education
to accommodate the demand for degree-level work. But a few
months after Labour came to power in October 1964, the new
Secretary of State for Education and Science, Anthony
Crosland, announced that the government favoured a binary
system based on the 'twin traditions' of the independent
universities on the one hand, and the leading technical
colleges, colleges of education and polytechnics in the public
sector on the other.[3] This was the line advanced in his White

Paper of May 1966, *A Plan for Polytechnics and Other Colleges: Higher Education in the Further Education System.*

The object was 'to reduce substantially the number of colleges engaged in full-time higher education', expanding provision while concentrating it in 'large and comprehensive institutions' under the control of local education authorities. Sixty-eight colleges would be amalgamated into thirty new polytechnics, including thirty-six colleges of technology, eighteen colleges of art, ten colleges of commerce and four specialist institutions. This prospect triggered immediate alarm among the art colleges, chiefly that they would be forced into polytechnics and lose their autonomy, but in a few cases that they might be left to wither outside.[4]

Staff and students came together in 1967 to mount a vigorous campaign against the plan to merge Hornsey with Enfield and Hendon Colleges of Technology in a new North London Polytechnic.[5] At Hornsey the struggle to maintain or develop an independent institution predated the sit-in and outlasted it, but, by bringing staff and students together in an organized political campaign it also helped to bring it about. Both Nick Wright, President of the Hornsey branch of the Students' Union, and the Principal, Harold Shelton – on the same side in 1967 – believed this to be the case. Wright reported that opposition had stimulated students into activity and Shelton, in retrospect, blamed Haringey Education Authority for taking 'a strong line' with them over the polytechnic issue. This had brought about 'a violent clash' between the college and the local authority in which 'for the first time the Hornsey students came together as one and formed an action committee'. It was 'probably their first realisation of their strength'.[6]

Most leading artists and educationalists were against the incorporation of art colleges into polytechnics and both Coldstream and Summerson verged on public opposition to government policy in 1966–7. On 19 November 1966 the Summerson Council conveyed to the Department of Education and Science its opposition to the plan as it stood, its desire to be consulted over mergers involving DipAD colleges, and its preference for free collaboration in 'a federated system' over 'a merger system'.[7] On 22 June 1967 Bryan Robertson, the Director of the Whitechapel Art Gallery, together with seven well-known artists, protested in *The Times* that the views of the Summerson and Coldstream Councils had been ignored.[8] A few days later Coldstream confirmed that his Council had indeed advised the Ministry that the proposals were 'not in its view in the best interests of advanced art education'. [9] Summerson and Coldstream discussed the question at length and in person with the Secretary of State, but Crosland conceded nothing.[10] The battle was lost.[11]

The case *for* polytechnics was most forcefully advanced in Eric Robinson's *The New Polytechnics: A Radical Policy for Higher Education*, published in June 1968.[12] Robinson argued that the divide between university and technical college replicated the two-tier system of grammar school and secondary-modern and carried it forward. On economic, social and educational grounds this was indefensible. It was necessary to establish a comprehensive reform of post-school education that would 'bring higher education out of the ivory towers and make it available to all': the comprehensive school must be followed by the comprehensive people's university.[13] Eventually both sides of the binary divide – the self-governing universities on the one hand, the local authority polytechnics and colleges on the other – would become part of a single university sector. In the meantime it was up to the polytechnics to offer a more radical model of what a university could be: 'Their cloisters must face outward, their doors must be permanently open and their facilities in constant use.'[14]

Robinson was strongly in favour of the incorporation of art colleges into polytechnics. In his view 'the new education in art' would have a radicalizing and leavening effect on other disciplines.[15] Art students would gain from access to the wider facilities of a polytechnic; students in other fields would gain from access to art facilities and teaching; and the resulting synergies would have the potential to foster new courses in journalism, television, film work, architecture, urban planning and industrial design.[16] In the art world, those arguing in favour of art-school mergers were in the minority (although Harry Thubron, a well-respected educationalist, and his wife, Elma Askham, put the case in *Studio International*).[17] Most shared with varying degrees of conviction the view expressed by Tom Nairn: 'Polytechnicization will be lengthy, stingy, and compromised in a hundred different ways. No less favourable conditions for art education can be imagined.'[18]

In April 1967 the Secretary of State invited relevant local authorities to submit proposals for the constitution and development of polytechnics. In May the governors at Hornsey resolved that merger would be against the interests of the college.[19] Staff and student agitation reached a peak in October, when the press reported 'open war' with Haringey Council, 'with resignations, protest marches, mud-slinging from both sides, and a threatened strike by students and staff'.[20] A special issue of *Gravy*, the college magazine, was turned over to the arguments. The position of staff, students and governors was almost unanimous: amalgamation would mean loss of autonomy, name and reputation; the colleges of technology – ignorant of the work of artists and designers and outnumbering them – would dominate resources and academic politics; there would be no unified campus in any case so that shared facilities and economies of scale would prove illusory; polytechnics were expected to leave research to the universities but Hornsey's public profile was based on its research activities; the merger would mean changing local authorities and moving further from London, making it harder to retain practising artists and designers as part-time staff; and planned or existing collaborations would be undermined. (Shelton, who claimed to be in discussions with Imperial College, Cambridge, and Salford College of Advanced Technology, said, 'I want to cooperate with everyone, of course. But I want to cooperate on my own terms'.)[21]

Haringey Council was due to commit itself at a meeting on 23 October 1967 which was picketed by the staff and student Joint Action Committee.[22] The governors expressed their view that incorporation 'would be gravely prejudicial' to developments that had 'raised the college to a position of national and international standing in design education'. They asked the local authority to join with them in exploring alternatives, 'for example, the creation of a specialist centre or the development of links with a university'. Since the local authority was heavily represented on the governing body, many of the governors were also councillors. They pressed their case at the Education Committee on 23 October, but by the casting vote of the acting chairman it was decided not to revisit the decision to join with Barnet and Enfield Councils in submitting the scheme that merged Hornsey College of Art with Enfield and Hendon Technical colleges in the new polytechnic.[23] The council's position was that Hornsey must go in.

On 12 November 1968, shortly after the college reopened after the sit-in, a special meeting of the Further Education Sub-Committee of Haringey Borough Council received a report from the Academic Structure Sub-Committee of the college's Board of Governors.[24] This raised yet again the question of Hornsey's absorption into the polytechnic, arguing that the college's national and international reputation implied that the logical next step was to cut numbers, restructure, and establish a specialist centre for design research.

Shelton and his supporters, wriggling on the hook, had come up with a plan whereby the college would be split: some levels of study (unspecified) 'could reasonably be transferred to the polytechnic without detriment to the students' while others 'related wholly or primarily to research and development' would be 'more appropriate to a specialist centre' which could establish its own academic links with universities or polytechnics as an autonomous body. It had long been Shelton's ambition to develop a postgraduate design research institute, something between the Bauhaus and the Royal College of Art, and he was an indefatigable, if ultimately unsuccessful, lobbyist for this at all levels of industry and government up to and including the Prime Minister.[25] Now it seemed to offer a way out of the polytechnic impasse and Haringey's Chief Education Officer was requested to send the proposal to the Secretary of State for his reactions.[26]

The Secretary of State – now Patrick Gordon Walker – was baffled. He pointed out that there were very strong educational arguments 'for associating art education, particularly education for design, with other disciplines in technology, sociology and economics. The divorce between them has for many years been a matter for concern to people interested in industrial design. . . . The Principal of the Hornsey College of Art has figured among the advocates of bringing them together.' The establishment of a polytechnic in north London 'could be expected to achieve the very synthesis which some of them have been advocating'.[27] Attempts to persuade him otherwise were rebuffed.[28] He was simply not prepared to agree to the establishment of a separately maintained, specialist institution, when in his view the reasons adduced in its support were the very reasons why advanced design technology should develop in a polytechnic.[29] Shelton was outflanked and in due course Hornsey was incorporated as the Faculty of Art and Design in Middlesex Polytechnic.

Meanwhile, much of 1967 and the early months of 1968 were dominated by the polytechnic campaign but not to the exclusion of other problems. Ten years after Shelton's appointment, the 'mouldering suburban hutment teaching pottery and basketmaking' had been extended and transformed into 'a sort of English Bauhaus'.[30] Outwardly successful, it was nevertheless embattled. While the college – staff, students and governors – was at loggerheads with the government over the polytechnic issue, Shelton was at loggerheads with the councillors and the Borough Treasurer over alleged financial irregularities, and the Students' Union was at loggerheads with the college administration and the local authority over control of the Union's funds. The threat of merger brought a temporary semblance of unity, as staff and students engaged in a campaign to preserve their independence while struggling internally with inadequate accommodation, poor management and strained resources.[31]

When the London Government Act (1963) led to the abolition of Middlesex County Council in 1965, Hornsey was precipitated from a large, experienced and congenial authority into the lap of Haringey Borough Council, a small, inflexible and reluctant one. Shelton made no secret of the fact that in his view the move to Haringey had precipitated 'a fairly rapid deterioration in the freedom of the college', and Alderman Bains admitted that 'there is a marriage between Haringey Council and the Hornsey College of Art which neither wanted' (although 'for the time being we shall have to put up with each other').[32] Had Shelton succeeded in persuading ministers, as he claimed to have persuaded Middlesex County Council, that some kind of advanced design institute should be funded directly from government, or could find support in whole or in part from business and industry, then this would have had the added advantage of freeing the college from Haringey's control.

But he was stuck with Haringey, and at the same time was fighting a rearguard campaign against the polytechnic, and lobbying for his design research institute, Shelton found himself investigated for financial irregularities. This concerned a protracted dispute over the general purposes fund (money raised from industry for special research projects) which had not been channelled through the local authority or audited by the Borough Treasurer.[33] Shelton's lawyers complained to the Chief Education Officer on 8 December 1967 about 'this colossal, intensive and apparently endless investigation'. Their client had been 'driven to the conclusion that the appointment of the new sub-committee [of inquiry]' was 'in effect, a form of persecution', intended as a riposte to his organization of strong opposition to the polytechnic scheme.[34] The dispute dragged on into the new year, when the council commissioned an independent report from Lewis Hawser QC and Shelton was summoned to an interview at the Civic Centre in March. It petered out in the summer of 1968, by which point it had been overtaken by the sit-in, and the Principal and the local education authority affected a more-or-less united front against radical opposition.[35] The souring of relations between them – over Haringey bureaucracy, inadequate resources, the battle against the polytechnic and the inquiry into the General Purposes Fund – together with Shelton's bitter disappointment at the thwarting of his ambitions for the college: all are factors, hard to calibrate, in the personal dynamics of the sit-in and its aftermath.

Over a relatively short period, Hornsey had expanded into a series of temporary annexes spread across ten square miles of North London. (Shelton would later claim that the accommodation, 'fought for almost room by room', was 'unquestionably .

. . the worst of any major college in the country'.)[36] There were three Victorian primary schools in Tottenham and Wood Green, the old 'Badminton Suite' at Alexandra Palace, offices, stables and an air-raid shelter at Bowes Road in Palmer's Green, and at various points a church hall and an abandoned fire-station.[37] Vocational students rarely visited the main college in Crouch End, and most diploma students visited only for General Studies and the obligatory fine art component of their course, known at Hornsey as 'Visual Research'. There was a shortage of purpose-built workshop space and shared facilities meant work had to be cleared away; there was no bar, or staff or student common room; library facilities were cramped and inadequate; there were long queues in the canteen; and tutorials and even interviews might take place in the corridors.[38] In 1964 vocational students at South Grove, in Tottenham, petitioned for better conditions: it was bitterly cold, there were no easels, no facilities for preparing food and lavatories shared with primary school children were 'revolting, disgusting'.[39] In 1966 one of the governors turned in desperation to Air Marshal Sir Christopher Hartley: could he, 'by any chance, think of a disused or semi-used RAF airfield in the home counties into which the school might expand, even if only on a temporary informal basis'?[40]

Shelton had repeatedly pressed Haringey for more resources and better conditions, arguing that without improved accommodation, facilities, staffing and administrative support, the college might not survive. But he was himself responsible for a lack of accountable structures and clear decision-making. The college's 'primitive organization', as the *Sunday Times* termed it, limped along 'by word of mouth between [the Principal] and his long-service department heads'. The Academic Board was nominated by Shelton and rarely met. The staff-student council, an advisory body, was 'toothless and impotent'.[41] Few were consulted, or represented; decisions were deferred, reversed, or simply not communicated. Things fell apart in 'a miasma of indecision' and 'corridor diplomacy'.[42] People 'got fretful and critical, bad-tempered, suspicious' and students began to feel that their successes 'were mere jewels round the neck of the Principal'.[43] 'Does Shelton know you?' asked the Student Action Committee, unimpressed by his claim to have been 'going to cocktail parties on your behalf'.[44]

Matters came to a head in April 1968. The Students' Union decided at a meeting on 30 April to set up a contingency fund to finance the President's sabbatical year and for legal costs 'incurred in establishing our autonomy and independence through law'.[45] They demanded that Arthur Pudney, the newly appointed Bursar and joint signatory to the Union account, should relinquish his position and surrender the cheque book to the Union treasurer. The request was refused. On 9 May they learned that Pudney had frozen the Union funds.[46] Immediately they consulted lawyers and contacted the National Union of Students, the governors, the Borough Treasurer's department and the local press.

Meanwhile Labour lost control of Haringey to a Conservative majority in the local elections. By May the college was without a governing body, except for the chairman, Alderman Bains, a local businessman and laundrette owner. Bains consulted Alderman Cathles, chair of the Education Committee, who consulted Peter Rigby, the leader of the council, and a decision to release the Union's funds was taken, probably on 23 May.[47] By this point the students had called an emergency protest meeting and built up a head of steam on this and other grievances. Unfreezing the funds was not enough to guarantee control of them. Union meetings on 21 and 22 May resolved to hold a 'critical seminar'. On 23 May Nicolas Wright and the Vice President of the Union, Peter Hayman, met with

Cathles and Rigby and informed them of the students' intention 'to hold a militant, radical and critical examination into the structure of the college and to bring forward a programme of far-reaching proposals for the reform of the content of courses, the democratization of the college academic structure and for the recognition of basic student rights'.[48] The Student Action Committee (SAC), in a draft discussion document apparently circulated on 28 May, condensed these points into the following motion:

> The Students of HORNSEY COLLEGE OF ART demand –
> 1. Complete control of the Union Funds;
> 2. Recognition of the principle of Sabbatical Student Union Officers;
> 3. Twenty per cent STUDENTS, and twenty per cent STAFF, participation on the Governing Body;
> 4. Course-content and course-policy Boards to have one-third Student participation;
> 5. Effective student participation in Administrative decision-making bodies.[49]

The 'teach-in' or 'critical seminar' was organized for 28 May.

THE GESTETNER REVOLUTION
28 May-12 July 1968

This is a revolution of Gestetners instead of guns,
meetings instead of marches, seminars instead of riots, old
movies instead of fresh massacres, cabarets instead of civil
wars, documents instead of slogans, microphones instead
of a mob in leather jackets.

Mike Bygrave[1]

This is a pure Chinese Red Guard effort and we are
not having it.

Alderman Bains[2]

May

The sit-in was planned to run from 4 p.m. on Tuesday 28 May,
beginning with a 'Mass Discussion on Student Autonomy' –
speakers to include Kim Howells and Nick Wright from Hornsey
and Digby Jacks from the Radical Student Alliance – after
which discussion would be open to the floor. 'Upon the
DECISION of the STUDENT BODY to OCCUPY the college',
a programme of seminars, mass discussions and entertainment
would run on through the night, ending at noon on Wednesday
29 May.[3] Bulletins were issued through the morning of the 28th;
cars were organized to bring students from the annexes; guest
speakers, press officers and stewards were briefed; a public
address system was installed; and typists, telephonists, electri-
cians, even plans to deal with an attack by the police, were put
on standby.[4] 'Quiet' rooms were set aside and students were

advised to bring blankets and sleeping bags. The programme promised twenty-four hour canteen provision, films (including classics by Fritz Lang and Charlie Chaplin), and performances by the Cartoon Archetypal Slogan Theatre and Pete Brown's Poetry Band. Various seminars were planned including a mass discussion of 'Students, Art and Society' at 10.15 p.m. Speakers were to include Tom Forthrop (Radical Student Alliance), Ron Ingles and Keith Grant (Hornsey lecturers), Robert Tusher (a journalist just back from events in Paris), and members of the General Studies staff (Michael Kullman, Tom Nairn and Alan Grant). There would be 'soft, smooth music' from 6–7 a.m., breakfast from 7–8 a.m., and at 9 a.m. an 'Open Discussion of Student Grievances' in Rooms A and B. Potential speakers included Stuart Brisley, Keith Grant, David Warren Piper, David Joseph and David Page (not all of whom had been consulted). The aim was to present printed copies of a 'Concluding Assessment' to the Principal, the Board of Governors, and the Education Committee of Haringey Borough Council.

Shelton, the Principal, had apparently persuaded the council not only to permit the protest but to lend it a five-gallon electric urn, no doubt with a view to keeping the students out of the kitchen. (After a symbolic lowering of the metal counter-blind, to satisfy the honour of the canteen manager, the kitchen was reopened as staff went home on 28 May.)[5] In the event, the atmosphere of a college *en fête* was accompanied by the bubble of long-standing grievances coming to the boil, and much of the entertainment was abandoned as frustration erupted in all-night debate. Students had been promised 'a chance to enforce long overdue reform within the college', but the focus on Hornsey's local problems had already widened to – had proved inseparable from – the analysis of art education nationally and the relations between artists, designers and society.[6] This had political ramifications, of course, but they were largely unacknowledged or nonaligned. Kim Howells, in whose rooms the sit-in was planned, was one of a number of students involved in the Vietnam protest movement. Many years later he admitted that they had 'wanted to replicate the events in Paris earlier that month'.[7] Student unrest was in the air. But for most participants the issue was art education: 'no one wanted to hear the old jargon' and 'overtly political speeches' were unwelcome.[8] More people were politicized by their experience of the sit-in than brought a focused politics to it in the first place.[9] There was a shared determination to *do* something if disagreement as to quite what: 'One group held that one could carry on while ignoring the old system. The other was for throwing the art schools in the dustbin and establishing centres for creativity and research.'[10]

Shelton was away in Manchester. When they could contact him, students conveyed the feeling of the meeting that he should return. They read out the train times and he was back in his office in the early hours of 29 May. He asked if they wanted to talk to him but was told that the moment had passed.[11] At dawn a group of students went to Covent Garden to collect fruit for the canteen. At 10 a.m. the general meeting reconvened. Rooms A and B were now packed with hundreds of students, squeezed onto the platform, on window sills and milling around the exits.[12] The programme had been clear: 'MIDDAY: SIT-IN finishes, normal college time-table to be resumed'. But the arguments went on and later that morning a seminar came up with the proposal for an elected senate in place of the Board of Governors, adding that: 'WE WILL STAY IN THIS BUILDING UNTIL THIS IS ACHIEVED.'[13] The college would not be given back.

It happened that the Staff Council was due to meet at 6 p.m. It turned out not to be quorate, but an informal meeting of twenty-four staff drew up a statement expressing 'a community of interest with the students' and a desire to work to lessen the 'alienation, fragmentation and tension' from which staff as well as students suffered. It was decided that there *was* a quorum of the executive committee of the Staff Council, which nominated six staff to meet with six elected student members the following day (Thursday 30 May). Shelton was invited to this meeting, and participated in drawing up a statement which recommended the setting up of a commission – consisting of six elected staff and six elected students – to restore confidence, investigate college policy, identify the decision-making structure and suggest changes that would foster the evolution of the college on lines acceptable to everyone. This was one of several points at which the sit-in might have been resolved.[14] Meanwhile, it having emerged that Shelton had spoken to the press and claimed to be in control of the college, the rugby team evicted him from his office and his outside line.[15]

The governors met on Friday 31 May and agreed to a number of initial demands: the Union President could have sabbatical leave, they would consider the request for a welfare officer, they would explore the question of disciplinary procedures and at their next meeting would discuss the composition of the governing body. They approved the 'formation of a democratically elected commission of staff, students and Principal to study educational curricula' and, in conclusion, they called upon students and staff 'to resume a programme of work in the interests of the future of the college' (as well as those of students, ratepayers, and art education in general).[16] By this point the debate had moved on, however, and also on 31 May the students issued a communiqué with an extended list of more radical demands: the elimination of GCE entrance qualifications, of exams related to academic studies and distinctions between vocational and diploma courses; the freedom to formulate and develop a more flexible 'network' structure of education; and an atmosphere in which grievances could be freely vented and changes introduced.[17] Neither the college nor the governors could meet many of these demands, since they were addressed to the structure of art education put in place by the Coldstream Council and administered by the Summerson Council. The students had been taking on the college administration, the senior staff, the governors and the local education authority; now they would have to make representations to the Department of Education and Science.

By 31 May it had been decided to unite the former staff and student bodies, the College Council and the Students' Union (already overtaken by SAC), in a new, inclusive and democratic organization: the Association of Members of Hornsey College of Art (AMHCA). This was to embrace all students, staff, administrators and technicians – even the board of governors – with all members eligible to vote and hold office.[18] It was intended to stress cooperation in a common enterprise – the education of students at Hornsey – over the old relations of authority between students, staff, Principal and governors. AMHCA would formulate the activities of the college in a flexible system intended to put 'the onus for discipline and decision making on the individuals rather than on some predetermined authority'.[19] Those opposed to the sit-in were quick to argue that it was undemocratic in practice, since only a minority was involved ('the Establishment on the one hand and a few militant students and staff on the other').[20] But this was to misunderstand the nature of participatory democracy, which can offer the opportunities – for representation, engagement or debate – but not, of course, the guarantee that they will be taken up or a means of gauging the strength of feeling in a silent majority.

June

Agreement on the proposal for a staff-student commission, to report by 14 June, had seemed to offer a way ahead. After this things became very confused.[21] A general meeting of students accepted the proposal (with some misgivings as to whether the Principal should have a place on the commission).[22] Sixty staff came to an informal meeting on Tuesday 4 June but others had not received an invitation and so a further meeting was called for Wednesday 5 June. About 160 staff were present in the main building when the Principal sent a message that he would like to address a full meeting of staff the *following* day, Thursday, at 2 p.m., together with a member of the governing body. Less than an hour before *that* meeting he pulled out: a telephone message from the Registrar confirmed that the Principal was in discussion with the local education authority, and in view of their advice it would not be possible for him to attend.[23] John Field, lecturer in art history, wrote to his parents that the Principal 'has done precious nothing. He has entirely lost the trust of the students and much of the staff as well. We are divided in our loyalty to our employers and our students and I suppose our jobs are in some jeopardy.'[24] Shelton retreated to his government-in-exile at Parkwood School, Wood Green, and except for a brief, symbolic occupation of his office at the end of the sit-in in July, disappeared from the college until it reopened – late – in the autumn term.

Meanwhile a new, temporary structure took over from the Student Union for the duration of the sit-in.[25] A pattern emerged of 'seminars feeding into general meetings, which threw detailed questions back to seminars for analysis'. Ideas thrashed out in groups of no more than twenty people, sometimes arguing late into the night, were appraised in 'a fug of Gauloises and blasphemy' in the grey morning light of studio F.[26] The largest meetings were held in Rooms A and B with the interconnecting doors pulled back. Rather than use the stage, a space was cleared in the centre of the floor and Alex Roberts handed round the microphone.[27] Tom Nairn described 'extraordinary explosions of debate, lasting literally and effortlessly from one dawn to another . . . as different in quality from conventional modes of discussion as a space-satellite is from an aeroplane'.[28] His colleague John Field brought a teenage daughter who was studying the French Revolution 'to observe a revolutionary constituent assembly in action'. (It was 'both interesting and extremely boring'.)[29] Feelings could run high, but there was a 'Procedure for All General Meetings for Maximum Effect', which stressed rational debate and the authority of the chair. Anyone engaged in 'persistent interrupting, temper losing and rebel rousing' would be asked to leave.[30] Everything had to be hammered out at the same time: a new educational policy, whether to buy another plastic slop bucket, whether to accept money from a sympathetic trades union, what to do with the window cleaners if they were really from MI5.[31]

Hornsey, its media profile honed by Shelton in terms of cutting-edge design, was now famous, or infamous, as a centre for sceptical debate. Staff, ratepayers and students from other colleges were invited to sessions with visiting speakers including Buckminster Fuller, Joan Littlewood, Sir John Summerson, Professor Nikolaus Pevsner, Sir Robin Darwin (Rector of the Royal College of Art), Professor Richard Wollheim and the radical psychiatrist R. D. Laing. Some were intended to be of interest for their own sake (Buckminster Fuller covered 'astrophysics, the gold-based economy, the fall-out of war technology, and education' in his first forty-five minutes); others were directly related to the politics of art and the structure of art education (an edited transcript of the Summerson seminar was published as Document 39). The

Hornsey Journal reported a seminar with artists Reg Butler, John Latham, Bernard Cohen, Bryan Kneale and Richard Hamilton, and a student's subsequent claim that 'we have learnt more in the last three weeks than in the last three years'.[32]

Jobs were taken by people prepared to do them. Administration was handled by a series of proliferating working parties: Front Office and Stewards (Kim Howells), Press (Martin Fryer, Terry Daniel, Ashley Bruce), External and Internal Liaison (Roger Hayden), Canteen (Dave Poston and Bee Crozier), and others in charge of the switchboard, document duplication, posters and mail.[33] Money began to come in from artists, designers and sympathetic businessmen, and the canteen (at lower prices but with no staff to pay) was turning a profit. The students opened a bank account and Prue Bramwell-Davis, the treasurer, turned to triple-entry book-keeping in the attic. ('I said I'd do it and got on with it. We opened a bank account in the name of AMHCA down the road. I just didn't want there to be any criticism about how the money was handled as a distraction from what we were trying to do.')[34] The sit-in gave rise to an enormous amount of writing. More than seventy documents, from one-page notices to substantial analyses of art education, were rolled off stencilled 'skins' on the Gestetner machine in those pre-photocopy days, tenderly repaired and reattached through copious reprintings.[35] In Studio D, 'strange, stray, silent figures' could be found lino-cutting in the poster workshop, 'still doing battle, ankle deep in chippings' at dawn.[36]

A 'Work Project' scheme was set up to coordinate work under way, draw up a list of new proposals and demonstrate to councillors and ratepayers that the college was 'viable, active, vital and alive'. A list of twenty-six projects drawn up on 10 June included toys for handicapped children; a workspace analysis of annexes and the main building; a high capacity irrigation pump; the AMHCA letterhead; a new design for level crossings; the recycling of waste products; injection-moulded, modular lavatories for trains; mass-produced or DIY sculpture kits; instrumentation displays for household goods; and a pneumatic helter-skelter. Larger projects requiring considerable collective research included an organization and method study on Oxford Circus tube station (jointly with London Transport); the documenting and graphic presentation of the new education system (involving a team of staff and students); a feasibility study for moving the whole college to Alexandra Palace; and a project to utilize low-cost materials in developing countries.[37]

Initially, councillors showed a measure of sympathy for student complaints. Alderman Cathles, chair of the Education Committee, came to the second general meeting of the sit-in at 9 p.m. on 28 May. He found the students 'very peaceful, very reasonable' and declared himself 'pleased to be able to go along and hear what they had to say'. He promised that there would be no victimization, and that all grievances would be looked into.[38] Alderman Bains, chair of the Board of Governors, told the *Guardian* that the students behaved 'like unprovocative, rational young people who are concerned about the quality of their education'.[39] On 9 June he wrote to each student, assuring them that 'the governors have much sympathy with your objectives, both educational and domestic'. He, personally, would 'always be pleased to listen to your views and [hoped] that now, together, we can work to maintain the pre-eminent position of the college.'[40]

As the sit-in continued, however, Cathles' and Bains's patience wore thin. They were dealing not only with sit-in protagonists but also with senior members of staff who found it a nonsense and wanted it stopped.[41] There was no precedent for this kind of thing and no model for resolving it. (Bains would later complain that it 'may sound silly to say so now, but at the time we were very conscious that a single false move might spark off a national revolt. We got no help from the Home Office, or the police, or the DES. We just had to handle it as best we could.')[42] Aldermen were businessmen and bureaucrats, used to a scaled-down version of parliamentary democracy. They couldn't understand the democracy of the students, in which representatives were not empowered to negotiate but only to refer points back to the general meeting. By the middle of June they believed that 'reasonable' demands had been met and that others were outside their remit and control.[43] Once the arguments had moved on to the national structure of art education they were a matter for the DES. The sit-in could not allow itself to be constrained by the limits of local government but, by the same token, the local education authority could not exceed them. In this sense, as *The Hornsey Affair* acknowledged, the sit-in 'fought the cultural revolution on the ground, against the wrong enemy, in the wrong way, and of course with the wrong result'.[44]

Relations deteriorated and Bains concluded that the sit-in was 'a pure Chinese Red Guard effort' that had to be crushed.[45] The college's reputation for 'stimulating fine design for export in industrial products' had been undermined; and since procedures for greater participation were in motion and domestic demands had been met there was no further justification for 'sitting in'. The affair had become 'revolt for revolt's sake, the ultimate aim being the wrecking of the college by a disgruntled minority of staff and students'.[46] The governors would be 'very strict and would stand no nonsense' next term.[47] For their part, staff who believed their motives and actions had been impugned consulted their solicitors.[48]

The Arguments

One of the first documents produced in the sit-in announced that students were now 'free to implement a new educational structure immediately'. Its basic principle would be 'the cultivation of the individual' and it would offer a degree of fluidity that was certainly ambitious and probably utopian. The aim was to arrive at an open system that would take account of all individual demands, with or without tutorial support, and with curricula in a continual state of flux. Tutors would be engaged for the duration of a project and on the basis of student evaluation (probably only technical staff would be employed full-time). All facilities would be available twenty-four hours per day, seven days per week. The idea was to continue the sit-in along these lines, both to develop a viable alternative structure and to resolve grievances directly, through action, rather than in negotiation with the authorities. A domestic dispute (control over Student Union funds and the President's sabbatical year) had precipitated a struggle for wide-reaching reform not only in education but through it: 'One must recognize that in setting up a new educational structure at Hornsey one is creating the working model for a fundamental re-organization of the educational system, and thus, in effect, the value and priority system of our present society.'[49]

The arguments were interlinked. A general critique of the structure and ambitions of the DipAD was driven by objections in particular areas: to the introduction of GCE entrance qualifications, which at a stroke divided vocational from diploma students and rendered them second-class citizens; to art history and complementary studies – the price of academic respectability – as obligatory and examinable components of the course; to the role of 'foundation', an introductory and diagnostic year from which many would fail to secure a diploma place; and to what was perceived as a linear, overspecialized curriculum by advocates for a 'network system' of maximum fluidity. Demands for greater student autonomy and meaningful representation were widespread at the time. At Hornsey, where 'petty dictatorship was the natural complement to the essential chaos of the whole situation', they were fuelled by the sense that students given a greater say in their education would make a better job of it.[50]

In replacing the NDD, increasingly moribund and impossible to administer, Coldstream had aimed at a liberal education in the arts. The argument now was not that the NDD was better, but that reform fell short.[51] Diploma courses were conceived in a form and at a time when the historical conditions that gave rise to them were crumbling. The muddle of NDD arts and crafts had been tidied into the four compartments of the new curriculum (Fine Art, Graphic Design, Three-Dimensional Design, Fashion and Textiles), just as the lines between them were blurred, as new technologies were being developed, as the turnover of styles and products intensified and fine art (especially through 'pop' and 'op') crossed over into consumer goods. A 'real revolution' in art and design had failed to find its counterpart in art education. Coldstream and his colleagues had been left behind, partly because they held before them 'the irrelevant mirage of the university'.[52] Education in art and design could no longer be a training in the styles and techniques of the past; it had to be a training in innovation itself: flexible, interdisciplinary, problem-solving, and carried out in a spirit of equal partnership between staff and students.[53]

Student Selection and the General Certificate of Education

The arguments are developed in more detail in the sit-in documents, in correspondence and in *The Hornsey Affair*. First, the question of the GCE entrance requirement. Noting 'the

Minister's policy that entrants to the diploma courses should have reached a satisfactory standard in general education', the First Coldstream Report (1960) concluded that the 'only practical way' of ensuring this was to recommend that applicants should have five passes at ordinary level – or the equivalent in combined 'O' and 'A' level passes – three of them in academic subjects. The authors of the report believed that this would not, 'within a few years, act as a serious deterrent to more than a small number of potentially good students', and the 'general rule' allowed of exceptions for candidates of 'outstanding artistic promise'.[54] There were thirty-six in one year, according to Summerson. 'It's a door-way,' he told the Hornsey students on 6 June, 'but you think it should be a triumphal arch.'[55]

There were two kinds of objection to the GCE entrance requirement: that it was an arbitrary method of selection in art and design and that it discriminated in favour of middle-class students.[56] It shifted the social composition of the college population and it hardened the distinction between diploma students (superior, creative) and vocational students (lower-class mechanicals). Document 11, among the sit-in papers, cited published sources suggesting that there was either no relationship, or an inverse relationship, between creativity and academic ability. In the first case GCEs were of doubtful value as a basis for selection and in the second they were positively misleading (a portion of the most gifted applicants was presumably excluded by them).[57] An analysis of figures from the Royal College of Art in the 1950s, before the introduction of the DipAD, revealed that 15.8 per cent of RCA students with five or more GCEs, and 17.4 per cent of those with less than five, gained first-class diplomas.[58]

Many of the artists who came to prominence in Britain in the 1960s were working class and almost exclusively first-generation college students.[59] On the other hand, it was in many respects an advantage to have educated and articulate designers and Misha Black, Professor of Industrial Design (Engineering) at the Royal College of Art, believed that design courses were 'more easily assimilated by those students who have at least a modicum of general education'. (The 'illiterate genius' trope was associated with fine art, and Black was a hard-nosed protagonist of the view that art and design education should be separated.) He believed that five GCEs represented 'a minimal standard which most children can achieve when they have the opportunity to do so'. In fact, only about one in four achieved it.[60] As David Page asserted in the *Guardian* in 1968, markers of GCE papers knew that 'schoolchildren who have been well taught do well, and children who have been badly taught do badly'.[61] Children who did badly were disproportionately lower class (and fine art applicants, on anecdotal evidence, disproportionately dyslexic). At this point local arguments about diploma entry met up with radical debates about the future of education nationally: about levelling the playing field in secondary education (through the comprehensives) and expanding the tertiary sector (through the new universities and the polytechnics).[62] Eric Robinson, in his book on polytechnics as comprehensive people's universities, suggested that taking a fresh look at the further education of mature adults could mean eliminating entry qualifications altogether.[63]

How, then, were students to be selected? In the mid-1960s, Hornsey had on average ten applications for every student place; ninety per cent had somehow to be filtered out, on entry requirements, on interview or on their portfolio. This, too, was an inexact science. The sit-in did not pretend to have found an answer. But Document 61, arguing that the factors leading to acceptance or rejection were rarely recorded and often unclear, suggested three approaches for testing the *efficacy* of a selection procedure. All applicants could be admitted or, given that that was probably impracticable, a random sample; or the fortunes of all rejected students could be followed up; or half the intake could be admitted according to existing criteria and the other half according to any scheme designed to bring about an improvement. In each case the point would be to engineer a systematic comparison between the outcome for those students selected with five GCEs and those emerging through other routes.[64] Meanwhile it was, of course, 'a satisfying historical irony' that the new regulations had brought into art colleges students who were not only articulate, but whose liberal arts training encouraged a healthy scepticism. The argument against GCE selection was conducted with fluency and verve by those who had had no trouble meeting it: that was the 'time-bomb' built inadvertently into Coldstream's new system.[65]

Diploma v. Vocational Courses

These students were, however, in the minority. More than 90 per cent of all art and design students were on other kinds of courses (vocational, foundation, part-time or day-release).[66] The First Coldstream Report of 1960, in establishing the terms of the DipAD, created at a stroke a two-tier system: a liberal arts education for diploma students and vocational training for the rest.[67] It claimed that 'in many fields of industrial produc-tion' there was a need for 'large numbers of workers who are not necessarily creative, but who are sufficiently responsive to the ideas of those who are, to be able to interpret their designs perceptively and sympathetically'. This view was confirmed in the Second Coldstream Report, on vocational courses, published in 1962.[68]

One of the first demands of the sit-in was for the abolition of this distinction.[69] In its original meaning, a 'vocational' course prepared the student for known employment – in this sense, medical students were 'vocational' – but it came to imply a distinction of level or merit.[70] Vocational students were often the Cinderellas of art education, second-class citizens with limited resources. Since most vocational courses did not demand five GCEs and were easier to get into, more working-class students were trained as 'mere technicians of the design processes'.[71] This was resented because it appeared to import the inequalities of class society into the college and, as a corollary, because socially disadvantaged students were denied the opportunity to develop their creative potential. Insofar as vocational courses were narrowly specialized, they were in danger of obsolescence in a rapidly changing society. In practical terms, what was needed was something more flexible: an education in design methods and problem-solving rather than a training in particular skills and techniques. In political terms, it was arguably 'the job of the education system to supply trained manpower only to the extent that this contributes to the well-being, the satisfaction, and self-actualization of the members of society'.[72] (Vocational students had the same rights to a self-realizing, liberal education as any of their peers.)

On the other hand, where vocational courses were ambitious and successful, competing with DipAD courses for students and funds, there was 'no reason whatsoever why vocational and diploma courses should not immediately be merged'.[73] (The 'Advanced Course' at St Martin's, where Anthony Caro taught, and the four-year Industrial Design course at Hornsey, were high-level vocational courses.)[74] Either they were poor relations, in which case they needed support; or they had equal standing, in which case they had similar rights to degree equivalence. The sit-in rejected Coldstream's division between creativity and mechanical skill in favour of what they called the 'only viable distinction': that between students required to demonstrate analytical and verbal abilities, as would-be teachers, for example, and the rest.[75] This was still a sizeable group, since only 24.5 per cent of DipAD graduates went directly into industry or design in 1966–8. Of the rest, 34.5 per cent moved directly into teaching or onto postgraduate teacher-training courses, and many of the 23 per cent who continued with postgraduate work at the Slade or the Royal College of Art were headed for teaching or part-time lecturing posts.[76]

Art History and General Studies

Coldstream had laid down that 15 per cent of the student's time and 20 per cent of the final mark should accrue to work in art history and in 'complementary' studies. At Hornsey, as elsewhere, this led to the recruitment of university specialists, the setting up of separate departments, the institutionalizing of a split between theory and practice and, potentially at least, tense relations with the studio staff. Thrusting young academics, many of them left-leaning, imbued with university traditions of scepticism and free speech, encountered a school-like atmosphere and saw their task as one of initiating debate on founding principles. 'Design for whom?' they were inclined to ask, and perhaps because of an interest in Edward de Bono and Buckminster Fuller, the Hornsey documents sometimes anticipate the 'design for need' answers in Victor Papanek's *Design for the Real World* (1971).[77]

Coldstream had encouraged schools to devise their own syllabuses. He had nevertheless assumed that these would embrace some serious study of the history of art ('in several significant periods of time'), specialist courses (such as history of costume or history of furniture), and studies 'complementary' to the studio area (to 'strengthen or give breadth to the students' training').[78] Pevsner confirmed in 1968 that complementary study was necessary because 'it occupies the intellect which does not get enough to bite on during studio hours and days'.[79] Studio staff of course felt patronized by any assumption that art and design were intellectually undemanding, and were aggravated to find high-flyers (or failures) brought down (or up) by marks awarded outside the studio.[80] Art history, assumed to be relevant, was often remote in practice from the interests of the studio, and its emphasis on painting and sculpture had little or nothing to offer design students (who were, after all, the majority). For Coldstream it was indispensible but Summerson's panellists, on college visits, detected 'a certain resistance to the whole idea, as if History of Art were some tiresome extraneous discipline', as for many it was.[81] Faced with a three-year survey from Byzantium onwards, the sit-in argued that art history 'should inform and permeate studies in art and design' and should be available 'throughout the course both formally and informally, but not compulsorily'.[82]

Pre-Diploma or Foundation Courses

The First Coldstream Report recommended that students take a preliminary course of at least a year before embarking on the DipAD. This was intended to be both introductory and diagnostic: students would be trained in 'observation, analysis, creative work and technical control through the study of line, form, colour and space relationships in two and three dimensions'; and their experience would enable them to make an informed choice between the four specialist areas of the DipAD.[83] With this in mind – but with only two terms to do it in – they would prepare a portfolio of work in the hope of an interview.

The college had to devise a course that would meet Coldstream's expectations, with the focus not on traditional skills (such as draughtsmanship and composition), but on some generic visual 'grammar' deemed appropriate to a range of activities in art and design. Many colleges, including Hornsey, adopted some variant of Basic Design, derived ultimately from the preliminary course at the Weimar Bauhaus in the 1920s, and adapted and developed in the 1950s by British artists and educators including Victor Pasmore, Richard Hamilton, Tom Hudson, Harry Thubron and Maurice de Sausmarez.[84]

Paradoxically, given that they were largely compulsory in the Coldstream scheme of things, pre-diploma courses were not subject to Summerson validation. And although it was widely assumed that successsful completion assured entry to a diploma course, this was not the case. The number of applicants greatly exceeded the places available and many students were disappointed.[85] First the Ministry (in 1964) and then the Coldstream Council, in an Addendum to its First Report, published in 1965, were obliged to make this clear, and Coldstream advised changing the term to 'foundation course' to minimize misunderstanding.[86] Sit-in participants railed against this wastage and uncertainty, rejecting the pressured nature of the average pre-diploma year (two terms, if that, before applications were due), in favour of alternatives such as an integrated four-year course.

In sum, the sit-in demanded that GCE entrance requirements be dropped; that the distinction between diploma and vocational courses be abolished; that academic assessments be abandoned; that the pre-diploma year be re-examined; that 'some more flexible system closer to the real needs' of design replace the DipAD system; that 'a very high degree of student participation' be introduced in the organization of work and the running of the college; and finally that research – including research into the educational process itself – be made an integral part of the curriculum. ('No system devoted to the fostering of creativity can function properly unless original work and thought is constantly going on within it.')[87] The 'network system' was to be the best means of bringing all this about.

The Network System

Perhaps surprisingly, among a plethora of documents there is none that maps in detail a sample curriculum. What the sit-in was obsessed with was structure, rather than content, and the sit-in advanced the idea of a 'network system' to maintain optimum flexibility.[88] The courses would be fitted to the students, rather than the other way round, such that the logical unit became 'not the class, but the creative group, embracing both students and staff in a common project'.[89] The diploma/vocational dichotomy would disintegrate across the spectrum, from a liberal design education to a more intensive industrial one. There could be specialization or no specialization at all. Irreversible decisions would be deferred as late as possible in a student's career. And the physical and conceptual barriers round departmental fiefdoms would be dissolved in the free flow of creative activity.[90] On the other hand, the structure had to have some shape. Buckminster Fuller was a tacit reference point here – self-described 'comprehensivist' and embodiment of 'an emerging synthesis of artist, inventor, mechanic, objective economist, and evolutionary strategist' – and the shape that comes to mind is that of his geodesic dome. The network system was not a 'complete option system of a random nature', but rather an extendable, operational structure, one in which the coherent group was an important source of motivation and support (so that the cumulative build-up of experience was worth preserving).[91]

The oppressive nature of the 'linear system' was constantly stressed. Students needed to think laterally, to correlate skills and disciplines in relation to the aims of particular projects.[92] One proposal, from David Warren Piper, suggested that the curriculum would have to be written in terms of two kinds of objectives: those concerned with design ability (including theory, methodology and history) and those concerned with skills (production techniques and practice at working with specific materials). Most staff would have two jobs, one relating to the first set of objectives and one to the second. Students would work on major projects, where the criteria for success were clearly stated but where there was room to interpret the objectives in terms of furniture design, or clothing, or ceramics, and in such a manner as to advance the acquisition of special areas of skill and knowledge. This would be overseen by a tutor responsible for the overall coherence of the student's programme, and for sending the student on courses run by a service department on particular materials and techniques. Running in parallel would be the design methodology scheme, introducing material from history, English, psychology and other disciplines relevant to the interests of art and design.[93]

According to *The Hornsey Affair*, reformers were often asked if changes were aimed at adapting students to the working environment or releasing individual potential. This they believed to be a false dichotomy. The linear system failed at both, at integrating art and design into the life of a modern, capitalist society (because in a period of change it was a training in outdated techniques and ideas) and in producing things good in themselves (regardless of commerce and fashion). The network system, they claimed, succeeded at both, because it offered a flexible training in generalized creative design, adaptable to changing circumstances, and because the imaginative qualities needed to produce the versatile designer of the future were 'no different from the ideal ones required to produce maximal individual development'.[94]

The objection to the network system was that it was incoherent, that 'no student would ever attain a proficient standard of skill in any one technique' and that something so fluid would prove impossible to administer.[95] (It was, perhaps, on one level a kind of fantasy: the expression of a compensatory desire for wholeness and freedom by those who found the college fragmented and inflexible.) Piper's response, in a later and more measured article, was that the network 'should not be confused with a cafeteria-style system in which students help themselves to courses catching their fancy'. The choices that students made would inevitably be qualified by their previous achievements. A network system was 'not the anarchic bogey it has sometimes been made out to be' but simply a way of relating courses together so that 'they form a greater number of sensible paths along which a student may progress'. Rather than starting from a fixed idea of what a course must be, and selecting or rejecting applicants to fit, the network was a dynamic system that aimed to provide a range of courses for the needs of people coming forward. (Quite how the needs, the people and the courses would be matched remained open to question.) In such a context the DipAD could be seen 'in its proper perspective' as one small part of the overall picture of art education.[96]

Alternatives

Some version of the network system was intended to establish at Hornsey an exemplary new structure for art education. GCE entrance requirements, the split between diploma and vocational courses, examinations in academic subjects and the one-year foundation course would all be abolished, and students would have a greater say in a more flexible education and in the running of the college. This was one position. But a second, more radical, questioned the relevance of an art college at all. One group imagined a series of interrelated communes, gathered around a central service core with teaching as a by-product; others felt that they should simply 'go out into society, armed with their own conviction, and change it from within', rejecting the art-object but drawing on their training in communication.[97] Reformists focused primarily on creativity and the educational structures necessary to develop it; radicals on the nature of art and its place in society.

Aneurin Thomas, who had been Vice Principal at Hornsey until 1967, proposed in 1973 that the DipAD should be abolished and art and design education split between the universities (art) and the polytechnics (design). The redundant art schools would then be able to take on a new role as 'centres for the new arts'. These would cater for those emergent, inter-disciplinary group activities that required a new attitude on the part of official bodies and a different kind of institution from the established gallery, theatre or concert hall.[98] The theme was taken up by Paul Oliver in 'Art Education for *What* Future?', an essay in the same collection. 'Let us assume,' he wrote, 'that there are no art schools as such', but rather art and design centres as 'the nodes of creative life' in a community.

These 'vital resources for creation and recreation' are complex, dynamic, and sometimes bizarre. They occupy warehouses, empty churches, dutch barns and village halls, augmented with tents, inflatables, and geodesic domes in local materials. They are serviced as far as possible through solar heating, water condensers, desalination plants and wind-powered generators. They house a nucleus of activities shared by eight-year olds, teenagers and retired businessmen, through which art and design activities (flower shows or light shows) are integrated into the life of the community.[99]

July

At a staff meeting at Parkwood School on 11 June, while noting that they were not in agreement with every proposal advanced by the sit-in, the majority of staff associated themselves with a movement aiming to 'rationalize and establish an improved structure in art and design education'. It was decided to elect from staff and students a steering committee, and a commission to 'enter into discussions on internal, local and national matters'.[100]

On Monday 1 July a meeting of the executive committee of the governors with four members of the AMHCA prepared a draft proposal for resolving the sit-in. This was to be presented to the steering committee on 2 July, to a governors' meeting on 3 July, and finally to a general meeting of staff and students on 4 July. The steering committee raised the question of how the commission was to be funded. It estimated that up to £2000 would be required, and suggested that the governors and representatives of AMHCA make a joint effort to raise the money. Bains seems to have misunderstood and, believing that the steering committee was asking for £2000 from the local authority, refused. The governors rejected the draft proposal and the college was officially closed at 7.30 a.m. on 4 July. The building was surrounded by security guards with dogs and the remaining students barricaded themselves in, rigging a loudspeaker at one of the windows and working methodically through their press list from the *Black Dwarf* to the *Christian Science Monitor*.[101]

The council had employed Bill Ray, of A1 Security Dogs, to clear the college after Securicor turned the job down. He told them that the only way to do this was with a double wire fence around the perimeter, eight feet high and ten feet apart. 'I could put my men and dogs into the no-man's land. We would put the place under siege. If the students tried to get in or out my dogs would rip them to pieces.' In fact the guards were soon ensconced in the canteen and the alsations eating corned-beef sandwiches. Ray said the place was like a warren with 'hundreds of entrances': six dogs and seven men were not enough, and how could they attack when 'we found the students polite and helpful?'[102] It was a token show of force, and counterproductive: it destroyed trust, questioned the council's political judgement and threatened the chance of a negotiated settlement.[103] (Haringey's Public Relations Officer was later reported as claiming that he had kept 'trying to get these grocers to see that they had the chance of running the best art school in Europe, and they blew it with a pack of guard dogs.')[104]

That evening a student and member of staff, elected from the general meeting, joined Bains, Cathles and Councillor Hitchens at the Town Hall. It was agreed that the dogs would be withdrawn, the services restored, and the draft proposal from 1 July put back on the agenda. Intense discussion over the weekend led to a general acceptance of the proposal with certain caveats. The question of finance was resolved with the promise of up to £10,000 from André Fer, of Cinex Ltd (later withdrawn).[105] On Monday 8 July Cathles, with council officers and the Principal, took part in an open meeting of the steering committee. He said that he believed the governors would agree to the revised proposals on condition that the Principal was a member of the commission. This was a sticking point: those against it felt it betrayed the sit-in; those for it believed it proper or expedient (it tied his hands). The governors reached agreement on eleven points submitted by the steering committee in time for a full council meeting that evening. Cathles promised to reopen the college and on Tuesday morning 'normality returned with a heavy stench of carbolic acid'.[106]

The switchboard was manned by college staff, the Principal reoccupied his office, but in fact the sit-in was not quite over. The students were indignant that Shelton was holding a meeting of departmental heads, not in the reopened building but at Parkwood School. Bains declined to give an undertaking, either that students' names would not be forwarded to their local authorities (threatening their grants) or that the autumn term would begin as scheduled on 23 September. His promise at the beginning of the sit-in, that no-one would be victimized, began to look thin. On Friday 12 July, without further discussion, the college was closed. Shelton's 'government in exile' continued at Parkwood School; the commission was obliged to meet elsewhere; students took holiday jobs or drifted home; and the rump of the sit-in transferred to David Page's house in Hanley Road.[107]

The ICA Exhibition

Meanwhile, amid the turbulence, students had been working on an exhibition and a conference, projects that came to fruition in early July. Michael Kustow, the new director of the Institute of Contemporary Arts, was just back from Prague when he joined a meeting as the sit-in began. After listening to 'stumbling but painstaking group discussions, discussions full of the tentative and repetitive utterances of people discovering their ability to speak a new language', he invited the students to take over half the Institute's gallery and extend their protest to a broader audience. Sympathetic, if not uncritical, siding with the dissidents meant that he 'paid his dues, as it were, to whatever questioning or "revolutionary" movement might be beginning on his doorstep', and allowed him to signal that the ICA retained its radical credentials, despite its grand new premises on the Mall.[108]

The exhibition – *Hornsey Strikes Again* – was assembled in two weeks by more than thirty people working round the clock. Part installation, part teach-in, part mobile canteen, it was intended as a didactic demonstration of the superiority of the network system over the conventions of the DipAD. A large Diploma in Art and Design in a gilt frame, surrounded by flashing lights on a silver easel, beckoned the visitor onto the DipAD course. This turned into a labyrinth of corridors, dimly lit, with 'an oppressive atmosphere'. In a formal interview room, three wooden figures fired taped questions from behind a desk ('How many O-levels do you have?', 'What does your father do?'). Pushing through a polythene passage, from which elements of the open system were partly visible, the would-be diplomate was faced with a choice of constricted pathways barely two feet wide (the limited options of the 'linear' curriculum). After squeezing through one of these channels and a section devoted to projects the visitor entered the territory of General Studies. Here were scrawls of meaningless notes on Leonardo, and a slide-test: images projected to the accompaniment of tedious questions on the history of art. Finally the visitor stepped out into an open area with general information, posters from the occupation, multi-screen projection of sit-in scenes and a miniature replica of the Hornsey canteen.[109] 'We were often there arguing with people,' David Page recalled, 'and trying to turn the ICA into our personal club. . . . It was a great attempt to do something different, but it preached to the converted – the ICA represented art radicals at the time [who] were broadly on our side anyway. But bless Michael Kustow for trying.'[110]

MORADE

The exhibition at the ICA opened on 5 July. From 8–10 July the newly constituted MORADE (Movement for Rethinking Art & Design Education) held a national conference on art/design education at the Roundhouse in Camden Town. This had been planned by representatives from fifteen colleges working in the tiny Vice Principal's office at Hornsey ('like the Black Hole of Calcutta'), and more than thirty colleges were represented.[111] Invitations were sent to principals, the DES, the LEAs, thirty MPs and thirty members from the House of Lords eliciting 'charming, warm, evasive' replies. 300 questionnaires went out to the design industry, to discover its views on education, and 200 went to colleges, to gather information on local power structures, staff-student representation and educational aims. The conference was to be 'the national manifestation of the general and particular grievances, questions and proposals art students/staff are asking all over the country'.[112]

On its second day, the conference passed a resolution in support of the 'Hornsey experiment' as of 'first importance to the future of art education in this country'. It appealed 'to the Secretary of State to intervene directly to ensure complete freedom for this work to continue in the next academic year. A live laboratory is worth any number of textbooks.'[113] It was crucial to shift the arguments out of the sphere of local politics and onto the national territory of the Summerson and Coldstream Councils and the DES. The feeling of the meeting, expressed in front of Sir John Summerson, was that his Council was defunct. He made no comment on this but suggested that regional centres, set up on an experimental basis outside the DipAD, could develop the work that Hornsey had pioneered.[114]

Finally, the conference proposed that art colleges be taken out of the control of local education authorities and funded directly (as universities were by the University Grants Committee); that this new central organization should negotiate with the DES and other national bodies; that colleges and departments should be free to establish their own academic and organizational structures; that they should be governed by staff and students via an elected executive committee; that the staff-student body as a whole should decide the function and responsibilities of the principal; that all students should have full grants; and that GCE entrance requirements and current assessment methods be dropped.[115]

AFTERMATH
1968-70

[This was] no way to run a college, or a whelk-stall for
that matter.

Lord Longford[1]

Assessments

By the end of August it was clear that the college would not
reopen until mid-October, or even November. The authorities decided that all the students must be reassessed as a
condition of re-entry and although there was some kind of
rationale for this (assessments had been cancelled or disrupted
in the summer term), there was something punitive about it,
too. Arrangements had to be made by post while the college
was closed and the students dispersed. An attempt to organize a
boycott failed as students were scattered and the NUS withdrew
its support. More than fifty students were told they could not
return when the college reopened.[2] Some had been away, some
could not be contacted, some refused on principle to attend.
One of the external assessors brought in to ensure impartiality
– the Marquis of Queensberry, Professor of Ceramics at the
Royal College Art – distanced himself from the whole affair. In
a letter to *The Times* he suggested that it was just an excuse on
the part of the governors to delay reopening and offered his fee
to the students instead.[3]

Haringey Education Committee proposed that grants be paid
monthly, rather than termly (making them easier to suspend),
and Shelton told the governors that assessing up to four

hundred students would take to the end of September at least.[4] When this was reported in *The Times* Sir Robin Darwin, Rector of the Royal College of Art, urged the London colleges to 'mark their disapproval' of Haringey's actions by giving temporary shelter to Hornsey students. He offered to take a hundred himself.[5] Cathles objected to Darwin's 'damaging' intervention and the Education Committee rescheduled: there would still be thirty-six weeks' tuition so the offer was redundant. Darwin, however, was 'totally unrepentant', and elsewhere the view was gaining ground that leading art colleges should not be subject to local control.[6]

The Commission

A joint staff-student commission was first suggested at the beginning of the sit-in, and the governors had agreed to it on 31 May. Through misunderstandings it failed to materialize, but a renewed proposal – for an elected commission of inquiry including staff, students and the Principal – was agreed at the governors' meeting on 7 June.[7] The terms of reference included identifying objectives for art education and drafting a new academic structure acceptable to everyone in the college. Its recommendations were to be put before a general meeting on 23 September, the first day of the autumn term, and sent as ratified by that meeting to the governing body and the Department of Education and Science.[8]

The commission consisted of eight elected students, eight elected staff, two co-options, a governor and the Principal (whose presence was controversial, but expedient).[9] Henry Moore contributed £500 towards the costs. It met throughout the summer, first under the chairmanship of Dr William Wall at the Institute of Education, and then at the Architectural Association under Lord Longford. Longford, an Anglo-Irish aristocrat, socialist and Catholic convert, had been a minister in several Labour administrations before resigning from government in January 1968.[10] *The Hornsey Affair* remarks on the odd role of this liberal public servant as 'referee in the battle between the students' ideas and the small-minded local administration', suggesting that where the college administration and Haringey Council were indifferent or malign, the 'higher echelons' were genuinely interested and 'really listened'. This liberal flexibility (though a well known tactic of absorption and control), could 'only be felt as useful and welcome in the unequal battle going on'.[11]

The atmosphere was good at the opening meeting, on 17 July, but progress stalled as the weeks went by.[12] Bains published a letter in the *Guardian* on 27 July, a governor's eye view putting the 'recent upheaval' in perspective and claiming that 'no firm or formal proposals' had yet emerged from the commission.[13] An interim report, 'Draft Recommendations for Interim Academic Structure '68–9', was sent to the governing body by 12 August with an outline programme for the first weeks of term.[14] Longford believed a 'solution could quickly be found' and matters could be 'settled in a fortnight'.[15] But the governors responded that due to an administrative backlog it would be impossible to open on 23 September and the start of term would be delayed.[16] Members of the commission were frustrated, both that academic discussion had been diverted by the need to engage with senior staff, governors and the local authority over the terms on which the college would reopen; and by the stalemate in which they found themselves. 'The official line seems to be that no plans can be made in the departments until the findings of the commission are known. On the other hand, the commission cannot make recommendations without having the *full facts* about decisions which have already been made.'[17] Heads of department were sent a list of questions: Would term begin on 23 September? What courses would open with which staff and students? Would new courses open or existing ones close? What changes in accommodation were in view? What decisions were being made about admissions, timetables and curricula? The Head of Fine Art, George Younson, wrote 'I don't know' against every single question.[18]

It was difficult to resolve points raised by the governors against the proposed structure when senior staff said one thing on the commission and another on the governing body. Shelton, for example, in favour of a tutorial system at meetings of the commission, opposed it at the governing board.[19] Students felt they had exchanged the 'constructive community and sympathy of the sit-in' for a 'clash of vested interests. . . Us and Them'. One complained that through more than twenty meetings, 'Contradiction followed contradiction and change after change of tactics came about with confusing regularity until I seriously did not know which side I was supposed to be on.'[20] For the students it felt a turbulent, even treacherous, transition from the atmosphere of the sit-in to that of the boardroom. Fault-lines appeared and recriminations set in.[21]

The governors had criticized the draft plan forwarded by the commission, chiefly on the grounds that the proposed tutorial scheme would be too expensive. (Haringey claimed it would cost a further £70,000 each year.)[22] This led to a further paper, known as the 'FitzPatrick Plan', which claimed to show in thirty pages of figures that such a system would actually be cheaper to operate.[23] Both papers were discussed with the sub-committee of Haringey Education Committee set up to consider the Hornsey issue. Heads of departments were asked to supply comments together with accurate figures related to teaching methods. Instead, on 3 October a document was presented to the commission under the title 'The Hornsey Commission – Proposed Structure for Hornsey College of Art 1968/69' (HD 5/2/10/68). Though uncredited, this had been produced by the heads of department, apparently in an effort to move things forward.[24] It was based on the original draft paper from the commission but with modifications, the most significant of which proposed a separate decision-making structure culminating in a College Executive (the Principal, Vice Principal and heads of department). Elected staff and students were limited to a purely advisory system in parallel ('a democratic façade that would leave the old power-structure intact').[25] This divided the commission, but in any case they were forestalled: on 7 October it emerged through the press that the governors had agreed to it and on that basis the college would reopen on 4 November, six weeks late.[26]

Staff and students were summoned to the Palace Cinema, on Tottenham High Road, on 5 November. (Clint Eastwood was starring in *Hang 'Em High* as a wronged man who takes the law into his own hands.) On the platform were the Principal (who was bland), the chair of the Board of Governors (who was firm), and Lord Longford (who made his celebrated remark to the effect that this was 'no way to run a college, or a whelk-stall for that matter').[27] The larger questions had had in the end to be postponed. A list of principles had been circulated but the commission's long-term brief – to propose a radical alternative structure for art education – was left to a series of working parties (and the reflections of Coldstream and Summerson).[28] Longford was confident that art education would 'change markedly in the next ten years', but his short-term brief was to 'examine as a matter of urgency such internal changes as are feasible within the existing national structure for the coming academic year'.[29] The authorities made it clear that the college opened on their terms or not at all. Longford urged them 'to create a vital spirit of cooperation' between staff, students and governors. Much goodwill was needed, and much had been lost. Suspended students should be readmitted, the position of staff whose contracts had not been renewed should be reconsidered, and the new system should be subject to testing and perhaps amendment 'so as to become more appropriate to Hornsey'.[30] There were cries of 'sell-out' and widespread indignation, but there was also a desire to have the college reopened.[31] In the end matters came down to the question of how many student representatives there should be on the new College Advisory Panel. The heads of department had said two, the commission had said seven, and seven was what the governors eventually agreed. In the words of *The Hornsey Affair*, 'a movement that had started by proposing a total revolution in education and the demolition of the old authority ended up begging for more representatives on the spurious parliament which that authority erected to disguise its educational bankruptcy.'[32]

The Select Committee

Some councillors, uneasy over the handling of the Hornsey dispute, wanted it referred to the Ombudsman, but the Labour leader's request for an independent inquiry was refused on 28 October.[33] On 13 November, following a year of student unrest, Parliament ordered a Select Committee on Education and Science (Student Relations). From this point Haringey's Chief Executive and Chief Education Officer maintained that no useful purpose would be served by a separate inquiry. Submissions were made to the Select Committee and students, staff, governors and councillors appeared before Sub-Committee B on 30 January 1969.[34]

Art students, who were only a small proportion of the student population, had been disproportionately active, articulate and prominent in the press. The Select Committee investigated four art colleges: Hornsey, Guildford and Brighton, all of which had experienced protests in 1968, and Manchester, which had not. The Committee's *Report and Evidence*, published in July 1969, contains extensive information on the causes and effects of student unrest. In the case of the art students, complaints were both national and local: the 'characteristic feature of student unrest in colleges of art was the debate on the content and purpose of art education' (the terms and effects of the DipAD); but they also objected to the terms of daily existence (at Hornsey, to the power of the Principal and his ruling élite, to the absence of decent amenities and the lack of an academic structure or plan).

For its part, the Select Committee noted that art and design teaching shared some peculiar features. There was no general agreement on course content or teaching procedures, a high degree of subjectivity in assessment and some uncertainty about occupational outcomes. An 'atmosphere of distrust and suspicion' had emerged during the process of taking evidence and it was clear that in some cases internal problems had been exacerbated by prolonged negotiations over polytechnic mergers. With hindsight it appeared that 'too little consideration' had been given to the destabilizing effects of the DipAD, the introduction of which had 'radically changed the character of the student population' and produced a situation in which strains were likely to develop.[35]

Local authorities were not best placed to manage these difficulties. The Committee noted that at Hornsey, 'the Principal, the college administration, the Town Clerk, the Borough Council, the Borough Education Committee, the Further Education Sub-Committee, and the governors were all involved [in a] ponderous chain of administration' that was 'ill adapted to present conditions', and Arnold Shaw suggested that Haringey Council had responded to the sit-in 'with as much subtlety as the Mayor of Chicago'.[36]

In all four colleges the introduction of 'general', 'complementary' or 'liberal' studies caused difficulties that were insufficiently thought-through. Shelton explained that it had been his idea to have a strong General Studies department, adding 'one makes mistakes. I have never been afraid of them.'[37] (The Report treads carefully here, but finds 'noteworthy' the fact that at Hornsey and Guildford 'the departments were reorganized and . . . some members of staff did not have their contracts renewed'.) The Committee did not feel itself competent to pronounce on the students' desire for a more integrated 'network system' but recognized that whatever the precipitating causes, discussions at Hornsey and Guildford had 'developed into a serious review of the purpose and place of art education'.[38]

It was immediately apparent, from the difficulty of agreeing on representative groups of staff, that staff were divided and this was especially marked at Hornsey.[39] Veterans of the sit-in argued for the wholesale transformation of art education nationally and clear policies, improved communications and representative government within the college.[40] Others distanced themselves from the 'revolution', believing it to have been destructive, or hysterical, or unnecessary (at least in their fiefdoms), while acknowledging problems in the college and looking to piecemeal reform. Jack Procter and Bernard Hancock, representatives of the Society of Industrial Artists and Designers and Shelton's allies, insisted that consultation and participation at Hornsey, implemented with goodwill, could bring about progressive development. Undue influence from extremists was to be avoided, both for its own sake and because it provoked a repressive response from the authorities. In their view, 'the militants do not want any system to work, and aim only at disruption for political ends.'[41]

This was also Shelton's position and he pursued it with a vigour and single-mindedness in direct proportion to the vehemence with which he felt himself attacked. He claimed in his evidence that the college was vulnerable to outside agitators because it was fragmented, with inadequate accommodation and poor facilities, for which he blamed the local authority. Political malcontents had taken advantage of this. The educational arguments were purely diversionary and had never been raised with senior staff.[42] He was not responsible, either for the alleged causes of the sit-in or for failing to help resolve it: he was merely in the wrong place at the wrong time, the victim of an international conspiracy seizing on the college's reputation as a means of fermenting student unrest.

To support this argument he advanced a number of subsidiary claims: that the sit-in had been planned in advance; that dissidents were politically motivated and local grievances not the issue; that there were links to radical organizations and outside agitators; and that visitors and staff sustained the sit-in. The evidence supported him, or so he believed, and certainly, it was not clear-cut. Even where facts were not in dispute, interpretation was open to question.

Shelton failed to see the sit-in as overdetermined. As far as he was concerned, the protest over union funds was not a catalyst, bringing simmering disaffections to the boil, but a demand that was met in full by 28 May. There was thus no reason for the sit-in to go ahead and the only explanation must be political. First, Nick Wright, who had never made any secret of his allegiance to the Communist Party, was determined to organize the Students' Union 'in an effective way as a fighting force'; and second, an 'emergent group of student militants', resolved to keep the Union up to the mark, had made plans for 28 May and carried them through.[43] Shelton claimed that the occupation was pre-arranged with outside support and was never intended to end as promised on 29 May. No evidence was laid before the Select Committee in support of this and the printed programme suggested otherwise.[44]

Politics was a prickly issue, present, but overstated if it was held to imply the advancement of a particular programme by known affiliates (rather than a general commitment to change). Wright was a Communist; David Page was 'some sort of unsectarian socialist'; Kim Howells considered himself an anarchist; Jim Singh-Sandhu was 'theoretically anarcho-syndicalist'; and Tom Nairn was a non-aligned Marxist associated with *New Left Review*.[45] A number of others were broadly 'on the left' and the majority probably nothing at all. David Warren Piper, Alex Roberts and Prue Bramwell-Davis were apolitical pragmatists interested in design solutions to social problems.[46] The issue was art education, first, and then the questions it opened onto: the place of art and design in society, what education was and who it was for. Participants were neither the 'Red Guard' imagined by Conservative councillors nor quite the political ingénus they appeared to student groups on the radical left.[47] They were 'scared to death of political interlopers' and refused to be corralled, although they believed that 'the lack of "political" education, the absence of dogma, placed us in a unique position *once the revolution had started*'.[48] (Tariq Ali was politely listened to and asked to leave, and visitors were informed as they entered the building that this was 'a protest against art education, not against Yanks in Vietnam'.)[49]

Shelton alleged that events at Hornsey were an integral part of student unrest, increasingly widespread in 1968: 'There is a definite pattern of procedure identifiable at both universities and colleges and the Hornsey action has followed the programme meticulously.'[50] The claim that outside agitators, militants and trade unionists had been repelled was 'a real hoax' and 'a cover for other activities'.[51] His submissions to the Select Committee complained that students were in constant touch with the Sorbonne, with Rome and Berkeley, and that unsolicited delegations had troubled staff in colleges elsewhere.[52] He forwarded literature from the Communist Party, the Radical Student Alliance and the Revolutionary Socialist

Student Federation. This, he said, had been picked up in the college, seemed 'to explain very clearly what the student unrest is really about', and proved the sit-in's covert connections with the wider movement.[53] Certainly this was quite explicit. The RSSF Manifesto called for the abolition of exams and grading and equal access to higher education but it was also opposed to imperialism, racism and immigration control, and supported national liberation struggles and workers' power as the only alternative to capitalism.[54]

On the one hand, political allegiance was strenuously denied – 'the telegram from the Beaux-Arts and the copies of *Black Dwarf* were nothing to do with it' – on the other, political interests were strongly asserted, both by opponents impugning motive (Shelton and Bains) and by activists and non-aligned dissidents concerned with mapping the broader picture (Howells and Page).[55] The difference was that for Shelton events at Hornsey were triggered by militants exploiting local grievances.[56] Politics caused the sit-in. For most participants it was the other way round. Local grievances led to the sit-in and the sit-in raised questions that opened onto political territory.[57] There was a certain pragmatism in keeping the public argument to education and staying out of sectarian politics.[58] Among many voices in endless debates, some would have agreed with the exclusion of politics reaching almost 'purge-like proportions', but others with the proposition that 'what we propose is a social revolution'.[59] How could the sit-in not be political? First, because it entangled staff and students in the machinery of local government and Parliamentary democracy (they did not think much of it); and second, because it sought to embody and precipitate social change (on a scale somewhere between the overthrow of capitalism and the overthrow of the DipAD).[60] 'The education debate was animated by a deep, instinctive conviction that the whole effort would be pointless and wasted unless it produced great changes *immediately experi-enced* in everyone's daily work and life. . . . This was what made the Hornsey upheaval "a revolution". . . rather than a "protest", or a demand for certain reforms. . . . This cellular change . . . without which "life" and "human nature" will retain their archaic character.'[61]

Whether the sit-in was, or was not, 'political', depended on context and how the term was used. There was slippage on both sides. The Labour government was at odds with Conservative councils up and down the country. Education was bound to be a political issue for local authorities charged with administering it. Bains, chair of the governors and a Tory councillor, could object to the politicization of education because he meant, presumably, that knowledge should not be shaped to sectarian interest. In a letter to staff that was published in the *Guardian*, he claimed that governors were 'regretfully forced to the conclusion that [the sit-in] was revolt for revolt's sake, the ultimate aim being the wrecking of the college by a disgruntled minority of staff and students'.[62] David Warren Piper wrote to object. 'One of the main responsibilities of educational estab-lishments is to foster progress – change – in our society. It is our job. To some of us it is a major interest. (That does not imply that we are interested in politics) . . . I am sure that many of my colleagues, both staff and students, share my dismay, bewilder-ment, and frustration at having our actions persistently perceived as political, and subversive. Our concern is educa-tion. This implies the pursuit of social change.'[63]

This was a red rag to Alderman Bains. Education, he wrote, concerned the development of 'principles, knowledge and skills'. It was a 'gross misconception' to claim that an educa-tional institution should foster progress. Piper, in admitting that social change was his major interest, had let the cat out of the bag: that was why he had taken a leading part in the Hornsey sit-in. He should look to achieve progress through the ballot-box, not through wrecking a progressive college: 'As we have seen in France, "direct action" can end in disaster, and the strong public reactions which are bound to arise may themselves give birth to a more totalitarian regime and the curtailment of the liberties which we should all carefully cherish.'[64]

Piper's response came two years later, in his two-volume edition of *Readings in Art and Design Education* (dedicated 'to Alderman Laurence Bains of Haringey Borough Council without whom I might never have summoned up the energy').[65] A sophisticated education system – that is, one that recognizes the inherent unpredictability of manpower requirements and technological development, and the right of students and workers to a degree of self-actualization – is necessarily, in Piper's view, 'an instrument of social and moral development'. He skirts the question of politics by attempting to keep the argument on educational territory (this involves keeping 'subversion' part of the dialectic of 'progress' in the interests of the polemic). 'In their role as independent critics, some educationalists, teachers or students might be expected from time to time to be at variance with powerful institutions; and as agents of social change, they might sometimes attack the existing social order. In this sense the educational system must be subversive in order to meet its obligations to society. If the educational system did not produce some people who occasionally bit the hand that fed them, then it would have failed in the task entrusted to it.'[66]

Piper was an educationalist, responsible for launching a new Industrial Design course at Hornsey with his colleague, Patrick Burke. When Burke left, Piper came to believe that the course was being undermined by other priorities, a view resented by some of his colleagues.[67] Shelton certainly felt that Piper had bitten the hand that fed him and included him in the allegation that General Studies staff had colluded in the sit-in and even encouraged it.[68] This was a source of tremendous bad feeling during the summer and vengeance after it, when staff were purged and the department was first exiled and later restructured under the erstwhile Head of Visual Research.

General Studies

The Coldstream Report brought numbers of university-trained lecturers into art colleges for the first time. This caused some friction. Studio staff could be defensive and jealous of their specialist skills. Oxbridge graduates could be appalled by poor resources, petty discipline and an apparent lack of interest in books.[69] Shelton's accusation, that the General Studies Department was disproportionately caught up in the sit-in, was not altogether wrong. It was situated in the main building, a place where students from different annexes came together for lectures and Visual Research. The head of department, David Joseph, kept an avuncular eye on student projects and saw it as the business of General Studies to stimulate reflection and verbal fluency (something that was managed with more or less investment and success). Once students had occupied the building – and given the lack of any specific direction from the authorities as to what they should do – he saw it as his duty to stay in contact with the students given that 'discussion, dialogue, conversation, listening [had to] go on'.[70] Discussion and dialogue were also the lifeblood of any General Studies seminar and despite moments of muddle and rant the sit-in at its best was an exemplary educational experience. Staff were alert to the fact that seminars had never approached this level of prolonged, impassioned, articulate argument and written productivity. Nearly all of them were present and 'to varying degrees sympathetic with the students' aims'.[71] Some – in particular David Warren Piper and David Page – 'made no secret of the fact that they saw the student upheaval as a possible way of bringing about changes in education for which they had fought in vain in the past, against the indifference and inertia of the system'.[72]

Joseph was more circumspect, but saw it as his responsibility to engage with the students and contribute to a negotiated settlement.[73] He refused to join the other heads of department in condemning the sit-in and was excluded from their meetings through the summer of 1968. Shelton put a sinister construction on the presence of Joseph's name in the list of speakers for 28 May although Joseph pointed out that the 'teach-in' was authorized, initially, and in any case his name had been added without his knowledge or consent.[74] In June, he tried to get Shelton to withdraw a possible allegation that the sit-in had 'directly resulted from the planned instigation of General Studies staff acting both individually and as a department'. And following a meeting with Shelton on 1 July, Joseph put in writing what had passed between them: that the Principal believed he had been misrepresented, that no such allegation had been made, that some of the educational arguments put forward during the sit-in were consonant with his own publicly declared strategy, and that he, Shelton, was prepared to contribute to a 'far-ranging educational debate'.[75]

When Joseph was allowed into the building in September, however, he discovered that the General Studies offices had been turned into a caretaker's flat and the files and furniture dumped in a studio. He no longer had a secretary, or even a typewriter, and his staff were exiled to Alexandra Park School two miles away.[76] In November he worked with his colleagues on a new curriculum, designed to satisfy the students, the studio staff and ultimately the requirements of the Coldstream and Summerson Councils (Hornsey was due its quinquennial review). He proposed an American-style credit system with course options in subjects including environmental study, philosophy, film, sociology, contemporary British history, the history of technology, design research methods, psychology, communication, and the study of music or literature. The idea was to maximize 'freedom of choice, flexibility of operation and the sense of personal responsibility . . . by the student'. But on 9 December it was 'irretrievably shot down in flames' at a meeting with the heads of department.[77] General Studies was to be split up and staff reallocated to studio areas. The following Saturday, 14 December, part-time General Studies staff received letters of dismissal (Joseph was neither consulted nor informed). Firing full-timers was trickier – it raised contractual issues and threatened scandal – but exasperated staff could see the writing on the wall. The department was shot from under him, as staff were dismissed, reallocated, or left to take up positions elsewhere.[78] In April 1969 he resigned.[79]

Complementary Studies and Art History were promptly merged with Visual Research and the new post of 'Head of Coordinated Studies' was advertised in the *Times Educational Supplement*. The whole procedure was rather brisk. Only two weeks were allowed for applications, no qualifications were listed and the four short-listed candidates were interviewed by Shelton and a selection of councillors and governors. There was neither internal nor external representation in the fields of Art History and Complementary Studies and Ian Simpson, the existing head of Visual Research, was appointed despite having no qualifications or experience in either of these areas. Perhaps this had always been the likely outcome: he was Shelton's ally and confidant, and the Further Education Sub-Committee had already noted the saving to be made if he was 'otherwise absorbed'.[80] Ironically, amid memos testifying to a lively debate among general studies staff in 1967, there is one to Joseph from

Warren Piper suggesting that General Studies and Visual Research be combined in the interests of a richer and more integrated programme. But this was not what happened in 1969, when a decimated department was merged for reasons of administrative convenience and control.

Shelton's Leadership

Shelton was, as Richard Wollheim observed, 'a peculiarly unpopular Principal'.[81] He had allies, of course, among the senior staff, and insofar as there were problems they were structural as well as personal. He was in a very different position by 1967 from that which obtained when he took over ten years earlier. In 1957 change was on the horizon, and Shelton had the backing of the governors and Middlesex County Council. He was about to expand the college, establish its reputation, gain DipAD accreditation and pursue his plan for an independently funded institute of advanced design.[82] By 1967 Hornsey had been transferred to Haringey Borough Council and was threatened with merger in the new North London Polytechnic. Relations with the local authority soured as Shelton pressed for more resources, the Borough Treasurer alleged financial irregularities, and staff and students mounted a vigorous campaign against absorption in the polytechnic.

When the Principal was turned out of his office on 30 May 1968, it was a practical and symbolic move that had nothing to do with personal animus. He was 'simply the titular head of an utterly frustrating system. . . . Hardly anyone had met him; some did not know who he was.'[83] Staff more than students had direct experience of the cloudy organization through which decisions emerged or failed to emerge, the lack of even a minimally effective committee structure and the poor communication across fragmented departments.[84] Shelton, for his part, did not see it as the Principal's job 'to deal with day-to-day detail, either academic or financial or clerical', but to forge relations with government, business and industry in pursuit of his educational ambitions.[85]

The problem was that the loose and vertical organization of a small suburban college, where people met in the corridors, was no longer adequate on a larger scale, across the annexes, or when there was increasing demand for staff and student participation. Legislation was pending, in 1968, that would require the local education authorities to draw up schemes of governance, subject to approval by the Secretary of State. Principals needed to command the respect and confidence of students, staff, governors and the local authority, as well as that of educationalists, industrialists, journalists and politicians. David Page insisted, in a paper to the commission set up in the summer of 1968, that 'normal British democratic procedure requires that any person at the head of an organization should be directly responsible back to that organization'. The model for the office of Principal should not be that of a ship's captain or a headmaster in sole control of a school but that of 'the chief executive of the policy-making body of the college'. This body should be elected democratically, and the governors should recognize themselves as purely advisory, in the position of a constitutional monarchy.[86] 'A Principal's first responsibility is to the students,' Eric Robinson wrote in 1968, and 'the first qualification for this post is moral courage'.[87]

Shelton was undoubtedly in a difficult position when the sit-in broke out. The demand for change on a national level exceeded his powers to meet it; and if communication in the college was 'tangled and uncertain', so was the web of relations outside it (between governors, the council, Haringey Education Committee and Further Education Sub-Committee, the Department of Education and Science and the dictates of Coldstream and Summerson).[88] That said, in absenting himself from the college, refusing dialogue with staff and students, taking refuge in conspiracy theories and absolving himself of responsibility, the Principal showed a lack of leadership and moral courage. He even planned to 'take advantage of the situation to create more freedom of action for myself' but failed to do so.[89] The *Sunday Times* got it about right. 'If Shelton had taken the sit-in by the horns, gone in and faced the students, it might have collapsed within the first day or so. But he ducked and delayed. It is no use having an authoritarian system if the man at the top can't wield his authority acceptably. In military terms, Shelton might be said to lack "officer-like qualities".'[90] Or in the words of *The Hornsey Affair*: 'If he was ever judged by the whole college, it was for his actions from 28 May on, not for the past. He could have led a victorious army: he chose to retire to a cottage.'[91]

The Quinquennial Review

The first cohort of DipAD students had enrolled in 1963 and graduated in 1966.[92] This meant that colleges recognized for the diploma in the first round of Summerson inspections were now due a quinquennial review. This required them to present evidence of their progress and to satisfy the NCDAD, both that the conditions and responsibilities of initial approval had been met, and that recognition for a further five years was justified.[93]

Page warned Shelton that the new arrangements for General Studies could threaten the college's DipAD status. In the past year, with decimated staff and no accommodation, it had been 'impossible to run a credible course in General Studies', and in the case of Art History 'some students literally did *no* work, went to no lectures, wrote no assignments etc.'.[94] He wrote to Summerson directly, but Summerson declined to 'interfere', as he put it, before the quinquennial review postponed until the autumn of 1969.[95]

The normal procedure for a review included meetings with the Principal and Heads of Department, with arrangements for consultation with other staff in the course of the visit. A report from the Visiting Board, drafted by the Chief Officer of the NCDAD, E. E. Pullee, would then be submitted to the full Council.[96] There was thus a report in writing for the NCDAD which does not appear to have been copied to the colleges under review.

NCDAD members visited Hornsey on 14 and 15 October 1969 and its DipAD status was subsequently renewed, but for only two years rather than five. This was bound to cloud the college's future and left open the question of whether it stood as a vote of no confidence in the present. A meeting between representatives of the NCDAD, Haringey Council and the governors, together with the Principal, took place on 16 January 1970. Following this, Haringey issued a press release insisting that limited recognition was based on administrative considerations, not on academic ones; it was now in a position publicly to deplore 'irresponsible and misinformed' allegations that the decision to renew DipAD status for two years represented a major criticism of the college that could lead to a permanent ban.[97]

On 20 March 1970, Richard Stranks, the Registrar, as secretary to the college's Academic Panel, asked for a written report that 'would be beneficial in allaying the uncertainties and rumours both internally and externally which continue to affect adversely the college and its future'. Members of the NCDAD promptly met again on the 'Hornsey situation' on 24 March and on 14 April, E. E. Pullee replied on behalf of the Council to A. V. Slater, Haringey's Chief Education Officer, in terms that failed to give this assurance. There was 'a lack of confidence in the academic organization, especially where consultation and decision making were concerned' and 'the senior specialist member of staff responsible for History of Art and Complementary Studies should be [made] a full member of the Executive Committee of the college'.[98] Slater replied to Pullee on 17 April, objecting that the new comments, taken in isolation, 'could give a quite unbalanced picture' of the situation as discussed on 16 January. But Pullee insisted that 'the communication made here on 16 January will not, I think, have left you or the governors and Principal in doubt that my Council's main anxiety is less in the matter of specific inadequacies or delays than in the general sense of malaise and low morale commented on by its Visiting Board'. (Pullee does not mention the fact and may have been unaware of it, but on 17 March the Hornsey Students' Union requested the blacklisting of their college and passed a unanimous vote of no confidence in the Principal and administration.)[99] Presumably the meeting on 16 January received the gist, if not the letter, of the Board's summary recommendations. Since these not only cast doubt on the college's academic and administrative structure but expressed a lack of confidence in the Principal as 'sensitive or alert to the priorities essential to raise the low morale amongst staff and students', it is perhaps more surprising that Hornsey's DipAD status was renewed at all.[100]

The Joint Report, 1970

In April 1968 the Summerson Council (the NCDAD) established a working party to make recommendations to the Coldstream Council (the NACAE) on the future development of art education.[101] This was overtaken by events as protest swept through the colleges in June, much of it directed at the structure of the DipAD.[102] Following a meeting of the Coldstream Council on 2 July, a public statement invited the submission of views from all interested parties, and in September the Secretary of State convened a Joint Committee of the NACAE and the NCDAD, under the chairmanship of Sir William Coldstream, to review the whole situation of art education in the tertiary sector.[103]

Summerson's response to what the *Joint Report* would refer to in passing as 'manifestations of unrest' was not to prescribe, but to invite principals to implement reforms. Colleges were sent a circular letter asking what they proposed to do about entry requirements, examining methods, student participation and the conduct of art history and general studies in their next five years. Summerson suggested that they might want to take into account the upsurge of new thinking on art education that had occurred over the summer of 1968: 'What we want them to do is to open the door to liberalization and to take the initiative in introducing innovations.'[104]

This was all very well, but it masked two problems. First, colleges were put in the position of speculating on innovations acceptable to the Summerson Council, and might well feel they were gambling with their credibility and DipAD status. Second, to put it a little too crudely, there had been a top-down imposition of the new Coldstream system followed by a (wide, but not universal) bottom-up rejection of it. What there had not been was a substantial piece of policy research on the basis of which the obvious questions might be answered and educational objectives developed: 'What kinds of designers exist? Can art colleges train them? Who do they work for? What do they earn? How many are needed? What social and economic conditions encourage an increased demand for good design [aside from the problems of students studying painting and sculpture]?'[105]

The *Joint Report*, published in 1970 as *The Structure of Art and Design Education in the Further Education Sector*, concluded that the 'general weight of the evidence submitted to us did not seriously challenge the fundamental concept of the DipAD'. The broad structure of the Coldstream system was maintained and the recommendations of the report were designed to buttress and extend it.[106]

The insistence in 1960, that every course should have a fine art component, was now quietly dropped, strengthening the growing autonomy of design. The position of art history in the academic segment of the curriculum was modified, prompting a formal 'note of dissent' from Nikolaus Pevsner.[107] Vocational courses were to be systematically restructured as 'design technician courses' geared to social need and known employment prospects in local industries. For the first time, and no doubt due to the fact that David Warren Piper had become a member, there was an emphasis on course objectives as the motor for course planning, although this was lightly sketched and not developed.

The most significant shift concerned the introduction of 'A' and 'B' courses: 'A' courses would offer a more flexible variant of the current diploma, and 'B' courses would involve placements of from three to twelve months and 'a substantial specialized technological content'. The stress on flexibility – in 'a more fluid system in which students may, if appropriate, pursue a broader range of studies which cross or overlap the boundaries of chief studies as hitherto conceived' – began to approach the demand of Hornsey students for a network system. This probably came from Piper and was certainly how he wanted it read: 'Whether or not DipAD courses remain fundamentally "linear" or not, the whole system, DipAD, technician, and general courses could be developed into a large network.'[108] The existing parameters of the DipAD were otherwise broadly confirmed.[109] The discussion of complementary studies and art history asked for closer integration with the studio areas, while maintaining the fifteen per cent proportion of examinable academic work.[110] Recognizing the level of public debate over the GCE entrance requirement, the report nonetheless insisted on it, asserting that the majority of those capable of completing a degree-level course would have at least five GCE passes. The distinction between diploma and vocational courses, bitterly resented at Hornsey, was now recast: four-year, Group B, sandwich courses, recruiting straight from school at 18, would have the diploma; two- to three-year design technician courses, recruiting at 16 and geared to work in local industries, would not. Towards the end of the report, 'extrinsic' and 'intrinsic' criteria for course development were set out: a demand from prospective students and a need for suitably qualified workers on the one hand, and the opportunity for 'personal benefits and satisfactions' on the other. But it did not look as though 'A', 'B' and design technician courses would meet these criteria in the same proportions and in the same way.[111]

The *Joint Report* was finally delivered to the Secretary of State – now Margaret Thatcher – on 24 June 1970. It met with hostile criticism and the introduction of 'A' and 'B' courses was never implemented.[112] The ATTI (the teachers' union) considered that it failed to 'constitute an acceptable basis on which the reorganization of art and design education should proceed'.[113] The NUS rejected it. And Richard Bourne's account in *Design* was headed 'Still at square one' (against a backdrop of continuing controversy the same establishment team had rejected radical change). The enumeration of 'A' and 'B' courses was now considered 'a stupid mistake' by Misha Black; and Shelton was quoted as asking for a different committee with more industrialists, and a better rationale, to secure the place of art and design in the polytechnics which the new proposals would make 'utterly chaotic'.[114] The Secretary of State took a year to issue her response: there would be another working party on design technician courses and further consideration on a number of other issues. Otherwise she batted the ball back to the NCDAD.[115]

RETROSPECT
Forty years on

[The occupation has] taken the term 'revolution' out of its
inverted commas, for the first time in recent British
history. Thus, a few North London crackpots achieved
more than the working class of this overwhelmingly
proletarian country . . . not by reasonable demands, but by
the technique of take-over . . . by the creation of a brief,
self-governing community that overthrew authority, and
took its life and work into its own hands.

Tom Nairn, 1968[1]

The Hornsey occupation's feverish idealism not only
carried away those responsible into the belief that they
were involved in a revolution but also attracted droves of
middle-class, middle-management, middle-of-the-road
apologists who thought they detected a reflection of what
they'd like to do but daren't.

Dave Rushton and Paul Wood, 1978[2]

How is the sit-in to be understood, and what did it achieve?
Both these quotations are from writers on the left. Nairn, a
supporter, well versed in Marxist political theory, was addressing
the readers of the *Listener* (with calculated provocation,
perhaps) in October 1968. Paris was a recent memory, the sit-in
still a pressing issue, the commission yet to report and the
college reopen; Coldstream and Summerson had established a
Joint Committee to review the future of art education and a

Parliamentary Select Committee was on the horizon. Rushton and Wood, on the other hand, were writing a decade later when the boom was over and the climate had soured. The report of the Joint Committee proved disappointing and the Ministry was slow to respond. Most of the major art colleges had been drawn into polytechnics and were now subject to a variety of pressures and cuts. Concessions on representation had helped to neutralize student unrest.[3]

The sit-in erupted when strains in the fabric of art and design education – related to, and exacerbated by, the perceived needs of corporate capital and the British economy – were compounded by inadequate resources, poor communication and a lack of leadership in the college itself.[4] Coldstream had 'sown some dragon's teeth' precisely because he had made things better. In Nairn's view the new system was 'a crystal-perfect example of the kind of reforming process doomed to end in a revolution, where – as De Tocqueville saw – each change merely generates a desire for more'. Reform opened a 'decisive gap', in Hornsey's case between its glossy profile and crumbling annexes, at a moment when 'vertiginous cultural change also impinged from outside'.[5]

Rushton and Wood have a particular aversion to the sit-in documents, finding only 'rambling speculations on education theory, leading to pie-in-the-sky recommendations, based on loose assumptions about the nature of societies, institutions and individuals'.[6] This is a little harsh (if politically coherent, against the backdrop of education cuts and rising unemployment at the tail-end of the Callaghan government, and given that they were allergic to 'a lot of self-serving claptrap about creativity').[7] They acknowledge in passing the tactical efficacy of keeping off sectarian turf, but probably underestimate the efforts and concessions required to forge a collective programme in the heat (or boredom) of the general meeting. They attack the educational arguments as 'typically introverted and mystificatory bourgeois theorizing', and they set out to provide a Marxist analysis of the ways in which the reform of design education, in particular, was linked to the developing needs of corporate capital.[8]

The links were not altogether efficient or complete. The DipAD was introduced in a liberalizing move to reform the old National Diploma in Design (which despite its name was chiefly concerned with fine art and the crafts). Coldstream was a painter in the figurative, Euston Road tradition, an establishment academic who still believed in fine art as the necessary adjunct to a training in design. (He told David Page that in 1960 there was hardly a decent library in any art school and that he 'just wanted a broad intellectual improvement'.)[9] Misha Black, Professor of Industrial Design at the Royal College of Art, argued for a separate diploma in design, but was over-ruled.[10] As Rushton and Wood point out, the membership of the Coldstream Council was set up to embrace the establishment tradition of fine art and liberal scholarship associated with the administrative classes, on the one hand, and a concern for the modernizing of design education associated with the needs of industrialists, economists, and the managerial classes on the other. In 1960 the First Coldstream Report was 'very much more arty' than the technocrats would have liked. Ten years later, after six years of a Labour government (committed, in Wilson's phrase, to the 'white heat' of technological revolution), and with the first signs of economic crisis on the horizon, the industrial lobby was in the ascendant and fine art as a core study was quietly dropped in the *Joint Report*.[11]

The sit-in, as a now-mythical event, lends itself, too easily, to one of two competing narratives: a political conspiracy aimed at bringing down a high-profile college is effectively fought off; or a triumph of collective action and radical pedagogy is successively betrayed. Rushton and Wood prefer to take the larger view. Design in the 1960s was no longer, as it was for the Bauhaus, part of a reforming social project and a necessary riposte to nineteeth-century academicism or 'art for art's sake'. Corporate capital, increasingly industrialized and centralized, aimed at a faster turnover of consumer durables. Local industries were in forced decline, and with them the need for specialized vocational courses adjusting their intakes to local firms. Designers were no longer to be involved predominantly in craft- or medium-based manufactures. They needed more flexible, abstract skills, and perhaps a sense of creativity – or at least novelty – derived from the idea of the fine artist (an artist freed under modern conditions from the constraints of patronage and the academic tradition).[12]

In a Marxist account of consumer society, designers are specially culpable. As Rushton and Wood point out elsewhere, under conditions of monopoly capitalism profits accrue from driving down costs while maximizing consumption. Fashion, industrial and graphic design, automotive design, interior design, advertising and packaging are all components of product turnover. The free play of creativity prized in the art schools is also an indispensable part of the economic system.[13] The Hornsey sit-in, in their view, failed to grasp this lesson. Hence the 'vaunted network proposals', the 'obsession with innova-tion', even the instance of a typesetter's education as already obsolete, cited in Document 11, were all arguments on the side of capital rather than against it.[14] Dissent was characterized by 'vagueness and idealism' because of 'the class position of the students (bourgeois); the economic context (boom); their isola-tion from the working class; and the related post-Stalinist vacuum' in socialist politics.[15] From this perspective the sit-in failed because of its inadequate political analysis, because the authorities were able to drive a wedge between revolutionary demands and pragmatic, issue-based reforms, and because of 'the impossibility of students in isolation changing . . . deeply embedded social institutions'.[16]

Ten years earlier, as Wood acknowledges, things 'probably didn't look like that at all'.[17] These were not the politics of the sit-in for several reasons. It stayed focused predominantly on local grievances (local to the college or specific to art education nationally). It had no *a priori* political position except, perhaps, a general sympathy with the anti-war movement and the student left. It included participants of every stripe and none. And if some were more equal than others – more articulate, charismatic or committed – it was nevertheless an item of faith to thrash out positions in extended debate at the general meeting. There was a popular front, in other words, rather than a sectarian manifesto or creed, and though it seemed pluralist and woolly to the ultra-left, it condemned that brand of politics in turn as authoritarian and stale.[18]

Kim Howells, as is evident in his contribution to *The Hornsey Affair*, would have agreed with the proposition that 'art was complicit in the bourgeois status quo' and needed to be transcended 'by a collective, revolutionary cultural practice that was not "art"'.[19] In May 1968 there was a groundswell of opposition to the gallery system among fine art 'plotters' in Crescent Road and the future of art and art education was a topical issue. But conceptual art was scarcely on their horizon (as it would be for Rushton and Wood) and never part of the political argument: Howells would later distance himself from 'cold, mechanical, conceptual bullshit' in contemporary art.[20]

As for design, was it for social need or commercial profit? Where Shelton had promoted his ambition for a graduate design research institute on the basis of its overwhelming advantages for manufacturing and the export trade, social theorists in the General Studies department were inclined to take commodity capitalism as something to be analysed rather than fed. Certainly there were tensions in the college and presumably in the design department that surfaced in sit-in documents. Was the complaint – about typesetters, for example – that students were trained to spin the wheels of profit or not trained to do it well enough?[21] Rushton and Wood were especially critical of the contributions of David Warren Piper and his erstwhile colleague, Patrick Burke. They had pioneered an industrial design course at Hornsey that focused on critical 'problem-solving', applicable in principal to any scenario, as opposed to a training in particular methods to particular ends. Rushton and Wood objected that ends were being bracketed out by system-atizing means ('state, solve, communicate, implement, validate'), and that problem-solving was not value-free. The aimed-for combination of flexibility and efficiency was after all a desideratum of British manufacturing in pursuit of increased turnover and maximized profits. There was no point developing effective problem-solving without some provision for estab-lishing whether the problem was worth solving in the first place.[22]

This was unfair for several reasons (if not from the perspective of the radical left). First, indifference to the problem to be solved was not a necessary corollary of understanding design as a systematic sequence of steps.[23] Second, Piper could respond that his job was to educate students in processes they would later develop and apply. It was not his job – nor was it in his power – to determine the work they were offered or chose to pursue. But third, unknown to Rushton and Wood, perhaps, was the depart-ment's strong concern with 'design for need': this was characterized by social projects – such as the design of thera-peutic toys for disabled children – which came to dominate the professional careers of Prue Bramwell-Davis and Jim Singh-Sandhu.[24] Students were quite explicit about the fact that they did not want 'to serve the society as it is now, because we know that we can do better than this'.[25] The concern with humanitarian or inclusive design at Hornsey was part of a growing recognition that designers should contribute long-term solutions to social problems, rather than short-lived products to a consumer economy.

On the one hand, design in the 1960s was directly related to a new phase in capitalist production involving corporate mergers, mass consumption and planned obsolescence. Larger companies with heavy investment, expensive technology and long production runs needed efficient control of the market. Design became 'an important link in the process of delivering consumers to producers'.[26] As Terence Conran put it: 'There was a strange moment around the mid-60s when people stopped needing and need changed to want. . . . Designers became more important in producing "want" products rather than "need" products, because you have to create desire.'[27] On the other hand, a figure such as Buckminster Fuller, especially influential at Hornsey, while deploring the cosmetic end of industrial design as 'a very tarnished affair', put design ahead of politics – or, at least, designers ahead of politicians – as the source of solutions to global problems. 'Making the world's totally available resources serve one hundred per cent of an exploding population may only be accomplished by a boldly accelerated design evolution. . . . This is a task of radical technical innovation rather than political rationalization. It is a task which can only be accomplished by the world's architects, inventors and scientist-artists.'[28]

These were some of the debates in design. Fine art was a different issue. Here Coldstream's reforms brought sweeping changes – an unintended consequence, perhaps – to the style and ambition of work in the studios. Small-scale, figurative work, often in the Euston Road tradition of Coldstream himself, dominated art schools in the 1950s. Now it was supplanted by large colourful abstracts, or influences from popular culture, or formal experiments with new materials and techniques.[29] Sought-after staff were younger, part-time, with a foot in the world of commercial galleries.[30]

College librarians updated their holdings and subscribed to *Artforum* and *Studio International*. By 1967, when the second cohort graduated, a reviewer was noting the influence of John Hoyland, Robyn Denny, Bernard Cohen and Morris Louis: the 'first and most startling fact' about the diploma shows was 'the ease with which many students pick up and imitate any idiom which is currently successful *today*'.[31]

There were still colleges, and corners of colleges, where traditional methods held sway; and others, such as Newcastle, Cardiff and Leeds, where under the influence of 'Basic Design' more adventurous curricula had long been in place.[32] But the introduction of the DipAD in 1963 marks the shift, symbolically, from an education still rooted in established skills in the figurative tradition to something more open-ended and investigative. This 'anti-academic' turn has been explored in an article of incisive brilliance by Thierry de Duve (though he acknowledges, of course, that in 'the everyday reality of art schools things are a lot more complex, more subtle, more ambiguous' than his schema lays out).[33]

In de Duve's analysis, the academic model can be understood as a tripartite structure linking 'talent – métier – imitation'. The academy believed in the uneven distribution of talent as something to be discovered and nurtured. Its pedagogic task was to train the apprentice artist of whatever talent in skills and techniques, that is, in art as a métier rather than a matter of inspiration and expression. Its procedures were rooted in the imitation of previous art and the observation of nature. This, broadly, was still the world of the NDD.

Over the course of the nineteenth century this model crumbled under the impact of industrialization, social upheaval, technological development (including the invention of photography), and the transformation of the cultural field (from the Salon des Refusés to the emergence of the avant-gardes).[34] In progressive quarters the old triad, 'talent – métier – imitation', was replaced by a new one, 'creativity – medium – invention'. An increasing interest in child and 'primitive' art encouraged the idea that creativity was innate (every man an artist, as Moholy-Nagy put it).[35] The task now was to establish the essential components of a visual grammar such that 'art itself, not merely skill' could be taught, 'and taught without resorting to a now obsolete tradition'.[36] It followed that an initiation into the basic grammar of art should precede more specialized study (as, on the Bauhaus model, the Foundation course preceded the DipAD).[37] The aim was not to train apprentices in their métier, but to encourage them to engage with the essence and resistance of the medium itself. The new pedagogy was no longer about imitation – of nature or canonical models – but about invention, in the struggle to discover what the medium 'has to say about itself and hasn't said yet'.[38] This was the Bauhaus model which, 'more or less amended, more or less debased', came to dominate art schools in the twentieth century.[39]

This in turn imploded with the collapse of modernism, and rather abruptly in comparison with the 'long-accomplished demise' of the academy.[40] A third constellation replaced the other two, 'attitude – practice – deconstruction'. Its origins lay in developments in art and art education from the mid-1960s including student unrest in 1968. First, attitude. Talent remained insufficiently egalitarian and creativity had come to seem mired in neo-romantic, bourgeois ideology. The most progressive art and teaching of the 1970s believed that art should be willed, whether as revolutionary rhetoric or as ideology-critique.⁴¹ A new politicized discourse dominated the most progressive (or fashionable) art schools of the 1970s and 1980s. The emergence of conceptual art – in the pages of the art magazines, in the short-lived Art Theory course at Coventry College of Art from 1969–71, and in Harald Szeemann's exhibition 'When Attitudes Become Form' in Bern in 1969 – represented a major paradigm shift from Greenbergian modernism (as from Pop, Op, and its other competitors).⁴²

Second, practice. The defining beliefs of modernist doctrine, de Duve argues, were the division of the arts according to medium rather than métier; Greenberg's reading of art's history in terms of 'a progressive surrender to the resistance of its medium'; and the emphasis on medium as a value in itself. One symbolic moment in the rejection of this paradigm came with John Latham's *Still & Chew*, 1966: pages from a library copy of Greenberg's *Art and Culture* were chewed and fermented and, in May 1967, on receipt of an overdue notice, returned in a glass phial. Latham was sacked the next day. This was art as 'practice' rather than métier or medium: a Duchampian gesture more than an academic skill or the modernist exploration of surface and support.⁴³

Third, deconstruction. From the 1970s, and partly under the diffuse influence of Jacques Derrida and Gilles Deleuze, students learned not to imitate, or even to invent, but to deconstruct.⁴⁴ This is where de Duve leaves us, with no solutions and in some despair. Students are learning to deconstruct before acquiring an artistic culture of any kind, and the new triad (attitude – practice – deconstruction), is not in his view a postmodern substitute for the old (creativity – medium – invention), but 'the same one, minus faith, plus suspicion'. It can yield strong works of art, but teaching in it is sterile.⁴⁵

So the sit-in took place at the same time as seismic shifts in art education, in criticism and in art itself: alongside the collapse of the Bauhaus model with its stress on medium specificity, and amid what Charles Harrison summarizes as substantial 'changes of direction and priority' in art between 1967 and 1969. (In the summer of 1967 *Artforum* published Sol LeWitt's 'Paragraphs on Conceptual Art', and in spring 1969 Harald Szeemann's 'When Attitudes become Form: Works – Concepts – Processes – Situations – Information' opened in Bern.)[46] These shifts were comparable to, and in a sense completed, those accompanying the rise of artistic modernism in Paris a century before.[47] The old debate, as to whether art could be taught, was supplanted by the more specific question of how art could be taught after modernism. As Louisa Buck puts it, 'How do you teach something that has no parameters? No subject, no medium, no process, no professional protocol?'[48]

These were not major issues for the sit-in, except insofar as they contributed to the turbulence of the period.[49] The impact of radical politics – of the student movement, events in Paris, and opposition to the Vietnam War – was more immediate, and the attack on the shortcomings of the DipAD and the college administration more pressing. Nor did the 1970s politics of race and gender emerge as significant issues.[50] Jim Singh-Sandhu's is the only non-white face in surviving photographs of the sit-in.[51] Plenty of women took an active part in it, but Prue Bramwell-Davis (unfazed, articulate, in 13-inch skirts) is the only one to appear consistently among the organizers, running the accounts, speaking to the press, serving on the commission and appearing before the Select Committee in 1969.[52] This was the nascent moment of 'second wave' feminism. Juliet Mitchell, a friend and colleague of Tom Nairn's, published 'Women: The Longest Revolution' in *New Left Review* in 1966; and in December 1968 Sheila Rowbotham was writing 'Women: A Call to Revolt' for a special issue of Tariq Ali's *Black Dwarf*.[53] But it is class discrimination rather than gender that figures in the sit-in documents, as in Paris (and nobody minded, on the whole, when pretty girls were arrayed for the press).[54]

But Hornsey was on the cusp of change and triggered, or prefaced, changes elsewhere. With money and support it might have done more. When the college initially failed to reopen the students resolved on a college of their own.[55] They wanted a flexible curriculum, with integrated staff-student project work and a 'network' of unfolding courses encouraging interdisciplinarity and student choice, together with a stress on socially inclusive design and, in fine art, alternatives to the production of 'bourgeois' commodities for the gallery system. It could have been an experiment testing and tempering the sit-in arguments but without substantial financial backing it never got off the ground.

It was easier to plan a radical course than a whole new institution. Three significant experiments in art education took place between 1969 and 1971: the 'Locked Room' at St Martin's College of Art (1969), the 'Art Theory' course at Coventry College of Art (1969–71) and the 'Women's Program' at California State University, Fresno (1970–1).[56]

By the mid-sixties the Advanced Sculpture Course at St Martin's, under the effective leadership of Anthony Caro, with occasional visits from Clement Greenberg and Michael Fried, had become the undisputed focus of sculptural innovation in Britain. Teaching centred on 'the crit'. Charles Harrison retained the impression of 'long sessions of struggle devoted to such issues as whether or not one more section ought to be added to some more-or-less arbitrary assemblage of scrap metal'.[57] But then Harrison was associated with a reaction against mainstream modernist art and criticism that set in from the mid to late sixties, including at St Martin's itself, where John Latham 'spat out' Art and Culture and the 'New Generation' sculptors (Philip King, Michael Bolus, Isaac Witkin, Tim Scott) were succeeded by a cohort rejecting Caro's concern with the sculptural object (Richard Long, Bruce McLean, Barry Flanagan, Gilbert and George). The undergraduate course was split in two: the 'B' course continued to be medium-based and closer to Caro's aesthetic; the new 'A' course, devised by Peter Kardia, aimed to open the sculptural field to influences from other disciplines including linguistics, phenomenology, cybernetics, psychology and cultural theory.

Kardia believed that habit was the greatest threat to creativity, and from the first day of the autumn term in 1969 the new students were locked in a white studio, for eight hours a day, for the rest of the term. They were provided with a particular material for an unspecified time – a bag of plaster, a roll of paper, a block of polystyrene – but given no instructions, no advice and no response. They were not allowed to leave, and they were not allowed to speak. Kardia's aim was deliberately to disorientate the students, 'to put them in an experiential situation where they couldn't grasp what they were doing'.[58] This was either one of the most radically inventive moves in art education, or what one of the students called 'an obtuse behavioural experiment', or some combination of the two: the sculptor Richard Deacon found it liberating and the film-maker Tony Hill, authoritarian and oppressive.[59] As pedagogy it bridged the last two models in de Duve's schema, merging a modernist exploration of medium with an emerging stress on process over the fine adjustment of the sculptural object.

At Coventry, the 'Art Theory' course was introduced by Terry Atkinson, Michael Baldwin and David Bainbridge, members of the Art & Language group, in October 1969. It drew on emerging critiques of mainstream modernism developed by conceptual artists on both sides of the Atlantic and 'lived critically and thus precariously within the institutional framework of the DipAD'.[60] It was not part of the 'complementary studies' required as an adjunct to studio work for the diploma, but neither was it 'studio activity' in the usual sense of the term. The course offered a deconstructive critique of the assumptions which, in its view, fatally compromised studio practice, including a belief in the primacy of the art-object, the importance of formal experiment in the medium, and the creative autonomy of artists and students.[61] This was a source of friction with other staff and administrators irritated by its influence and sceptical of its claims.[62] Baldwin and Bainbridge were dismissed, and the course dismantled, in 1971, after the Summerson Council confirmed that only 'studio work' in 'its commonly accepted meaning, that is to say the production of tangible, visual art objects' was acceptable for assessment.[63]

It seems reasonable to suppose that despite the radicality of these courses – and perhaps because of its vehemence – neither was in a position to escape what Paul Wood calls 'a faultline of endemic sexism' across art-college culture in general.[64] As the sculptor Reg Butler put it, bluntly, to the Slade students in 1961, the question was whether 'a woman [can] become a vital creative artist without ceasing to be a woman except for purposes of census?'[65] Robert Strand, from the perspective of the Summerson Council, admittedly unsympathetic, claimed that at Coventry many students were 'virtually brainwashed and disoriented' by a theoretical programme beyond their reach.[66] Trudi Gurling, at St. Martin's in 1966–9, recalled that women sculpture students 'received little support and encouragement' and had to 'survive the course (literally) by negotiating a way between those overbearing male egos'.[67]

It was because the American artist Judy Chicago believed that 'art educational systems are allowing the potential of women to remain untapped' that she organized the 'Women's Program' at Fresno State College in 1970–1.[68] As an experiment in art teaching this offers an instructive contrast to courses at St Martin's and Coventry (closer to avant-garde developments

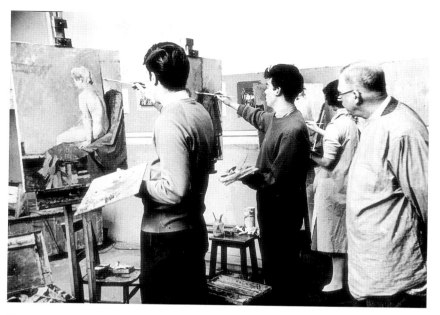

ABOVE: Jesse Cast, teaching a life-class at Hornsey College of Art, c.1957. HCA Archive, Middlesex University Learning Resources.

LEFT: Harold Shelton, c.1957. HCA Archive, Middlesex University Learning Resources.

Sir William Coldstream
photographed by Jorge Lewinski,
1963. © The Lewinski Archive.

Sir John Summerson, photographed
by Walter Bird, 1966. © The
National Portrait Gallery.

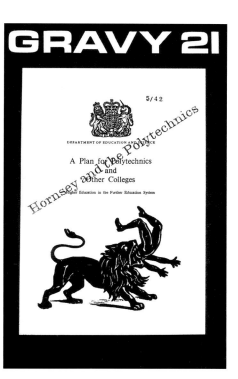

LEFT: *Gravy 21*, 'Hornsey and the Polytechnics', 1967. HCA Archive, Middlesex University Learning Resources.

BELOW LEFT: Gestetner machine. Photograph © Alex Roberts.

BELOW: *Smash the System*, linocut, reproduced from the *Listener*, 4 July 1968.

Open Forum, screenprint, 58.3 × 45.5 cm.
Royal Water Colour Society Archive,
Bankside, London.

Talk With Us, letterpress, 68.5 × 46.75 cm.
Royal Water Colour Society Archive,
Bankside, London.

Power Must Not Crush, linocut, 65.5 × 43.5 cm.
David Page Archive.

Please Avoid the College, linocut, 61.5 × 40 cm.
David Page Archive.

Kim Howells (speaking) and Alex Roberts during a sit-in meeting. Photograph © John Rae.

Prue Bramwell-Davis and David Poston during the sit-in. Photograph © Alex Roberts.

LEFT: David Warren Piper (speaking) and Alex Roberts during a sit-in meeting. Photograph © John Rae. RIGHT: Bill Ray of A1 Security Dogs. BELOW: Buckminster Fuller speaking in Rooms A and B, 21 June 1968. Photograph © Steve Ehrlicher.

LEFT: A security guard, called in to close the college on 4 July 1968 is given a cup of tea by the students. Photograph © Evening Standard/Getty Images, Hulton Archive.

BELOW LEFT: Demonstration demanding the reopening of the college, 23 September 1968. From John Goldschmidt's film *Our Live Experiment is Worth More than Three Thousand Textbooks*, 1969, courtesy of John Goldschmidt and ITN.

BELOW: Lord Longford at the Palace Cinema, 5 November 1968. From *Our Live Experiment . . .*, 1969, courtesy of John Goldschmidt and ITN.

TOP: Lawrence Bains and Harold Shelton at the Palace Cinema, 5 November 1968. From film *Our Live Experiment . . .* , 1969, courtesy of John Goldschmidt and ITN.

MIDDLE: The Ones Who Left. From 'What Really Happened at Hornsey', *Sunday Times*, 13 September 1970. Back row, left to right: Alex Roberts, Paul Harris, Richard Fletcher, Dennis Kelly; second row: Stuart Brisley, James Meller, David Joseph, Tom Nairn, Fred Scott; third row: Alan Grant, Clive Latimer, Eirian Short, June Jackson, Neil Van Allen, Joe Darracott; front row: Michael Kullman, Linda Stillitz, David Page. Photograph © Peter Laurie NISyndication Ltd, 1970.

BELOW: 'Weep-in', Crouch End Hill, 1 April 1969. A funeral procession of around 250 students complete with pall-bearers and a riderless horse with boots reversed, symbolises the death of the sit-in's hopes at the hands of Haringey Council. Photograph © Alex Roberts.

outside the classroom as both of those undoubtedly were).[69] Chicago was not uncritical of her students' tendency to lack self-confidence and a professional attitude toward their work, but she ascribed this to 'role-conditioning', to their socialization *as women*. She saw them 'sit in classes taught primarily by men, look at slides of work done almost exclusively by male artists, and . . . asked to work on projects that have little to do with their lives and concerns'. If they did try to work out of their own experience they were 'put down, ignored, laughed at, or rejected'.[70] Students on the St Martin's 'A' course worked with their given materials, in silence, locked in the studio by tutors who watched but said nothing. Students on the Art Theory course, working with language, were immersed with fiercely articulate tutors in a critique of mainstream, medium-based modernism. Neither course was concerned with traditional 'skills' and both were opposed, in their different ways, to the idea of 'self-expression'. In this respect the Fresno course was pedagogically old-fashioned but to particular ends. The students met as a group, off campus, away from the men. They went to the theatre, cinema and concerts together, read books and talked. 'At the end of two months we were ready to stop talking and start preparing art.'[71] In a modified form of consciousness-raising they worked first on themselves (as their own raw material), giving each other permission to draw on their experience as women without being 'laughed at, or rejected'. They did not develop the kind of analysis that animated the Art Theory course, or influenced later feminist artists, but they brought their own critique of the values and institutions of mainstream modernism to bear on art education with productive effects.

In Britain in 1968, fine art students made up 42 per cent of the final-year DipAD cohort and in 1969 just under 40 per cent of these were women.[72] In some respects they had been better served by the tail-end of the academic tradition or by the

Bauhaus model. The academies began by excluding them, at least from the life-room, but once they gained a foothold a sense of métier and structured discipline sustained them (think of Gwen John at the Slade).[73] The Bauhaus or modernist model, too, could prove productive, extending to women the idea of a basic training in visual grammar and experiment with the medium (think of Lee Krasner with Hans Hofmann).[74] The 'attitude – practice – deconstruction' model was more of a challenge, at least at first. To put it schematically, in terms of how women were perceived by themselves and their peers, in the academic model the principal sticking point was talent (did they have it?); in the Bauhaus model, invention (could they do it?); and in the post-Bauhaus model, attitude (were they up to it?).

In their sociological study of Coventry College of Art, Madge and Weinberger noted the observations of a colleague on the pre-diploma students enrolled in 1968–9. They fell into 'three main categories of roughly equal size': 'firstly, those whose self-confidence was severely shaken; secondly, those who though confused were not so worried by this; and thirdly, those who had positively gained in confidence and understanding. . . . In the first group were a majority of girls, in the last a large majority of boys.'[75] Like other writers, Madge and Weinberger stress the central place accorded to the 'crit': the more or less combative event in which students are required to articulate and defend the direction of their work. The art student is in their view 'driven to behave as though he [sic] had access to a charisma which may not be his to command; and he has to justify this, to himself and to his peers and teachers, in intellectualized terms and under conditions of almost unbearable ambiguity'.[76] The goal was no longer manual competence, but the possession of certain kinds of knowledge and the ability to occupy a particular position.[77] The additional ambiguity for female students was that 'attitude' – requiring the forceful assertion of one's work and identity as an artist – was at odds with the commonplace assumption that girls were essentially decorative and compliant. Lacking in virility and invention, their destiny was to marry artists, take teacher-training courses, or find some other way to square the circle until they could face the contradictions down.[78]

There is a considerable psychological literature on the distribution of supposedly 'masculine' and 'feminine' traits in the art and art-school population. One study, funded by the Calouste Gulbenkian Foundation and published shortly before the sit-in, acknowledged that 'although an *interest* in art is a feminine trait in our culture . . . young women quickly learn at art college that *practical, professional* art is a male preserve.'[79] In 1985, Griselda Pollock concluded that women had trouble in art schools because they were 'the bastion of reactionary ideas about art, teaching, self-expression and above all individualism' and that the 'positions sustained by these ideas are difficult if not impossible for women to adopt without some severe distortion or negation of aspects of their particularity as persons'.[80] Madge and Weinberger noted at Coventry that an 'emphasis on the freedom of the individual was regarded somewhat cynically by some students who were subjected to quite persistent bullying by some staff'. Women's names do not emerge in accounts of the short-lived Art Theory course which helped initiate conceptual art as a pedagogic project.[81] But conceptualism, a moment of 'radical fissure' around 1968, proved fertile for women.[82] Attitude, practice and deconstruction came together: deconstruction, as a tool turned to the analysis of cultural meanings and effects (especially around gender and sexuality); practice as a new political aesthetic (often combining images and texts); and attitude as a confident staking out of the ground (supported by a shared conversational community).[83] That art schools are not what they were is an achievement as well as a source of regret.

POSTSCRIPT

I have no doubt that in this unsophisticated world the
authorities will win – or say that they have done so – in
the end.

John Siddeley to Harold Shelton[1]

The sit-in was, and was not, defeated. The old régime was
restored and attempted to secure a return to its own definition of normality through 'a number of compromises and acts of
repression'.[2] Staff were persecuted, or sacked; students who
failed to present themselves for assessment were excluded; the
General Studies department was exiled; and the main college
'fortified' with security alarms and steel bars.[3] Page, who hung
on until 1970, bemoaned the 'survival in power without
casualty or shame of those shown to be incompetent and
lacking in common humanity'. He found it, in short, 'a worse
place than it was before': the 'Academic Panel' was only
advisory, the 'College Executive' had met once, decisions
mysteriously took themselves and it was 'all extremely
familiar'.[4] On the other hand, automatic acquiescence had
disappeared – 'a subtle, permanent change had taken place' –
and on the national stage there were signs that a complete
review of art education was on the horizon.[5]

The *Joint Report* was a disappointment, but many of the sit-
in's local aims were reached, or withered, in the following
years.[6] *The Hornsey Affair* made large claims for the sit-in: 'We
were taking over a new world, not just a few rooms in one part

of a North London college. Ten or fifty years from now, the form of art education – and possibly of society at large – will prove we were right.'[7] A decade later 'Hornsey', now the Faculty of Art and Design in Middlesex Polytechnic, stood on the brink of the Thatcherite eighties and successive cuts in education (known as 'rationalization' or 'driving down the unit of resource'). Design departments had flourished or dwindled according to student demand and the extent to which their polytechnic masters were minded to nurture them. In fine art, conceptual, performance, installation and video work were institutionalized under headings like 'Time-based Media'. Whatever the difficulties – they were many, and various – neither Hornsey nor other colleges incorporated as polytechnic faculties of art and design suffered quite the same combination of local authority politics, starved resources, autocratic admin-istration, internal division and erratic leadership that led to the sit-in.[8]

Like any historical event, and unsurprisingly, the sit-in was a different experience for different people. Staff, students, admin-istrators, governors, the Principal and the local education authority were differently placed, before their particular frustra-tions, ambitions and allegiances played themselves out at the time and in retrospect.[9] There were those who were for or against the arguments, or for the arguments but against the methods. There were those caught up in the excitement of 'a real, lasting, valuable, indelible, active, transforming, future-oriented, inspiring, adult *education*', and those who thought it 'revolt for revolt's sake'; those who lent conditional support from a distance, and those who waited it out at home.[10] Tony Judt concludes that the French events of May 1968 had 'a psychological impact out of all proportion to their true signifi-cance'.[11] A similar verdict, adapted to the circumstances and on a more local scale, could be passed on Hornsey. The impact on participants – as much as any measurable cause and effect in institutions – was for long a crucial part of *its* significance. As *The Hornsey Affair* puts it: 'Even the most unsuccessful and ingenuous attempts at direct control of a collective destiny, at "direct action" or "direct democracy", even those which end in apparent chaos and indecision, possess a humanity, a grandeur, an educative potential which dwarfs the most imposing bureaucracy.'[12]

The authorities seemed to win, in the short term, but history is not always written by the victors or even kind to them (as David Page put it, 'we knew we could beat them to the history because they weren't going to write a book').[13] We may need an open verdict on the sit-in now, as something essentially hybrid and ambiguous – neither 'introverted and mystificatory bourgeois theorizing' nor quite the 'bonfire of the old order and beacon for the new' it hoped to be – and as something not fixed and finished in the past but part of our constellation in the present.[14] What art is and can be for, the role of design, in the interests of commodity turnover or a better life, the best means of educating students in either or both: these are still questions for us now. History is Janus-faced: its meaning is in the use to which it is put.[15]

GLOSSARY

ATTI	Association of Teachers in Technical Institutions
DES	Department of Education and Science
DipAD	Diploma in Art and Design
GCE	General Certificate of Education
LEA	Local Education Authority
MORADE	Movement for Rethinking Art and Design Education
NACAD	National Advisory Council on Art Education ('Coldstream Council')
NCDAD	National Council for Diplomas in Art and Design ('Summerson Council')
NDD	National Diploma in Design
NUS	National Union of Students
SIAD	Society of Industrial Artists and Designers
UGC	University Grants Committee

NOTES

Preface & Acknowledgments (pages 7–10)

1   Singerman (1999), p.1.

2   The Summerson Report (1964) noted: 'There is a temporary shortage of suitably qualified art-history teachers. But we are inclined to think that it is not necessarily the art historian with the highest academic qualifications who is the best teacher of art history in a college of art.' Extracted in Ashwin (1975), pp. 11–12. See also NCDAD papers in the National Archives, DB4/40, History of Art Panel, minutes of meeting 21 Nov. 1967, which note discrimination in postgraduate applications between students with university degrees and those with the diploma and express the view 'that the DipAD should be seen as a University Degree equivalent and eligible for postgraduate studies in a University'. Particular individuals were influential too, of course, beginning with the calligrapher Donald Jackson, teaching Saturday morning classes at Ealing Art College, who recommended Hornsey as an ambitious institution. I embarked on the Fine Art course at the end of my pre-diploma year with Clive Tickner and Mick Dunn, and I remember our friendship with gratitude and affection. The Sculpture department was a miserable place to be a female student but the General Studies staff, stimulating and convivial, made up for the rudeness or indifference of the studio. David Joseph, John Field, Joseph Darracott, Suzanne Lang and eventually Nikolaus Pevsner, external examiner at Hornsey and Chair of Summerson's Art History Panel, encouraged my interest and supported my passage to postgraduate research.

3   Karl Marx, *The Eighteenth Brumaire of Louis Bonaparte* [1852], London: Progress Publishers, 1977, p.10.

4   It is unlikely that the Principal would have agreed to my employment had he known otherwise.

5   My telephone number, among others, is in Shelton's papers; my signature is in one of the sit-in visitors' books; and David Page (the General Studies lecturer who lived at 14 Hanley Road), still has the *Atelier Populaire* poster we brought back to Hornsey from the École des Beaux-Arts, from a trip to Paris that coincided, quite fortuitously, with the May *événements*.

6   I aim for a 'good enough' history and lay no claims to omniscience or the studied neutrality of the classic realist text. This is to touch on extensive debates in historiography, of course. Since there is no one authoritative position from which the truth of the past is discovered or experienced, the best we can expect is a field of generous, intelligent and sceptical conversation about it, adequate to the evidence, conducted in good faith, impelled by the investments of the present but not disabled by them. 'Good-enough' history is borrowed from D. W. Winnicott's concepts of good-enough mothering and the good-enough holding environment in psychoanalysis.

7   Karl Figlio, 'Oral History and the Unconscious', *History Workshop Journal* no. 26, 1988, pp. 120–32 (quotation p. 129). *The Hornsey Affair*, put together by participants and completed in November 1968, was rushed out as a Penguin Education Special in 1969.

8   On 'social dramas' see the anthropologist Victor Turner, *Drama, Fields and Metaphors: Symbolic Action in Human Society*, Ithaca, N.Y.: Cornell University Press, 1974. On the 'microphysics of power' and its 'capillary forms' see Michel Foucault, *Discipline and Punish: the Birth of the Prison*, transl. Alan Sheridan, New York: Routledge, 1979, pp. 29-30; and *Power/Knowledge: Selected Interviews and Other Writings 1972–1977*, ed. Colin Gordon, Brighton: Harvester Press, p. 39. For a succinct account of 'microhistory', on which there is an extensive literature, see Giovanni Levi, 'On Microhistory', in Peter Burke ed., *New Perspectives on Historical Writing*, University Park, Pa.: Pennsylvania State University Press, 1991, pp. 93–113.

Epigraph (page 11)

1   Document 3a in DP Box 4, Hornsey College of Art, 31 May 1968.
2   Editorial in the Wood Green, Southgate and Palmers Green Weekly Herald, 27 Sept. 1968, quoted in The Hornsey Affair (1969) p. 207.

Back Story: NDD to DipAD (pages 13–19)

1   Tom Stoppard, *Rock 'n' Roll*, London: Faber and Faber, 2006, pp. 106–7.
2   The jeweller Gerda Flöckinger, who taught at Hornsey until 1967, quoted in Peter Laurie and Roger Law, 'What Really Happened at Hornsey', *Sunday Times Magazine*, 13 Sept. 1970, pp. 36–47 (quotation p. 36).
3   Tom Nairn, 'On the Subversiveness of Art Students', *Listener*, vol. 80, 17 Oct. 1968, pp. 491–2 (quotation p. 492). The claim was contested elsewhere on the political left, for example by Dave Rushton and Paul Wood: 'The whole enterprise at Hornsey . . . reek[ed] of spontaneist naïveté from top to bottom' (in Rushton and Wood (1978), p. 26).
4   See for example Crick and Robson (1970), p. 82; Fraser (1988), p. 248; Kurlansky (2004), p. 253; and at greater length, Crouch (1970), pp. 111–14. For accounts by participants see *The Hornsey Affair* (1969) and Tom Nairn and Jim Singh-Sandhu, 'Chaos in the Art Colleges', in Cockburn and Blackburn (1969), pp. 103–18.
5   Minutes of the Governing Body of Hornsey College of Art and Crafts, 14 Mar. 1957. Shelton's Principal's Report, 31 Oct. 1957, refers to a meeting with Her Majesty's Inspectors on 30 July to discuss the proposals agreed by the governing body for the expansion of the college. HCA Archives, HCA/1/01/C/1 1956/7.

Hornsey School of Art was founded as a private venture by Charles Swinstead in 1882 and housed in purpose-built studio accommodation on Crouch End Hill in North London. By 1904 it was under the joint control of the Board of Education and the Middlesex County Council. In 1920 the County Council took over full financial responsibility for the School, reconstituted the Board of Governors, and ran it until 1965 when it was transferred to Haringey Borough Council. See Ashwin (1982), pp. 9–10, 18, 24. Charles Swinstead (Headmaster 1882–90) was succeeded by his son Frank Swinstead (Headmaster and then Principal, 1890–1927), by Frank's deputy John Moody (Principal 1927–47), then by John Platt (1947–57) and finally by Harold Herbert Shelton (Principal from 1957 until 1 Jan. 1973, when Hornsey College of Art was merged with Enfield and Hendon Colleges of Technology to form the new

Middlesex Polytechnic). Shelton (1913–94) had studied design at the Royal College of Art (1936–9), joined the Air Ministry as a trainee engineer in 1939, and in 1941 became a personnel officer with the Ministry of Supply. After the war he worked as a designer for F. W. Grafton & Co. in Manchester, designing and costing new ranges of clothes. He was Principal of Carlisle College of Art from 1948–57, and Assistant Director, Middlesex Polytechnic (until 1975 also acting Dean of Art and Design), from its inception in 1973 to his retirement in 1978.

6   By 1957 there were 190 schools, colleges and departments of art in the public sector, 140 of which entered students for the Intermediate Examination and 110 for the National Diploma. See the very thorough account in Strand (1987), p.7. I am indebted to Robert Strand's book and to the work of Clive Ashwin (1975, 1982).

The first DipAD courses were launched in 1963; the last NDD was awarded in 1967. For student numbers see Clare Francis and David Warren Piper, 'Some Figures about Art and Design Education' in Piper (1973), pp. 26–9.

7   Medley (1983), p. 221. Medley was head of painting at Camberwell School of Art and later a panel member for the Summerson Council (the NCDAD). Acknowledging that the 'new order was not born without trauma' he nevertheless believed it responsible for 'an outburst of creative energy in the art schools that was a fuelling element in the resurgence of British art in the sixties'. The artist Peter Blake, on the other hand, regretted the passing of the old Intermediate/NDD training although it 'had been a very strict, Victorian-style examination' ('A Drawing Lesson' in Hetherington (1996)). Ashwin (1975), pp. 83–6, gives the list of fifty-five design and craft areas, and sample questions.

8   Strand (1987), p.6. Norbert Lynton recalled that 'a whole year of sculpture students failed because the external assessor appointed by the Ministry, an RA sculptor whose affections [did] not stretch to anything post-Carpeaux, just did not like the work.' 'Waiting for Coldstream', *Studio International*, vol. 178, Sept. 1969, pp. 58–9.

9   Dave Rushton and Paul Wood are keen to stress that far from the introduction of the DipAD being 'an isolated innovation, comprehensible solely in terms of a struggle . . . against the straitjacket of the NDD system' it should be understood as 'an epiphenomenon of [the] Cold War'. See Rushton and Wood (1978), pp.9–10. But they also point out that the NDD threatened to implode if colleges withdrew from the system in favour of their own locally recognized courses (p. 17). They conclude that 'the core of the NDD was under threat from two directions': from the monopolization of large-scale industry, at the expense of ties between local schools and local manufacturing; and from the university fine-art lobby, concerned with the cultural heritage. Both axes – the industrial and the cultural – were aimed at transforming the NDD but, as tensions emerged between them, the influence of the culture lobby tended to dilute and confuse the aims of the industrialists (p. 10). See also Paul Wood, 'Between God and the Saucepan: Some aspects of art education in England between the middle of the nineteenth century and the end of the twentieth', *The History of British Art* vol. 3, *Art and the Modern World: From the Victorians to Now*, London: Tate Publications, forthcoming, 2008.

10   Ashwin (1982), pp. 90–1. One of Shelton's first tasks as Principal was to assess how the college might best prepare itself for the changes ahead. The Principal's Report for June 1957 set out his *Recommendation for the Development of the Hornsey College of Art*, HCA/1/01/C/1 1956/7.

11 Principal's Report, June 1957, HCA/1/01/C/1 1956/7. The government had announced in 1957 that advanced work would be concentrated in nine élite Colleges of Advanced Technology (CATs). These would focus on degree-level work, shed part-time and lower-level courses, and enjoy national rather than regional status and catchment areas.

12 Ministry of Education Circular 340, 14 July 1958. HCA/1/01/C/1. The first task of the NACAE, appointed by Lord Hailsham in January 1959, was to consider the Report of the National Advisory Committee on Art Examinations within the framework of Circular 340.

13 Since acronyms are indigestible and less easily distinguished, I refer to the Coldstream Council and Summerson Council rather than (more correctly) the NACAE and the NCDAD. In March 1960 Shelton reported to his governing body that: 'Both staff and students are aware that changes are imminent, and there is a restless feeling,' although interested students hoped to be able to take one of the new courses. Principal's Report 17 Mar. 1960. HCA/1/01/C/1. Some students were taking evening GCE courses in readiness.

14 There are useful extracts from the First Coldstream Report (1960), officially the *First Report of the National Advisory Council on Art Education*, in Ashwin (1975), pp. 93–103. It is discussed in Strand (1987), pp. 8–13. The Second Coldstream Report on Vocational Courses in Art and Design, appeared in 1962; the Third Coldstream Report, on Post Diploma Studies in Art and Design, in 1964; and an Addendum to the First Report, on the question of pre-diploma courses, in 1965. On Coldstream, figurative painter and Slade Professor of Fine Art, see Laughton (2004); and also Julian Bell's judicious and sympathetic treatment of Coldstream as artist and administrator in his review of Laughton, *London Review of Books*, 2 Dec. 2004, pp. 23, 25. Christopher Frayling suggests that 'the Coldstream people seem to have had at the back of their minds the Slade as a model for fine art teaching (still the centre of the curriculum), the Courtauld as a model for scholarship, and the Royal College as a model for professionalism.' Frayling (1987), p.174.

15 Hornsey would need to gain full accreditation to maintain its position. Shelton noted that work would need to be grouped into major areas of study under an experienced Head of Department. At this point there was only one recognized department, 'Women's Crafts', and a number of sections with lecturers or senior lecturers acting as 'Heads of Department' (Principal's Report, 27 June 1957, HCA/1/01/C/1). The Department of 'Women's Crafts' included 'dress design, fashion drawing, dressmaking and tailoring, needlework and lingerie, millinery, embroidery and lace making, hand loom weaving, spinning and dyeing' (Ashwin (1982), p.29).

16 Full-time students on degree or degree-equivalent courses had a right to maintenance grants from their local educational authorities which could be taken up at any institution that offered them a place.

17 In Shelton's view, inadequate accommodation and equipment were rapidly prejudicing the status of the college. It needed to expand to embrace a wider range of work and to consolidate advanced courses. He looked to the possibility of erecting purpose-built studios and workshops across the road, but the Ministry's plans were developing at a speed that outstripped its building programmes.

18 See paras 54, 55, 57, 58, extracted in Ashwin (1975) pp.100–1. The 'development

in art schools of new full- and part-time courses of a more strictly vocational kind . . .
is likely to prove necessary when the [DipAD is] introduced. Other types of courses suit-
ed to local conditions will, no doubt, suggest themselves.'

19 Ashwin (1982), pp. 23–4. See also Bell (1963); Macdonald (1970); and Callen
(1979). Photographs of the Slade at the turn of the century show the Professor, Fred
Brown, surrounded by women in a sea of hats.

20 Ashwin (1982, pp. 13, 35). Ashwin does not give sources, having hoped at the time
to provide 'a more detailed and comprehensive history' with full references 'in due
course' (p.7). The college was then known as the Hornsey School of Art.

21 Circular 340, 14 July 1958: 'This is no less important, whether it takes the form of
full-time work at a lower level, or courses for part-time students vocational or non-
vocational. Art schools have much to contribute to the raising of standards of artistic
performance and to a growing appreciation of art throughout the country.' See also
Ashwin (1975, p.102), *First Report of the National Advisory Council on Art Education:
Addendum*, August 1965.

22 The Summerson Report questioned whether colleges 'attracted by the financial
and academic advantages of diploma courses' had sufficiently considered 'how, or
whether' these could be combined with lower-level work (para. 20, extracted in Ashwin
(1975), p.107). Part-time provision helped secure a college in its community as local
residents came in for evening or afternoon classes, and the loss of this connection no
doubt hindered relations with local ratepayers at the time of the sit-in. Shelton's
Principal's Report for 17 March 1960 noted a continued increase in the number of full-
time students (HCA/1/01/C/1).

23 Ashwin (1975, pp. 104–113), discusses the Summerson Report (1964), officially
the *First Report of the National Council for Diplomas in Art and Design*. Summerson was a
distinguished architectural historian, Curator of the Sir John Soane Museum and lecturer at Birkbeck College, University of London.

24 There were twenty-six members, six of whom were also members of the NACAE
(the Coldstream Council) in order to facilitate cooperation between the two bodies.
On the NCDAD and its visits see Strand (1987), pp. 13–21. The Fine Art panel chair
was Professor Claude Rogers, the Graphics chair William Stobbs, the Fashion &
Textiles chair Edward Pullee, the Three-Dimensional Design chair Professor R.Y.
Goodden, and the History of Art and Complementary Studies chair Professor Nikolaus
Pevsner.

25 Strand (1987), p.13. The National Council for Technological Awards received a
Royal Charter in 1964 as the Council for National Academic Awards. The NCDAD
merged with the CNAA in 1974, becoming its committee for art and design, and under
the terms of the merger the DipAD became a BA (Hons.).

26 Summerson Report (1964), para.4. In other words it offered a limited emancipation from the common syllabus and centralized assessment of the NDD system that still
stopped short of the freedom enjoyed by self-validating universities.

27 The invitation from the Summerson Council to submit course proposals was
extended in Memorandum No 1, July 1961. The Summerson Report is extracted and
discussed in Ashwin (1975, pp. 104–13) and Strand (1987), pp. 19–20.

28 An unnamed County Education Officer and Summerson panel member, cited in
Richard Wollheim, 'Should Art be Respectable?', *Sunday Times Magazine*, 8 Sept. 1968,

p.22. Dr Richard Beeching (1913–85) was appointed by the Conservative government in 1961 to cut spiralling losses of around £140,000,000 per year on the British Rail network. His report, *The Reshaping of British Railways* (1963), proposed axing a third of the network.

29 One college withdrew and thirteen were ruled out by the Ministry on administrative grounds.

30 By 1969 forty colleges had achieved DipAD recognition. See Macdonald (1970), for a list of these colleges and courses in Appendix B. In Fine Art, Hornsey was approved for Painting with Drawing and Sculpture with Drawing. Subsequent reviews approved courses in Three-Dimensional Design and Fashion & Textiles.

31 Strand (1987), p.19. Some local education authorities took action and made fresh applications, others turned to a range of non-diploma courses instead. Rushton and Wood (1978), p. 19 point out that despite the Summerson Council rhetoric of 'standards' as their sole criterion, exactly, or almost exactly, one third of courses were recognized in each of the four Coldstream 'areas' (the slightly smaller percentage in Fashion & Textiles precisely balanced by the slightly larger percentage in Three-Dimensional Design). This seemed to them too tidy a coincidence. Hundreds of assessors were crisscrossing the country in small groups, but their views were fed to a sub-committee of only seven members – the chairs of the five panels together with the chair and vice-chair of the Summerson Council – which made the final recommendations to Council.

32 Strand (1987), pp. 26–8. As late as the summer of 1967, the Chairman of the Association of Art Institutions, at its annual conference, remarked on the diminishing number of topics for discussion unless there should be 'some great upheaval of which we are not, thank God, aware'. This was quoted, ruefully, by M. R. T. Cowern in his address the following year (15–17 July 1968), extracted in the NSAE [National Society for Art Education] Bulletin for October 1968, unpaged (Hornsey papers, Bankside Gallery).

The Polytechnic Question (pages 20–31)

1 Bryan Robertson *et al.*, letter to the editor of *The Times*, 22 June 1967, quoted in Laughton (2004), p.245.

2 The Government set up a Committee of Enquiry under Lord Robbins in 1961. Its report, published in 1963, led to the creation of six new universities and the upgrading of ten Colleges of Advanced Technology to university status. About 8.5 per cent of the relevant age-group was in higher education in Britain if teacher-training and technical colleges were included. See Sampson (1965), pp. 218–19.

3 Crosland's views were made known in a celebrated speech at Woolwich Polytechnic on 27 April 1965, copies of which were circulated to all local education authorities and colleges on 6 May 1965. See National Archives ED206/3, NACAE minutes (66) 2. Crosland later regretted alienating the vice-chancellors – he had referred to the 'snobbish, caste-ridden, hierarchical obsession with university status' in Britain – which made negotiation with them difficult and laid him open to the charge that he was effecting a two-tier system in higher education of the type that comprehensive schools were designed to eliminate in secondary education. These points are made, and Crosland's arguments at Woolwich summarized, in Kevin Jefferys, *Anthony Crosland*, London: Richard Cohen, 1999, pp. 108–9.

4   The White Paper sought to assure them that there would be 'no question of creating a rigid or ossified pattern irrespective of traditions and individual circumstances' but they remained largely, and justifiably, unconvinced. See *A Plan for Polytechnics and Other Colleges: Higher Education in the Further Education System*, HMSO, May 1966, 'Summary of Proposals', 28 (i) – (vi). Strand (1987), p. 56, notes the concern of members of the Summerson Council that art departments would lose out in the competition for resources with larger and more powerful departments of science and technology. Robinson (1968), pp.31–2, notes that the White Paper was also attacked by the technical college lobby, 'because it left the excluded colleges in limbo', and by the universities, 'belatedly appreciating the implications for them of the growth of a new state university system'. (In Appendix A he reprints Crosland's Parliamentary Statement, 5 April 1967, with the list of colleges to be merged.) For the art colleges, due in part to their recent history – no school or department of art that was part of a technical college had gained DipAD recognition – association with technical colleges meant failure and independence was a necessary condition for success. See also Strand (1987), pp. 54–69, on the White Paper and ensuing developments, including correspondence from Coldstream to the editor of *The Times*, and from Summerson to the Secretary of State, the relevant local authorities, and the principals of art colleges likely to be incorporated into polytechnics. The Alex Roberts Papers include a 'Report on North London Polytechnic Situation July 1968: Diary of Events Concerning Hornsey College of Art'. This begins with consideration of the White Paper at a governors' meeting on 3 June 1966, to which the Principal reported staff concerns, and continues through the formation of a committee (four governors, five staff and the Principal), on 17 May, to prepare a draft scheme for the future of the college.

5   This had become Middlesex Polytechnic by its inception in 1973. Staff encouraged student participation in the anti-poly campaign in 1967, and made facilities in the Graphic Design department available for printing leaflets and banners. This led to bad feeling in 1968, when access to graphic equipment was refused, and sit-in posters had to be produced with more primitive linocut and basic silkscreen techniques. (Communication from David Page, 16 Nov. 2005.)

6   Wright, reported in notes on a meeting at Woolwich Polytechnic, 18 Oct. 1967, HHS Archive, Victoria and Albert Museum Art and Design Archives, AAD/1997/9 (hereafter HHS) Brown Box 7. Wright claimed that Hornsey College of Art, an institution of international repute with four DipAD areas, one hundred pre-diploma students, seventy teacher-training students, five annexes and a special film and television course at Alexandra Palace, would be swallowed up in a polytechnic and perhaps lose DipAD recognition. Shelton is quoted from the Memorandum of the Principal to the Select Committee on Education & Science, Sub-Committee B, Hornsey College of Art, 30 Jan. 1969 (inquiring into student unrest), HHS Brown Box 4. His notes for this memorandum (Brown Box 6) claim that 'the promotion of a successful student revolution depends upon selecting an educational establishment which has obvious underlying reasons for discontent' before going on to identify the 'violent clash' as providing an opportunity to radicals pursuing a political agenda of their own. See also Tom Nairn and Jim Singh-Sandhu, 'Chaos in the Art Colleges' in Cockburn and Blackburn (1969), pp. 103–18: 'Although smiled on by the authorities, this agitation [against the polytechnic] had the effect of generating the one thing the system normally conspires to keep hidden: a feeling that it was *possible* to change things by intelligent, direct common action. A few months later, the fruit was harvested in the shape of the famous sitin' (p. 113).

7   Strand (1987), pp. 56–7. Nikolaus Pevsner (member of the Summerson Council and chair of its Art History panel) wrote to Shelton, 8 Nov. 1967: 'As you will have realized at the meeting of principals, the Summerson Council for the last nine months or so has regarded it as its principal job to protest against the idea of the merger of colleges of art with polytechnics. The Department of Education [and Science] has never budged and now, all that can be hoped for is the publicity given to individual cases.' HHS Brown Box 4 contains a range of correspondence on the polytechnic issue in a green card folder.

8   Bryan Robertson *et al.*, letter to *The Times*, 22 June 1967, quoted in Laughton (2004), p.245.

9   Coldstream's response in *The Times*, 28 June 1967, is printed in full in Strand (1987), p. 62.

He believed that the art colleges were just 'getting into their stride' after the introduction of the DipAD. The DES letter to Coldstream enclosing a copy of the *Future Pattern of Higher Education within the F. E. System*, and Coldstream's response are in the NACAE Papers, ED206/3, (66) 2 and 3 [i.e. second and third meetings in 1966]. Coldstream complains of lack of time to consider the proposals, and insists that experience shows colleges of art to be generally the most suitable environment for art and design education: there should be no pressure on local authorities to integrate major art colleges with other further education establishments just because they are close by.

10 Strand (1987), p. 60. Summerson's deputy and eventual successor, Stuart Mason, was also present. Presumably this meeting took place at some point in or around July 1967.

11 On 11 Aug. 1967 Summerson wrote to all the DipAD college principals that it was now a matter of safeguarding the freedom of art colleges within the new system (letter reprinted in Strand (1987), p.60). Summerson had conveyed to Crosland, in a letter dated 1 Aug. 1967, the 'widespread sense of despondency, even demoralization' resulting in some quarters from 'the polytechnic issue and the particularly unhappy impact it has had in the field of art education'. Goronwy Rees replied for the Department on 18 Aug., suggesting that 'the despondency may be lifted when it becomes more widely understood that polytechnics will be substantially different institutions from the traditional technical colleges' and arguing that art colleges would gain 'from the greater opportunities for cross-fertilization between art and technology and social studies' (Strand (1987), pp. 57–8). The Hornsey campaign could of course point to the fact that colleges falling within the remit of the Inner London Education Authority – including Chelsea, Central and St. Martin's – were not being forced into mergers; why could Hornsey not also retain its independence? A fierce if belated attack on the 'polytechnicization' of art colleges was launched by the painter Patrick Heron under the heading 'Murder of the Art Schools' in the *Guardian* on 12 Oct. 1971. Heron was a member of the Fine Art Panel of the Summerson Council and he persuaded many of his colleagues into a mass resignation. Strand sees this as a futile gesture: 'To jump overboard in stormy seas is seldom the best way to save the ship or to change its course' (p. 65). His own view, with the benefit of hindsight, is that the advantages of being drawn into

a polytechnic outweighed the drawbacks (he acknowledges that this is 'a question on which no neat balance sheet can be drawn up', p. 64).

12 Robinson, *The New Polytechnics: A Radical Policy for Higher Education*, London: Cornmarket 1968, p.11. Robinson was a former President of the ATTI and academic head of the Faculty of Arts at Enfield College of Technology.

13 Robinson (1968), pp. 9, 10. 'The creation of the polytechnics is . . . an attempt to create a new type of institution with new educational forms and new systems of government which, if it is successful, could be the basis of a comprehensive reorganization of higher (or rather tertiary) education in fifteen or twenty years' time' (p. 173). This is exactly what university administrators at the other end of the political spectrum felt threatened by: 'The whole aim of the scheme was to set the universities in a position where at a later stage they could be reduced to the same degree of "social control" as the polytechnics on grounds of unresponsiveness to social needs, expensiveness, exclusiveness, of playing the kind of socially divisive role the independent secondary schools are supposed to do, and so on' (D. C. Watt, 'The Freedom of the Universities. Illusion and Reality, 1962–69' in C. B. Cox and A. E. Dyson eds., *Black Paper Two: The Crisis in Education*, London: The Critical Quarterly Society, 1969, pp. 119–125, quotation p. 122).

14 Robinson (1968), pp. 46, 47. Polytechnics could bring about change in universities only if they did not aspire to be like them: they should open out to the community; make bids for local radio and television stations; extend to computing, marketing and industrial design courses; and run parallel offices offering services to local firms that could make use of their expertise. Robinson (1968), pp. 39, 133.

15 Robinson (1968), p. 89. Since Robinson regretted the shadow that university academicism cast back onto the secondary school curriculum, he approved of the fact that the 'leaders of art education have even made efforts to keep their potential students out of grammar school sixth forms' in order to protect them from it.

16 Robinson (1968), p. 153. Robinson also pointed out that in 1964 the Summerson Report had advocated the value of collaboration between art and technical colleges and encouraged development of advanced education in technology, commerce, art and pedagogy on single campuses. There was little or no reference to this in the battles over 'polytechnicization' in 1967 (*First Report of the National Council for Diplomas in Art and Design*, 1964, para. 22, cited Robinson (1968), p. 184).

17 Elma Askham and Harry Thubron, 'The Case for Polytechnics', *Studio International*, vol.174, Sept. 1967, pp. 82–3. Askham and Thubron argued that the divisions and constraints that had bruised the experience of art departments in technical colleges need not be taken as precedents, since polytechnics would be neither technical institutions nor third-rate universities but something larger and quite distinct. Integration with larger institutions was a necessary stage in the further evolution of art education. Geri Morgan wrote in response from Hornsey College of Art that the Thubrons' 'closer relationship between art and other disciplines' was already happening at Hornsey. Engineering and science departments in the new polytechnics would produce technocrats, not creative individuals with whom an art college dialogue would be possible. 'For and Against Polytechnics', *Studio International*, vol. 175, Jan. 1968, p.8.

18 Tom Nairn, 'The Death of Art Education', *New Statesman*, 6 Oct. 1967, reprinted in *Gravy* 21, pp. 9–10.

19 *Gravy* 22, p.1. 'Interview with Ken Garland' by Clare Francis. Garland points out that while the Tory councillors were all opposed to Hornsey going into the polytechnic, one of the majority Labour group of councillors, who as a governor had also been opposed to the merger in May, introduced a contrary motion in an education meeting a few weeks later, suggesting there had been pressure on the majority group to change their minds.

20 HHS Press Cuttings 1968, clipping 10 Nov. 1967 from the [Hampstead and Highgate?] *Express and News*. Shelton is quoted as pointing out that most of the college's money – *c*. £650,000 – came from the Department of Education and Science, with Haringey providing only the remaining £60,000, and 'I don't think the councillors really understand this form of higher education at all'.

21 'Hornsey and the Polytechnics', *Gravy* 21, undated but from internal evidence October 1967; edited by Jim Singh-Sandhu, Roger Haydon and Terry Scales (HCA Archive). *Gravy* was mainly financed by the Student Union, but this issue was completely supported by the college. There were some dissenting, or at least cautious, voices. Alan Grant, a lecturer in General Studies, suggested that 'we think very hard before rejecting altogether' the polytechnic idea (better in than out, perhaps), and others were keen to distinguish their opposition to Hornsey's incorporation from an opposition to polytechnics in general. See Grant in *Gravy* 21, p.3, 'Now about this Poly business . . .' and David Joseph, Head of General Studies, *Gravy*, 21 p.2, 'Poly Wolly Diddle'. (Joseph suggested that art colleges may only have been included in the White Paper 'at the eleventh hour' after earlier drafts had left them out.) There was some awkwardness about the fact that the ATTI, the Association of Teachers in Technical Institutions, was in favour of the polytechnic, and thus opposed to the views of its own membership among staff at Hornsey College of Art. Shelton is quoted in 'Poly-Art?' by Fiona McCarthy, an undated clipping from the *Guardian* reproduced in *Gravy* 21 immediately before page one. He was furious at having learned that Hornsey was to be merged in a polytechnic through an informal call from a colleague, rather than in a letter from the Department or a visit from the local authority.

In fact there seems to have been more debate and less unanimity earlier, or behind the scenes. General Studies staff, as academics with a commitment to weighing pros and cons in reasoned argument, were especially motivated to engage in debate and to see the possibilities in the polytechnic system. See 'A Case for Going into the Polytechnic', unattributed and undated, DP Box 8. The author (not David Page) points out that the 'other parts of *this* poly are not dominated by technological Neanderthalers. They have very strong Social Science sections. . . capable of understanding and collaborating with Art & Design staff and students: they are on the whole young, energetic, and challenging in their thinking. . . Hornsey *could* go into the poly at a high level of energy, demanding certain things & expanding rather than contracting. (For instance, a film school; the incorporation of music, drama, architecture etc.)'

David Joseph, Head of General Studies, assured Shelton that he was 'open-minded', and that 'though I may wish to assume the role of devil's advocate in order to test the durability of objections to the concept of a polytechnic, which are based on highly subjective experiences or a priori assumptions, I do not wish to appear to be at the head of a faction pressing for the acceptance of polytechnic proposals'. Memo to Shelton from David Joseph, 19 Oct. 1966. See also 'Comment on the [15] Points Raised for the

Formation of a Polytechnic' and 'Comment on the [32] Points Raised Against the Formation of a Polytechnic', D.J.W.P [i.e. David Warren Piper], 8.11.66 (many of them developed or reproduced in *Gravy* 21, 1967, p.13); and 'Polytechnic: a comment on the arguments for and against' by D.J.W.P., dated 14.11.66 (all in DP Box 2). Piper thrashes out the arguments and acknowledges the principal fears – that the college would lose its autonomy in a polytechnic as well as lose out in the struggle for budgets and resources – but concludes that the 'solution to these problems lies in enlightened and competent government of the polytechnic and on the successful creation of a new kind of institution which is unlike either present day art colleges or colleges of technology. Much of the case for and against the establishment of a polytechnic hinges on the likelihood of such enlightened college government materializing' (p.2). These papers largely embrace the points made in 'A Brief Summary of the Objections of Hornsey College of Art Students and Staff to the Proposed North London Polytechnic' (unattributed, undated) and 'Art Students and the Plan for Polytechnics' by Nicolas Wright (President of the NUS at Hornsey), 7.2.68 (NW papers); and Shelton's 14 points against incorporation in 'Notes relevant to the proposed polytechnic', 22 May 1967, HHS Archives, Brown Box 9.

22 The staff and student Joint Action Committee was dedicated to 'the development of Hornsey College of Art as an autonomous institution' (*Gravy* 21, p.8). There was also a Staff-Governors Committee and a College Council representing the staff. See the Joint Action Committee's announcement of a 'Polytechnics Action Day Monday 23rd October 1967', flyer dated 18 October 1967, over the names of D. J. Warren Piper for the Staff Association and Nicholas Wright for the Students' Union. This urges a mass lobby and picket of the council meeting on 23 October, in order 'to persuade the members of the Haringey Borough Council that Hornsey College of Art has a viable educational case for staying out of the North London Polytechnic and to show the press, the council and the people of north London that the students and staff are united in their desire to maintain the autonomy and reputation of the college', HCA/3/3/Ingles. See also 'Memorandum to all staff. Polytechnics', October 1967, from the Action Committee, 19 October 1967, HCA/3/3/Ingles (which promises an eight-foot Union banner, campaign badges and a decorated truck). Staff are urged to write to their MPs and local council members, to solicit the support of the National Society for Art Education, and to contribute £1 each to a fighting fund for the publication of a brochure. This appeared as a separately printed version of 'Some points in the argument. . . ', published in *Gravy* 21, pp. 6–7, together with a sprightly motif – a man being swallowed by a lion – that was now the emblem of the campaign. HCA/3/3/Ingles. Councillor Vic Butler responded immediately: 'Yes, opposition is well known. There is little evidence, other than that "closed minds" prevail at the college. . . . Would it not be more sensible to support the council in its determination to get the best possible conditions for the Hornsey College of Art within the proposed polytechnic so that its status and service to staff and students is still further enhanced?' Butler to the Action Committee, 18 Oct. 1967, HHS Brown Box 9.

23 As reported in the *Hornsey Journal*, undated clipping reprinted in *Gravy* 21, p.12. There was one dissenter on the governing body, Councillor L. A. Vitoria, who having originally favoured autonomy changed his position and supported the merger. See also bound volumes of Council Minutes, vol. 4, 22 May 1967 – 29 April 1968, Minutes of

Education Committee, 2 Oct. 1967, in which, while noting the views of the governing body, the council resolved that 'in view of the decision made on 10 July 1967, no useful purpose would be served in pursuing at this stage the consideration of alternative schemes or organization for the college.'

24 Further Education Sub-Committee Minutes, 1/LBH/C14/1, 12 Nov. 1968. In October, the Further Education Sub-Committee had received a statement from the Principal setting out the alternatives to incorporation and had agreed to defer the question until the views of the governors were received and to consider them at a special meeting on Tuesday 12 Nov. convened for this purpose. The specialist design research centre would be financed ultimately through a combination of fee income and industrial support.

25 See for example Shelton to A. W. Tillman, Engineering Industries Association, 24 Nov. 1964, HHS Box 1, labelled 'Papers 1960s', Folder 2. His proposed 'University or College of Design Technology' would embrace television, film, advertising, packaging, fashion, textiles, ceramics, metalwork, furniture and design for light and heavy engineering, extending eventually to architecture and town and country planning, in close association with the needs of industry and commerce. A similar letter to Sir Maurice Laing, 4 July 1967, sought support for a 'new form of National Institute for Design Research and Development'. HHS Brown Box 8, contains extensive correspondence on variations of this proposal with the DES, the Board of Trade, the Chancellor of the Exchequer, the Prime Minister, sundry MPs, the National Export Council, Harrods, Courtaulds, the Engineering Industries Association, the Amalgamated Union of Building Trade Workers and others. Ministers were unpersuaded: see Tony Crosland, Minister of State at the DES, to William Hamling MP, 30 Sept. 1965; and George Darling, Minister of State at the Board of Trade, to Shelton, 4 Feb. 1966. Because there was already the Royal College of Art, and the Summerson Council had in addition designated Manchester, Birmingham and Leicester as centres for the development of post-Diploma work, the DES ministers saw no reason to hive off Hornsey's research activities in a separate institution. Drawing a blank at the DES, Shelton switched to the Board of Trade and the Prime Minister. He clearly hoped that following Labour's return to power in 1964, Harold Wilson's public enthusiasm for a 'white hot technological revolution' would lead to his support. Shelton complained to Wilson (20 Dec. 1965), that his rejected proposals were '*not properly understood*'. He followed up with a document (27 June 1966) outlining a joint 'Government and Industry Establishment of Design Research and Product Development' which would *not* be an educational establishment although it would provide facilities for training design technologists. The principle, he insisted (31 Aug. 1967) was 'to establish a new creative design policy in partnership with industry to complement the present intensive technological and scientific development programme . . . [in comparison with which] the new creative element as related to design technology and its application to new products has barely been initiated'. He told James Callaghan, Chancellor of the Exchequer (16 May 1967), that a 'continuous flow of new products must be a priority objective if the export market is to be substantially improved and consistently maintained'. He even approached the Duke of Edinburgh with a view to persuading him to sponsor a project development unit involving a partnership between education and industry (HHS Box 1, folder 2, draft letter to Sir Donald Stokes and others, undated, enclosing 'A New Approach to Design in

Industry'; Box 1, folder 5, letter to Commander Parker, 29 Dec. 1966). Tony Benn, Minister of Technology, wrote to Donald Swann on 10 Jan. 1968 that Shelton had 'made numerous approaches directly and indirectly to ministers and the Prime Minister about the future of his College for which he has, at various times, suggested university, para-university, national college or independent status' but now seemed to have changed tack to 'something in the nature of a Government-sponsored design consultancy service', by which neither the Ministry of Technology nor the DES was convinced. After the sit-in, Shelton approached Shirley Williams (31 Oct. 1968), Keith Joseph (14 Apr. 1969) and Margaret Thatcher (undated, but c. Dec. 1969) in support of his proposal for a specialized design research institute outside the polytechnic. The governors agreed to this but it was turned down by the Secretary of State in February 1969. (All this correspondence is in Brown Box 8, with the exception of the letter to Thatcher, which is in a tape-tied file with no box or code number.) See also Haringey Council Minutes, vol. 5, 20 May 1968–6 May 1969, pp. 249–51, Report of Education Committee, 18 Nov. 1968; Further Education Sub-Committee Minutes (1/LBH/C14/1), agenda papers, 13 Mar. 1969.

26 Shelton assured the Hornsey College of Art Academic Panel on 17 Dec. 1968 that the 'decision to set up a design research centre would not cut the college in half or diminish its strength'. In any case the plan had first to be approved by the DES. HCA/3/3 Ingles, Minutes of Academic Panel, 17 Dec. 1968.

27 Patrick Gordon Walker to Sir Eric Fletcher MP, 22 Nov. 1967, copy in DP Box 2. Gordon Walker could only assume that the college's objections were due to a misunderstanding of the Government's intentions for polytechnics as comprehensive, national institutions of higher education with more independence of governing bodies leading to greater academic freedom, including for the art colleges incorporated within them. But Shelton's particular vision for Hornsey as a design research institute, closely linked with business and industry, would also have served his personal ambitions: it would free him from local authority control and confirm his status as head of an autonomous, postgraduate institution. This was a goal that long predated the threat of merger which made it urgent. Shelton must have known that his chances as an inaugural polytechnic director were slim. (He applied to Newcastle and Middlesex but was unsuccessful at both.)

28 He conveyed the same points in person at a meeting with representatives of the governors and the Haringey Education Committee in December. Further Education Sub-Committee Minutes, 1/LBH/C14/1, 12 Nov. 1968. See also the letter from Shirley Williams, Minister for Education and Science, 3 Jan. 1969, to Alec Heath, Chairman of the Board of Design Education, Society of Industrial Artists and Designers, insisting that the directions for governance in the new polytechnics would give adequate representation to art and design. HCA 3/3/ Ingles.

29 Letter dated 10 Feb. 1969, quoted by A. V. Slater, Clerk to the Governors, in his 'Report on Representations to the Department of Education and Science', Agenda Item 4 (b), meeting of the Governing Body of Hornsey College of Art, 18 Mar. 1969, HCA/3/3/Ingles. (This page is inscribed – by whom? – 'Governors say go ahead if its [sic] all industry money'.) See also Further Education Sub-Committee Minutes, 1/LBH/C14/1, 13 Mar. 1969: 'The Secretary of State expresses considerable doubt about the viability of a small institution concerned with research and design development but divorced from the main stream of advanced studies in the field of art and design as a whole.' The Education Committee, while regretting this decision, 'agreed that all possible progress should be made towards the formation of the proposed North London Polytechnic'.

30 Peter Laurie and Roger Law, 'What Really Happened at Hornsey', *Sunday Times Magazine*, 13 Sept. 1970, pp. 36–47, quoting Gerda Flöckinger (p.36), who taught jewellery. Between 1957 and 1968 the college expanded from about 200 full-time students to 860, developed new courses and projects, attracted money from industry, and won a number of international awards: Shelton liked to cite the mobile shelter, which won a prize at the Milan Triennale, plans for an electric car, links with industry such as those with Standard Telecommunications, and the popularity of the college with overseas visitors. John Rae, among the General Studies staff, remembers a stimulating period in which 'lots of glittering things' were happening – Hornsey was 'quite a happy ship' (and Shelton a capable medium-paced bowler in the staff cricket team) – but resentments were building as these were paid for by money bled from less favoured departments (conversation with John Rae, 1 Dec. 2005). In his Principal's Report, 8 Nov. 1967, Shelton wrote that communications were strained to the limit, staff were overburdened, there was insufficient administrative support and the buildings were worse than those of any major college of art in the country. Hornsey was 'passing through a crucial stage and it will either emerge as a continuing force in art and design education, or it will disappear completely'. HHS Brown Box 9.

31 That the students were fighting simultaneously against the college authorities and alongside them is neatly encapsulated in the injunction on the last page of *Gravy 21* (undated, c.1967, HCA 3/3/Ingles): 'Support your Union in its legitimate claims for autonomy, greater student representation at all levels; its fight against polytechnics; its fight for a sabbatical year for its President'.

32 The London Government Act (1963) transferred responsibility for education to the fifteen outer boroughs. Hornsey was moved from the jurisdiction of Middlesex (pop. 2,250,000) to that of Haringey Borough Council (pop. 246,570) on 1 April 1965. See Shelton to E. E. Pullee, Chief Officer NCDAD, 5 Dec. 1967, HHS Brown Box 6. As *The Hornsey Affair* points out (p. 143) Hornsey was 'a national college, supported by national finance, awarding a national degree to students from all over the country' in the hands of a local education authority. (The NCDAD, granting or withholding accreditation, was 'a fairy superstructure perched ornamentally far above what happens, and exercising very little day-to-day control'.) Shelton did not consider himself responsible for problems of accommodation and equipment, or for administrative and clerical breakdowns, which were the province of the local education authority. Bains's remarks were reported in the *Hornsey Journal*, 20 Dec. 1968, HCA Press Cuttings 1968.

33 HHS Brown Box 9, 'Papers, 1960s', 'General Purposes Fund. Private and Confidential Statement in Reply to Terms of Reference to Council'. HHS Large Cardboard Box 1, 'Papers, 1960s', Folder 6, includes the copy provided for Shelton of a letter from the Borough Treasurer to the Chief Education Officer, 6 June 1967, expressing his concern over incomplete information and apparent discrepancies between payments and receipts in the general purposes fund. He complained that letters to Shelton and the college had received no response.

34 HHS Brown Box 9, 'Papers, 1960s', 'General Purposes Fund. Private and Confidential Statement in Reply to Terms of Reference to Council'.

35 The Education Sub-Committee looking into the affair in turn commissioned a report from Lewis Hawser QC. This did not recommend legal action but left further decisions to the committee which decided to do nothing, so that, according to one former councillor, 'The whole affair was hushed up effectively indeed.' The *Hornsey Journal*, 13 Feb 1970, photocopy of clipping in HHS Box 6; this alleges that money from the fund was also used for staff parties and leaving gifts.

36 HHS Brown Box 4, 'Papers 1960s + Harold Wilson', 'Memorandum of the Principal of the Hornsey College of Art' (black tape-bound typescript) submitted to the Select Committee on Education and Science. Sub-Committee B. Hornsey College of Art, 30 Jan. 1969, p.3. According to Shelton (p.4) the expansion of the college had been planned in concert with a building programme agreed in 1961, but interrupted with the transfer from Middlesex County Council to Haringey Borough Council in 1965. Existing plans for extending or rehousing the college would presumably have been dropped in 1966 as a result of the proposal to merge Hornsey in a North London Polytechnic. Instead there was to be a new building at Cat Hill, in Cockfosters, but it was clear by the spring of 1968 that this was unlikely to be ready until 1970 at the earliest.

37 The annexes were 'linked intermittently by the imperial edict and the 41 bus' as Tom Nairn puts it (*The Hornsey Affair*, p.20).

38 HHS Brown Box 4, translucent blue plastic folder, pages associated with Shelton's submission to the Select Committee on Education and Science, Sub-committee B. 1969.

39 HHS Large Cardboard Box 1, Folder 15 (only Box 1 has numbered folders). In the same folder is a memo to Shelton from head of department Leslie Roberts, about accommodation problems causing 'real distress', and forwarding memos from other staff including David Joseph, Head of General Studies, who described the 'generally demoralizing effect which whips through the students like an infectious disease'.

40 It was, he wrote, ludicrous that Hornsey's ambitions as a university of design should be 'thwarted by small-scale local government politics'. HHS Large Cardboard Box 1, Folder 2, unsigned letter from a college governor, 1 Nov. 1966. After the sit-in started Douglas Smith, a governor and Haringey councillor, claimed that the council had long been disturbed by the college facilities, 'many of which made Dotheboys Hall look like a luxury hotel'. *Hornsey Journal*, 31 May 1968, clipping in Jenny Cole scrapbook, HCA Archive.

41 HHS Brown Box 7, Student Action Committee, no. 5 in a list of grievances. See DP Box 4, Minutes of Staff-Student Council, Thur. 15 Feb 1968: Nick Wright, President of the Student Union, 'sought guidance on the function, aims and powers of the Council. He felt that unless it had executive powers there was little point in further time being spent in such meetings.' See also NW Box 2, 'Notes on the Academic Structure of Hornsey College of Art/1967/1968.' This alleges that the ostensible structure – departmental boards of study beneath the Academic Board – 'existed *only* on paper'. Annexes ran largely as independent fiefdoms. The Principal and key administrators constructed 'a climate of opinion in private discussion' that was then implemented by individuals. Students, junior and part-time staff were excluded from decision making. The staff-student council had no executive powers. The Students' Union took to sending memoranda to the governors (on the budget, a sabbatical presidency, a common room and welfare facilities) which were largely ignored. Communication was exclusively vertical, 'placing the greatest responsibility for a disproportionate number of decisions on the principal' who then avoided them. A working party of the Hornsey commission, in July-August 1968, was unable to establish whether the Fine Art, Three-Dimensional Design or Graphics Boards of Study had ever met. The Academic Board met for the first time in 1968 and made no recorded decisions on academic policy. 'Few departments identified the educational aims of the courses as problems which should be discussed and clarified' and even where boards of study were active there was 'general doubt among students' as to the relevance of their courses and the educational thinking behind them. Alex Roberts papers, Interim Report of Working Party 2, Jane Oldfield and Roger Haydon.

42 As summarized in Peter Laurie and Roger Law, 'What Really Happened at Hornsey', *Sunday Times Magazine*, 13 Sept. 1970, drawing on a series of interviews with staff and students. This was not just the view of a disgruntled minority: see DP Box 2, motion passed (22 for, 2 against) at an Extraordinary Meeting of the College Council with several heads of department present, 17 Jan. 1968: 'Council objects to the way in which decisions are made which affect the educational practice in this college with specific reference to the lack of consultation between the administration and the departments . . .' The main points in the debate, involving several heads of department, included the lack of planning in allocating space, the impact of outside projects on the regular teaching programme, the lack of a consistent selection policy, the lack of coordinated decision-making, the Principal's reluctance to decide on pressing issues and delays in ordering goods and equipment. See also DP Box 2, 'Memorandum. Staff & Students at Hornsey' probably dated 1969 and written either for A. V. Slater, the Chief Education Officer, or for the Parliamentary Select Committee into student relations: 'Mr Shelton was (and is) pathologically averse to decision-making, or perhaps to being *seen* to make a decision. He would go to the governors, say "The college wishes to do such and such". The governors having agreed, he would return to the college and say, "My governors have decided such and such." . . . On internal matters he would create an atmosphere without making a ruling' (to be interpreted by the Registrar or the Vice Principal). Poor communication was exacerbated by the (necessarily) high proportion of part-time staff. The problem was endemic in ambitious art schools and helped foster an autocratic style of administration at Hornsey and elsewhere.

43 Quoted from interviews with staff and students in Laurie and Law, 'What Really Happened at Hornsey', *Sunday Times Magazine*, 13 Sept. 1970.

44 DP Box 5, 'Student Action Committee (SAC). . . Grievances' [undated but c.28 May 1968]. Item 7 in a list of sixteen grievances including refusal of union autonomy, lack of participation in college affairs, questionable exam and entry conditions, lack of union or sports facilities, lack of a welfare officer, lack of a common room, poor catering facilities etc. But see also HCA/3/3/Ingles, 'The Hornsey College of Art "Sit-in" – Background Factors', a copy of notes by 'Alan' [unknown] for 'Jack' [probably Procter] as passed to an MP. 'The Principal was continually under criticism from [a] minority on the grounds of being an addict to fame and self-seeking opportunism. *In this they totally ignored the hours he spent in negotiations to establish the opportunities for College enterprises.*' Although he was the connecting link between the college, the governors and the local education authority, Shelton did not consider it his responsibility to run the college on a day-to-day basis, but rather to forge links with government, business and industry: to face outwards rather than inwards, in other words. In easier circumstances, with better management and good communication, a division of labour of this kind between Principal and Vice Principal might have been sustained. But Shelton failed to allay a widespread perception (justified or not) that he was more interested in public relations, and disengaged from the daily problems of the institution. Internally, departments felt differently favoured. Some resented what they perceived as the 'glossy supplement' image of external projects distorting the college's work and paid for, in effect, by privation elsewhere (the 'plethora of modern equipment in the Film and Television Department' underwritten by 'the peeling plaster and 1880 lavatories' of South Grove, as Tom Nairn notes in *The Hornsey Affair*, p.22). There were tensions between teachers and administrators, between studio staff and General Studies academics, between thrusting part-timers with gallery contracts and a full-time old guard, some of it sclerotic and suspicious, now in positions of administrative power. Leslie Roberts, Head of Three-Dimensional Design, was one of the old guard, patrolling the corridors and laying down rules for types of project and hours of work (though he was a benign figure compared with Jack Shaw, the unpopular and autocratic Vice Principal). Derek Boshier was one of the new whizz-kids from the Royal College of Art. We waited a long time for him one 'outdoor study day' at South Kensington tube station, while he was photographed by Lord Snowdon for *Private View* (London: Thomas Nelson, 1965).

45 The following account is based on Student Union papers in HHS Brown Box 7: a pink sheet referring to decisions taken at the meeting on Tues. 30 April 1968 and its aftermath; a blue sheet with the agenda for a student representative council on Tues. 14 May; and a white sheet, the Hornsey College of Art Student Union General Bulletin for 20 May 1968. Since the autumn of 1967 the union had supported the college authorities (in the campaign against the polytechnic scheme) while struggling against them (for union autonomy).

46 The Student Union was chiefly financed by a compulsory subscription, collected by the college, in most cases from the grant-awarding authorities, along with the tuition fees each year. At Hornsey, where the sum due for 1967/8 was around £2,130, they subsidized the rugby club, the film society, and *Gravy* magazine along with dances and other leisure activities (see *Gravy* 22, p.13, DP Box 8). Robinson (1968), pp. 120–1, points out that college student unions, though they might have 'effective control of their own finances, subject to audit by the local authority' were 'frequently subject to petty interference and regulation'. Sabbatical officers, paid for by union funds, were increasingly common by this point but Nick Wright, the President at Hornsey, had to scrape by on the charity of friends. In an interview with Frederika Adam (23 August 2001) he suggested that the government withheld his sabbatical grant because of his political position (he was a Communist Party member, the only known member involved in the sit-in). It was rather the case that Pudney, as college Bursar, refused to sign off the money as an appropriate use of Union funds.

47 HHS Brown Box 9, letter from Shelton to Harold Evans, 12 Nov. 1970, following publication of 'What Really Happened at Hornsey?' Slightly different dates are given in the surviving documents. What is not disputed is that the funds had been released and this information conveyed to the union, Shelton claimed in his office on 24 May, but certainly before the sit-in started on the 28th. But 'through a combination of irreversibility and enthusiasm the protest went ahead with the knowledge of the college administration' (DP Box 3 'The Hornsey Commission. . . AS(ST)/4/RSF 29/10/68').

48 DP Box 4, 'Hornsey College of Art Student Union Bulletin', dated 23 May. Wright and Hayman asserted the students' right to take direct action in pursuit of just demands. On the other hand, where memos had been ignored and attempts at negotiation frustrated in the past, they hoped that a new council administration might help them achieve their demands. Cathles expressed support for student control of Union funds and suggested that he would recommend acceptance of this point to a newly constituted board of governors, due to meet in early June (it actually met on 31 May).

49 DP Box 5, Student Action Committee, 'Student Participation in College Government. Student Union Autonomy'. Draft discussion document, undated but from internal evidence 28 May 1968. See also HHS Brown Box 7, for a longer list of requirements including common rooms, welfare facilities, adequate toilets, better transport between annexes, better library and sports facilities, a better canteen, proper machinery maintenance, longer working hours, art shops with a range of materials and student discounts and adequate diploma show facilities. SAC was formed in the week before the sit-in, following the meetings of 21 and 22 May, by implication from frustration with what others saw as the Union's slow progress in realizing its demands. See Jed Bailey's evidence to the Parliamentary Select Committee, *Minutes of Evidence Taken Before the Select Committee on Education and Science. Sub-committee B*, 30 Jan. 1969, p. 10: 'The Union seemed completely ineffective. . . [it] did not seem to be getting anywhere with these problems.' Nick Wright believed himself 'completely marginalized' by SAC (conversation, 29 Oct. 2005).

The Gestetner Revolution (pages 31–58)

1 DP Box 2; also in HCA/3/3/Ingles: Mike Bygrave, ed. of *Scenes*, a flyer from the Institute of Contemporary Arts, July 1968, inviting information on 'happenings/events/lectures/ publications/festivals/courses/causes/crises/catastrophes/ explosions', and listing the sit-in exhibition which opened at the ICA on 5 July. The 'Gestetner', a mimeograph machine, was central to administrative life – and radical politics – before the introduction of the photocopier (although the Hornsey sit-in was a physical occupation first, of course, before it was a 'Gestetner revolution'). Patricia Holland's *The Hornsey Film* (1970), has frequent recourse to Gestetner imagery and one student recalls how she loved printing on it while the others were asleep.

2 Alderman Bains, in an interview with the *Hornsey Journal*, 2 Aug. 1968, quoted in *The Hornsey Affair* (1969), p.186.

3 HCA/3/3/Ingles, 'Student Action Committee (SAC)', original plan for the sit-in dated Mon. 27 May 1968. The following paragraph draws on this document but it is worth bearing in mind that not everything happened at the time and in the order laid down. According to the *Evening Standard* on 29 May, 500 of the college's 800 students stayed the night and pickets were in position at the annexes the following morning to encourage others to join the protest at the main building, although third-years facing assessment were exempt. (See a range of clippings for late May and early June 1968 in the Jenny Cole scrapbook, unnumbered pages, HCA archive.)

4 *The Hornsey Affair*, p.31.

5 The canteen was the 'vibrating heart of the revolution'. The partition between staff and students was torn down, hot food was provided throughout the sit-in, the white walls were repainted in oranges and yellows, and – after a difficult visit on 17 June – the Chief Public Health Inspector mollified that hygiene was being maintained. See *The Hornsey Affair*, pp. 40, 156–7, and *New Society*, 13 June 1968, 'Sorbonne, N8': 'Good food is served at low prices by stunning girls.' HHS papers, Press Cuttings Box 1968.

6 HCA/3/3/Ingles, 'Student Action Committee (SAC)', original plan for the sit-in dated Mon. 27 May 1968. See also one version of Doc. 3 quoted in *The Hornsey Affair*, p.35: 'A person who designs should be a person who is capable of having meaningful relationships; a person with imagination; a person with insight into and an understanding of the world around him and an ability to communicate. . .[or] he will not be able to relate what he produces to his social environment.'

7 Kim Howells, quoted in Paul Lashmar, 'Shades of '68', the *Guardian*, 5 June 1993 (i.e. twenty-five years on), p.30. Howells, a twenty-one year old fine art student, lived at 2 Crescent Road, opposite the main college, where members of the Student Action Committee plotted the sit-in (about fifty, according to the press, but around fifteen to twenty, according to Howells). The house belonged to a Mrs Kafka, a relative of Franz. Howells entered Parliament as Labour MP for Pontypridd in 1989 and has been Minister of State at the Department of Transport (2003–4), the Department of Education and Skills (2004–5) and the Foreign and Commonwealth Office (from May 2005). The student occupation of the Sorbonne was followed by barricades and clashes with the police that peaked on the nights of 10/11 and 24/25 of May. This was widely reported in the British press on Sunday 26 May, and on 2 June the *Observer* ran an article headed 'Inside the Sorbonnne' (pp. 6–7). This claimed that Paris and indeed the whole country were discussing the autonomy of the French university system in relation to the government's centralized administration of education; the participation of students in university administration; the reform of courses, teaching methods and examinations; and the question of how to widen access, improve the relation between courses and jobs, and embed the universities in the rest of the working world. These aims corresponded closely with those of the sit-in and were typical of radical student programmes elsewhere.

8 *The Hornsey Affair*, p.32.

9 This was true for David Warren Piper, for example (conversation 7 Dec. 2005), and for Martin Walker and other students speaking in Patricia Holland's *The Hornsey Film* (1970).

10 *The Hornsey Affair*, p.39.

11 Proposals for reform, drawn up on Tuesday 28 May to present to him, were for some reason not passed on. The aims were that no student should do set project work without agreement, and without the structure of the course being discussed by staff and students; that all workshop facilities should be available to students (if necessary with the support of technical staff); that no student or staff member should be expelled from the college without going before a staff/student committee; and that students should be on the committee for selecting staff with whom they would be involved. *The Hornsey Affair*, p.43.

12 *The Hornsey Affair*, p.44, claims 'upwards of 600 students'. As always in such situations there was constant disagreement over numbers, and thus over the level of support enjoyed by the dissidents.

13 *The Hornsey Affair*, p.45. This would be a mediating body between the college and the council – five staff, five students, five councillors, five outsiders – elected every three months. It is important to remember that students from different annexes, and part-time staff, had often never met each other before; there was exhilaration that by this point the building 'was suddenly warm, it had a heart. . . . Everyone spoke to everyone. . . . We had become a community.' *The Hornsey Affair*, pp. 43–4. See also DP Box 6, 'The First Four Days', pp. 29–57, typescript for *The Hornsey Affair*, but not identical with it.

14 The commission's report would be presented to a general meeting of staff and students on Friday 14 June. DP Box 1, 'A Staff Statement of Recent Events', Thurs. 6 June 1968; DP Box 5, loose page of proposals dated 30 May 1968 over the names of six staff (R. Robbins, D. Joseph, L. J. Roberts, D. Warren Piper, A. Grant and D. Page), six students (N. Wright, R. Jerram, C. Francis, A. Roberts, K. Howells and M. Walker) and the Principal (H. H. Shelton). Richard Robbins, chair of the Staff Council on 29 May, questions the account in *The Hornsey Affair* (Memoir, p. 39). He recalls that a number of those present supported the students but he, at least, while sympathizing with their aims, was opposed to the sit-in as means of resolving frustration in the college. He felt that 'good people became involved and made a fool of themselves'. As the son of Lord Robbins – author of the Robbins Report and facing problems of his own at the LSE – he may have been especially sensitive to the damaging consequences of student unrest.

15 *The Hornsey Affair*, p.48. On Thurs. 30 May the *Daily Telegraph* announced that control of Hornsey College of Art was being claimed by both students and college authorities, 'thirty hours after more than 500 students took over the college switchboard, canteen and most of the building'. Shelton's secretary had read a statement on his behalf from the college steps, claiming that the protest had been authorized in consultation with the local education authority, that he was still in control, and that eighty percent of the students were carrying on their normal work. When Kim Howells, Jim Singh-Sandhu and others entered his office he left without protest. He was offered a room elsewhere in the college but left the building and set up an administration in exile at Parkwood School in Wood Green.

16 *The Hornsey Affair*, p. 52. DP Box 5, Minutes of the Governing Body, 31 May 1968.

17 HHS First Box, 'To whom it may concern', communiqué from Hornsey College of Art, N8, Fri. 31 May 1968. See also *The Hornsey Affair*, pp. 47 (Doc.3), 53. The Room F seminar ran through Thursday night, after a rushed examination of the Coldstream Report in the afternoon, and proved unstoppable: 'As if anyone wanted to stop it. As if, come to that, the members of staff present could be anything but enthralled by a seminar on a theoretical subject – the basic principles of education – which ran for six hours and ended with students demanding when it could continue.' (Some of its conclusions were written into Document 11.)

18 The open letter of Friday 31 May, beginning 'The students of Hornsey College of Art have taken over the direct control of the College', was sent out by AMHCA. See also the Outline Constitution (undated) in HCA 3/3/Ingles. The 'supreme governing body of the Association' was to be the general meeting, but an elected executive committee would coordinate and execute the Association's activities. This executive committee would have a student coordinator, with a sabbatical year, a secretary, a treasurer and six committee members. It would meet at least every three weeks. AMHCA's finances – including the money previously paid into student union funds by local education authorities – would be administered by a finance committee and audited annually. Ordinary general meetings would be held at least once a term, with a quorum of 200 members or one-fifth of the total, whichever was the smaller. See also DP Box 1, Doc. 22, 'HCA Association. The Constitution (proposed).'

19 DP Box 4, 'Statement to the Meeting of Staff of Hornsey College of Art, to be held on 11.6.68. Parkwood School, Trinity Road, Wood Green, N22. Issued by the AMHCA 10.6.68.' The Association was also intended to give formal recognition to staff support. According to *The Hornsey Affair* (p. 146), 'about twenty members of staff were by now taking a full part in the debates and activities, while a much larger number were extremely sympathetic.'

20 HCA 3/3/Ingles, draft of letter from 'a practising designer' (probably Jack Procter) to Alderman Bains, undated. It continues: 'The great majority of students and staff want to carry on working and at the same time bringing about progressive improvements in the system by reasoned discussion and negotiation.' See also undated, unsigned page, also in HCA 3/3/Ingles: 'It is monstrous, in our view, that the work of a major institution in the field of design education should be totally wrecked by activities instigated by a handful of politically motivated people with no knowledge or experience in the field of art or design. . . . We believe in a democratically elected staff body, and a democratically elected student body, maintaining close contact through a joint committee; but we cannot accept the dictates of the so-called Association [i.e. AMHCA], which is democratic neither in composition nor in operation. We believe that the great majority of staff and students would welcome a return to a programme of work, uninterrupted by continuous "dialogues" (which are mostly monologues), under the established senior staff and subject to modification and improvement by close cooperation. That the present system has faults we are well aware. . . . Therefore we say: end the present deadlock, and let us all resume our activities at the point where they were so ruthlessly interrupted in May – with guarantees of goodwill and the desire to cooperate on both sides.'

21 See David Joseph's evidence to the Select Committee. It was 'a very sensible, a very restrained and a very constructive meeting', at which staff and students shared Richard Robbins's peppermints and thrashed out a proposal for the commission. 'In this atmosphere of considerable goodwill and geniality a possible formula for solving the situation was produced quickly. I cannot analyse exactly why it did not come off. . . . [The situation] became increasingly worse within a period of a week or ten days.' HCA 3/3/Ingles, Confidential Proof, *Minutes of Evidence taken before the Select Committee on Education and Science (Sub-Committee B), Thursday, 30 January, 1969*, p.40.

22 *The Hornsey Affair* p.52. The students were uncertain as to whether the Principal, as part of the problem, could be part of the solution: they felt that the old structure had reasserted itself in the meeting. Sympathetic staff, however, had wanted to commit Shelton to a process of consultation by including him.

23 A full staff meeting would be called 'at the earliest possible moment'. DP Box 1, 'A Staff Statement of Recent Events', Thurs. 6 June 1968. The 119 staff in the building responded that they were present at the express invitation of Shelton himself, and dissociated themselves from any views expressed by the heads of department who had met with Shelton that morning at the offices of the Haringey Education Committee. Shelton, for his part, had misunderstood a message from the staff as coming from the AMHCA, and by the time this could be clarified was committed elsewhere.

24 John Field to his parents in the USA, 7 June 1968 (quoted in correspondence 21 Jan. 2007). 'This little would-be revolution is not essentially a political matter but an educational one . . . Personally, I sympathize with most of the student complaints, but I have little confidence in any sort of positive proposals yet put forward by them.'

25 This loose and fluctuating group was often still referred to in shorthand as 'SAC', but SAC was entering a period of planned obsolescence as decisions were referred to the general meeting. See HHS First Box, 'Hornsey 1960s'. The 'Agenda for General Meeting of Student Body', undated, proposed a motion to this effect and another inviting formal recognition of the working parties.

26 *The Hornsey Affair*, pp. 35–6: 'The later into the night the discussion continued, the greater became the lunatic fringe. Everybody turned from lunatic to cool appraiser and back at some stage during the twenty-four hours.' See also DP Box 4, Doc. 19, 'Programme for Tuesday 4 June'. At 10 a.m. SAC collates feedback from the previous evening's seminars and forms the agenda for the general meeting. At 1.30 p.m. the general meeting discusses the feedback and votes if necessary, after which SAC advances new problems and problems unresolved or not voted on for that evening's seminars.

27 Alex Roberts cannot now recall why control of the microphone – effectively the means for chairing the meetings – fell to him, except that he was a bit older than the other students who made assumptions about his maturity and experience of the world. John Rae recalls that in the earliest meetings students were harangued by speakers at the front, but that David Warren Piper was a key figure in effecting a shift towards discussion with the chairs pulled into something more like a circle. (Interview 1 Dec. 2005.)

28 'They make the Oxford Union look ridiculous.' Tom Nairn, 'The Crouch End Commune', *New Statesman*, 7 June 1968, clipping in Jenny Cole scrapbook, HCA Archive, unpaged. Nairn is a distinguished political philosopher and social theorist, credited, along with Perry Anderson, with introducing Antonio Gramsci's work on hegemony to Anglophone culture. The author of a number of books on nationalism and the state, he is currently Associate Director of the Globalism Research Institute and Professor of Nationalism and Cultural Diversity at RMIT University, Melbourne.

29 John Field to his parents, 7 Jun. 1968. On 18 Jun. 1968 he wrote: 'It is interesting to observe the give and take of democratic debate and voting, but also it becomes frustrating and boring when it is so long drawn out'; 25 Sept. 1968: 'Meanwhile, I seem to be on paid vacation, which is very handy for moving house'; 6 Nov. 1968: 'A great deal of contention and ill-feeling remains. I am increasingly demoralized by the situation at Hornsey.' All quotations from correspondence 21 Jan. 2007.

30 DP Box 4, 'Procedure for All General Meetings for Maximum Effect'. This paper also asks for shorthand volunteers, at least three, to work in eight-hour shifts.

31 *The Hornsey Affair*, p.36. Shelton denied that there was any link to the Special Branch during the sit-in, as was rumoured, and as some staff and students believed. Peter Laurie and Roger Law ('What Really Happened at Hornsey?', *Sunday Times Magazine*, 13 Sept. 1970, pp. 36–47) concluded that Special Branch did take an interest but wrote off the whole affair as a clash of personalities. Margaret Bird, archivist at the Metropolitan Police, has found no Operations Orders or other reference to the Hornsey sit-in, in Special Branch or other surviving papers (communication 12 Aug. 2004). On the other hand John Goldschmidt, who was making a film about the sit-in for BBC Omnibus, learned from his car-hire company that Special Branch had been asking questions about him. When he told the BBC that he thought he was being followed they cancelled the programme, on the grounds that the arts department was not allowed to stray into current affairs. Goldschmidt, furious, took it to Granada instead.

Visitors to the college were warned about drugs, weapons, and jumping on political bandwagons; students were issued with legal advice in case of arrest; and as for the regular police, Superintendent Collier of Y Division, Wood Green, was not inclined to take sides unless there were breaches of the peace (treating it like an institutional 'domestic'). See DP Box 6, 'Education in Action', p.25; duplicated legal advice in the Alex Roberts papers; and papers in HHS Brown Box 8 (handwritten notes on a meeting at Keith Grant's studio) and HHS second tape-tied file (letter from 6 Camden Studios [Keith Grant] to Shelton, 21 June 1968).

32 DP Box 6, 'Education in Action', pp. 30–1. Despite the assertion here that visiting seminars, which took place from around 6 June, were intended as occasions for communication with the professional art world and 'not an attempt to make our action culturally respectable', a scribbled page among the Alex Roberts papers, headed Liaison Committee (undated), suggests 'inviting outside speakers (artists, dealers – Kasmin?) who have considerable public reputations and who would be sympathetic (someone on the Arts Council). VERY HELPFUL AND IMPORTANT TO NOT JUST MAINTAIN BUT POSSIBLY INCREASE PUBLIC RELATIONS [and] BOOST IMAGE.' A *Guardian* correspondent, aware that on a previous occasion 'Bucky' had talked for eight hours, left weakly after the first 45 minutes: see clipping from the *Guardian*, 22 June 1968, also the *Hornsey Journal*, 21 June 1968, both in HHS Press Cuttings Box 1968.

33 *The Hornsey Affair*, pp. 37, 49, 54. There was considerable interest from the press, radio and television (all the archives contain copious press-cuttings including from the regional press). See also HCA/3/3/Ingles for a spider diagram of the sit-in structure with Coordination at the centre ('We know what is happening'), surrounded by External Liaison; Gestetner Printing; Press Office; Treasury, Canteen and other financial commitments; Public Address and Disc Jockey; Reception, switchboard, car pool, project office, internal events and incoming mail.

34 Prue Bramwell-Davis in *The Hornsey Affair*, p.175, and correspondence 23 Jun. 2007. Outgoings included £80 per day on food, Gestetner paper and ink, film hire, photographic costs, the public address system, printing bills, train fares and petrol money for delegations to other colleges, paper, paint and repairs to the fabric. See also DP Box 6, 'Education in Action', p.27.

35 DP Box 6, 'Education in Action', pp. 9–10. All documents were supposed to be numbered, but not all of them were, and sometimes two different ones ended up with the same number. Because they were constantly reprinted, repairing tatty skins and reattaching them to the Gestetner machine was a necessary skill.

36 DP Box 6, 'Education in Action', pp.45–6; *The Hornsey Affair*,p. 74. Images were posted in the corridors (which was rather preaching to the converted) and sometimes sold at the college entrance or through sympathetic local shopkeepers. 'Smash the

System' was reproduced on the cover of the *Listener*. 'Don't let the bastards grind you down' was taken by five thirteen-year old girls to put up in their school. Some silkscreen posters were printed outside, but others were improvized in the college using an orange-box, a sheet of glass and a torch. Some students at least would have been aware of the French posters produced by the Atelier Populaire at the École des Beaux-Arts, on strike since 8 May: Clive Tickner and I had brought some back from Paris; others were reproduced in the British press (there is an image of a poster studio in 'Inside the Sorbonne', the *Observer*, 2 June 1968, pp. 6–7); and emissaries from the École des Beaux-Arts visited Hornsey with David Robins during the sit-in (but were not long detained). For a selection of these 'weapons in the service of the struggle' see *Texts and Posters by the Atelier Populaire: Posters from the Revolution. Paris, May 1968*, anon., London: Dobson Books, 1969.

37 DP Box 4, Doc. 52, 'Initial List of Projects Requiring Interaction between Departments. . . Please add further ideas to pool situated to the right of Liaison.' Also in DP Box 4 and numbered as Doc. 52 is a statement on the 'Importance of Work Projects'. This urges students to be seen to be working constructively, as the most practical form of participation in the educational experiment, and so that councillors and ratepayers will see that they are capable of organizing themselves to good effect. DP Box 4, Doc. 18, 'Important', dated 3 June, solicited work from before 28 May that could be considered 'a perfect example of the restricted set-project work we are against' to compare with work post-28 May 'which complies with our aim of freedom to formulate and develop our educational ideals'. On the feasibility study into Alexandra Palace see DP Box 6, 'Education in Action', pp. 43–4, and *The Hornsey Affair*, p. 155. Moving to Alexandra Palace would have brought the college under one roof, solved its various accommodation problems, and moved it from Haringey's remit into that of the Greater London Council. The idea was to make Hornsey the nucleus of an educational centre but Haringey's planning department refused to provide the necessary information and plans, neither the chair of the Board of Governors nor the Principal replied to correspondence, and Reginald Marks – the chairman of the Alexandra Palace Committee – refused to enter into discussion once decisions had been postponed for financial reasons. It was decided instead to write a general report for the GLC to add to its existing feasibility study on the future of Alexandra Palace. See also HHS Box I, Folder 15, Shelton to A. V. Slater, Chief Education Officer, 6 Mar. 1968, re accommodation pressures and the hopelessness of more makeshift annexes fitted out at expense on a temporary basis, together with correspondence relating to an attempt to gain more space at Alexandra Palace (where the Fine Art department already occupied the Badminton Suite). This includes *Notes in Favour of Accommodating Hornsey College of Art Within Alexandra Palace*, 1p., undated.

38 HHS Press Cuttings Box 1968, *Daily Telegraph*, 29 May 1968; see also in this box a clipping from the *Wood Green Herald*, 31 May, in which Cathles is quoted as saying that the students 'made a number of perfectly normal student complaints', but that he had told them they would be better off working with the local education authority in joint opposition to the polytechnic merger. See also *The Hornsey Affair*, p.37. Cathles, who attended the meeting with Councillor Rigby, asked the students to tell him what was wanted (at which point a member of staff said: 'You'd better ask for what you want, only for god's sake ask for the moon, don't ask for sixpence. Then they'll decide if they can give it to you'). He reminded the students that the local authority had given permission for the 'teach-in' providing it finished, as planned, at noon the next day.

39 HHS Press Cuttings Box 1968, *Guardian* 6 June 1968 (although Bains objected to the news that the Board of Governors had been declared 'defunct': 'I am not defunct and I have no intention of being defunct'). Cathles was later seen as taking a stronger line with the sit-in than Bains. See DP Box 4, 'Notes of telephone conversation, 3 a.m. 25 June, between Councillor Hitchens and Prue [Bramwell-Davis]'.

40 *The Hornsey Affair*, p.154. Feeling that 'precise, unambiguous offers' were not forthcoming, the students set out the points that needed to be met in a letter to Bains of 12 June (Doc. 50) to which no reply was received.

41 See the complaints from Industrial Design in HCA 3/3/Ingles; and also HHS Box 1 Folder 10, a 'further detailed statement' in addition to reports provided for the chair of the Board of Governors and the Chief Education Officer, objecting to 'increasing intimidation' of staff and students, the picketing of annexes, the tearing down of the canteen partition, and haranguing by an 'agitator with Welsh accent' [i.e. Kim Howells], who told the Fashion and Textile staff and students that they were 'bloody fools' selling themselves down the river. Julian Robinson, Head of Fashion and Textiles, was a vociferous opponent of the sit-in. Fine Art, at Alexandra Palace, Interior Design, at South Grove Annexe, and Graphic Design, at Bowes Road Annexe, all lent support to the sit-in and made proposals for course reform. See DP Box 4, Doc. 51, 'Points for Discussion in Fine Art Seminar. 14 June 1968'; DP Box 4, Doc. 54, 'Hornsey College of Art. Interior Design. South Grove Annexe', re meeting 14 June 1968; DP Box 5 'Points/Proposals & Questions for Bowes Road', undated. The Teacher Training students at Page Green School gave conditional support – 'because in this department we have mutually satisfactory liaison and communication' – so long as the sit-in remained nonviolent and looked to a negotiated settlement. This support was withdrawn on 10 June, it being considered that the conditions had not been met and that 'no solutions can emanate from the present atmosphere of crisis and non-cooperation'. DP Box 4, Doc. 42, 'Department of Teacher Training and Education Studies', 7 June 1968 and Doc. 55a, 'Department of Teacher Training and Education Studies', 10 June 1968.

42 Bains quoted in 'What Really Happened at Hornsey', Peter Laurie and Roger Law, *Sunday Times Magazine*, 13 Sept. 1970, p. 43. It is possible to feel some sympathy for Bains here. Tony Judt, with hindsight, concludes that the May Events in Paris 'had a psychological impact out of all proportion to their true significance', offering the spectacle of a rather telegenic revolution with ultimately 'quite unthreatening' demands (Judt (2005), p.412). But this was not how it seemed at the time: 'France Faces Civil War' and 'France: A Hair's Breadth from Revolution' were headlines in the *Sunday Telegraph* (pp.1, 17) on 26 May 1968. Nor is it the view of a recent historian, Kristin Ross (2002), who points to the unique relation in France between student and sustained industrial militancy and argues that the May events have been ideologically reclassified as cultural rather than political.

43 DP Box 4, Doc.58. 'Report on Seminar held at 10 p.m. on Friday 14th June in Rooms A & B'. In Cathles' view reasonable demands, within the Council's remit, had been met. The discussion on art education in progress could be continued on condition that the switchboard reverted to the authorities, Shelton and the administrators were given back their offices, and work continued only in rooms A and B. It was pointed out that under these conditions things could not continue as they had been. He replied that he would only be as reasonable as he had been if he was met half way. He later complained that it was impossible to reach agreement with the students because they would not nominate a leader. The *Hornsey Journal*, 12 July 1968, cited in *The Hornsey Affair*, p. 161.

44 *The Hornsey Affair*, p.144.

45 Alderman Bains, in an interview with the *Hornsey Journal*, 2 Aug. 1968, quoted in *The Hornsey Affair*, p.186. Shelton's relations with Haringey Council had been increasingly strained since the transfer from Middlesex in 1965 and over the polytechnic campaign in 1967.

46 DP Box 2, draft page from Bains dated 24 July 1968. Bains also claimed that students and some staff failed to understand the purpose of the college as a practical training ground for teaching and industry, for both of which 'some personal discipline is necessary, and anarchic procedures during training would be a disservice to the students'.

47 HHS Press Cuttings Box 1968, Bains quoted in the *Hampstead and Highgate Express*, 26 July 1968. He claimed that the sit-in had been supported by around 200 out of 850 students – i.e. a minority – but a spokesman for AMHCA was quoted as claiming 60 per cent, not 25 percent, support. DP Box 3, 'The Hornsey Commission' AS(ST)/4/RSF 29/10/68, claims that the average number of students present in the main college buildings in any 24-hour period over the six weeks of the sit-in was approximately 60, with day-time numbers sometimes reaching 120 staff and 300 students.

48 DP Boxes 2 and 11 contain correspondence, July–Aug. 1968, between or relating to various staff (including James Meller, David Page and David Warren Piper); from M. A. Polden, of their solicitors (Polden, Bishop & Gale); from the Town Clerk on behalf of Alderman Bains (sliding out of the proposal for a conciliatory meeting); and from Hugh Rossi MP (with whom Page raised Bains's 'scurrilous and defamatory letter about David Warren Piper', published in the *Guardian*).

49 *The Hornsey Affair*, p.47, Doc. 3, produced on Wed. 29 May and taken to the general meeting on Thurs. 30 May. This document threatened to call for a general strike across art colleges should any person or institution threaten to sabotage such a structure (either by force, or by withholding funds or services).

50 DP Box 8, 'On the Reasons for a Revolution: a Study Paper by the Association of Members of Hornsey College of Art, England' (received 6 Dec. 1968), *Leonardo*, Pergamon Press, vol. 2, pp. 193–8 (quotation p. 195). This also exists in typescript in DP Box 4. It offers a cogent summary of the arguments as they stood at the end of 1968. The account that follows is drawn from this, in particular the section titled 'The False Consciousness of Art and Art Education', and from other documents produced during the sit-in. In hundreds of hours of debate there were of course diversions, disagreements and dead-ends, but general consensus on the principal points.

51 The DipAD promised a radical transformation of art education, but in its insistence on a fine art component to design courses and some knowledge of the humanities, and in its claim to intellectual respectability, it also looked back to the aspirations of the eighteenth-century academies. It was perhaps no coincidence that Nikolaus Pevsner, influential on both the Coldstream and Summerson Councils, had published a study of *Academies of Art Past and Present* in 1940 (reprinted 1973).

52 DP Box 8, 'On the Reasons for a Revolution: a Study Paper by the Association of Members of Hornsey College of Art, England' (received 6 Dec. 1968), *Leonardo*, Pergamon Press, vol. 2, pp. 193–8, p. 195. These points are also made in Doc. 46, cited in *The Hornsey Affair*, pp. 124–6. Elsewhere, of course, the radicals were inclined to condemn 'a voracious appetite for appearances, a desire for constant and novel stimulation' as capitulation to the needs of commodity capitalism.

53 Marshall McLuhan is quoted with approval in *The Hornsey Affair*, p. 105: 'Education must shift from instruction, from imposing of stencils, to discovery. . . The teach-in represents an attempt to shift education from instruction to discovery, from brainwashing students to brainwashing instructors. It is a big, dramatic reversal.'

54 First Coldstream Report (1960), quoted in *The Hornsey Affair* p.109.

55 DP Box 4, Doc. 39, 'Sir John Summerson – Seminar, June 6th, 1968.' See also *The Hornsey Affair* pp. 79–80. Summerson conceded that there was a case for criticizing art and design education and that the foundation courses were 'in a mess, as you know'. Asked why the GCE barrier had been set up, Summerson said that it was 'to make art education respectable . . . There was the question of degree equivalence, because people had a passion after the war for having letters after their name.' Education could not be planned exclusively for 'the type of people' in his audience, people 'completely absorbed and dedicated in the problems of art education'. The total number of DipAD students in 1968 was 1669, of which 36 would represent around 2 per cent (Haringey Papers 1/LBH/C14/1: Further Education Sub-Committee, 10 Nov. 1969, Appendix III, information on student destinations issued by the NCDAD; see also the *Second Report of the NCDAD* Appendix 4, which gives a figure of 1.9 per cent). Principals were requested by the NCDAD (the Summerson Council) to verify GCE certificates, ensuring that entrance requirements were met, and to submit applications for exceptional entries to the Secretary immediately after interview (i.e. 'exceptional' entry was not in the college's gift). See AR papers, 'National Council for Diplomas in Art & Design [Summerson Council]. Confidential. Revised and issued March 1967.' See also DP Box 10, Doc. 6, which proposes that 'the college in no way considers the obtaining of GCE [a necessity] in entrance to any course', although it misleads in claiming that Coldstream 'does not specify that GCE be necessary for admission to the diploma'.

56 In addition to the underlying objection that the new entry requirements had been imposed without 'any real research or investigation' into the needs of art and art education or into what was expected of them. DP Box 8, 'On the Reasons for a Revolution . . .', p. 194. In this context the authors regretted what they called 'the *assimilation* of the bohemians into conventional higher education'. There is an ambiguity here that turns on whether the bohemians in question are the same people (people with, or without, GCEs). Perhaps it comes to the same thing: some actual or potential bohemians are excluded because they can't meet the entry requirements, those who are not excluded are assimilated through the pressure of academic respectability. Either way, no leavening of the social dough by 'bohemian' creativity. Every so often a rather romantic notion of the artist as outsider erupts, even in hard-nosed discussions addressed to design students.

57 I. Macfarlane Smith, *Spatial Ability*, London: University of London Press, 1964; D. W. McKinnon, 'The Nature and Nurture of Creative Talent', in B. Semeonoff, ed., *Personality Assessment*, Harmondsworth, Middlesex: Penguin, 1966; and others quoted in *The Hornsey Affair* pp. 134–6.

They might have added Robert C. Burkhart, 'The Relation of Intelligence to Art Ability', *Journal of Aesthetics and Art Criticism*, XVII, 2 (Dec. 1958), pp. 20–41: 'In summary, intelligence tests are not good predictors of art ability . . . In general, aesthetic factors are not related to intelligence beyond the third-grade level'. The authors of *The Hornsey Affair*, p.87, make the further claim that although 'the literary-discursive character of university education is not the appropriate standard by which to judge art education' this is not the same as concluding that 'artistic and intellectual skills are, by nature, divisible and irreconcilable. This belief is shared alike by Summerson and Coldstream, and sometimes by ourselves' (Doc. 11).

58 DP Box 1, Doc. 11, cited in *The Hornsey Affair*, p. 130. Appendix 1, with an analysis of figures from the RCA Annual Report (1959), covering the years 1950–9, is reproduced on p. 132. About the same number with, as without, five or more GCEs gained upper second class diplomas.

59 Barry Curtis, 'A Highly Mobile and Plastic Environ' in Stephens and Stout (2004), pp. 46–63, quotation p. 58.

60 Misha Black, 'Notes on Design Education in Great Britain' in Piper (1973), vol. 1, p.42. Statistically, five GCEs presented more of a barrier then than now. The one in four statistic is from Paul Oliver, 'Art Education for *What Future?*' *ibid.*, pp. 140, 142. Clare Francis and David Warren Piper, 'Some Figures about Art and Design Education', in Piper (1973), vol. 2, p.32, say one in five. Robinson (1968), p. 55, claimed: 'The child from a lower working class home who even contemplates GCE is exceptional.' According to government figures, 61.5 per cent of year 11, age 16, pupils gained five A*–C grades in 2007 (46.5 per cent including maths and English). Anthea Lipsett, 'GCSE gap is narrowing, says minister', *Guardian*, 19 Oct. 2007, p.10.

61 DP Box 1, letter DP to the *Guardian*, 14 June 1968: the GCE barrier, in discriminating against the less verbally gifted, automatically debars a proportion of the most visually gifted and at the same time, children from poorer homes.

62 Barry Curtis, 'A Highly Mobile and Plastic Environ' in Stephens and Stout (2004), p. 58, points out that by 1969 there were three times as many universities and four times as many students as there had been thirty years before.

63 Robinson (1968), p.132.

64 Revising 'O' and 'A' level teaching in line with art college curricula, increasing the information available to potential applicants, and improving 'the recognised unreliability' of interview techniques would all help develop a fairer and more rational selection process. DP Box 4, Doc. 61 and Doc. 39 (quoting Sir John Summerson, 6 June 1968, to the effect that the NCDAD wanted 'a really effective A-level in Art'). See also *The Hornsey Affair*, pp. 110–1, 114.

65 DP Box 2, untitled MS in DP's hand: 'Coldstream built a timebomb into the Art Educational System.'

66 See Clare Francis and David Warren Piper, 'Some Figures about Art and Design Education', in Piper (1973), vol. 1, pp. 17–39. Table 11 (p.21), shows the distribution of students through the art and design education system in 1970 (100,000 plus). DipAD students accounted for only 7 per cent of the total. Nearly 60 per cent were on courses that did not lead to a nationally recognized qualification. A further 30 per cent were on 'non-advanced' courses (half of them on foundation courses). See also the tables reproduced in vol. 2, *After Coldstream*, pp. 138–52.

67 Or as David Joseph puts it in Patricia Holland's *The Hornsey Film* (1970), a division between the brilliant ones who have the ideas but smudge the ink and can't draw their lines straight, and the mechanicals who will do that for them. Joseph, Head of General Studies at Hornsey, resigned in 1969 when his position became untenable. He moved first to the Arts Faculty at Enfield College of Technology and then to the Open University.

68 Quoted in *The Hornsey Affair*, pp. 93–4.

69 DP Box 10, Doc. 3, quoted in *The Hornsey Affair* p. 121. See also Doc. 46 (more lower-class vocational students) and Doc. 11 (no reason not to merge), cited pp. 121–2.

70 Coldstream and Summerson in their *Joint Report* (1970) noted that this was unfortunate, both because it implied that DipAD courses were *not* vocational in the sense of leading to gainful employment in art or design, and because it suggested that vocational courses were inevitably secondary and subordinate. See Strand (1987), p. 34.

71 Doc. 46, cited in *The Hornsey Affair* p.122. See also DP Box 3, 'You gotta have art schools', a review in the *Education Guardian*, 8 Aug. 1972, of *The Employment of Art College Leavers*, Jane Ritchie assisted by Chris Frost and Sue Dight, Office of Population Censuses and Surveys, Social Survey Division (London: HMSO, 1972). This revealed the continuing class differential in art and design education: 50 per cent of diploma students and 26 per cent of vocational students came from grammar schools; 17 per cent of diploma students and 45 per cent of vocational students came from secondary modern schools. Of the vocational leavers 23 per cent had no GCEs at all and 43 per cent had two or less.

72 David Warren Piper in Piper (1973), vol. 1, p.22. Individuals should be enabled to make judgements independently of employers' or government's views as to what those needs were.

73 Doc. 11, cited in *The Hornsey Affair* pp. 121–2.

74 In fact St Martin's, powerhouse of British sculpture in the 1960s and 1970s, and with the support of Clement Greenberg and Henry Moore, failed, initially, in its bid for diploma recognition. The Hornsey Industrial Design course entailed day-release in engineering at Hendon Technical College. Prue Bramwell-Davis thought it 'brilliant' – she graduated from it in 1969 –but it was loathed by the head of department, Leslie Roberts (correspondence 24 June 2007).

75 DP Box 2, Doc. 6, 1 June 1968. William Morris, and the Arts and Crafts movement generally, had denounced the separation of creative design from execution since the late nineteenth century. See also DP Box 7, DP to Mr Richardson, 2 Sept. [1969?] soliciting the official inspectorate view on general studies for vocational students. (He had been informed, erroneously, by Harold Shelton, that the inspectorate advised against it and would even penalize vocational courses including general studies.)

76 See Haringey Papers 1/LBH/C14/1, Further Education Sub-Committee, 10 Nov. 1969, Appendix III: information on student destinations issued by the NCDAD. Of the rest, 3.5 per cent took up work that was unconnected to their art training, 0.8 per cent were foreign students returning home, 0.8 per cent emigrated, and the destinations of 7.4 per cent were unknown.

77 The authors of *The Hornsey Affair* complained of 'a dismal, schoolroom discipline in what should be a centre of creation and experiment' (p.195). They wanted collegiality, and collective debate. Staff who had taught design for many years, or were practising designers concerned to forge Hornsey's links with industry, found the social (if only tacitly political) scepticism of students and colleagues impertinent and irrelevant. In Patricia Holland's film of *The Hornsey Affair*, a student complains of being set 'ridiculous projects' for an elite minority when they should have been contributing to society as a whole (Jim Singh-Sandhu, in particular, was interested in design for the developing world). Victor Papanek's *Design for the Real World* was not published in the USA until 1971 and in the UK until 1972, but these concerns were widespread in the 1960s, partly through the influence of Vance Packard's books, *The Hidden Persuaders* (1957), *The Status Seekers* (1959) and *The Wastemakers* (1960). Papanek's book has an introduction by his friend R. Buckminster Fuller, which is dated '1963–71' (Fuller lectured at Hornsey during the sit-in and on at least one other occasion). In his preface (1972, p. xxi), Papanek claims: 'There are professions more harmful than industrial design, but only a very few of them. And possibly only one profession is phonier. Advertising design, in persuading people to buy things they don't need, with money they don't have. . . Industrial design, by concocting the tawdry idiocies hawked by advertisers, comes a close second.' Fred Scott, who also taught industrial design, was involved with the Archigram group and also believed in design solutions to social problems. John Rae recalls that Edward de Bono was regarded as 'almost a God' by enthusiasts at Hornsey. His book *The Use of Lateral Thinking* was published by Jonathan Cape in 1967, and he is referred to by David Warren Piper in the course of a discussion of creativity in Piper (1973), vol. 1, pp. 146–7.

78 First Coldstream Report (1960), cited in Strand (1987) p.12.

79 Quoted from the *Journal of Liberal Studies* (Spring 1968) by Dick Field (1970), p. 93. Pevsner also said: 'I think it is good for anyone if during his education he is forced to use his brain' (*Sunday Times*, 14 July 1968, Jenny Cole scrapbook, HCA Archive). This seemed to imply that brain work was not required in art and design. Perhaps it would have been less offensive to speak in terms of context, and of the need for students working in art and design to gain some breadth of knowledge, historical and critical, to extend and enrich their studio activity. Attitudes to General Studies among students and studio staff were ambivalent: some found it stimulating, others irrelevant to their main concerns, but many resented the assumption that art education needed this pinned-on brooch of academic respectability.

80 *The Hornsey Affair*, p. 86, suggests that the 'introduction of liberal studies to art colleges would have made more sense if twenty per cent of a degree course had been devised in free expression, from which many university students would surely have benefited'.

81 *The Summerson Report* (1964) extracted in Ashwin (1975), p.112: 'Somehow, the atlas of historic time has to be made vivid and comprehensible while at the same time the student's interest must be engaged at once in the real stuff of art history – the objects of art with which it and he are concerned.'

82 The interest and relevance of art history (and complementary studies) varied from institution to institution and depended in part on the warmth and vitality of the lecturer and a certain breadth of interest in the student. Design history developed as a discipline in the polytechnics, largely out of a perceived need to meet the interests of studio students. The 1967–8 Hornsey College of Art Prospectus (p. 11) outlines a three-year survey course in the history of art that must have seemed dreary to design students: year one, Ancient Byzantine and Mediaeval art; year two, Renaissance onwards with in-depth study of great masters including Leonardo, Michaelangelo, Raphael, Rembrandt; year 3, Modern Art, Primitive and non-European Art (Nick Wright Papers, Box 1). The comment on art history from Doc. 11 is quoted in *The Hornsey Affair*, p. 131.

83 First Coldstream Report (1960) quoted in Strand (1987), p. 29. In *its* First Report (1964) the Summerson Council referred to the widespread misconception that successful completion of a pre-diploma course guaranteed a place on a diploma course. In fact, foundation courses produced more students than diploma courses could absorb (in 1964, when the DES asked local education authorities to make this clear, there were 3030 pre-diploma students and only 1480 DipAD places available).

84 The preliminary course at the Weimar Bauhaus was developed largely by Johannes Itten, Josef Albers and Laszlo Moholy-Nagy. Moholy-Nagy's *The New Vision: From Material to Architecture* (1929) ran through several editions from its translation in 1932 (New York: Brewer, Warren & Puttnam); and Itten's book *Design and Form: the Basic Course at the Bauhaus* was published by Thames and Hudson in 1964. Other currents fed into Basic Design, including the writings of Paul Klee, D'Arcy Thompson's *On Growth and Form* (Cambridge 1917, revised ed. 1942, abridged ed. 1961), Gyorgy Kepes' *The Language of Vision* (Chicago, 1944) and an interest in child art influenced by Herbert Read's *Education Through Art* (London: Faber, 1943). The emphasis shifted from a training in skills, expressed in the production of a particular artifact (such as a life drawing), to a more open-ended process of discovery (exploring the properties of particular materials, forms, colours and shapes). For a useful overview see David Thistlewood, 'A Continuing Process: the New Creativity in British Art Education 1955–1965, in Thistlewood (1992). (This slightly reworks his earlier essay in A *Continuing Process*, exh. cat., ICA, London, 17 Mar.–19 Apr. 1981.) John Walker discusses his experience of Basic Design as a student of Victor Pasmore and Richard Hamilton at Newcastle, in Walker (2003), pp. 14–16, bibliographic references p.61. See also Hamilton (1982). Maurice de Sausmarez brought an enthusiasm for Basic Design to Hornsey, where he was head of the Fine Art Department, but outside the foundation course it had largely petered out by the time Richard Robbins joined the fine art staff in 1961. De Sausmarez's papers and Basic Design material from Newcastle and Leeds can be found in the Bretton Hall collections, University of Leeds (accessible online).

85 In 1966 there were 4,599 Foundation students and 2,326 admissions to DipAD courses; in 1969 the numbers were 5,826 and 2,526 respectively. Clare Francis and David Warren Piper, 'Some Figures about Art and Design Education', in Piper (1973), vol. 2, p. 29.

86 Ministry Circular 15/64, 21 May 1964; *Addendum to the First Coldstream Report*, August 1965; Strand (1987), p. 37.

87 *The Hornsey Affair*, pp. 196, 197.

88 The structure of the network system was frequently addressed. See in particular two versions of Doc. 70 (DP Box 1), 'A Network System. A study paper', Dennis Kelly, 7 Jul. 1968 and 'The Implementation of "A Network System"', Colin Cannon, Dennis Kelly, 21 Aug. 1968; Doc. 47 (DP Box 2) 'The Information System in a Network', John Dicks; and Doc. 55 (DP Box 5) 'Study Paper . . . Quick thoughts on the network', David

Warren Piper. These form the basis of the account in *The Hornsey Affair*, pp. 119–21, together with elements from Doc. 4 and Doc. 46. See also Doc. 21a, cited in *The Hornsey Affair*, p. 115, which explains that with the 'network or flexible system' the one-year pre-diploma or foundation course would disappear, and with it the problems of stress and wastage from which it suffered. Indeed, under the new scheme, there could be a choice of routes through the institution varying in length from three to five years.

89   Doc. 46, cited in *The Hornsey Affair*, p.120. The Architectural Association was a possible model here (cited in Doc. 30, 'Report from Seminar in Room H Tues. 4 June'), and the example of Archigram in particular. 'Archigram regarded the student not as an empty vessel to be filled with knowledge, but as an active agent of change. . . . Spurning traditional master/pupil interaction, Archigram members cultivated something more like the relationship between a rock band and its fan base' (Simon Sadler, 'Archigram's invisible University', *arq* vol. 6, no. 3, 2002, pp. 247–55, quotations from pp. 247, 254). See also J. Gowan ed., *A Continuing Experiment: Learning and Teaching at the Architectural Association*, London: Architectural Press, 1975. James Meller and Fred Scott, who taught industrial design at Hornsey, were both associated with the AA and David Warren Piper and Prue Bramwell-Davis went on to teach there. (Piper had resigned from Hornsey before the sit-in, with effect from the end of the academic year; he moved to Bradford University in 1968 and to the Institute of Education at London University in 1970, ending his career as Professor Emeritus at Southampton University.)

90   Piper, as an educational psychologist, was particularly concerned to promote alternatives to what he called a 'drop dead' system, in which failure from the eleven-plus exam on was hard to recoup: 'what you needed were choice points, so you could always recover' (interview 3 Mar. 2007). The 'network' concept, largely advanced by Piper and colleagues in Industrial Design, was attractive to artists on parallel grounds. Coldstream's traditional 'fine art' categories – painting and sculpture – were beginning to be challenged in the schools by instances of film, performance, installation, or proto-conceptual art (such as Clive Latimer's 'Light Sound Workshop' at Hornsey, loosely associated through its participants with the Pink Floyd). Stuart Brisley, the performance artist who taught in 'Visual Research', was convinced that 'departmentalization in art education is property and territory based, promoting the sense of division and separation of creative activity categorized by medium which was and is absurd, being contrary to contemporary vocations of the artist while fostering bureaucratic attitudes in the faculties'. The Hornsey protest was in his view partly 'an expression of the refusal of this condition' (correspondence 30 Oct. 2006).

91   Doc. 70, cited in *The Hornsey Affair*, pp. 119–20. James Meller, who taught in Industrial Design, was close to Fuller and edited *The Buckminster Fuller Reader* (London: Jonathan Cape, 1970). Fuller, who addressed the sit-in on 21 June 1968, enjoyed almost legendary status at this point. He had lectured at the ICA in the 1950s, where the Independent Group was interested in him, at the Royal College of Art, Cambridge University and the Royal Institute of British Architects. He was widely known for the US Pavilion at the Montreal Expo in 1967 (a geodesic dome), and he received the RIBA's Gold Medal for Architecture in 1968. He had no formal qualifications but set out in 1927 to become a 'comprehensivist' in an era of specialization. He joined the staff at Black Mountain College in the summer of 1948 and 'carried on a non-stop talkathon, for which his classes (on Architecture and Industrial Engineering) were the merest warm-up'. Geodesic dome experiments, light-sound workshops, John Cage 'happenings', collaborations between Robert Rauschenberg, Merce Cunningham, Cage and Fuller, and other interdisciplinary forays were all part of the expansive and interactive Black Mountain experiment. See Martin Duberman, *Black Mountain: An Exploration in Community*, London: Wildwood House, 1974 ('nonstop talkathon', p. 284); Thomas T. K. Zung, ed., *Buckminster Fuller: Anthology for the New Millennium*, New York: St Martin's Press, 2001; and *Starting at Zero: Black Mountain College 1933–57*, exh. cat., Arnolfini Gallery Bristol, 5 Nov. 2005–15 Jan. 2006 ('emerging synthesis', p. 54).

92 Doc. 4, cited in *The Hornsey Affair*, pp. 120–1. See also Doc. 11 cited pp. 117–8: 'The linear structure of the present courses militates against versatility and particularly against the emergence of the bridge personality who can make vital connexions between apparently disparate disciplines.'

93 DP Box 5, Doc. 55, 'Study Paper . . . Quick thoughts on the network', David Warren Piper. Variations are proposed in DP Box 1, Doc. 70, 'A Network System. A study paper', Dennis Kelly, 7 Jul. 1968. These include the idea of three types of knowledge course: technical, general studies and professional. Short, three-month technical courses would be taught by technical staff training students to learn and exploit particular skills, materials and machines. Professional courses would relate directly to the student's future career: 'market research, chemical compounds of glazes, advanced industrial processes and so on'. General studies courses would run for a term, in some cases longer, and would cover a broader range of subjects than at present.

94 *The Hornsey Affair*, p. 116. Herbert Read, in *Education Through Art* (London: Faber and Faber [1943], 1958, p.5) had already argued that the purpose of education was 'to develop, at the same time as the uniqueness, the social consciousness or reciprocity of the individual' – society needs individuation and it needs it to be integrated – thus resolving (rather too easily in the context of commodity capitalism) an implicit tension between individuality and social need. See also Doc. 11, cited in *The Hornsey Affair*, p. 130, which gives as an example of 'educating for obsolescence' the training of type-setters. Those whose livelihoods are only maintained by restrictive practices would not see computerized photo-setting as a threat if they had been educated differently. The innovative and adaptable designer will survive, the designer 'sewn up in a particular technology' will vanish with it. This was a fair point but it was true, as the *Sunday Times* pointed out, that students were in the position of complaining both that they were being processed for a squalid materialistic rat race (and bought off with diplomas), and that they were not being processed efficiently enough. Peter Laurie and Roger Law, 'What Really Happened at Hornsey', *Sunday Times Magazine*, 13 Sept. 1970 pp. 36–47 (p. 47).

95 Hannema (1970), p. 123. Professor Misha Black, an influential member of the Coldstream Council, agreed that the really brilliant student might flourish in a network system 'but ninety per cent will flounder' (quoted in Peter Wilbur, 'What the Art Students Want', *Observer*, 6 Oct. 1968, Jenny Cole scrapbook, HCA Archive). In her evidence to the Parliamentary Select Committee, after Roger Jerram had acknowledged that the term network was 'a bit vague', Prue Bramwell-Davis suggested that it was 'a bit of jargon we have been using'. It stood for better communication between departments and improved access to shared facilities: 'It was not necessarily any kind of terminal solution at all.' *Minutes of Evidence Taken Before the Select Committee on Education and Science. Sub-committee B*, 30 Jan. 1969, p. 17.

96 David Warren Piper in Piper (1973), vol. 2, pp. 55–6. Piper believed that the recommendations of the Coldstream and Summerson Joint Report (1970), to which he had contributed, provided the basis for experiments with a network scheme, given the support of the NCDAD and changes in the eligibility rules for student grants. Opponents, such as Misha Black, believed that a network system would produce only dilettantes. He was on the side of the specialists against the generalists. He singled out Buckminster Fuller, who had advocated the generalist position with 'Messianic fervour' across the world, but who had had a specialist training in engineering and whose major achievements, in Black's view, were rooted in engineering and mathematics. Misha Black, 'Notes on Design Education in Great Britain', in Piper (1973), vol. 1, pp. 38, 39.

97 DP Box 2, MS in DP's hand describing the twice-weekly meetings of the 'rump' of the sit-in at his house over the summer vacation.

98 Aneurin Thomas, 'The future of the DipAD' in Piper (1973), vol. 2, pp. 71–7. Thomas was at this point Director of the Welsh Arts Council.

99 Paul Oliver, 'Art Education for *What* Future?' in Piper (1973), vol. 1, pp. 136–7. See also from a more conservative position Hannema (1970), who claims that modern art 'exists only in the form of a well-organized publicity stunt' and that there is 'no room for the artist-prince in a democratic society'. He praises the work of the Artists' Placement Group (which, founded by John and Barbara Latham, put artists into non-art organizations and businesses), and suggests that artists should be trained primarily as the teachers most of them will become, with only the most gifted eligible to apply after two apprentice years to postgraduate courses in art and design.

100 HCA/3/3/Ingles, letter from A. V. Slater, Chief Education Officer, to members of staff present at the 11 June meeting at Parkwood School, confirming the proposal to form a new college body inaugurating a democratically elected commission. Staff also suggested departmental seminars to discuss such student proposals as could be implemented immediately. See also HHS Brown Box 4, papers 1960s + Harold Wilson, 'Diary of Main Events in "Sit-in"', and *The Hornsey Affair*, pp. 158–9. The steering committee met on 28 June, submitting to the chair of the Board of Governors a list of eleven points, on the basis of which a return to normality could be negotiated. These included recognition of the steering committee and the terms of reference of the commission; facilities for planning an exhibition at the Institute of Contemporary Arts and a national conference; clarification of financial responsibility for the sit-in; assurances in relation to staff contracts and student grants; discussion of allegations of the political motivations of staff and students; reform of the governing body; better communication through the college and between the college and the governors; and Document 50 as the basis for a discussion of college affairs. HCA/1/01/D 'Hornsey College of Art Steering Committee. Areas of Discussion', 28 Jun. 1968. The steering committee was apparently unaware of the fact that the eleven points had evolved in a secret negotiation between a small group and Alderman Bains to whom, as chair of the Board of Governors, they were now submitted. *The Hornsey Affair*, pp. 158–9.

101 DP Box 6, 'Education in Action', p. 24.

102 *Daily Mail*, 5 July 1968, p.3 (mis-labelled *Sun* in Jenny Cole scrapbook).

103 *The Hornsey Affair*, pp. 161–3, citing an interview by Alexander Mitchell with Bill

Ray in the *Sunday Times*, 14 July 1968. Ray complained that the council had refused to authorize the use of dogs in writing. 'If they'd given me full backing, I would have charged into the college like a bull at 2 a.m. and set the dogs among them. I could have cleared the place in an hour.' The whole episode was something of a fiasco and widely reported. See *inter alia* the *Daily Mail*, the *Sun*, the *Daily Mirror* and *The Times*, 5 July, and the *Wood Green Herald*, 12 July 1968.

104 Reported in 'What Really Happened at Hornsey', Peter Laurie and Roger Law, *Sunday Times Magazine* 13 Sept. 1970, p. 43. MPs protested in the Commons about the use of guard dogs and Labour councillors called it 'highly deplorable' (*Daily Mail* 6 July 1968; *Hornsey Journal* 12 July 1968, Jenny Cole scrapbook, HCA Archive). Cathles complained in evidence to the Select Committee on Student Relations, 30 Jan. 1969, that the authorities received no assistance from the police, the Home Office or the DES, and that in Counsel's opinion it was necessary to close the college in order to take legal action against the dissidents. *Minutes*, pp. 82–3. The security firm had been ordered not to touch or go near the students. The total cost was £100.

105 He offered to underwrite the commission with up to £10,000 but later withdrew, feeling his motives had been questioned in the press, and offered a Bolex camera instead.

106 *The Hornsey Affair*, pp. 170–3. Shelton had in fact moved back on Friday 5 July and left his office locked that evening, but after a general meeting decided that the return to work should be delayed until 9 July, students had broken in through the window.

107 With the exception of the Teacher Training Department (which was related to the Institute of Education), all parts of the college were declared closed, such that 'any persons remaining or entering without express permission will be trespassers and liable to legal proceedings' (notice in Alex Roberts papers over the name of Lawrence Bains, chair of the Board of Governors). Students melted away not (or not only) through indifference, but from necessity because they needed to work, or pragmatically because there were others to carry on (what social theorists call the 'free rider' problem). On the 'Hanley Road Commune', a short distance from the Main College, see *The Hornsey Affair*, pp. 200–3. The files and Gestetner machine were moved into Page's studio, and those who were left organized themselves as best they could to continue the arguments and build support in other colleges and among the public. There was widespread bitterness that the unilateral closing of the college had broken both the spirit and letter of the agreement that the students believed they had reached with the council. See also DP Box 3, Doc. 7, 'The 28th May Movement'. This was a liaison and information group intended to forward the ideals of educational reformers, fight their victimization and feed information to the National Union of Students. It was instigated by Hornsey participants at the MORADE conference in July, and issued literature over the addresses of Page (at 14 Hanley Road) and Kim and Jane Howells (at 2 Crescent Road). The aims are set out in an unidentified clipping in the Jenny Cole scrapbook, HCA Archive. DP Box 10 contains a buff folder marked 'File 1 May 28th Documents' including 'Newsletter No. 2' reporting on an exhibition at the Battersea Gallery, organized to raise money, with work donated by Derek Boshier, Stuart Brisley, Bernard and Harold Cohen, Richard Hamilton, David Hockney, Henry Moore, Eduardo Paolozzi and Patrick Procktor, among others. There was 'a non-Bond Street type opening party' on 22 August, a Thursday, chosen to coincide with the evening opening of the local jellied-eel shop. See also HHS Press Cuttings Box 1968, the *Guardian*, 22 July 1968.

108 Kustow (1975), pp. 73–4. He recalls that he 'just said "use your imagination: here's a space"' (telephone conversation, 30 Jan. 2005). The lease for the new ICA location in Carlton House Terrace (a fine Nash building backing onto the Mall), had been secured with the help of Jennie Lee, Britain's first Minister for the Arts, Lord Goodman, Chairman of the Arts Council, and Robert Maxwell, then a Labour MP, in 1966. *Hornsey Strikes Again* opened on 5 July 1968. Kustow felt that he had 'transported their creative vigil into the hallowed centre' but was struck by 'an eminently British tone of common sense' (in contrast to the Sorbonne insurrection and 'the *corrida* conflicts' with riot police in the Latin Quarter). Eventually the 'art-school uprising was absorbed into the time-honoured British machinery of a commission of inquiry and the production of a report' (pp. 74–5).

109 I am indebted here to DP Box 6, 'Education in Action', pp. 67–9 and the brief account in *The Hornsey Affair*, p. 171. This was only the second exhibition put on at the ICA in its new venue and 'hundreds of art students came from all over the place to see it' (p. 171). The ICA offered £50 towards the cost. According to a review in the *Hampstead Express* (undated, HHS Papers, Press Cuttings 1968), there was also a blackboard inscribed with selected quotations from sit-in opponents, including : 'You've nothing to offer the world except brazen impudence, bad manners and permissive sex' and 'This is a show of stunted satire, almost lapsing into Dada but not even achieving that convincingly.' Discussions were organized on the evenings of 8–12 July: Coldstream, Summerson, Jonathan Miller, Anthony Caro, Cedric Price, Bridget Riley, William Turnbull, Barry Flanagan, Adrian Henri, Harry Thubron, Alan Bowness and Norbert Lynton were among the outside speakers invited. (List on ICA notepaper in HHS Large Cardboard Box 1, Papers, 1960s, Folder 11 – a few names were provisional and may not have been confirmed. Folder 10 contains an unsigned carbon note, objecting that photographs of work supposedly carried out in the network system had been completed as part of the normal timetable before the sit-in.)

110 David Page, correspondence 27 July 2006.

111 DP Box 6, 'Education in Action', p.61. MORADE was set up following a meeting and press conference called by several London colleges in Hornsey's support, at the Royal College of Art, on 19 June 1968. Its aims were to democratize art colleges; to examine the function of art and design education and circulate the results of that research; to examine the allocation of funds to art colleges and discrepancies between student grants in different areas; to examine the place of art and design education within the structure of further education; to set up an executive body to implement these aims; to establish a system for collating and distributing information; and to seek the support of practising artists, architects, designers and educationalists. It was not to have any particular political affiliation. MORADE grew out of connections forged in the early days of the sit-in, when it was necessary to build alliances in the debate with Coldstream, Summerson and the government. A stream of documents left 'External Liaison' at Hornsey including an eight-point communiqué sent to every art college in Britain. On 4 June the 'Northern Delegation' set off for colleges in Birmingham, Liverpool, Carlisle, Newcastle, Sunderland, Hull, Leeds, Bradford and Sheffield, and a few days later the 'South-West' delegation left for Exeter, Winchester and Portsmouth. Messages of support arrived from many London colleges including the Architectural Association, the Royal College of Art and the LSE. The École des Beaux-Arts sent a delegate from their Paris occupation. On 11 June the *Guardian* reported 'Art students still top of protest league' following disruptions at Croydon, Birmingham, Bristol, Brighton, Keele, Edinburgh, Essex, Norwich and the Royal College. Clearly the tinder was dry: protests were sparked spontaneously as well as by Hornsey's example. By the end of the summer term there had been demonstrations at thirty-five art schools across the country. See HHS Press Cuttings Box, unnamed clipping, 1 June 1968; DP Box 6, 'Education in Action', pp. 53–60; DP Box 5, 'To the Students of the Hornsey College of Art' from the École des Beaux-Arts, published as Doc. 13; and the editorial introduction to Richard Wollheim, 'Should art be a respectable occupation?', *Sunday Times Magazine*, 8 Sept. 1968, p.22.

112 *The Hornsey Affair*, p. 172. AR papers, 'Movement for Re-Thinking Art & Design Education', 4 July 1968. The student questionnaire asked about administrative structures and participation, whether students had any say in staff appointments and the relation of administration to the well-being of the college. It solicited proposals for educational change, and asked recipients whether they thought it likely that 'a satisfactory form of Art and Design Education' could be achieved under the present structure involving local education authorities with the Coldstream and Summerson Councils. Designers turned out to be largely indifferent to the structure and content of art education, except for those who regretted the lack of effective communication between colleges and industry. The organizers of the MORADE conference included representatives from Hornsey, Manchester, Birmingham, Guildford, Brighton, Camberwell, Exeter, Hammersmith, St. Martin's and Central Colleges of Art, the Slade School of Fine Art and the Royal College of Art. See also AR papers, 'Movement for Re-Thinking Art & Design Education', inscribed 24 June in red ballpoint.

113 HCA 3/3/Ingles, 'The National Conference on Art and Design Education . . . Chairman's Report Monday Tuesday 8th 9th July', Geoffrey Bocking; 'Chairman's Report Wednesday 10th July', Andy Elton. There is slightly different wording in *The Hornsey Affair*, p. 172. A BBC Radio 4 programme, recorded and compiled from interviews at the conference by Meg Sheffield and Tony Gould, was broadcast as 'What's Wrong in Art Education?' on 25 Sept. 1968. A copy is in the National Sound Archive: NP1341R. There is no linking narrative and speakers are not identified (although Kim Howells' voice is easily distinguished). The main themes are those of the sit-in: the relation of art to society, the need for college autonomy, a limit to bureaucracy, better communication, critiques of the DipAD, the advantages of a network system, and the need to develop the Hornsey experiment since 'some mild form of revolution would have to happen to bring any real change'.

114 HCA 3/3/Ingles, 'The National Conference on Art and Design Education . . . ' ; *The Hornsey Affair*, p. 172.

115 *The Hornsey Affair*, p. 172. MORADE was still active in October, when *The Times Educational Supplement* published two articles by Geoffrey Wansell under the heading 'Thinking aloud on the vexed subject of art'. These reported discussions at a meeting of about thirty people, held at the Royal Society of Arts and apparently instigated by MORADE with the *TES*. Shirley Williams, William Coldstream and John Summerson were among those present and it was chaired by Richard Wollheim. *TES* cuttings 4 and 11 Oct. 1968, HCA Press Cuttings.

Aftermath (pages 59–82)

1   Lord Longford, Chair of the Hornsey Commission, addressing staff and students at the Palace Cinema, Tottenham, 5 Nov., reported in *The Times*, 6 Nov. 1968. HCA Press Cuttings 1968. Longford was concerned that a member of staff with fourteen years' service could get no clear answer as to why her contract had not been renewed, but his words were taken – and perhaps intended – as applying to the administration of the college as a whole. Shelton had undertaken to inform staff by 3 Aug. if there was any doubt about their contracts being renewed for the next academic year. 'Commission for Hornsey College of Art. Record, July 17', AR papers.

2   In the end, twenty-eight students were excluded ('militants' and others), but there was an overwhelming vote for their reinstatement at a meeting of the whole college at the Palace Cinema on 5 November. At the governors' meeting three days later, twenty were reinstated on two months' probation. Eight who failed to present themselves for assessment were permanently excluded. Among them was Nick Wright, President of the Hornsey branch of the NUS, whose claim that he was not an assessable student but a union official was over-ruled. HHS Press Cuttings Box 1968: *The Hornsey Journal*, 8 Nov. 1968; the *Guardian*, 6 Nov. 1968; the *Evening Standard*, 9 Nov. 1968. Bains had also undertaken to review the position of part-time staff whose contracts were not renewed. After the governors' meeting on 8 Nov., Cathles told the *Evening Standard* that part-time staff would be cut by 54 as there were 110 fewer students (recruitment being down). There were 27 who had applied for re-engagement but would not be taken on because of the reduction in numbers, a change in subjects being taught, and – allegedly – the need for an injection of new blood into the college. Another 58 did not wish to be re-engaged and 31 new part-time staff had been taken on. Astonishingly, in evidence to the Select Committee on Education and Science, Cathles recalled his 'no victimization' pledge, accepted by the governors, the Education Committee and the council, and claimed that it had been 'scrupulously observed throughout in respect of both staff and students'. *Minutes of Evidence Taken Before the Select Committee on Education and Science Sub-Committee B*, HMSO, 19 Feb. 1969, p.58. There is a folder of papers relating to individual student assessments in DP Box 1.

A related issue was the vetting of students for the Art Teachers' Certificate. Selection had always been the sole responsibility of the Teacher Training department. In 1968 Shelton and Shaw, his Vice Principal, insisted that all applications be routed through their office and anyone who had been active in the sit-in, or who 'looked dangerous', was blocked. Apparently Bains thought it 'a sensible procedure' to exclude the trouble-makers. Peter Green, the head of department, and his staff, strongly opposed this action. There was 'much unpleasant argument' but after what was probably 'the quiet intervention of the Institute of Education' the matter was reluctantly dropped. Green afterwards found himself very unpopular with the loyalists and was subsequently 'more engaged in the general debate for change and less of an "establishment" head of department'. (I am grateful to Peter Green for communication on this issue, 15, 23 and 27 Dec. 2005.) The teacher-training students had offered their conditional support to the sit-in on 7 June, while making clear that in their own department they enjoyed 'mutually satisfactory liaison and communication'. Three days later it had been withdrawn, citing an 'atmosphere of crisis and non-cooperation', when they found the governors' proposals a satisfactory basis on which the main college should return to work. DP Box 4, Docs. 42 and 55a.

3 *The Hornsey Affair*, pp. 205–6 (Queensberry is not mentioned by name). Queensberry's letter to *The Times*, 26 Sept. 1968, provoked comment in the *Daily Telegraph* the following day. See HHS Press Cuttings Box 1968. His fee was £20 per day.

4 At a special meeting of the Haringey Education Committee, Labour councillor Mrs Lillian Angel called the delay 'criminal' and expressed concern that assessments would be used as a route to victimization. After an hour's discussion the Committee went into secret session. *Hornsey Journal*, 30 Aug. 1968, Jenny Cole scrapbook, HCA Archive.

5 AR Papers, press clippings, *The Times*, 27 Aug. 1968 and response from Sir Robin Darwin, 29 Aug. 1968.

6 AR Papers, press clippings, *The Times*, 31 Aug. 1968: 'The warmth with which Sir Robin is now being told from Haringey to mind his own business shows that his point has not been missed.' Darwin had suggested that the Summerson Council help in the distribution of students to other colleges but Summerson wrote immediately to say that this would be quite improper. In its editorial, *The Times* expressed some sympathy for local authorities with 'a revolt on their hands which they have been slow to comprehend, and which arises from factors only partly of their making'. The students were largely justified in their complaints but provocatively impatient and contemptuous of authority, while local councils had 'shown about as much subtlety as the Mayor of Chicago in dealing with protests at Hornsey and Guildford'. (Mayor Daley had allowed the Chicago police to break up the protest marches at the Democratic Convention of 1968 in brutal fashion.) Bains acknowledged that neither Haringey nor Hornsey had wanted their shotgun marriage and that removing the college to the remit of a regional body, or something like the University Grants Committee, would be much more sensible (the *Hornsey Journal*, 20 Dec. 1968, HCA Press Cuttings 1968). After Cathles had objected that the students' 'idealism' had led to damage of £1500 to the roof, Keith Grant, a lecturer in the Fine Art department, pointed out in *Studio International* that 'the authorities talked in terms of political motivation and material damage without reference to the costs of their own decisions to send in guard dogs, cut off and reconnect services, commission expensive security measures round the building, employ external assessors and send administrative staff home on full pay'. Nowhere had they accepted the contribution of the Hornsey experiment, and he was 'grieved when I think of the thousands of pounds the council has wasted [when] . . . I may not give a free tube of paint or a free brush to needy students' (*Studio International* vol. 176, Nov. 1968, pp. 179–80).

7 *The Hornsey Affair*, p.183.

8 DP Box 6, 'Further Thoughts of Chairman Bains'.

9 See HCA/1/01/D, handwritten notes on General Meeting, Monday 8 July. David Warren Piper is reported as saying that the governors would not accept a commission without the Principal on it; that public opinion would see his presence as reasonable on the part of the AMHCA; that if the commission's report was not accepted in September public opinion would accept a renewal of the sit-in; and that agreement had been sewn up in such a way that neither the governors nor the local education authority would be able to back out. 'I believe we have won and wouldn't like to see all we have fought for thrown away.' Kim Howells reported to the meeting that Shirley Williams had said that the commission's findings should be reported directly to the Coldstream Committee during the summer and (unofficially) that a working party under an independent chair could deal with the problem of the governors and how the college was run. The Alex Roberts Papers contain commission agendas, records [brief, of meetings] and reports from working parties, July 1968–Jan. 1969, together with a copy of *Unity and Variety: Current Problems in Art and Design Education. Report of The Hornsey Commission*, 26pp., undated. DP Box 4, Doc. 69b, lists the student members (elected from 23 nominations): Alex Roberts, Prue Bramwell-Davis, Martin Walker, Jed Bailey, Brian Forster, Roger FitzPatrick, Roger Haydon and Jane Oldfield. The staff members included Joe Darracott, James Meller, David Warren Piper, Eirian Short, Ian Simpson and probably John Wormold and Peter Green (whose names appear in the records of meetings) although Richard Stranks, the registrar, and Jack Shaw, the Vice Principal, were on two of the working parties. The names of Anthony Horrocks and Clive Latimer are also recorded (but people sometimes attended as observers or stood in for colleagues). The governor was Councillor Hitchens, and the two co-options Dr M. L. J. [Jane] Abercrombie of the Educational Research Unit at the Bartlett School of Architecture, University of London, and Dr C. R. R. [Richard] Joyce, a psychologist described as a 'medical education reformer'. A plan to coopt two practising designers, strongly recommended by the chairman, Dr Wall, to give substance to the commission's conclusions, did not materialize. The DES preferred to send a representative who could answer questions and provide information rather than nominate another cooption. Students and part-time staff were paid £10 per week, including expenses, for their attendance.

10 Dr Wall, Dean of the Institute of Education, resigned on 2 Aug. due to pressure of work. Lord Longford, who succeeded him, had been Colonial Secretary (1965–6), Leader of the House of Lords (1964–8) and Lord Privy Seal (1966–8). He was a noted public figure dedicated to social and penal reform.

11 *The Hornsey Affair*, pp. 196–9, quotation p.197. Because the sit-in 'did not appear as too much of a threat on the national level . . . there was an odd alliance between the student movement and these ruling-class figures for the duration'.

12 HHS Press Cuttings 1968, clipping from the Guardian, 18 July 1968, quoting Dr Wall after the first meeting: 'the atmosphere was very good. I was very pleased'.

13 DP Box 6 'Education in Action', loose page, 'Further Thoughts of Chairman Bains'. The letter, circulated to staff, was published first in the *Hornsey Journal* and then in the *Guardian*. D. Warren Piper replied in the *Guardian* on 30 July (quoted in *The Hornsey Affair* p. 185).

14 See AR Papers, 'Hornsey Commission. Record of meeting 6th August.' This notes that the recommendation drafted by the commission at a meeting on 2 Aug. was unacceptable because it put the commission into a position of negotiation and because the college was unlikely to agree to the proposed Academic Board which would delay reopening. A detailed timetable to get the college working again was preferable. This was the suggestion (originating apparently with Prue Bramwell-Davis): a general meeting at the town hall on Mon. 23 Sept. to discuss the commission's recommendations; departmental meetings on Tues. 24 Sept. to decide changes to the administrative structure; reports from the departments to be presented to a coordinating committee consisting of one staff member and one elected student together with technical staff from each department on Wed. 25 Sept.; collation of these reports by the coordinating committee and discussions with the Principal, Vice Principal and Registrar on their implementation on Thurs. 26 Sept; the coordinating committee to report back to departments on

Friday 27 Sept. before teaching started the following week.

15 Longford quoted in the *Hornsey Journal*, 27 Sept. 1968, Jenny Cole scrapbook, HCA Archive.

16 *The Hornsey Affair*, p.189. The governors also 'took the unprecedented step' of asking *other* local authorities 'to pay grants to Hornsey students monthly, instead of by the term', a ham-fisted move that, as the *Observer* pointed out, was 'calculated to cause further trouble, not prevent it' (1 Sept. 1968, quoted p. 189). On 23 Sept. two hundred staff and students, who had gathered outside the locked gates on what should have been the first day of term, marched to Wood Green Civic Centre to demand the reopening of the college. They also hoped to raise the money to open a college of their own (*Daily Mirror*, 24 Sept. 1968, Jenny Cole scrapbook, HCA Archives).

17 DP Box 2, 'Hornsey Commission. Report from the Working Party on arrangements. . . for next term', undated. 'See also HCA 3/3/Ingles, Confidential Proof, *Minutes of Evidence taken before the Select Committee on Education and Science (Sub-Committee B)*, Thurs. 30 Jan. 1969. The Association of Teachers in Technical Institutions, which had members at Hornsey, submitted three papers, in the second and third of which they noted that although the authorities claimed they could do nothing until the commission reported, many serious decisions – about security measures, accommodation, staff-student assessments and future courses – were actually taken during this period without any consultation at all.

18 DP Box 2, *ibid.*

19 DP Box 3, R. S. FitzPatrick, 'The Hornsey Commission. . . a recommended academic structure to be implemented in the Hornsey College of Art. . . on 4th November 1968', AS(ST)/4/RSF 29/10/68. A document prepared by commission member R. S. FitzPatrick based on documents PR2, AS(ST)/2, AS(ST)3, CS1 and CS2, the discussions of the commission and written and oral depositions of a number of its members. A handwritten note in the Alex Roberts Papers, headed Aug. 29 2.30, records that Shelton – in favour of a tutorial system at commission meetings – opposed it (together with Ian Simpson) at the governors' meeting on 20 August.

20 'R.H.' [Roger Haydon] in 'Life on a Commission', *The Hornsey Affair*, pp. 180–2.

21 John Woodrow, acting chair in a brief interim between Wall and Longford, wrote to the governors on 16 Aug. explaining that the commission's 'apparent slowness in making interim proposals' was due to the fact that it had been obliged to turn its attention to the problem of ensuring the reopening of the college, 'rather than to its proper function of making academic recommendations'. Alex Roberts Papers. See also HCA 3/3/Ingles, letter from Kenneth Palmer, a part-time lecturer, to Alderman Cathles, chair of the Education Committee, 19 Sept. 1968. Palmer claims that there is now deadlock 'with the governors and administration on the one hand and the "sit-in" supporters on the other'. A third group, 'consisting of a majority of staff and a large number of students desire certain reforms in art education, but realise that these cannot be brought about in one short-term operation'. And HHS Press Cuttings Box 1968, report in the *Hornsey Journal*, 2 Aug. 1968, claiming that the dissidents are determined to make AMHCA the supreme authority in the college while the governors are equally determined to contain it in an advisory role; that there is a secret blacklist of staff supporters; and that the agreement under which the sit-in ended has been breached by the governors and administration side-stepping the commission.

22 Memorandum of the Council of the London Borough of Haringey and the Governors of Hornsey College of Art, submitted to the Select Committee, *Minutes* p.59.

23 With the commission's Agenda for 14 Aug. 1968 came 'Proposals for an Interim Academic Structure 1968/9' (AR Papers). This was a five-tier tutorial system consisting of Tutorial Groups (not more than eight students), a Course Tutorial Directorate, an Area Directorate, Coordinating Panels and a College Directorate. See also DP Box 6 'Education in Action', 'Further Thoughts of Chairman Bains', which notes that the 'Statistics Regarding Implementation of the Interim Academic Structure' were presented to the governors on 11 Sept.

Six heads of department attended a commission meeting on the same day: Ian Simpson, Romek Marber, George Younson and Harold Hussey expressed themselves in favour of a tutorial system in principle but claimed that the proposed structure would prove unworkable in practice; David Joseph and Peter Green supported the proposal enthusiastically and Green added that a similar structure at Teacher Training showed evidence of a reduction in the administrative load. Commission Agenda for 17 Sept. with notes of meeting on 11 Sept. 1968, AR Papers.

24 See HHS Brown Box 4, 'Papers 1960s + Harold Wilson', 'Diary of Main Events in "Sit-in"': in Shelton's account, a group of senior staff decided in September that it was necessary to move things on; they compiled a structure based in part on the commission's draft which was accepted by the governing body as a means of progress. In a circular letter to the students on 28 Oct. 1968 (DP Box 5), Bains claimed that no firm or formal proposals had emerged from the commission and that the heads of department proposals, including an improved tutorial system and a new college structure with staff-student advisory panels, would be the basis for reopening. The proposals were in line with recent agreements between university vice-chancellors and the National Union of Students, and the commission had in general accepted them 'although there is naturally some reservation on some issues'. (This was promptly refuted by some members of the Commission.)

25 *The Hornsey Affair*, p.197. The original commission paper was AS(ST)/2. The problem was exacerbated by the distrust that had built up over several years towards the Principal and a small group of senior staff who controlled policy but did no teaching and did not seem to consider themselves accountable to the wider college.

26 DP Box 3, R. S. FitzPatrick, 'The Hornsey Commission. . . a recommended academic structure to be implemented in the Hornsey College of Art. . . on 4th November 1968', AS(ST)/4/RSF 29/10/68.' See also CS/1/RSF 8/10/68, 'Comments on a document received from some of the Heads of Department of Hornsey College of Art'. The commission spent the rest of October negotiating with the governors to change the heads of department document, for example to increase the number of students on a College Advisory Panel. This was frustrating to members who felt it was failing its terms of reference, that it should be drawing up a blueprint for the whole future of art and design education. A motion to put the commission back on this course was put to the vote (the only vote of its existence) and defeated. A revised version of a draft report on 'Problems in Art and Design Education' was finally accepted for publication by the commission at its last meeting on 27 Jan. 1969. See *The Hornsey Affair*, p. 182, summary by J.C.D. (Joseph Darracott): 'the first six objectives are groundwork for improving the immediate situation' (including alternative structures for art colleges); the next two 'are interim measures for better information services'; the last two 'are for future action'. 'The need for more and better informed discussion is stressed, and a preference is stated for creating a new national body, with different terms of reference from what now exists.' HCA 3/3/Ingles contains an earlier draft by E. Short, J. C. Darracott, P. Bramwell-Davis, J. J. Oldfield and B. Forster, 'On the Problems in Art & Design Education', a Short Report to the Hornsey Commission, dated 9 Dec. 1968 and marked 'under revision'. Much of this was incorporated into the commission's report, *Unity and Variety: Current Problems in Art and Design Education*. Appendices to this report remarked on the inadequacy of communal facilities for art students (sports, union facilities, bars, common rooms); the absence of clear relations between Coldstream's intentions, set out in the First Report of 1960, and the objectives of higher education subsequently set out in the Robbins Report of 1963; and the need for improved interchange of information and ideas between teachers, artists, designers, industrialists and policy makers (it was thought that a periodical along the lines of the American *College Art Journal* would be useful).

27 I have borrowed here from *The Hornsey Affair*, p. 198. Longford's comment about the whelk-stall was reported in the *Times*, 6 Nov. 1968, HCA 'Press Cuttings 1968'. Edward Short, the Secretary of State for Education and Science, had been asked to intervene in the dispute (but declined to do so), and a formal complaint, drawn up by solicitors, with over 700 signatures, had been handed in to the Ministry. Jack Straw and a colleague from the National Union of Students were present at the meeting and 'noted the recommendations made by Lord Longford on behalf of the commission' (DP Box 6, letter from E. C. Garraty, NUS, to DP, 5 Nov. 1968). Longford was, according to Piper, 'an absolutely brilliant chairman' who made a very good speech in presenting his report (telephone conversation, 23 Nov. 2005).

28 A 'Short List of Principles', associated with the commission agenda for 31 Oct. 1968, AR Papers, presumably corresponds with that referred to by Longford as 'submitted to you all as members of the college' in his chairman's report. This appears to be a draft for *Unity and Variety* or for his address to the Palace Cinema meeting or both. The 'Short List' includes the following points:

> College policy should be based on a clear statement of objectives.
> The college should be primarily concerned with preparing people to produce effective and creative solutions to problems.
> Courses should be organized according to aimed-for performance rather than according to traditional boundaries of subject or materials.
> There should be an emphasis on learning design techniques rather than memorizing specific information.
> Direct interaction between students and staff across courses and years should be encouraged.
> The main aim of the assessment should be feedback with a view to improvement.
> Participation in decision-making should be maximized.
> There should be as many options open to the student as possible for as long as possible.

The Association of Members of Hornsey College of Art, properly constituted
and recognized by the local education authority, should have the right to
discuss any college matter.

Students should be given a probationary period with right of appeal before
any disciplinary action is taken.

29 Longford was right to anticipate that his report would be criticized as overcautious
(*Unity and Variety*, pp. 1–2, AR Papers). Where it had more radical ambitions – and it
was divided on this, Shelton urging it to 'take a firmly radical line' on 26 Sept. – the
commission could not effect change on its own. This required consultation with other
colleges, legal and educational experts, the Coldstream and Summerson Councils, staff
and student unions, the DES and professional bodies such as the SIAD. The 'Exploratory
Group on problems in art and design education' effectively recognized this (AR Papers).
The only alternative – not, apparently, seriously entertained – was to persuade the LEA
and senior staff to risk ceding DipAD status in pursuit of success as an independent institution committed to educational experiment. A draft 'Report on the problems in Art &
Design Education' (9 Dec. 1968), by Eirian Short, Joe Darracott, Prue Bramwell-Davis,
Jane Oldfield and Brian Forster, was finally submitted to the Hornsey commission for its
meeting on 27 Jan. 1969, and to the Joint Committee of the Coldstream and Summerson
Councils, reporting in 1970. This seems to have been the last meeting of the commission, which in Nov. 1968 had already had an inconclusive discussion about its future
(record of previous meeting attached to agenda for 26 Nov. 1968, AR Papers).

30 Chairman's Report, AR Papers: 'More radical proposals have been made at the
commission, and some members . . . hope that the structure as proposed will be amended during the year, so as to become more appropriate to Hornsey. This structure is a first
step, not as big a step as the commission originally hoped, but nevertheless a step forward'. Longford appears at the Palace Cinema in John Goldschmidt's film, urging that
the termination of staff and students be reconsidered in the interests of recovering good
will: 'I respectfully but firmly make this request. And I implore the governors to give
effect to it.' In his response, Bains says: 'I do not speak with animosity. I do not speak
with hostility' (but insists that he cannot go back on the decision without a full meeting of the governors).

31 Alex Roberts recalls the barracking and that it was rather alarming to be on the
platform at the Palace Cinema (conversation 6 Nov. 2005). Nonetheless, according to
Roger Jerram, interviewed in Jan. 1969 by the Select Committee, the 'conclusion that
the students came to at the cinema was that we all wanted to go back to college. . . .
Therefore we would show every bit of goodwill that we could in order to get this plan
working.' (He did not feel there had been enough support and goodwill from the other
side.) *Minutes*, p.18.

32 *The Hornsey Affair*, p. 198.

33 Haringey Council Minutes Vol. 5, 20 May 1968–6 May 1969, p. 309, Report of the
General Purposes Committee Part B, 30 Dec. 1968. See also HCA Press Cuttings 1968,
'Refer College of Art Dispute to Council's own Ombudsman', the *Wood Green Herald*,
1 Nov. 1968. This records that Councillor Mrs Sheila Berkley-Smith, the Labour
Leader, moved formally on 28 Oct. that there should be an independent inquiry into
the handling of the dispute, but was defeated.

Parliament had ordered a Select Committee on Education and Science on 13 Nov. 1968.

34 This was one of four sub-committees of the all-party Select Committee appointed to inquire into student relations with universities and colleges. The members were Gilbert Longden (Chair), Ronald Bell, Kenneth Marks, Arnold Shaw and Frederick Willey. See *House of Commons. Minutes of Evidence Taken Before the Select Committee on Education and Science. Sub-Committee B*, 30 Jan. 1969, HMSO, 19 Feb. 1969. There are copies in the Alex Roberts Papers, and in the British Library. Student representatives were Roger Jerram, Jed Bailey, Roger FitzPatrick, Alex Roberts, John Clifford and Prunella Bramwell-Davis. Staff representatives were Ian Simpson, Douglas Lowndes, David Joseph, Alin Braund, Jack Procter, Bernard Hancock, Richard Robbins and Jeremy Eldridge. David Warren Piper and Alan Grant, former staff now teaching elsewhere, were also questioned. Shelton and two heads of department, Julian Robinson and Leslie Roberts, appeared with the councillors and governors: Ald. Cathles, Ald. Bains, Cllr Mrs B. S. Remington, Mr George King (governor), Mr A. V. Slater (Chief Education Officer) and Mr E. F. Cooley (Assistant Education Officer). The ATTI, the SIAD, Shelton, the students and Haringey Council also made written depositions. The students objected at the end of their evidence that too much time had been taken up with questions of political motivation, the polytechnic issue and other events prior to 28 May, at the expense of questions relating to academic responsibility and representation. The meeting seems to have broken up with some impatience on both sides. Panel: 'We hope you have said all you want to say?' Students: 'We have not said anything we want to say.' Piper subsequently wrote to suggest that the process had 'leant more towards the debating procedure of the Law Courts, than towards, say, the kind of enquiry a management consultant would make in order to analyse the structure and working of an organization.' The Select Committee had been thorough but the students 'failed to say much of what they thought'; others, more experienced, 'were able to capitalize on the situation'; and even where the facts could have been elicited witnesses 'were not required to substantiate more thoroughly' the assertions that were made [DWP papers].

35 I have consulted original papers but cited where possible from Ashwin (1975) which is much more accessible. This includes relevant extracts from the *Report of the Select Committee on Education and Science (Student Relations)*, 1969, pp. 114–22 (quotations here from paras. 219–23, pp. 115–16). The Select Committee also visited Glasgow School of Art but took no formal evidence there. The *Report and Evidence* of the Select Committee appeared in several volumes in July 1969. It recommended the formation of a statutory Higher Education Commission, exceeding the powers of the UGC, to implement its proposals, provide a national forum for debate, and pave the way for an end to the binary system. There were 58 recommendations on a wide range of issues, some of them meeting demands raised in the sit-in or at other centres of student unrest. These included the approval of disciplinary arrangements and student union constitutions, the promotion of research (including research into teaching methods) and the instigation of inquiries into unforeseen problems. It recommended full student participation in the management of welfare services, that teachers should be subject to the opinions of students as well as peers, that there should be better student representation and that staff might receive some managerial training. The Report concluded that there was a *prima facie* case for an independent inquiry at Hornsey, Guildford, Essex and the LSE, noting that it received little evidence to support any theory of an international conspiracy to promote student unrest in Britain. (It was not within the remit of Sub-Committee B, of course, to comment on the structure of the DipAD or on alternative modes of art and design education.) Haringey Papers 1/LBH/C14/1, Further Education Sub-Committee Minutes, 10 Nov. 1969, Appendix II, gave members a summary of the main points.

36 Para. 226, extracted in Ashwin (1975), pp. 116–7. In his opening remarks Cathles questioned, and made clear that he did not welcome, the extension of the Select Committee's remit into the realm of local authority-managed education. *Minutes*, pp. 77–8. Shaw's comment was quoted in the *Hornsey Journal*, 7 Feb. 1969, Jenny Cole scrapbook, HCA Archive.

37 *Ibid.*

38 Paras. 484–5, extracted in Ashwin (1975), p. 118.

39 Para. 482, extracted in Ashwin (1975), p.118. In his evidence, Alan Grant suggested that the 'government in exile' was over-represented among the staff witnesses. *Minutes of Evidence* p. 50. See also DP Box 11, David Page to [Cyril] James, Clerk to Sub-Committee B of the Select Committee, undated ('Friday'), arguing that 'an approach to the staff organizations in the College is not perhaps the best way to identify staff who have evidence to give' (partly because of divisions over the sit-in and partly because a number of those who had something to say – including David Warren Piper, W. Patrick Burke, Ron Jackson, Vernon Mills and Alan Grant – had already gone elsewhere). Piper and Grant both gave evidence (perhaps as a result).

40 One student claimed that the aim of the sit-in had been 'to reduce the restricting, absolute power of the nine or so senior staff over the 1,200 staff and students'; and other evidence acknowledged 'the distrust, which had built up over several years' in this ruling élite, aggravated by an unsympathetic handling of internal disputes and after the sit-in by a hardening of positions on both sides. *Minutes of Evidence*, Sub-Committee B, 30 Jan. 1969, p.2, extracted in Ashwin (1975), pp. 119–20. Management was not much studied, or even taken seriously as an activity requiring particular skills and competences, in educational or indeed many other types of institution in the 1960s.

41 HCA 3/3/Ingles, *Memorandum to the Sub-Committee of the Select Committee on Education and Science*, from the two SIAD representatives on the staff group appearing before the Sub-Committee on 30 Jan. 1969, dated 29 Jan. 1969. Procter, part-time lecturer in the Advanced Studies Department, was a Fellow and Vice-President of the SIAD; Hancock, Senior Lecturer in the Graphic Design Department, was an Associate of the SIAD. They pointed to the SIAD submission to the Joint Committee of the NACAE (Coldstream) and NCDAD (Summerson) Councils, called to look into unrest in the art schools and the future of art education nationally, which advised greater flexibility together with an avoidance of dilettantism. Eight staff members gave evidence on 30 Jan.: the other six were Ian Simpson, Douglas Lowndes, David Joseph, Alin Braund, Richard Robbins and Jerry Eldridge. David Page had offered to give evidence, quoting from a letter he had sent to Shelton on 28 Feb. 1966, following a meeting at which the Principal had asked for concrete proposals for improving student morale. Page had suggested student common rooms, regular dances, a bar, cross-departmental seminars on design work etc., and had endorsed

Joseph's long-term effort to stimulate activity through the film society, the debating society and *Horn* (the student magazine). Shelton never replied. DP Box 1, DP to Cyril James, Clerk to Sub-Committee B, 22 Dec. 1968. DP Box 2 contains a ten-page commentary, sent to James on receipt of a copy of the *Minutes of Evidence* for 30 Jan. 1969.

42 HHS Brown Box 4, 'Papers 1960s + Harold Wilson', *Select Committee on Education and Science. Sub-Committee B, Memorandum of the Principal of the Hornsey College of Art* (typescript bound with black tape), p. 10: The sit-in 'was without doubt pre-arranged and apparently planned with outside support'. 'Every opportunity by participants has been taken to suggest that the Hornsey sit-in was unassociated with the main trend of student unrest and that it was concerned with art education policy' but the students 'made no approach at any time to senior staff' with serious criticisms of national policy and discussions had focused solely on control of Union funds and a sabbatical year for the Union President. Once this was agreed, by 24 May, Wright 'advised the Principal that this would end the trouble and he need not cancel an engagement in Manchester'. Shelton made similar assertions to a Special Council Meeting of the NCDAD on 1 July 1968: the disruption to the college was catastrophic, and ugly, but a matter of external provocation and contributions from staff who by the nature of their academic interests had no normal creative outlets. He did not consider that student unrest was fundamentally based on attitudes to art education in general or the DipAD in particular. Sir Robin Darwin countered that in his view the disturbances were a healthy and welcome sign of student vitality. National Archives, NCDAD papers, DB4/20, 1 July 1968. For his part David Page asserted in a letter to the *Guardian* (18 Oct. [1969], DP Box 4): 'The whole argument of the sit-in at Hornsey, as the documents show, was about the nature and purpose of education, not Student Union facilities. But that wasn't what the Select Committee were interested in, to the great regret of students and staff'. Even Kim Howells, who recalled that he was 'very keen on storming buildings, [and] really saw myself as a Red Guard when I went in and told the Principal he had to leave his office,' felt that 'in fact, the debate about creativity was in many ways even more fundamental to me than the directly political debate'. He added that his ideas about creativity were 'strongly reinforced by the occupation and all that led up to it. Painting pictures and making sculptures was just bourgeois individualism!' (Quoted in Fraser *et al.* (1988), pp.248–9.)

43 HHS Brown Box 4, 'Papers 1960s + Harold Wilson', *Memorandum of the Principal of the Hornsey College of Art, ibid.*, p.6.

44 In his evidence to the Select Committee, David Joseph said that he had been left with the distinct impression the Friday before, 24 May, that 'there was a big question mark' against the sit-in going ahead at all. HCA 3/3/Ingles, *Memorandum to the Sub-Committee of the Select Committee on Education and Science*, p. 34. Kim Howells confirms that he and the other dissidents 'had no idea what would happen' on 28 May (interview, 27 Feb. 2006).

45 Wright had always been open about his CP membership. Page thought of himself as an anarchist after the sit-in. Howells, described by several people as on friendly terms with the Crouch End International Socialists, insists that on the contrary he was an anarchist. Jim Singh-Sandhu, though theoretically 'anarcho-syndicalist', claims that 'conventional politics and organized religion were an anathema' to him as 'sources of problems for humanity, definitely not solutions' (communication 24 Feb. 2006). There was disagreement on the radical left as to whether students were, or could be, part of a revolutionary vanguard (even if they felt themselves alienated from the educational process in parallel with workers alienated from the process of production). One issue was their actual or potential class position and another their inability to inflict serious economic damage or disruption, compared with that of miners, dockers or transport workers who chose to withdraw their labour. Nick Wright, as a Communist, did not consider the sit-in a truly revolutionary situation (just as the leaders of the French Communist Party dismissed the Paris events, in May 1968, as a party, rather than a revolution). Tom Nairn, on the other hand, argued that it was the art students who had 'provided something of an avant-garde for the rest of the student movement' and 'taken the term "revolution" out of its inverted commas, for the first time in recent British history' ('On the Subversiveness of Art Students', the *Listener*, vol. 80, 17 Oct. 1968, pp. 491–2). See also Nairn, with Jim Singh-Sandhu, 'Chaos in the Art Colleges', in Cockburn and Blackburn (1969), pp. 103–18.

46 Neither Page nor Piper knew Kim Howells, the lynchpin of SAC, before 28 May. Piper hadn't known anything about plans for a 'teach-in' but, being in the building, had wandered along. He was concerned with the quality of the students' education and, with others, felt too high a price had been paid for Hornsey's public profile, with staff and technicians tied up in prestige projects for venues such as the Milan Triennale. He describes himself as 'quite ignorant of political things' although 'the *experience* politicized me and woke me up a bit' (telephone conversation, 23 Nov. 2005). Those aligned on the Piper axis, including Roberts and Bramwell-Davis, were apolitical in the sectarian sense (Bramwell-Davis was interested in Zen and eastern philosophy, the politics of William Cobbett, the ideas of Buckminster Fuller and Marshall McLuhan and the radical pedagogy of Paulo Freire). David Page called them 'engineers at heart', adding 'I would cheer at that, rather than sneer', though the more politicized saw it as misplaced Enlightenment optimism (correspondence 27 July 2006). On the other hand they shared a commitment to what is sometimes called 'inclusive design': to solving or alleviating the social problems associated with disabilities, or third-world development, or environmental issues. Design education was itself a design problem: something to be rationally analysed and, through a series of 'critical pathways', resolved. Those aligned on the left, the Page/Nairn/Howells axis, were politicized with different allegiances to different effect. This is evident in the history of *The Hornsey Affair*. Page, like Piper, had always insisted that the sit-in was primarily an educational experiment with educational objectives. He signed the contract for the book with Penguin and wrote the section on 'The First Four Days'. Prue Bramwell-Davis, notably systematic, organized the documentation. The manuscript was then re-edited by Tom Nairn and Vicky Hamilton, to the consternation of Bramwell-Davis, who felt that 'David and I and others had sweated blood all that summer to get it written and then they were going to put some kind of gloss on it that had nothing to do with that process' (communication 23 June 2007). This included framing the narrative with Marxian quotations and preambles.

47 Bramwell-Davis was amazed to discover, in the early days of the commission, that she and Piper had been thought 'the central core of the hard core of the Red plotters' by William Wall when at moments in the sit-in 'we were practically *lynched* for being so reasonable'. Bramwell-Davis to Piper, 13 Aug. 1968.

48 DP interviewed by Frederika Adam, copy provided by Dr Adam; DP Box 6 'Education in Action' typescript, p. 39; *The Hornsey Affair*, p. 63.

49 DP Box 4, Doc. 71A. Tariq Ali was the editor of *Black Dwarf* and a leader of the Vietnam Solidarity Campaign, responsible for major demonstrations in March and October 1968 and a common reference point for student protest groups internationally. Visitors from the École des Beaux-Arts were listened to respectfully, but blankly (interview with David Robins, who came with them, 3 Jan. 2006). See also Alex Roberts Papers, letter from Page to the editor of the *Hornsey Journal*, undated [mid-June 1968]. 'Let us be clear that there are no outside agitators involved. Obviously various political persons have tried to use the student action for their own purposes: the quiet ones have been politely listened to and their arguments refuted; the noisy ones have been escorted out of the college. . . .There is no need to feel, as your leader does, that democracy is in peril. This action took place precisely because of an undemocratic state of affairs. The answer is more democracy.' Students made the same points in their evidence to the Select Committee. When the chairman claimed that the programme for 28 May suggested people 'highly skilled in organizing disturbances', they pointed out that 'posters, publicity, pressure and so on' were part of their professional stock in trade (*Minutes*, p.12). David Joseph and Richard Robbins, among the staff, confirmed that feelings appeared to change as a result of discussions during the night of 28–9 May and that 'the emergence of a sit-in from the teach-in was in no sense premeditated or planned' (Joseph, *Minutes*, p.32).

50 There was a sit-in at the LSE in March 1967 and fighting between police and demonstrators outside the US Embassy in Grosvenor Square in October 1967 and March 1968. Events in Paris, in May 1968, had an international resonance. The American civil rights movement provided a further model, and television and newspapers what Margaret Thatcher would later call the oxygen of publicity. A sit-in poster, 'Bureaucracy. Smash the System', was reproduced on the cover of the *Listener*, 4 July 1968, alongside John Sparrow's article on 'Revolting Students' which cited disturbances at universities in California, Columbia, Rome, Paris and Berlin, and in Britain at Leicester, Kent, Hull, Essex and the LSE. By the end of 1968 there had been protests at seventeen universities and six local-authority colleges in the UK. Student unrest has been attributed to a range of local causes (confrontation with the authorities over discipline, or student union autonomy, or institutional representation, or politics), underpinned by long-term developments (unprecedented economic growth, high employment, the demographic 'bulge' of a post-war baby-boom, the emergence of a self-conscious youth culture facilitated by the expansion of capitalist markets, the growth of higher education absorbing a larger proportion of the teenage population (from 2.7 per cent of their age group before the Second World War to 11 per cent in 1967), above all by the changing profile of western capitalism: now more corporate, increasingly technologized, requiring more skilled and white-collar workers and fewer unskilled manual workers. See Fraser *et al.* (1988), Cockburn and Blackburn (1969), Crick and Robson (1970), Kurlansky (2004), and Judt (2005, especially Chapter XII, 'The Spectre of Revolution'). The Hornsey sit-in was part of the temper of the times, but it was not aligned with the sectarian left. It was devoted specifically and often pragmatically to the reform of art education and although several of its protagonists were broadly on the left, its politics emerged largely through its analysis of the social context of art and design.

51 DP Box 11, David Page to the Clerk to Sub-Committee B of the Select Committee [Cyril James], 25 Nov. 1969, citing an interview with Shelton in the *Guardian*, 21 Oct. 1969.

52 HHS Brown Box 4, 'Papers 1960s + Harold Wilson', 'Further Memorandum of the Principal of Hornsey College of Art' [to the Select Committee]. Shelton claims that complaints about Hornsey students spreading unrest were made by other principals at a meeting of the National Society for Art Education, at the Victoria & Albert Museum, on 6 July 1968, and to him personally.

53 Since Shelton was absent from the building for most of the summer this must have been gathered on his behalf. His papers contain a great deal of sit-in literature but the documents were forwarded to him by participants. It is not clear how some students' private and personal correspondence came into his possession. This may have occurred during a period in which college mail was rerouted by the post office to the 'government in exile' at Parkwood School. The Radical Student Alliance was an independent organization, formed in 1967 to protest against the raising of overseas students' fees, seeking educational revolution not reform. There is a flyer in HHS First Box, 'Hornsey 1960s'. It collapsed after about eighteen months, partly due to sectarian differences between Leninists, Trotskyists and libertarian anarchists (Fraser *et al.* (1988), p. 111). Kim Howells was a member of the Revolutionary Socialist Students' Federation (*ibid.*, p. 358) formed in June 1968. Its efforts were also hamstrung by sectarian division. Meanwhile the NUS, run hitherto by moderates to the right of the Labour movement, was itself becoming more radical. Jack Straw, elected to the presidency in April 1969, was a left-Labour candidate who had long argued that students should radicalize their own union and not splinter into left-wing sects (*ibid.*, pp. 250–1).

54 HHS First Box, 'Hornsey 1960s', RSSF Manifesto, adopted by the second RSSF conference, London, 10 Nov. 1969; HHS Brown Box 7, Founding Conference of RSSF, LSE, 14–15 June 1968: 'Events in France have shown the huge revolutionary potential that exists in Europe. . . . Even in Britain a wave of unrest is sweeping the universities. An organization of revolutionary socialist students can both expand and link this unrest to other sorts of struggle.'

See also Jack Woddis, '"Red Bases" in the Colleges', reprinted from *Comment*, a weekly journal of the Communist Party. This credits the student movement with two concerns: the democratization of the education system and, by contributing to revolutionary struggle, the overthrow of capitalism. HHS Brown Box 3, copies sent with covering letter 23 Apr. 1969 to E. E. Pullee (Chief Officer of the NCDAD), Councillors Hitchens and Bains, and Cyril James (Clerk to Sub-Committee B of the Select Committee, which had not yet published its report).

55 DP Box 6, 'Education in Action', p. 23. Kim Howells was quite explicit, on film (standing in front of a Che Guevara poster) and in *The Hornsey Affair* ('Against the Art Object', pp. 69–72), that artists were guilty of collusion, producing luxuries for 'the decadent bourgeois elite'. ('I say shit on their art world, I want nothing of it.')

56 HHS Diaries Box, undated typescript, apparently by Shelton: 'The promotion of a successful student revolution depends upon selecting an educational establishment which has obvious underlying reasons for discontent.'

57 See *The Hornsey Affair*, p. 53, on the Room F Seminar, 31 May, at which one speaker claimed: 'The whole ramshackle structure of art and design education is teetering. It never had a foundation anyway. With one good hard push we can bring it tumbling down. Once that is down the whole education system in this country, with its immoral barriers and its distorting early specialization, will be shaken. . . . And when we change education, we change the whole of society.' And also pp. 68–9: 'We have always emphasized the purely educational character of our protest, but . . . it would be misleading to gloss over the fact that many of us are also protesting against aspects of the art world. . . . We object to being "educated for obsolescence" but we also object to being trained for demand by an art world gone capitalist.'

The sit-in attracted support from the Haringey branch of the Socialist Party of Great Britain. See AR Papers, 'To the Students of Hornsey College of Art', May 1968. 'We hope that your efforts to improve your working conditions, to raise the quality of your training and to obtain a more effective voice in college affairs will succeed. The problems against which you contend are symptoms of a society which cannot effectively serve human needs based as it is upon the class monopoly of the means of production, and the profit motive. . . . Art is the Cinderella of capitalism. . . . Only in a socialist society will the artist be free from domination by the values and pressures of a profit-seeking society.'

58 Apart from keeping disparate positions better united, it was the education question that best elicited public sympathy and brought the students high-profile support. According to the *Sunday Telegraph*, 23 June 1968, HHS 'Press Cuttings 1968': 'If any students have a genuine grievance, it is those at the schools of art. . . . They have a clear case for a close re-examination of the entire system of art education.' (The *Sunday Telegraph* also noted that Enoch Powell, the day before, had used student unrest as an argument against the growth of higher education.)

59 *The Hornsey Affair*, p.186 (many students felt they should disaffiliate from the National Union of Students). The second quotation comes from a red notebook, which appears to contain notes taken in sit-in meetings, in Shelton's papers, HHS First Box 'Hornsey 1960s': '*Courage*, we all recognize the real problem. It's not [at] our local authority level. What we propose is a social revolution. . . . It's a national issue and has to be fought on a national front.' Keith Grant's letter in the *Guardian*, 11 June 1968, HHS 'Press Cuttings 1968', also referred to Hornsey College of Art as a microcosm for social revolution.

60 DP Box 6, 'Education in Action', p. 73: 'The Hornsey affair took staff and students into the Houses of Lords and Commons. Our reaction was: government by professionals pretending to be amateurs. . . . The whole place is reminiscent of Hornsey in its makeshift unplanning, and when we suggested to one group that they needed to instigate a bit of a sit-in, they agreed, without demur.' (MPs and Lords were, however, 'both interested and helpful'.)

61 *The Hornsey Affair*, pp. 107, 108. This passage argues that a failure to recognize how the sit-in set out to transform everyday experience 'points to a weakness' in the position of more self-consciously revolutionary groups.

62 *The Hornsey Affair*, pp. 182–3, *Guardian*, 27 July 1968. This view was also advanced by Cathles in evidence to the Select Committee in 1969: 'It is our considered opinion that . . . the intellectual impetus came from a small group of staff without whom [the sit-in] would not have been prolonged' and also 'that despite appearances and the genuine belief of many students the sit-in was not spontaneous' but built on 'the preparatory work of a small group of staff and students whose avowed intent was to use this educational establishment as a means of enforcing social change'. *Minutes*, p.60.

63 *The Hornsey Affair*, pp. 184–5, *Guardian*, 30 July 1968. Page was more explicit, in drawing together again the terms that Piper so carefully kept apart. See DP Box 3, 'Notes towards a Red paper in education', published in the first issue of the *Leveller* (undated), p. 12. 'A way of changing society, anyhow, is to change education; contrariwise you can't change society and leave education alone. I might add in passing that people still show amazement when they stumble on the obvious fact that education is politics' (p. 12). The *Leveller* was planned as a quarterly for the non-sectarian left.

64 *The Hornsey Affair*, pp. 187–8, *Guardian*, 12 Aug. 1968. See also DP Boxes 2 and 11, for legal correspondence with Polden, Bishop and Gale, solicitors, over Bains's remarks. M. A. Polden (undated letter to Bains, Box 11) tried to mediate on behalf of James Meller, David Page, David Warren Piper and David Joseph who felt that their motives had been misconstrued and their professional reputations impugned because of their involvement in 'recent events'. Polden suggested a meeting but Bains replied through the Town Clerk that since he was aware of no such allegations he could see no useful purpose in a meeting (Box 2, letter from M. A. Polden to David Warren Piper copied to Page, 8 July 1968). Page wrote to Hugh Rossi MP on 15 Aug. 1968 referring to 'the scurrilous and defamatory letter about David Warren Piper written by Alderman Bains and published in the *Guardian*. It inevitably raised doubts in our minds as to Alderman Bains's fitness for his office. . . . How are we expected to act in this atmosphere of petty malevolence?'

65 These volumes (1973) were based on symposia organized at the Institute of Contemporary Arts in April and May 1971.

66 Piper (1973), vol. 1, p. 23. Piper, responsible for a new industrial design course at Hornsey with his colleague Patrick Burke, joined the Management Centre of the University of Bradford in autumn 1968. He was appointed a member of the NCDAD and participated in drawing up the *Joint Report* of the Summerson and Coldstream Councils in 1970.

67 HHS Diaries Box, memo from Piper to Leslie Roberts, 27 Feb. 1968, complaining of poor physical conditions and alleging that the industrial design course was no longer that outlined by Patrick Burke (so that the students could sue). It was 'completely indefensible, that technicians' time and even students' time should be taken up on work [that may draw] public attention to the college but which has little or no educational content. . . . I am of the opinion that the college is morally in the wrong.' Shelton, on the other hand, alluding to Piper, told the Select Committee that new staff arriving after the introduction of the DipAD failed to recognize that the college was preparing students for industry and commerce. Piper had criticized work on the electric town car although 'he was not an industrial designer' and 'he influenced students to withdraw from this and also from another project on behalf of the national body, Action for the Crippled Child, which up to that time certain students were most enthusiastic about'.

68 Shelton described Piper as a 'clever and dangerous psychologist' and alleged to the Select Committee that he 'slept in the college and in his Ford Thames Mini Bus parked outside.' (Piper lived within walking distance with his wife and children and this was quite untrue.) For the first, see Peter Laurie and Roger Law, 'What Really happened at Hornsey', *Sunday Times Magazine*, 13 Sept. 1970, p. 43, and for the second, 'Further

Memorandum of the Principal of Hornsey College of Art' [to the Select Committee], HHS Brown Box 4, 'Papers 1960s + Harold Wilson'. Shelton also claimed that David Warren Piper and Alan Grant had promoted the College Council only as 'a power structure for furthering their own ideas and objectives and an organization for discussing and promoting personal grievances' (*ibid.*).

69 Richard Robbins, unpublished *Memoir*, pp 3–4: 'It was a shock to teach in an art school after my time at Oxford. . . . In the morning a senior member of staff stood at the door checking in staff and students. Classes started at 9.30 and at 9.40 a red line was drawn so that late arrivals could be identified. Students were not meant to go out to lunch. Registers were conscientiously marked.' Richard Robbins, a painter and sculptor now retired from teaching, joined the Fine Art Department in 1963. I am very grateful to him for the loan of this memoir, compiled apparently in two stages (1985 and 1992). See also Tom Nairn's account of arriving at Hornsey in *The Hornsey Affair*, pp. 15–25.

70 HCA 3/3/Ingles, Confidential Proof, *Minutes of Evidence taken before the Select Committee on Education and Science (Sub-Committee B)*, Thursday, 30 Jan. 1969, p. 36. Following on from Bernard Hancock and Ian Simpson, whose evidence implied that distinguished individuals had 'dabbled' in the protest and thereby extended it, Joseph objected to the contrary that the presence and interest of figures of the calibre of John Summerson, Nikolaus Pevsner and Robin Darwin 'was an expression of their sense of responsibility and concern'. Asked if he was suggesting that the Principal, the governors or the local authority were in some way impeding the work of his department, Joseph replied that since the sit-in he had lost the sympathy and support he formerly enjoyed. 'I have felt I have been held responsible to an extraordinary degree for encouraging, aiding and abetting the students' and 'a number of extraordinary allegations' have been 'made about my activities'. The Principal 'has failed to protect me and my department from a situation which has rendered it almost impossible for the department to function'. The ATTI, in a written submission to the Select Committee, also pointed out that the Principal, the administration and a high proportion of senior staff withdrew at the beginning of the sit-in: a collective failure of leadership, in its view. Staff attitudes varied, of course. Some, no doubt, were simply curious (Marc Vaux); some were opposed (Trevor Frankland); some were sympathetic to ends but not to means (Richard Robbins); some were ardent supporters and contributors (in their different ways, Piper and Page). Dr Suzanne Lang was probably more alarmed than anyone: a refugee from Nazi Austria, she associated the student revolution with the *Anschluss* (John Field, communication 21 Jan. 2007).

71 *The Hornsey Affair*, p. 212. In the early 1960s the General Studies Department housed an assortment of highly intelligent and forceful academics, among them Joseph Darracott, John Field, Hannah Gavron, Alan Grant, John Hayes, David Joseph, Michael Kidron, Michael Kullman, Suzanne Lang, Tom Nairn, David Page, David Warren Piper and John Rae. During these years, in favoured areas at least, the college was an ambitious and vital place in which to work.

72 *The Hornsey Affair*, p. 211.

73 Bains, in evidence to the Select Committee, claimed that staff, especially General Studies staff, provided intellectual coherence and the drive to keep the sit-in going. But he did not blame Joseph: 'I think he was a bit like the Duke of Plaza Toro, leading his troops from behind' (*Minutes*, p. 85).

74 Shelton claimed in his evidence to the Select Committee that Joseph's name on the list incriminated him (*Minutes*, p. 28).

75 HHS Large Cardboard Box 1, Folder 10, Joseph to Shelton, 27 Jun. 1968. Joseph said that he would have to take legal advice if this allegation was not 'absolutely and without reservation refuted'. HHS Second Box, 'Hornsey, Countryside Association, 1960s-1980s. Design', Joseph to Shelton, 2 July 1968, following their meeting the day before in the members' room at the Royal Institute of British Architects. Joseph confirmed that Shelton dissociated himself from the so-called 'loyalty oath', circulated among senior staff, claiming to have had no part in its production.

76 *The Hornsey Affair*, p. 212. The art historians were allowed to continue in 'an attic warren' at the main building, condemned as a fire hazard. Apart from Joseph Darracott, a member of the Commission, they were not caught up in the sit-in and thus considered relatively 'safe'. See also DP Box 7, ink manuscript in Page's hand outlining events in the autumn of 1968. Alexandra Park School was cleared out during the third week of November but the block release system drawn up to take students there for one day per fortnight was abandoned. Page points out that timetable clashes that led to this could have been resolved in the six weeks during which staff were 'on call' before the delayed reopening of the college.

77 DP Box 1, 'Art History and Complementary Studies. Interim Arrangements for Complementary Studies', undated but Nov./Dec. 1968. Students would need to amass eighty-four credits over three years from courses worth twelve credits per term. DP Box 1, Joseph to Page, 9 Dec. 1968, concerning the meeting at which a 'compact majority', including Romek Marber, Bernard Hancock, Jack Shaw, Julian Robinson and Tom Robb, 'extracted from Mr Shelton a decision that Art History and Complementary Studies should from now on be arranged separately with reference to individual departmental requirements. These requirements could well include such intellectually stimulating options as "Creative Tax Avoidance". This last was supposed to be a subject of great importance and relevance to future graphic designers.' Shelton would later claim that relocating General Studies in the departments was designed to integrate it more closely with work in the studios: 'This was based on an educational argument and was to overcome the total stagnation which was growing within the General Studies area.' HHS Brown Box 8, 'Papers 1960s', typescript of a reply apparently sent to a letter from Jack Straw, Deputy President, National Union of Students, to Councillor G. Murphy, chairman of the Haringey Education Committee, 29 May 1969.

78 *The Hornsey Affair*, p. 214, quoting the Christmas 1968 edition of *Revelations*, a dissident college publication: 'Already three have gone, and others are applying for every available job elsewhere. There may be some people who think: "General Studies! So what, isn't that just a few boring lectures and seminars less all round?" But this is to miss the point completely. . . . It's not being axed because some students were bored. It's being liquidated because of what it has come to *represent*. . . .The capacity of people to think and act for themselves, to behave critically and constructively instead of just doing what they are told* [italics in original].' The part-time contracts of Linda Stillitz, Neil van Allen, Tom Nairn and Vicky Hamilton were not renewed. (The Select Committee asked Cathles about part-time staff who were not re-engaged and he claimed that this was normal. Was there any relation to the sit-in? 'No, no relationship at all'. *Minutes*, p. 87.) The part-time lecturer Victor Perkins and the full-time staff Alan Grant, David

Warren Piper, Joseph Darracott, Suzanne Lang, John Rae and David Joseph all resigned in 1968–9. Page remained, until in March 1970 the governors upheld Shelton's decision not to renew his contract. Bains insisted that the decision was 'based on academic considerations put before us by the Principal after consultation with his senior academic colleagues', bearing in mind declining numbers in Page's classes, and had 'absolutely nothing to do with [his] penchant for publicly criticizing the college administration, nor his contribution to the 1968 sit-in'. (Alan Beattie, however, claimed that Simpson had told him the real reason was Page's status as a political nuisance, but sufficient academic reasons could probably be established.) See on this DP Box 11, extensive correspondence with the ATTI, and *Inside Hornsey*, vol. 2, no. 3, 9 Mar. 1970, a special issue intended to 'clear the air' over Page's contract and the resignation of Alan Beattie. And also DP Box 4, 'To the Principal from Members of the General Studies Department', a memo objecting to the dismissal of part-time staff and to the bypassing of the consultative machinery now supposedly in place in the college: 'How can you believe that this sort of action does not produce suspicion and resentment?. . . It also adds weight to the growing body of rumours that suggest that you are about to arrange for the closure of the General Studies Department as a department' (with grave consequences for the future of the college). The authorities at Hornsey were canny enough to avoid the more public scandal at Guildford School of Art, where seven full-time staff were dismissed in addition to thirty-five part-timers. See letter from Peter Hall and Kay Hunt, *Studio International*, vol. 176, Dec. 1968, p. 239.

79 DP Box 1, 'To Members of the College and Other Interested Persons', a statement on Joseph's resignation by David Page and John Rae, 28 Apr. 1969. This warned that General Studies staff would no longer have a general view of the college or staff the stimulus of belonging to a multi-disciplinary department; students would lose a common meeting ground, a forum for wide-ranging discussion and a spring-board for extramural activities; and the college would lose resident specialists, its intellectual reputation and – if it failed to satisfy the Quinquennial Review – its DipAD accreditation. David Page had written to Shelton on 18 Mar. 1969 (DP Box 1), complaining that the programme had been hamstrung from the start of the year 'by lack of facilities and absurd conditions'. The college's licence to run diploma courses was in jeopardy. 'When I last saw you with David Joseph you informed us that you were not responsible for the co-ordination of the departments of the college, and that you were no longer able to make executive decisions. I cannot accept this as an adequate explanation. If you feel unable, for whatever reason, to carry out your duty to the College, then I must remind you that you have only one honourable recourse.'

Letters replying to their dismissal from Tom Nairn and Vicky Hamilton and Alan Grant's resignation letter from Fine Art are reproduced in *Revelations* V (an unofficial student publication, unpaged). Copies of Joseph's resignation letter and James Meller's from Industrial Design are in David Warren Piper's papers. Nairn considers his dismissal 'an unintended tribute' and the sit-in 'the most valuable educational experience of my career'. Hamilton regrets that Shelton and his allies 'have crushed the great upsurge of creative thinking' following 28 May and considers that Joseph has been 'treated abominably'. Grant refers to 'the almost hysterical attempts to prove political motivation for the sit-in, which in fact stemmed from real failings in our college'. Joseph points out that he has been 'placed in a position where I cannot effectively attempt what I was originally appointed to do'. And Meller resigns 'solely because the cumulative effects of the decisions taken by you [Shelton] and your associates have created a situation in the Industrial Design Section in which I find education is no longer possible.'

80 Haringey Further Education Sub-Committee (1/LBH/C14), agenda papers for 21 May 1969, Item 13A. Ian Simpson became Principal of St Martin's College of Art in September 1972. DP Box 1 contains the advertisement for the Head of Coordinated Studies inscribed *Times Educational Supplement*: 'This is a newly created post resulting from the realization by the Main [i.e. presumably Studio] Areas of the College of the need to achieve an integrated programme of Visual Research, Complementary Studies and History of Art and Design'. Notes in Page's hand record his fury that this reproduced yet again the division 'between *teaching* and *administration* of a department'. At a meeting with Haringey, Jack Straw and others from the National Union of Students expressed 'grave disquiet at the methodology and educational philosophy behind this decision' but to no effect. See DP Box 8, Straw (now President of the NUS) to Edward Short (Secretary of State at the DES), 20 Apr. 1970, glossing events that led to the NUS decision to blacklist Hornsey and Guildford Colleges of Art from 21 Apr. 1970. DP Box 1, memo from Warren Piper to Joseph, 17 Nov. 1967.

81 Richard Wollheim, 'Should art be a respectable occupation?', *Sunday Times Magazine*, 8 Sept. 1968, pp. 22–4, 28 (quotation p. 22). Relations at Hornsey were amiable enough in the early 1960s (John Rae and Jonathan Miller both confirm this), but by 1967–8 – embroiled in his own troubles and following the departure of Aneurin Thomas, who had helped keep things together – Shelton seems to have become too detached to recognize, let alone respond to, the atmosphere of frustration and mistrust in less favoured parts of the college. More than one ex-member of staff has described him, privately, as autocratic, indecisive, deluded and even rather unstable in this period.

82 Shelton expanded the college from around 200 full-time students in 1957 to 860 in 1968, increasing departments, resources, and high-powered staff. Peter Laurie and Roger Law claim that since higher education principals were paid per capita, like pig farmers, this also increased his salary by over £1000 per year. 'What Really Happened at Hornsey?', *Sunday Times Magazine*, 13 Sept. 1970, p. 36.

83 *The Hornsey Affair*, p. 51.

84 Page's claim – that Shelton 'ruled by vague indication, so that he could disclaim responsibility for any actual decisions, which were always made by secondary people who thought they were reading his mind' – is confirmed by others.

85 HHS Brown Box 9, 'Papers, 1960s', maroon folder containing a 'Private and Confidential Statement' in reply to the council's terms of reference for the inquiry into the general purposes fund. The day-to-day running of the college was the responsibility of the Vice Principal in concert with the Registrar and college administration. By contrast Bains, in a letter to staff dated 22 July 1968, claimed: 'The Principal is specifically responsible for the internal organization, management and discipline of all departments' (AR Papers).

86 DP Box 1, 'The Office of Principal, the Board of Governors. A Study Paper', typed with amendments in Page's hand, 19 numbered points. 'Clashes like the sit-in occur when an organization has no satisfactory machinery for the examination of diverging [views] and their resolution into an agreed policy.'

87 Eric Robinson, *The New Polytechnics* (1968), p. 169.

88 Peter Laurie and Roger Law, the *Sunday Times Magazine*, 13 Sept. 1970, p.47. Piper told the Select Committee that it was Shelton's characteristic style of management 'to get people into his room singly, so it was impossible later to substantiate exactly what had been said, what suggestions had been made and what bargains had been struck'. *Minutes*, p. 49.

89 Memorandum to the Select Committee from Alan Grant, *Minutes*, pp. 42–4. Grant resigned in May 1968 over poor relations and lack of communication between staff, students and administration, dating to the departure of the former Vice Principal, Aneurin Thomas, early in 1967. In his view Shelton had 'lost control of his college, and since then he has been able neither to regain it, nor to accept the genuineness of the need for radical reform and democratization in matters of policy and teaching'. Richard Robbins recalls Shelton also making a remark to him about turning the sit-in to his own advantage.

90 Peter Laurie and Roger Law, the *Sunday Times Magazine*, 13 Sept. 1970, p. 45.

91 *The Hornsey Affair*, p. 51. Shelton must have felt outflanked by the sit-in as well as bemused. Speaking as the new President of the National Society for Art Education in 1963, he had referred to the new era brought in by the DipAD as an 'opportunity for the complete overhaul of the art education system'. The revolution had already taken place (with the switch from the NDD) or it would happen on different terms (when he became head of a design research institute somewhere between Hornsey's Advanced Studies Department, the Bauhaus and the Royal College of Art). He would later claim that it was only after the students took over his office and broke into his files that they moved from local grievances to challenge the whole system of art education. But if he felt that they were using his own ideas against him, he was underestimating the extent to which the sit-in developed when specific frustrations boiled over (and also the extent to which it was set up as a critical 'teach-in' from the beginning). He was temperamentally both indecisive and autocratic, and facing outwards in pursuit of his vision for the college he neglected to look over his shoulder to the welfare of his troops. After the sit-in he applied unsuccessfully for jobs elsewhere while denying that there was any truth in the rumour that he was leaving (see various unidentified press clippings in the Jenny Cole scrapbook, HCA Archive). In a bid to become Director of Newcastle Polytechnic he had to acknowledge that he was known for 'very strong views' on the 'polytechnic idea' but insisted that these were merely 'statements of concern', limited to the Hornsey case. Applying for the post of Director of the Architectural Association he insisted that his application 'in no way' related to 'the present matter of student unrest' (he had been thinking of a change and eight months earlier had been shortlisted for the post of Director of the Spastics Society). See HHS Brown Box 4, 'Papers 1960s + Harold Wilson', application to Newcastle 15 Oct. 1968; and Second Box, 'Hornsey, Countryside Ass., 1960s–1980s. Design', undated pencil draft of application to the Architectural Association.

92 Foundation Courses had been set up at Hornsey and elsewhere in 1962 to prepare students for the DipAD.

93 DP Box 2, 'National Council for Diplomas in Art and Design. Quinquennial Review 1968/9. General Arrangements'. Reviews were carried out between October 1968 and April 1970.

94 DP Box 4, Page to Joseph, 5 July [1969]. Things were very much worse in General Studies than for 'loyal' staff in other departments. Whereas Bernard Hancock (graphics), Douglas Lowndes (film) and Jack Procter (industrial design) told the Select Committee that the new arrangements were working smoothly, David Joseph said that 'in trying to trace or unravel the source of a decision one invariably finds it disappears'; and Alan Grant claimed that 'students are now immeasurably worse served in educational and human terms than before the sit-in. . . . The college authorities have behaved irresponsibly, reckless of agreements openly reached in the summer, and regardless of student welfare.' *Minutes*, pp.35–6, 42.

95 DP Box 1, two letters from Summerson to Page, 21 Mar. and 22 May 1969. Once Piper was appointed to the Summerson Council in October 1968, concerns about the college could be aired directly inside the Council. In Apr. 1969 Piper urged that the situation with General Studies was far from satisfactory, given that most staff had left or were in the process of leaving. National Archives, NCDAD papers, DB4/13, Council Meetings nos. 51–3, 1 Apr. 1969.

96 DP Box 2, 'National Council for Diplomas in Art and Design. Quinquennial Review 1968/9. General Arrangements'.

97 DP Box 8, 'Statement' issued by Brian Darby, Press and Information Officer, London Borough of Haringey, 13 Feb. 1970. The fact that the move of certain departments to Cat Hill had been postponed until early 1970, made it difficult for the Visiting Board to form an accurate picture of college facilities. Summerson was reported as appreciating that a range of difficulties had arisen since the disruptions of 1968.

98 This and the following information is taken from DP Box 7, *Inside Hornsey*, vol. 3, no. 3, 8 May 1970, in which Councillor Gerald Murphy, now chair of Haringey Education Authority, released letters exchanged between Haringey and the NCDAD (Summerson Council) in a bid for transparency. The implication of the reference to a 'senior specialist' staff-member responsible for Art History and Complementary Studies was that these areas should no longer be represented at executive level by a non-specialist, i.e. the Head of Co-ordinated Studies, the ex-Head of Visual Research. The college believed that the press release issued on 13 Feb. had been agreed with NCDAD and also, wrongly as it turned out, that they had understood on 16 Jan. the full extent of NCDAD's reservations. In his introduction to the published letters, Murphy claims that after Stranks had asked for fuller details that could be used as a blueprint for change, and NCDAD had reconvened on 24 March, it 'produced a "blueprint" which not only changes the emphasis but is also at some variance with that discussed in January'. In his letter to Pullee of 17 Apr., Slater also complained of damaging statements in the *Guardian* in December, attributed to 'unauthorized disclosure' from NCDAD proceedings and confidential exchanges of view on a number of issues. Pullee's reply is dated 27 Apr.

99 DP Box 6, unsigned letter from the NUS to Edward Short, Secretary of State, DES, 20 Apr. 1970, setting out reasons for the blacklisting of Hornsey and Guildford and again requesting a major inquiry into events at both institutions. At Hornsey, the writer cites uncertainty about the polytechnic merger, poor student morale, the vicissitudes of the Industrial Design section of the Three-Dimensional Design Department, NUS suspicion of the 'dual structure' leaving actual executive power unchanged, postponement of the move to Cat Hill with inadequate preparation for the shortfall, the alteration of term dates and alarm over the massive restructuring of General Studies. See also DP Box 7, *Inside Hornsey*, vol. 2 no. 4, 18 Mar. 1970, reporting on the Union meeting of more than 200 students which called for more participation in college government, asked the NUS to blacklist the college (which it did, from 21 Apr.) and passed a vote of no confidence in the Principal and college administration. See also DP Box 2, 'A Boycott on the 28 May' [1969], reporting the Union's demand that Shelton immediately resign 'as he has shown himself incompetent to run the college'. DP Box 8, *Inside Hornsey*, vol. 3 no. 1, 20 Apr. 1970, contains a piece by Shelton, 'What does blacklisting mean?', arguing that because of a motion passed by only a small minority of the 700 students at the college, 100 additional students would be without places, the Students' Union would lose around £250 in annual subscriptions, other colleges would be reluctant to accept Hornsey students, staff would look for alternative appointments, diminishing numbers would threaten courses, standards would drop and students might even face problems finding employment. Staff and some students rallied with a petition against the blacklist. But Digby Jacks defended the Hornsey Students' Union, writing to Shelton on behalf of the NUS: 'I draw your attention to the recommendation of the Parliamentary Select Committee on Education and Science that, prima facie, there is a case for a public enquiry into the college, this combined with a major vote of no confidence, passed by the Hornsey Union, in yourself, combined with [the Summerson decision to reinspect], lead us to ask, when will you cease regarding the troubles at Hornsey as a "left-inspired plot" to get at you rather than a genuine mixture of grievance and concern that will not fade away of its own volition?' DP Box 6, Jacks to Shelton, 27 Apr. 1970.

100 NCDAD Papers, Modern Records Centre, University of Warwick, GB 152, MSS.322/AD, NCDAD 56/69. Agenda Item No. 5. Hornsey College of Art, *Summary of the Recommendations made by members of the Visiting Board in the Report submitted to Council*. I am grateful to James King, Senior Assistant Archivist, for a copy of this report. Strand (1987) discusses the quinquennial visit – by an unusually large team of fourteen including the Vice Chairman and six other members of Council – rather too complacently, on pp. 98–9.

101 Strand (1987), pp. 86–7, points out that the question of possible changes to the DipAD was raised within the NCDAD in 1967, after some discussion in the art press but well in advance of student disruptions in 1968. A letter from Andrew Forge, a member of the Fine Art Panel, in November 1967, led to a joint panel meeting on 8 February and ultimately to the setting up of a NCDAD working party on 25 Apr. 1968. Forge suggested that Coldstream's original prescription for fine art as a core study in the design areas was a source of restiveness, at the same time as fine art activities were increasingly diversified. Misha Black, a signatory to the *Joint Report*, believed that student unrest had sparked conviction into action but that three fundamental changes to the situation in 1960 had brought about the need for review: the automation of formerly craft-based industries such as textiles, ceramics and furniture, the development of industrial design courses, and the demand for a popular and accessible art that was not restricted to an aesthetic élite (he quoted Kim Howells from *The Hornsey Affair*). Black, 'Notes on Design Education in Great Britain' in Piper (1973), vol. 1, p. 32.

There had already been extensive discussion of the DipAD in *Studio International* from 1966, when the first cohort graduated. Victor Willing's 'What kind of art education?' (vol. 172, Sept. 1966, pp. 131–9), contained interviews with Richard Hamilton, Misha Black and Herbert Read: Hamilton favoured an emphasis on thinking rather than intuition; Black wanted separate categories of art and design but considered the ideal would be schools of human ecology linking studies in different aspects of the environment; Read suggested that art schools should be abolished and reoriented to design, or merged in institutions in which painting, sculpture, music, theatre and dance were studied outside an examined curriculum. There were follow-up articles in October 1966 (vol. 172, pp. 166–7, including a splenetic contribution from Roy Ascott, in favour of cybernetics and damning the 'mythical swinging scene'); November 1966 (vol. 172, pp. 226–7); January 1967 (vol. 173, pp. 4–5, including Tom Hudson, insisting on common ground between artists, designers and architects); March 1967 (vol. 173, pp. 117, including Christopher Cornford's counterblast to Black's 'educational apartheid' between art and design); and Sept. 1968 (vol. 176, pp. 65–6: Tom Hudson's 'Points in a reconstructive primer for the creative individual' which incorporate a number of issues raised in the sit-in). 'What kind of art education?' was a question indissolubly linked, of course, to 'What kind of artist? Or designer?'

102 Both Summerson and Pevsner, chair of the Art History Panel, visited the Hornsey sit-in in June. See also National Archives ED206/5 NACAE (68), letter from Coldstream to members of the NACAE, 19 Jun. 1968. 'You will of course be aware of the unrest which exists at a number of colleges of art. The issues involved are in many cases of purely domestic relevance. . . . There does, however, seem to be some dissatisfaction with certain aspects of art and design courses on which I think it is important that we as a Council should have a view.' The minutes of the meeting on 2 July (*ibid.*) indicate that Coldstream had been to see the Minister, Shirley Williams, 'and told her that he thought his Council should set up a working group to take the views of students and others'. Since it appeared that this would overlap substantially with the NCDAD working party, which was collecting the views of colleges on possible modifications to the DipAD, the two were merged.

103 See Nat. Archives, ED 206/5, NACAE (68) 3rd meeting. Nikolaus Pevsner's letter in the *Listener*, vol. 80, 18 July, p. 83, 'Hornsey's Revolution', solicited submissions and explained: 'Both Councils are naturally aware of views being currently expressed and they feel that there should be an opportunity for the current structure to be looked at and, if necessary, reassessed.' See also the *Joint Report of the National Advisory Council on Art Education and the National Council for Diplomas in Art and Design: The Structure of Art and Design Education in the Further Education Sector*, HMSO, 1970. Selections are edited and introduced in Ashwin (1975), pp. 123–36. The Joint Committee was smaller than either the NACAE or the NCDAD, and consisted of 19 members: Coldstream, Summerson (the Vice Chair), D. Bethel, M. Black, R. Darwin (resigned 19 May 1969), A. Forge, M. W. Hawes, Ald. Mrs M. J. Keeble (the only woman), G. W. R. Lines, A. MacIntyre (resigned 2 Dec. 1969), S. C. Mason, M. Pattrick, N. Pevsner, D. J. Warren Piper, S. Shelton (no relation), W. G. Stone, R. A. Strand, E. Walker, N. Ward. Seven were drawn from the NACAE, eight from the NCDAD, and four had positions on both. The Joint Committee met on 48 occasions including one weekend session and its report, published in 1970, was longer and more comprehensive than those appearing previously from either of its constituent bodies (over 60 pages, more than 160 paragraphs with statistics attached). The *Select Committee Report* (1969) specifically recommended that the joint review should include the administrative, social and other problems arising from the introduction of diploma courses and involve consultation with those directly involved in teaching art (this point was drawn out in the summary in Appendix II, 1/LBH/C14/1, Further Education Sub-Committee Minutes, 10 Nov. 1969). By the end of July 1968 the Joint Committee had already received 136 submissions. There is extensive material from principals of colleges, designers and lecturers in the National Archives including sample curricula. See for example ED206/12 NACAE (SC) 1968 (which includes a letter from Richard Robbins, 20 July 1968, as 'a member of Hornsey College staff who has not been in support of the sit-in'); ED206/13 (including a letter from John and Barbara Latham with a 'Proposal for a Department of Eventstructure, Hornsey, June 1968'); ED206/15 (including a 'Report of discussions by a panel of staff and students formed to consider the present structure of art education' from St. Martin's College, and a submission from Aneurin Thomas, who had left Hornsey to run the Welsh Arts Council early in 1967 but still felt 'very concerned about developments'); and ED206/17 (which includes the draft report of the Hornsey commission working party, 'Problems in Art and Design Education. Objectives, and Action to be taken'). ED206/17 NACAE (SC) (69) 7 records a meeting of the Joint Committee with NUS members including Jack Straw, the Deputy President, Nick Wright, ex-Hornsey student and member of the NUS Art Colleges Advisory Panel, and David Poston, Acting President of the Hornsey Students' Union.

104 AR papers, Press Cuttings, Richard Bourne, 'Art courses "must use new ideas"', *Guardian*, 12 Aug. 1968; and HHS 'Press Cuttings Box 1968', *The Times*, 4 Sept. 1968, 'Power plan for art students', quoting Summerson: 'We do look for change. . . We don't regard the excitement among students as one enormous rag. It's a very serious matter. There is plenty of evidence that art colleges are radically rethinking their DipAD syllabi.'

105 HCA Press Cuttings, C. E. W. Deacon in the *Listener*, 15 Aug. 1968, with reference to Nikolaus Pevsner in the issue of 18 July. The same point was developed by David Warren Piper in Piper (1973), vol. 2, p.57. The NACAE, by then and for the time being suspended by the Secretary of State, had had no servicing unit to prepare information for it to consider but relied on the informed opinion of its members. The NCDAD was concerned to inspect colleges and uphold the standard of the DipAD. Neither was actively responsible for educational policy and, insofar as it was too remote, nor was the DES.

106 Extracted in Ashwin (1975), p. 125.

107 *Joint Report* regretted the division between Art History and Complementary Studies, expressed a desire to bring them closer together, and then concluded that the history of art and design was *part* of Complementary Studies. In his 'Note of Dissent' Pevsner insisted that the fifteen per cent of time devoted to academic studies in the DipAD curriculum was 'a dire necessity'. 'It is clarity of thought and expression, it is unbiased recognition of problems, it is the capacity for discussion and it is ultimately understanding – they must achieve. But to understand one must know the facts; to know the facts one must learn the facts, and to choose the relevant facts one must command a surplus of facts. That is the unpalatable truth' (extracted in Ashwin, 1975, pp. 135–6).

108 D. W. Piper, 'Art and Design Education', *Studio International*, vol. 181, May 1971, pp. 194–7 (quotation p. 196). Piper wrote the final chapter of the *Joint Report* but came close to not signing it and submitting a minority report instead (conversation 23 Nov. 2005). He believed that two important 'network' principles were put forward there: that 'irrevocable decisions about specialization should be delayed as long as possible' and that the emphasis should shift 'from selection of students for courses to the selection of courses for students' (p.196). These were presumably wrested from Misha Black, who claimed that generalization must develop from specialization and not the other way around; that a flexible network system could only produce dilettantes in a three-year course; and (in a dig at Piper) that those who promoted it were not practising designers but inexperienced students or academic theoreticians. Black acknowledged that given the rate of technological change, specialist skills were threatened with obsolescence, but insisted that the core curriculum must still retain an intense concentration on known techniques while acknowledging their transient value. See Misha Black, 'Notes on Design Education in Great Britain', in Piper (1973), vol. 1, pp. 29–45. Black had been appointed Professor of the new School of Industrial Design (Engineering) at the Royal College of Art in 1959. Up to that point 'the kind of industrial designer who knew about engineering – as opposed to the kind of designer who had emerged from the craft tradition – was still part of a very rare species' (Frayling (1987), p. 142). Around 1970 students studying industrial design (engineering) were still only about` two per cent of the full-time art and design total (cited in Misha Black, *ibid.*, p. 39).

109 A deputation from the NUS, including representatives from Guildford, Hornsey, Birmingham, Brighton and Oxford colleges of art, had met with Shirley Williams and DES officials on 8 July 'to discuss the recent events in art education' and the proposed working party, under Coldstream, that subsequently became the Joint Committee. The deputation presented their views on the causes of student unrest and outlined vital reforms they hoped would be introduced without delay. The Minister apparently suggested that the Hornsey commission should pass its findings to the Coldstream Council as promptly as possible. NW Papers, Box 1, 'A Summary of NUS Meeting with Mrs Shirley Williams and DES Officials – Monday 8 July 1968'.

110 Pevsner wrote an informal, five-page paper on 'History of Art and Complementary Studies in Colleges of Art', included with the Joint Committee minutes, ED206/11, NACAE (SC) (68) 9. He was in favour of increased student representation. Students had been on the Board of Governors at Birkbeck College, where he taught, for a generation, and were 'invariably helpful and enlightening'. Students could not just do what they enjoyed: all university subjects required elements that were more or less to the taste of particular individuals. Exams should stay. Nevertheless, the argument that the history of art had been too much a history of painting and sculpture was valid: 'The textile designer needs no Giotto (or a little will go a long way).' More design history in the specialist areas was needed. But even an obscure corner of art history could be illuminated by the lecturer's passion: it was true that in art colleges it had been 'too unenthusiastic, too antiquarian, in short too dull'.

111 The proposed distinction between 'higher' or 'B' and 'lower' or 'design technician' courses recognized in part a *fait accompli*, in that certain colleges denied recognition for the DipAD had developed specialized, high-level, non-diploma courses of their own.

112 On the reception of the *Joint Report* and debates leading up to it see: Norbert Lynton, 'Waiting for Coldstream', *Studio International*, vol. 178, Sept. 1969, pp. 58–9;

Norbert Lynton, 'Coldstream 1970', *Studio International*, vol. 180, Nov. 1970, pp. 167–8; Roy Ascott, 'The Coldstream Report', *Studio International*, vol. 181, Jan. 1971, p.6; Ray Watkinson, 'Coldstream Report', *Arts Review*, vol. XXII, 10 Oct. 1970, p. 640; 'NUS Seminar on the Coldstream Report' and 'Comment on Coldstream', invited responses from a number of college principals including Shelton, *Arts Review*, vol. XXII, 21 Nov. 1970, pp. 766–9; D. W. Piper, 'Art and Design Education', *Studio International*, vol. 181, May 1971, pp. 194–7. Lynton believed that the 'old' system had scarcely been tried: that Summerson had 'accepted all the kicks that were going with a willingness' he found culpable (1969). Now 'the sloppy past' of the NDD was sliding back, flavoured with the demagoguery of 1968 (1970). Watkinson claimed that despite high-minded sentiments the 'vicious philosophy' of the *Joint Report* would 'destroy most of the good effects' of the DipAD. An NUS seminar, at the ICA on 3 Nov. 1970, unanimously rejected it (although David Hockney left after asserting that it did not matter whether art-school teaching was good or bad, since artists just evolved). Shelton, who found the absence of co-opted industrialists 'a serious omission', wanted two diplomas: a Diploma in Art and Design (General) and a more specialized Diploma in Design (Professional). Ascott, arguing that the committee had 'failed to respond to the cultural impact of new scientific thought and technology', asked for 'research into the relevance and methodologies of visual learning and the variable conditions for creative behaviour'. Digby Jacks, President of the NUS, called the *Joint Report* thoroughly contradictory: 'Of course it is. It is well known that several members of the committee have directly opposite viewpoints and each is catered for' (quoted by Stuart Macdonald in Piper (1973), vol. 2, p.99). Piper, though not uncritical, nonetheless wrote in its defence: 'Sweep away the verbiage, . . . look behind the compromises, and there is an outline plan for future development.' The NUS *Policy Statement on Art/Design Education* (1971) was reviewed in *Studio International* by Linda Morris (vol. 183, Nov. 1971, p. 168).

113 HHS Brown Box 9, 'Comments on the Coldstream/Summerson Report 16. 12. 70'.

114 DP Box 3, unpaged cutting from *Design*, no. 265, Jan. 1971. Compare the proposals of the 'Board of Design Education [of the SIAD], Evidence for submission to the joint Summerson & Coldstream Working Party [final draft] Jan. 1969'. These include separate diplomas for art and for design, four-year courses with a common first year, network options in the second and third years, organization and management skills as an additional area of study, high-level vocational courses, security of tenure for part-time staff and an education research body concerned with art and design.

115 Coldstream had written to the Secretary of State on 5 Feb. 1971 to 'clarify certain points' in the *Joint Report* 'which appeared to have given rise to misinterpretation' (Nat. Archives ED206/8 NACAE (71) 1). There is a copy of Thatcher's response to the Joint Report, Circular 7/71, 12 Jul. 1971, in ED206/8 NACAE (71) 2. Rushton and Wood argue that 'the Joint Committee's preoccupation was to keep the flag fluttering over the independent fortress of art education when in reality that position was already subverted', not merely by absorption into the polytechnics, but through the changing staff-student ratios, part-time staff reductions, budget constraints and increasing bureaucracy which this entailed (Rushton and Wood (1978), p.29).

Retrospect (pages 83–99)

1   Tom Nairn, 'On the Subversiveness of Art Students', the *Listener*, vol. 80, 17 Oct. 1968, pp. 491–2 (quotation p. 492).

2   Rushton and Wood (1978), p. 25.

3   The Select Committee had recommended a greater level of student participation and the government had stressed the necessity of proper administrative structures and instruments of governance, particularly in the new polytechnics. Rushton and Wood see this as a 'straightforward liberal tactic of appeasement' endorsed by a reformist NUS, and quote from the proceedings of a 1969 conference on *Student Unrest and Technical Education* (Coombe Lodge Report, vol. 2, no. 7, 1969), in which participation is described as 'the only way to absorb student unrest. . . . Better to institutionalize it and to dissipate it in the administrative routine. . . than to face a violent unexpected explosion' (pp. 24, 25).

4   On 'strain' in Durkheim and social theory, see Hermann Strasser and Susan C. Randall eds., *An Introduction to Theories of Social Change* (London: Routledge Kegan Paul, 1981), p. 83. N. J. Smelser's *Theory of Collective Behaviour* (New York: Free Press, 1962) is discussed on p.222. Smelser's determinants on collective behaviour are listed as structural conduciveness; structural strain; the spread of a generalized belief; particular precipitating factors; the mobilization of participants for action; and the operation of social controls anticipating or restraining collective behaviour. In the case of the sit-in, 'structural conduciveness' was a matter of the increasing vociferousness of students in general, the example of Paris, and the experience of the anti-polytechnic campaign. Sources of 'structural strain' included ambiguity (over the purpose of art education and the status of art students post-Coldstream), contradiction (between 'colour-supplement' projects and inadequate resources in less favoured annexes), and conflict (between Haringey Council, senior staff and the rest of the college, and between students and authorities). A 'generalized belief' identifying these problems and leading to action developed through *Gravy* (co-edited by Jim Singh-Sandhu), union meetings, the informal growth of SAC, and finally the 'teach-in' of 28 May. The 'precipitating factor' was the witholding of Student Union funds. Participants were 'mobilised for action', first in SAC and then with the motion to continue the sit-in from 29 May. There were no 'social controls' in place to anticipate these developments; they were developed on the hoof, and patchily, as the sit-in continued. Despite Longford's impassioned plea for goodwill at the Palace Cinema on 5 November, measures were developed to repressive effect in the winter of 1968–9. What gives this model explanatory power is the interweaving of structural conditions with individual agency (see Alex Callinicos, *Making History: Agency, Structure and Change in Social Theory*, Cambridge: Polity Press, 1987, pp. 6–7).

5   Nairn, 'On the Subversiveness of Art Students', *Listener*, vol. 80, 17 Oct. 1968, pp. 491–2 (p. 492). See also Robin Blackburn's review of *The Hornsey Affair* in the *Listener*, 5 June 1969, pp. 793–4: 'Before May 1968 the college was a byword for modish design. . . . In a context of industrial stagnation, the "spectacle", the organisation of appearances, acquires a special urgency. Britain, the most laggard capitalist nation, clogged by archaic social forms, needs the stimulus and distraction that the spectacle supplies with its dizzying succession of fashions, life-styles and pseudo-dramas. Before it became a storm centre of the art revolt Hornsey was a major source of spectacular production. The connection between these two facts is not hard to discover.'

6 Rushton and Wood (1978), p.26.

7 Rushton and Wood's perspective in the 1970s was broadly neo-Trotskyist, affiliated to the politics of the Socialist Workers' Party, Rock Against Racism and the Anti-Nazi League. They were writing with hindsight after the first miners' strike, amid rising unemployment and education cuts, with Thatcherism 'just around the corner'. They valued 'action over debate, politics over culture' and were allergic to 'a lot of self-serving claptrap about creativity, which years of involvement in art education and conceptual art had inoculated us against'. In retrospect, Wood feels that they were both right and wrong: that theirs was a justified response to the context but that an ultra-leftist position may have 'failed at that point to allow enough relative autonomy' to the cultural field. The SWP, Rock Against Racism and the Anti-Nazi League were 'more-or-less workerist' – compared with the theorists at *New Left Review* (Perry Anderson, Tom Nairn) or the Eurocommunist wing of the CP which had 'a strong sense of the import of culture and media' (Raymond Williams, Stuart Hall). I am grateful to Paul Wood for a very eloquent account (communication 28 Feb. 2006), and for his generosity in setting out a view of what he notes is 'slightly tricky territory' so that I can argue with him.

8 Rushton and Wood (1978), p. 4. In their view, post-war art education took 'the form it has, and espoused the aims it has – both real and professed – in response to the forces of the productive system as a whole . . . in complex ways, determined by contradictions within capital itself' (p. 39). They argue that most 'theorizing about art education has been couched in terms of "creativity" and its putatively beneficial effects' without any analysis of how that might be assessed in the context of any particular set of social relations. In their view a misunderstanding – that the education issues were not political – 'played no small part in the relative ease with which the rebels were eventually suppressed'. On the other hand, they note the emergence in the documents of a situationist vocabulary of 'spectacle', 'so that Hornsey's anti-politicism in fact does sit within a quite well defined political tradition, and isn't merely the natural channel into which a lot of bright young things' rebelliousness flowed' (p. 26).

9 Coldstream himself came from a professional family of doctors, lawyers, soldiers and civil servants: his father was a doctor, his brother a brigadier, and his first cousin Secretary to the Lord Chancellor (Laughton (2004), p.1). Page recalled his words in correspondence, 27 July 2006.

10 Black was appointed to the new school of Industrial Design (Engineering) at the Royal College in 1959. In 1962, the Society of Industrial Artists urged Summerson to encourage hybrid design/engineering courses at undergraduate and postgraduate level 'to bridge the gap between the "two cultures"' and meet the needs of a rapidly expanding market. See Jane Lidderdale and Mary Nicholson, *First Report: Education for Industrial Design: with reference to the policy of the Society for Industrial Artists*, Feb. 1962 (quotation p. 54). (The Society added 'and Designers' to its name in 1963.) Also in 1962 and in anticipation of Coldstream's reforms, the *Sunday Times Magazine* ran a cover-story on art students (Janice Elliott, 'The Reality Behind the Art-Student Image', 1 July 1962, pp. 2–11). This noted 'a trend away from the life class into design' – only about 2000 of a total of 130,000 art students were studying painting – and claimed that 'British art schools have woken up to the real importance of a thoroughly professional approach . . . in the applied arts and in industrial design' (pp. 5,2).

11 Rushton and Wood (1978), p.59. They point out that the industrial lobby was already critical of the capacities of diploma graduates emerging from 1966.

12 These are Rushton's and Wood's arguments, *ibid.*, p.15. In their view 'the Coldstream Council's liberal humanist illusionism veils multi-dimensional pragmatic utilitarianism' (p. 16). During the 1960s fine art and various kinds of design did indeed – as Pop and Op-Art became ubiquitous – draw closer together.

13 David Rushton and Paul Wood, 'Art-Learning' in Batchelor *et al.* (1979), pp. 22–7 (p. 24).

14 Rushton and Wood (1978), p. 27.

15 *ibid.*, p. 24.

16 *ibid.*, p. 28.

17 Wood, communication 28 Feb. 2006.

18 Interview with Kim Howells, 27 Feb. 2006. Howells recalls a delegation of Hornsey students at the LSE occupation of October 1967 (timed to coincide with a major demonstration against the Vietnam War) dismissing the politics of the LSE student left as 'stale' on these grounds. He suggests that 'formal politics played very little part in the genesis of the occupation, or in the occupation itself'. Prue Bramwell-Davis also has no memory of sectarian divisions emerging in sit-in debates. The rhetoric of the documents, with talk of 'spectacle', sometimes seems to echo that of the French Situationists, but in his most recent essay Paul Wood is sceptical of the view that the sit-in was 'an English manifestation of Situationist critique': 'this is a weight [that] Hornsey can scarcely bear'. 'Between God and the Saucepan', 2008, forthcoming.

19 Paul Wood, communication 28 Feb. 2006. For Howells see 'K.H.', 'Against the Art Object' in *The Hornsey Affair*, pp.69–72: 'The gallery system itself is struggling to avoid its inevitable end. It is riddled with the "you know so-and-so" set of creeping pseudo-intellectuals and public-school drop-outs, all desperately searching for the rich clientele and the mythical jackpot. Yet this is the home of British modern art, this is the world inhabited by our "brilliant" young artists. It is the creation of the boss class and their lackeys; it cannot exist without them. . . I say shit on their art world, I want nothing of it' (p. 71). Howells, the son of a communist lorry-driver, makes the same points to camera in *The Hornsey Film* (1970). In 1969 he failed, or was 'unassessed' for his diploma, having submitted a 20–minute film about politics and riots in Paris, Tokyo and the USA. *Hornsey Journal*, 1 Aug. 1969, Jenny Cole scrapbook, HCA Archive.

20 Opposition to the gallery system among the fine art students who formed the core of SAC, planning the sit-in in Kim Howells's flat before 28 May, was conveyed by Howells on 27 Feb. 2006. In May 1968, *Studio International* published a collage of quotations, unattributed, under the heading 'After Art School?' (eds. Gordon Richardson and Ted Hawkes, vol. 175, pp. 238–40): 'The big question is: Are we ready for a completely new attitude to art? Have we the courage to face a really radical reassessment of the role, even the definition, of the "artist"?' In Paris, at the same time, artists opposed to the gallery system advanced an ideological programme attempting 'to combine (not without a certain glorious confusion) the Marxist critique of capitalist society, the Dadaist rejection of the legitimacy of culture . . . and the surrealist aspiration to all forms of liberation' (Raymonde Moulin, 'Living Without Selling' in *Art and Confrontation: The Arts in an Age of Change*, various authors, Greenwich, Connecticut: New York Graphic Society, 1968, pp. 121–36, quotation p. 133). Howells's comments on the Turner Prize (2002) can be found at http://news.bbc.co.ul/1/hi/entertainment/

arts/2379975.stm (accessed 13 Oct. 2005). Rushton was a student at Coventry College of Art on the controversial Art Theory course introduced in October 1969 and Paul Wood followed a similar if less systematic course under Keith Arnatt at Newport.

21 Sit-in documents claimed that educating more flexible, problem-solving designers would ease the introduction of new technology, for example computer typesetting. Wood (2008) who points out that the 'defeat of the print unions was as significant as the related defeats of the steel workers and the miners' in annexing new technology to corporate interests in the Thatcherite 1980s, finds this socio-economically naïve.

22 Rushton and Wood (1978), p. 26, quoting W. Patrick Burke from *Learning Design*, published by the Welsh Arts Council in 1967 when he was still teaching at Hornsey (he left before the sit-in). Piper is condemned (pp. 31–2) for prioritizing problem-solving means over the question of whether or not the ends are desirable. See also p.31, where they relate the systematization of problem-solving to 'planned programme budgeting', taken up by the DES and local authorities in the late 1960s, and to systems analysis in the USA.

23 See Doc. 62, D. J. Warren Piper, 'Notes on Problem-Solving in Design', in which the stages in the design cycle include the consideration of value judgements and conflicting constraints. Like science and technology, 'design' can of course be harnessed for social benefit or social harm: essential to commodity capitalism in promoting the rapid turnover of goods, it has an important role in the development of solutions to ecological, technical and social problems.

24 Bramwell-Davis, a specialist in Education Design, became Senior Tutor in Industrial Design (Engineering) at the Royal College of Art, the first industrial design course to appoint anthropologists to teach ethnographic research. Her interests in design for developing economies, and in prioritizing user-centred factors in design solutions, were influential in setting the agenda of the Helen Hamlyn Research Centre for Inclusive Design at the RCA. Singh-Sandhu, born in Malaya during the Japanese occupation, studied medicine in India for a year before coming to England. He was badly beaten in a racist attack in 1962 and had a corneal graft in St Thomas's Hospital. His interest in disability dates from this event (communication, 27 Feb. 2006). He founded the Special Needs Unit at Northumbria University and the British (now European) Institute for Design and Disability. At Hornsey, together with Roger Hayden, he developed the use of inflated polythene tubing as a play environment for disabled children at a day-care centre in Greenwich (*Sunday Times*, 27 Apr. 1969, Jenny Cole scrapbook, HCA Archive). An earlier *Sunday Times* article, 'What the Kids are Doing this Year' (22 Aug. 1965, p. 27), featured Alex Roberts, James Meller, David Warren Piper and others from the industrial design course with a range of toys developed for children disabled by thalidomide. On humanitarian or inclusive design in the 1960s see among others *The Buckminster Fuller Reader*, ed. James Meller, 1970; Victor Papanek, *Design for the Real World*, with introduction by Fuller, 1971; and Paul Oliver, 'Design for What Future', in Piper (1972), vol. 1, p.131: 'Do we have to be reminded that the immediate future is one of *environmental crisis?* . . . The responsibility facing designers to devise new ways of containerization, to employ organic, recycling systems in disposable materials. . . to design plant that will purify, desalinate, reuse and in every way reduce the levels of contamination and waste – this responsibility is scarcely reflected in our schools of design.'

25 AR Papers, printed fragment, 'To the Authorities Whoever they Are', undated, uncredited. See also DP Box 5, Jim Singh-Sandu, Peter Young, 'The Easy Way Out. Or . . .': 'A person who designs should be a person who is capable of having meaningful relationships; a person with imagination; a person with insight into and an understanding of the world around him and an ability to communicate. . . It is up to us as students to bring about a fundamental transformation of the student *role* from passive consumer of the "fact-factory" to an active participant within an intellectual community.'

26 John Hewitt, 'Good Design in the Market Place: The Rise of Habitat Man', *Oxford Art Journal*, vol. 10 no. 2, 1987, pp. 28–42 (quotation p. 35). See also Nigel Whiteley in the same issue, 'Toward a Throw-Away Culture: Consumerism, "Style Obsolescence" and Cultural Theory in the 1950s and 1960s', pp. 3–27. Whiteley points out (pp. 8, 17), that high mass consumption in Britain in the 1960s, following that in the US in the 1950s, was fuelled by a rise in disposable incomes, a fall in real terms in the cost of many consumer items, and a massive increase in hire-purchase debt. Between 1955 and 1969 retail prices rose by 63 per cent but average weekly earnings by 130 per cent.

27 Quoted in Hewitt, *ibid.*, p. 40. In 1964 Herbert Marcuse, in *One-Dimensional Man* (a book widely read in the US and the UK), rued the extent to which people had come to 'recognise themselves in their commodities; they find their soul in their automobile, hi-fi, split-level home, kitchen equipment. . . . Social control is anchored in the new needs, which it has produced' (Boston: Beacon Press, 1991, p. 9).

28 R. Buckminster Fuller, 'World Planning' 1963, reprinted in *The Buckminster Fuller Reader*, ed. James Meller, London: Jonathan Cape, 1970, pp. 362–8 (quotation p. 362). See also 'The Designers and the Politicians' (1962) in *ibid.*, pp. 355–61, in which he suggests that great world dilemmas have not been, and will not be, solved by politicians. (Presumably we are now broadly agreed that political will is a necessary if insufficient condition of social change.)

29 The Euston Road tradition of directly observed, point-to-point figuration, largely shorn of its interwar interest in documentary subjects and focused in the studio, continued to influence the curriculum at the Slade, where Coldstream was Professor, at Camberwell and elsewhere. In 1985 Linda Morris asked Coldstream why the Slade kept its life rooms when the effect of the first Coldstream Report had been to shut them down across the country. He replied that: 'While the committee was sitting Victor Pasmore organized the Developing Process exhibition with Harry Thubron, Richard Hamilton and Tom Hudson, at the ICA [*A Continuing Process. The New Creativity in British Art Education 1955–65*]. They were very successful with the Bauhaus idea and there was little I could do against the tide of opinion. . . . It should have been called the Pasmore Report, then people would have understood what was happening.' *http://thehornseyproject.omweb.org/modules/wakka/LindaMorrisPaper*, accessed 9 Nov. 2006.

30 Glynn Williams recalls that when he left art school in 1964 it was possible to get a college post almost anywhere: 'There was almost an unspoken form of state sponsorship for the young artist' as these were the staff with which to impress a Summerson panel. Williams in Hetherington (1994), p. 24.

31 Bruce Laughton, 'Artists with Diplomas', *Arts Review*, vol. 19, 8 July 1967, pp. 239–50. Colleges were drawn closer to the market when ambitious students encountered successful young staff, but this also produced a backlash, in antipathy to the gallery system (as expressed by Kim Howells) and in forms of conceptual, performance, or installation art less easily traded in it (at least at first).

32　Victor Pasmore, Richard Hamilton, Harry Thubron and Tom Hudson were key figures here, anticipated and influenced by Olive Sutton at the Manchester School of Art and William Johnston at the Central School of Art in London (who had brought in Pasmore and Hamilton as well as Eduardo Paolozzi, William Turnbull, Alan Davie). See Thistlewood (1981).

33　Thierry de Duve, 'When Form Has Become Attitude – And Beyond', in De Ville and Foster (1994), pp. 23–40, henceforward referred to as De Duve (1994). See also the version published in German as 'Das Ende des Bauhaus-Modells', in *Akademie zwischen Kunst und Lehre: Künstlerische Praxis und Ausbildung – eine kritische Untersuchung*, ed. Denys Zacharopoulos (Vienna: Akademie der bildenden Künste Wien, 1992). Thierry de Duve spent three years working on the project for a new art school for the City of Paris which was subsequently abandoned for financial reasons. I have not been able to do his argument justice in this very condensed précis but have benefited from reading it alongside two pieces by Charles Harrison: 'L'Enseignement de l'Art Conceptuel' in Douar and Waschek (2004) and 'Conceptual Art, the Aesthetic and the End(s) of Art', in Perry and Wood (2004).

34　De Duve (1994), p. 23. There are numerous studies on the secessionist groups of the nineteenth-century and the early twentieth-century avant-gardes. On the increasing autonomy of the cultural field see Pierre Bourdieu, *The Field of Cultural Production: Essays on Art and Literature*, a collection of his translated essays edited by Randal Johnson (Cambridge: Polity Press, 1993), and *The Rules of Art: Genesis and Structure of the Literary Field* [1992], trans. Susan Emanuel (Cambridge: Polity Press, 1996). On cognate shifts in the institutions of modern art and in the market for it see Robert Jensen, *Marketing Modernism in Fin-de-Siècle Europe* (Princeton, N.J: Princeton University Press, 1994).

35　Moholy-Nagy insisted that 'everyone is talented' and 'any healthy man can become a musician, painter, sculptor or architect'. László Moholy-Nagy, *The New Vision* [1928], 4th rev. ed., and *Abstract of an Artist* (New York; Wittenborn, Schultz, 1947), p. 67, cited in Singerman (1999), p. 117.

36　De Duve (1994), p. 25. Major modern art theorists (Herbert Read, E. H. Gombrich, Rudolf Arnheim) also explored the perceptual and psychological bases for a 'visual language', as de Duve points out, and pioneers of modernism (Malevich, Kandinsky, Klee, Itten, Moholy-Nagy, Albers), were all associated with teaching programmes based on the premise that a fundamental syntax immanent to the medium could be discovered or developed (p. 26). The *Vorkers*, the core course in design, was retained in various forms in each of the Bauhaus Schools in Germany and the USA. Richard Wollheim, giving the first Maurice de Sausmarez Memorial Lecture, denied that there was such a thing as a visual grammar: the units existed (line, dot, colour, plane etc.) but not the syntax (there were no rules of combination). See 'The Art Lesson', *Studio International*, vol. 181, June 1971, pp. 278–83. Craft skills, no longer taught in serious art-classes, found a home in 'how-to' books for amateurs. In Elkins (2001), he instances 'How to paint young animals', 'How to paint barns', 'Successful marine painting' and 'Painting weathered textures in watercolour' (p. 141).

37　De Duve (1994), p. 28, suggests that there is a blatant contradiction here: 'Many art schools yield to the particularly perverse illusion . . . that they produce or fabricate artists, while at the same time considering that their incoming students are artists already, even though only potentially. In fact all teachers know by experience that talent exists and that creativity is a myth.' Although some elements of academic discipline, including perspective, anatomy and drawing from casts, were dropped when the NDD was instigated in 1946, by the 1960s residual elements of the academic model coexisted with the Bauhaus model, including at Hornsey. Maurice de Sausmarez had introduced Basic Design into the Fine Art department before the introduction of the DipAD, but after he left in 1962 its influence waned, except – characteristically – on the one-year Foundation course. Meanwhile despite the impact of more up-to-date manners and means (Pop, Op, spray-painting, welded metal sculpture) remnants of the old Euston Road figurative style persisted among staff and students.

38 De Duve (1994), p. 29. 'The métier gets practised, the medium gets questioned; the métier gets transmitted, the medium communicates or gets communicated; the métier gets learnt, the medium gets discovered; the métier is a tradition, the medium is a language; the métier rests on experience, the medium relies on experimentation' (p. 20). What comes with this is a distrust of technical skill, an insistence on the specific properties of the medium, and a contradictory emphasis on doing something new with it. Phyllida Barlow, at Chelsea School of Art in 1960–3, was on the cusp of this shift from the academic model in sculpture when George Fullard arrived after Henry Moore left. Before, they had worked on the figure in clay (women were kept out of the welding room). Now Fullard got rid of the life model and encouraged the use of salvaged materials. These were plentiful as the King's Road leases were coming to an end and old shops gutted to make way for new boutiques. 'Learning Experience', interview with Phyllida Barlow by Mark Godfrey, *frieze*, no. 101, Sept. 2006, special issue on 'Art schools then and now', pp. 168–75 (p. 170).

39 De Duve (1994), pp. 26–7. In America, art education shifted from its base in specialist art schools and artists' studios to the university in the postwar period. Harold Rosenberg remarked that only one abstract expressionist painter had a degree (and not in art), compared with most of the 'thirty artists under thirty-five' in the *Young America 1965* exhibit at the Whitney Museum of American Art in New York in 1965. He believed that the liberal university setting was partly responsible for the cool, impersonal art of the 1960s. Rosenberg, 'Educating Artists' in Battcock (1973), reprinted from *Art News*, vol. 69 (Feb. 1971), pp. 92–3. See also the excellent study by Singerman (1999), who argues that art on campus cannot be a calling or vocation, nor can it be a craft or technique (as it was in the guilds and academies), nor can it be purely inspirational or expressive: in its university setting it has to be an object of knowledge, a discipline and a department like the others (pp. 5, 198).

40 De Duve (1994), p. 31. 'Who among us hears the word creativity without wearing an ironic smile? Who among us still dreams of a utopian visual language à la Kandinsky, some Esperanto composed of red squares, yellow triangles and blue circles? Who still believes in the purity or the specificity of the medium, in the manner of Greenberg? Who, perhaps with Warhol in mind . . . or Steve Reich, will deny that as much contemporary art of quality has been produced through repetition as through invention?' De Duve suggests (p. 32) that the 'last art school with a strict Bauhaus ideology (though already considerably amended) was the Black Mountain College, and its best "fruit" was Rauschenberg'.

41 De Duve (1994), p. 34. The most progressive art and teaching of the 1970s believed that art should be willed, whether as revolutionary rhetoric or ideology-critique. Attitude was essentially a blank 'volition without content', but invocations to Lukács, Adorno and Althusser were intended to convey its critical edge.

42 De Duve (1994), p. 34, claims that conceptual art was acknowledged for the first time by a major institution with the 'Information' show at the Museum of Modern Art, New York, in 1970. Szeemann's exhibition ('Attitudes') was recast by Charles Harrison for its London showing at the ICA in August 1969.

43 De Duve (1994), p.36. See also John A. Walker, *John Latham: The Incidental Person – His Art and Ideas*, London: Middlesex University Press, 1995, pp. 84–6. (Walker says that Greenberg was known for dismissing most contemporary British art as in 'too good taste', and Latham decided to invert this and see if Greenberg's writings 'tasted good'.) De Duve remarks that today 'he could do the same performance with the principal's blessing, and the librarian wouldn't even bother to reorder *Art and Culture*'. Events and performances have been absorbed into the art schools, many of which have institutionalized 'multi-media' or 'interdisciplinary' or 'time-based' work in departments which indicate that 'the teaching of art no longer rests on an aesthetic commitment to the specificity or the purity of the medium'. Greenberg's *Art and Culture* (1961) reached a wider audience after it appeared in paperback in 1965. As Harrison points out (in Perry and Wood (2004), p. 65), the modernist account of modernism – in Greenberg or Fried for example – came late, at the end of a century stretching from Manet to Morris Louis or Kenneth Noland. The very act of defining it helped provoke its antithesis (and Latham's response).

44 De Duve (1994), pp.38, 39, observes that deconstruction was poorly understood and assimilated but seemed to suggest that the polarity between imitation (the academic model) and invention (the Bauhaus model) needed to be rethought. In a 'post-medium' age it was also consonant with Duchamp's rising influence (his exhibition at the Tate Gallery, organized by Richard Hamilton in 1966, was a significant moment here). Singerman (1999), p. 204, notes that by 1978, 101 colleges and universities across America offered courses in conceptual art.

45 De Duve explains that he offers a diagnosis, not a cure (1994), pp. 39, 40, 44. Singerman (1999), p. 212, citing Bourdieu's argument that under modern conditions the structure of the cultural field is invoked in every new act of production, argues that 'the frame and the field of work have become precisely the métier, the craft skills with which work is made'. As Robert Motherwell put it, 'every intelligent painter carries the whole culture of modern painting in his head. It is his real subject' (quoted p. 153). What this means is that the new arrival at art school is more sophisticated and less skilled. As Paul Huxley puts it, 'At eighteen she will already know from television that Jackson Pollock threw paint, that Andy Warhol traced round photographs, that Marcel Duchamp just made choices and that a number of artists with considerable cachet from Yves Klein onwards appear often to have ideas but do nothing at all with their hands. The student will be very resistant to the grinding discipline which was once the only source of invention.' 'Confronting the canvas – in the studio and tutorial room', in Hetherington (1994), p. 72.

46 Sol Lewitt's 'Paragraphs on Conceptual Art' appeared in *Artforum*, vol. 5, Jun. 1967, along with pieces from Robert Smithson and Robert Morris and a rearguard action from Michael Fried ('Art and Objecthood').

47 Harrison, in Perry and Wood (2004), p. 58. See also Victor Burgin, 'Situational Aesthetics', *Studio International* vol. 178 (Oct. 1969), pp. 118–21: 'Some recent art . . . has tended to take its essential form in message rather than in materials. In its logical extremity this tendency has resulted in a placing of art entirely within the linguistic infrastructure which previously served merely to support art' (p. 118).

48 Louisa Buck, 'Art is Not a Career' in Bonaventura and Farthing (2004), p. 73. The idea that art cannot be taught goes back at least to early modernism (see for example Clive Bell's *Art*, 1914) and survives with modifications in the present (see Elkins (2001), especially pp. 97–105). It made no sense in the academy, for which art was a métier requiring a set of skills with which to earn a living, rather than a vocation through which to transform the cultural field. Why some moments proved particularly fertile in particular places remains an open question, as Harrison points out. Was it a particular educational system, a charismatic teacher, or the accidental coincidence of compatible individuals that led to a flowering of pop art at the Royal College of Art c.1960, abstract sculpture at St Martin's during the 1960s, conceptual art at Coventry around 1969–71, or the Young British Artists at Goldsmiths in the 1990s? (Charles Harrison in Douar and Waschek (2004), p. 153).

49 The fine art students were concerned with how they were taught, and here their brief and entirely reasonable demands throw light on how casually and chaotically fine art departments were sometimes run. (Why would they not have a right to adequate resources, technical help and regular tutorials, the outcomes properly recorded and conveyed?) Their objections were otherwise directed predominantly to the gallery system and expressed most vehemently in Kim Howells's denunciation of art works as commodities for the bourgeois elite. Howells's argument found support in Sjoerd Hannema's curious book, *Fads, Fakes and Fantasies: The Crisis in the Art Schools and the Crisis in Art* (1970). Hannema considered student unrest a 'spiritual malaise' and a 'staggering misdirection and squandering of adolescent talent' (p. 5) and he was against the network system (p. 123). But he also believed that art was caught up in a speculative market for luxury goods, that painting was outmoded, that the highbrow concept of fine art was already extinct, and that the artist's task was to 'render service to the common good' through design (in the tradition of the Arts and Crafts Movement, the Deutsche Werkbund and the Bauhaus) (pp. 5–7, pp. 60–4). Pierre Bourdieu would later argue that symbolic and cultural capital, like economic capital, are unequally distributed among social classes and class fractions, and that cultural consumption is a mechanism of social distinction: see *Distinction: A Social Critique of the Judgement of Taste* [1979], trans. Richard Nice (Cambridge, Mass.: Harvard University Press, 1984).

50 Tony Judt, writing on events in Paris in May 1968, remarks that: 'There were no women among the student leaders. In contemporary photographs and newsreels girls can be seen prominently placed on the shoulders of their boyfriends, but they were at best the auxiliary foot soldiers of the student army. The youth revolt of 1968 talked a lot about sex, but was quite unconcerned with inequalities of gender.' Judt (2005), p. 412.

51 The few Black and Asian students at Hornsey in the 1960s included a Nigerian woman who graduated in sculpture in 1966, and the black painter visible in Gerry Cranham's photograph for the *Observer*, reproduced in Barrie Sturt-Penrose's *The Art Scene* (London: Paul Hamlyn, 1969), pp. 106–7.

52 Kim Howells thinks there were as many women as men (and no staff) in the original group of fine art 'plotters': he mentions Janet Unwin, Kathy Hilton and his wife, Jane Perryman (interview 27 Feb. 2006). This group numbered more like 15 than the 50 mentioned in the press.

53 *New Left Review*, no. 40, reprinted in modified form in Juliet Mitchell, *Woman's Estate* (Harmondsworth, Middlesex: Penguin, 1971). On Rowbotham and *Black Dwarf* see Tariq Ali and Susan Watkins, *1968: Marching in the Streets* (London: Bloomsbury, 1998), p. 209.

54 Kristin Ross observes from her reading of the documents that women activists in Paris in 1968 tended 'to self-identify as any number of things – as workers, as members of different groupuscules or political tendencies, as German Jews, as the "pègre", as activists or citizens – rather than as women per se' (Ross (2002), p. 155). Prue Bramwell-Davis is quoted in Paul Lashmar, 'Shades of '68', *Guardian*, 5 June 1993, p. 30: 'We did pamper the media. In filmed debates, the boys were at the back looking serious and girls would sit on the floor in their miniskirts'. Gender is subsumed with class in Kim Howells's call for 'a new culture – not for a Chelsea or Hampstead elite – but a culture by and for ordinary men and women. To achieve it means revolutionary social changes by housewives, students, workers' (in *The Hornsey Film*).

55 See the *Daily Mirror*, 24 Sept. 1968, following what should have been the first day of the autumn term, Jenny Cole scrapbook, HCA Archive. This predated the editorial on 'Student Unrest' in the *Bulletin* of the National Society for Art Education (Oct. 1968, unpaged) which demanded the prompt withdrawal of financial aid by the authorities, suggesting that 'zealous inexperienced innovators' should justify their claims by finding 'the financial means necessary to run their own institution for a period of not less than five years'.

56 No doubt there were others. Alan Kaprow's solution to the problem of teaching art in a changed climate was based on assemblage: 'an art of distinguished traditions . . . manifestly open to incredibly rich transformation . . . a lingua franca of the present time'. See Alan Kaprow, 'The Effect of Recent Art upon the Teaching of Art', *Art Journal*, vol. 23, winter 1963/4, pp. 136–8. The student would begin by working in a restricted range of materials assigned by the tutor, where the subject matter was the material itself, before moving to a second, more difficult kind of assemblage, with a greater emphasis on imagery and 'literary' meanings. Kaprow admired Hans Hofmann's school, which shared the academic view that craft skills, if not Art, could be taught, and the Bauhaus view that 'all art obeys certain fundamental syntactical principles'. In his scheme, as in Hofmann's, students would be expected thoroughly to familiarize themselves with the art of the recent past, and to separate disciplined study in class from free creative experiment at home.

57 Harrison (2001), p. 234: 'If I strike a sceptical note in remembering such scenes, it is because . . . the reaction against mainstream Modernism which set in during the mid-to-late 1960s was in part a reaction against just such images of rigour and self-criticism as those which the sessions at St Martin's were supposed to inculcate.'

58 Kardia (originally Atkins), quoted in Hester Westley, 'The Year of the Locked Room', *Tate etc.*, no.9, Spring 2007, *http://www.tate.org.uk/tateetc/issue9/yearlocke-drooom.htm*, accessed 9 July 2007. This brief article draws on the substantial archival and oral research in Westley's Ph. D., *Traditions and Transitions: St Martin's Sculpture*

Department 1960–1979 (Courtauld Institute of Art, 2007). It was linked to a Tate Britain display, devised by Westley and Clarrie Wallis, on 'St Martin's Sculpture Department 1964–71'. The course was taught by Kardia, Garth Evans, Gareth Jones and Peter Harvey and 'reconstructed' for a BBC documentary by Christopher Burstall, *A Question of Feeling*, in 1970. As Westley puts it, Kardia's paradoxical pedagogy aimed to liberate students by imprisoning them. At the end of the term, outraged that such a radical course was nonetheless to be bureaucratically assessed, Richard Deacon, Ian Kirkwood and Ted Walters installed a chicken coop in the studio in their stead, suggesting the chickens might just as well be assessed in their place.

59 Quoted in Westley, *Tate etc.*, no. 9. See also Ian Kirkwood quoted in the report of a symposium on *The Problem of Documenting the Creative Process*, *http://www.dispatx.com/make/comments.php?item=2700*, accessed 10 July 2007. He found the experience both 'liberating and alarming': he and his fellow students 'oscillated between feeling subject to an obtuse behavioural experiment to more positive realizations that they were undergoing a cathartic process where the engagement with material, the *doing*, became the work itself'.

60 Harrison and Orton (1982), p.26.

61 I am grateful to John Mitchell, who taught on it, for some recollections of the course and to Fred Orton for comments on Coventry in the mid to late sixties. Harrison (2001), p. 269, refers to five areas of study: Art Theory, Audio Visual, Epistemology, Romanticism and Technos. Mitchell (conversation 29 Aug. 2007) remembers two main parts, Art Theory, which was seminar-based with reading and discussion topics set in advance (eg 'What is Ontology?'); and Technos, which involved projects set in such a way that students producing objects were drawing on material in the Theory part of the course.

62 Staff and students on the Art Theory course were clear that 'its position was not only to consider its own "problems", "interests" and "answers", but in some sense to set the intellectual tone of the course by raising questions within other parts of the course'. Philip Pilkington, Kevin Lole, David Rushton, 'Some Concerns in Fine Art Education', *Studio International*, vol. 183, Oct. 1971, pp. 120–2 (p. 121 note 1). Atkinson and Baldwin later published an essay on 'Art Teaching', derived from the experience of the Art Theory course (*Art-Language* vol. 1 no. 4, Nov. 1971, pp. 25–50).

63 The internal politics were complex, and disputed. On 29 July 1971 Edward Pullee, Chief Officer of the NCDAD, wrote to Sir Alan Richmond, Director of Lanchester Polytechnic (in which Coventry was now merged), confirming that the Council required 'the production of tangible, visual art objects' for assessment. See Harrison (2001), p. 70; and Harrison and Orton (1982), pp. 26–7. The course was defended in two issues of *Studio International*: Philip Pilkington, Kevin Lole, David Rushton, 'Some Concerns in Fine-Art Education', *Studio International*, vol. 183, Oct. 1971, pp. 120–2; and 'Some Concerns in Fine-Art Education II', vol. 183, Nov. 1971, pp. 168–70. It was revisited in 1972 ('Four Midland Polytechnic Fine Art Departments', vol. 184, Nov. 1972, pp. 176–9, and 'Remarks on Art Education', pp. 179–81). Paul Wood ('Between God and the Saucepan', 2008) points out how 'the emergence of what subsequently came to be ratified as *post*modernist art was indigestible, to a system covertly premised on modernism itself'.

64 Paul Wood (*ibid.*, 2008). Two of the twelve students on the 'A' course were women and most of those on the Art Theory course were men.

65 Reg Butler, *Creative Development: Five Lectures to Art Students*, London: Routledge and Kegan Paul, 1962, p. 21. See also p. 11: 'Again I am quite sure the vitality of a great many female students derives from frustrated maternity, and most of these, on finding the opportunity to settle down and produce children, will no longer experience a degree of passionate discontent sufficient to drive them constantly towards the labours of creation in other ways'. These lectures were delivered in June 1961, i.e. after the Coldstream Report but before its implementation.

66 Strand (1987), p. 98. Clearly some students responded with enthusiasm and Philip Pilkington, Graham Howard and David Rushton went on to contribute to the work of Art & Language in the early 1970s. Strand claims others were 'neither temperamentally inclined nor intellectually capable of responding to the new programme'. Mitchell recalls that the Art Theory course was very demanding, that about half the students had dropped out by the end of the year, that there were fewer women to start with 'and some of them were struggling to make it comprehensible'. (It was nevertheless in his view the first major development in art education after Thubron's Foundation course at Leeds.) Fred Orton, who left Coventry in 1967 for the Courtauld, confirms its 'macho' atmosphere at that time (communication 5 June 2007). David Page, teaching in the Fine Art Department at Hornsey in 1969–70, found 'no shape to the course, mixed with severe sexism from many male staff' (communication, 27 July 2006). This had certainly been my experience at Hornsey in 1963–6.

67 Trudi Gurling, email response to BBC website on Vanessa Engle's documentaries on *Art & the 60s*, *http://www.bbc.co.uk/bbcfour/documentaries/features/ask-vanessa-engle*, accessed 3 May 2007. Gurling asked Engle if she had 'thought about challenging the St Martin's myth makers' and Engle replied that she was 'aware that it was tough for women on the course. . . . There is another story to be told, which is what it was like to be a woman artist in the 60s.' Some women did survive with a degree of professional success, notably Wendy Taylor and Katherine Gili, and it is only fair to point out that Trudi Gurling was not on the 'A' course and Deirdre McArdle, who was, recently commented: 'In a way, it was a charming game for Peter and his staff. Although we could baulk at its discipline and intensity, we could see how it helped our attention to focus, and I think we were flattered by the atmosphere of seriousness.' Quoted in Hester Westley, 'The Year of the Locked Room', *Tate etc.*, issue 9, *http://www.tate.org.uk/tateetc/issue9/yearlockedroom.htm*, accessed 9 July 2007.

68 Judy Chicago, *Through the Flower: My Struggle as a Woman Artist* [1975] Harmondsworth, Middlesex: Penguin, 1993, p. 91. Fresno State College, as it is popularly known and as Chicago refers to it, is properly California State University, Fresno.

69 At St Martin's, generally, and at Coventry with the Art Theory course, art education was more closely linked to the cutting edge of contemporary practice and liberated into multi- or inter- or anti-disciplinary fields from the modernist concern with the medium-based object. See Lucy Lippard, *Six Years: The Dematerialization of the Art Object from 1966 to 1972* (New York: Praeger, 1973). This followed her article on 'The Dematerialization of Art', co-authored with J. Chandler, in *Art International*, Feb. 1968. In Singerman's view (1999), p. 175, this 'dematerialization' was linked in the USA to the development of university art courses with visiting lecture programmes, since the university 'offered a room and an audience for work that was in one way or another transitory' (such as happenings and performances, film and video screenings, site installations and so on). Such developments had yet to make an impact at Hornsey in 1969 when Kim Howells – suspended and then reinstated at the Palace Cinema meeting in November 1968 – was failed, or 'unassessed', because the film he presented was considered 'not fine art'. He left in disgust, diploma-less, for the South Wales steelworks. (Interview 27 Feb. 2006.)

70 Chicago, p. 91, also comments that women had problems because they were unfamiliar with basic skills deployed by men. After Fresno, Chicago moved to the California Institute for the Arts and taught the Feminist Art program there with Miriam Shapiro. For the collective *Womanhouse* project students had to acquire the skills necessary to renovate a run-down Los Angeles mansion before they could use it as a studio and turn its rooms into installations. For feminist art initiatives in the UK see Rozsika Parker and Griselda Pollock, *Framing Feminism: Art and the Women's Movement 1970–85*, London and New York: Pandora, 1987.

71 Judy Chicago, interviewed by Judith Dancoff. See 'A Feminist Art Program', *Art Journal* vol. 31 (Autumn 1971), pp. 48–9 (quotation p. 48). Chicago talks in terms of an authentic self-expression here: 'I also decided that a great many of my ideas about art-making were based on male ideas . . . [*sic*] I began to feel a tremendous need for identifying with women.'

72 See Piper (1973), vol. 2, p. 138. In 1968 there were 1746 Diploma entries: 42 per cent in Fine Art, 24 per cent in Graphics, 17 per cent in Fashion & Textiles and 17 per cent in Three-Dimensional Design. The gender breakdown in Table 15, Appendix A, p. 148, is for 1969: Fine Art, 1772 men and 1169 women; Graphics, 920 men and 704 women; Fashion & Textiles, 137 men and 887 women; Three-Dimensional Design, 835 men and 508 women. Piper also notes (p. 30) that assuming equal numbers applied, women had a poorer chance of being accepted onto diploma courses: they outnumbered men on foundation courses but except in Fashion & Textiles were outnumbered by them in the other studio areas.

73 The most recent biography is Sue Roe, *Gwen John: A Life*, London: Chatto & Windus, 2001. See also my essay '"Augustus's Sister": Gwen John: Wholeness, Harmony and Radiance' in *Gwen John and Augustus John*, exh. cat., London: Tate Publishing, 2004, Tate Britain, 29 Sept. – 9 Jan. 2005, pp. 29–45.

74 See in particular Anne Wagner, *Three Artists Three Women: Modernism and the Art of Hesse, Krasner, and O'Keeffe*, Berkeley, Los Angeles, London: University of California Press, 1996.

75 Madge and Weinberger (1973), p. 35.

76 A successful and supportive 'crit' can enhance the social cohesion of the group and its capacity for reflection and debate. There are two problems: first, that crits can be abrasive, crushing the student or calling forth a combative response; alternatively, that in a gentler mode they can become a therapeutic prop the graduate finds it hard to do without. This second point is made by Charles Harrison ('Educating Artists', *Studio International*, vol. 183, May 1972, pp. 222–4). He continues: 'This is the irony of art education – in England at least: the art student is encouraged to see himself as blessed with a particular freedom, with the ability and opportunity to express himself, and with the right to a form of production entirely his own. There is another view: that art schools act as institutions in which the educationally homeless, the destructive, the work-shy, the non-specialist intellectual, the intelligent artisan and other potential threateners of the status quo are incarcerated for a period of years and occupied "therapeutically" with the production of essentially functionless commodities – the tokens of their "individuality" and their "freedom".'

77 Singerman (1999), p. 173.

78 The emphasis on the crit takes the place of the focus on medium in the Bauhaus model, and métier in the academic model. As Singerman points out (1999), pp. 144–5, the assignment and response are no longer aligned or in the same language as they are in the academic model (as in 'make a life drawing'), but separated (as in 'make a void'). The instruction is, in effect: 'Surprise us with something we hadn't thought of but in terms that we're prepared to recognize, and defend it.' He quotes Madge and Weinberger (1973), p. 145, who observed that tutors 'did not spell out what exactly it was they expected or wanted from students . . . [and] quite deliberately did not explain their criticisms'. Many women art students before 1970, and some after, have branded in their memories the moment when a particular tutor reminded the whole group that whereas men could become artists, women were destined to become wives, mothers, or secondary-school art teachers. In my case it was Keith Grant, anti-Vietnam war protester, vociferous supporter of the sit-in and a middling sort of painter of Nordic landscapes. There were usually a few sexual predators among art-school staff (*la vie de bohème* and so on), and the only fine art student to gain a first-class diploma at Hornsey in 1966 was in a relationship with one of the tutors. Page respected Richard Robbins (with whom he was at odds over the sit-in) because he was a man of principle, and because he gave equal tutorial time to *all* his students. The only woman among the sculpture staff, the late Astrid Zydower, was part-time, marginalized, and somewhat bruised by the experience.

79 Peter Stringer, 'Masculinity-Femininity as a Possible Factor underlying the Personality Responses of Male and Female Art Students', *British Journal of Social and Clinical Psychology*, vol. 6, 1967, pp. 186–94. A 'battery of cognitive and personality measures' was administered to 74 male and 115 female students at four major English art colleges (unnamed). Most were studying graphics or fine art. Stringer predicted that both male and female students would show marked deviation from general sex-role norms, the men in the direction of the female norm, the women in the direction of the male norm, and that women's deviation would be the greater. Citing Phyllis Greenacre ('Woman as Artist', *Psychoanalytical Quarterly*, vol. 29, 1960, pp. 208–27), he wonders whether the 'relative lack of successful female artists' might be 'due to an inability in women in Western culture to sustain sex-role deviation' (p. 193). American examples are discussed by Howard Singerman in *Art Subjects* (1999), ch. 2, 'Women and Artists, Students and Teachers', esp. pp. 42–7. The arguments are often circular, since authors tend to import into their analysis the very terms they set out to investigate (artists are at the 'feminine' end of the occupations scale because an interest in culture – as opposed to business or sport – is already characterized as a feminine attribute). Singerman points out that in the United States the professionalization of art education in university departments (from the 1930s), the practical and ideological impact of the GI Bill, offering free college places to returning ex-servicemen (from the 1940s), and the rapid public acceptance of Abstract Expressionism (in the 1950s), all confirmed the image of the artist as essentially, even ruggedly, masculine (pp. 128–9, 244 n. 15).

Postwar British art – abstraction, neo-romanticism, kitchen-sink expressionism, with Hepworth and Bacon as prominent figures – was perhaps more ambiguously gendered and sexed.

80 Griselda Pollock, 'Art, Art School, Culture: Individualism and the Death of the Artist', *Block*, no. 14, 1985/6, reprinted in Bird (1996), pp. 50–67 (p. 63). As she points out elsewhere, the peaks and troughs of women's achievement are not the same as men's, and often invisible to them. See 'Feminist Perspectives in Fine Art Education' in Hetherington (1996).

81 Lynn Lemaster contributed to Art and Language in the mid-1970s.

82 Pollock lists abstraction, surrealism and minimalism as other 'moments of radical fissure' ('Art, Art School, Culture. . . ', in Bird (1996), p. 63). 'Conceptualism' – a blurred and capacious category – has also been fruitfully exploited by artists with a stake in postcolonial issues.

83 Pollock, ibid., pp. 50–1, although she notes that this has led to recurrent crises over the assessment of such work by tutors, often male and educated in an earlier modernist paradigm, who are unfamiliar with it.

Postscript (pages 100–2)

1 AR Papers, letter from John Siddeley to Shelton, 25 June 1968, copied to Roberts with covering note. Siddeley takes the side of the sit-in 'because I believe that basically they are right in their stand', and regrets that he 'cannot continue helping you on the advisory panel'.

2 *The Hornsey Affair*, p. 194: 'The system reasserted itself . . . as death, as the unconvincing shadow of its former self, as a ghost performing constitutional rituals nobody believed in.' See also the quotation from Adolphe Thiers who successfully repressed the Paris Commune of 1871 (p. 145), used in the following pages to map the trajectory of the Hornsey sit-in: experience shows that the first thing to do is to applaud the revolution, stressing its idealism and generosity; then the revolutionaries must be made to feel that it would be a striking gesture of reasonableness for them to lay down their arms; then, once the revolution is disarmed criticisms can be allowed to emerge; then it is necessary to hammer home that 'the great revolution' was actually 'a sinister criminal undertaking'; finally, 'in the prevailing fear and stupor, the time is ripe to undo all the work of the revolution and punish those responsible for it'.

In May 1969 Jack Straw, President-elect of the NUS, addressing a crowd of around 700 students at the culmination of a march to Speaker's Corner, accused the college and local authority of implementing 'a ruthless policy of attrition' from the autumn of 1968. He claimed that the Union was investigating rumours of forty-two nervous breakdowns and nine suicide attempts among the students. Shelton replied that he knew of only ten cases of students under treatment, some from before the disturbances, and two attempted suicides, both by students who had made previous attempts. *The Times*, 29 May 1969, Jenny Cole scrap-book, HCA Archive.

3 Both Cathles and Bains had promised 'no victimization'. See HHS Press Cuttings Box 1968, Cathles reported in the *Guardian*, 31 May and Bains in the *Hampstead Express* 26 July 1968. See also HCA Press Cuttings 1968, *The Times* 20 Dec. 1968, letter signed by nineteen academics objecting to the 'sacking' (or non-renewal of con-

tracts mid-session) of Tom Nairn, Vicky Hamilton, Linda Stillitz and Neil van Allen without the knowledge of David Joseph, Head of the General Studies Department. Signatories included Parveen Adams, Tessa Blackstone, Herbert Butterfield, Leon Kossoff, R. D. Laing, Ralph Miliband and Juliet Mitchell. (The contracts of other part-time staff were also not renewed, without warning and six weeks after term should have started, making it impossible for them to find work elsewhere.) Nick Wright was one of those students 'presumed withdrawn' because he had not presented himself for assessment and offered 'no satisfactory explanation', despite the fact that he had been Student Union President in 1967–8. See DP Box 6, letters from R. J. Stranks and H. H. Shelton to Wright, 7 and 25 Oct. 1968, and Wright's response to Stranks, 8 Oct. 1968. The minutes of Haringey Education Committee for 7 Oct. 1968 record approval of the chairman's action in relation to expenditure of more than £6000 'to obviate fire risks and to improve security' at Hornsey College of Art (bound into Haringey Council Minutes, vol. 5, 20 May 1968–6 May 1969, p. 120). 'Security measures' included lockable fire doors, steel bars on lower windows, steel spikes on drain pipes, outside lighting, security alarms and a live-in caretaker.

4   DP Box 2, DP typescript 'Memorandum, Staff & Students at Hornsey', undated but probably prepared for the Parliamentary Select Committee at the beginning of 1969. See also Joseph's evidence to the Select Committee, HCA 3/3/Ingles, Confidential Proof, *Minutes of Evidence taken before the Select Committee on Education and Science (Sub-Committee B)*, Thursday, 30 Jan. 1969, p. 36: there is 'still some uncertainty as to how decisions are taken in the college, decisions which do not appear to have gone through the machinery. . . . When one tries to trace or unravel the source of a decision one invariably finds it disappears.'

5   Events at Hornsey were chiefly responsible for making art education a pressing issue – for the Coldstream and Summerson Councils, the Department of Education and Science, the Parliamentary Select Committee and the unions (the National Union of Students and the Association of Teachers in Technical Institutions). Nick Wright was on the Art Colleges Advisory Panel of the National Union of Students and 'a long ovation greeted his coming to the microphone to speak on the structure of art education' at the NUS Conference in November 1968 (HCA Press Cuttings 1968, *Times Educational Supplement*, 29 Nov. 1968). Over the summer of 1968 the NUS became heavily involved in the art college cause. Whereas before there had been little representation from the art schools, which were small in size and lacking in funds, students had now become more articulate and inclined to participate (which the Union attributed to the introduction of the DipAD). It was evident through MORADE and the Round House conference of 8–10 July, at which 63 colleges of art and further education were represented, that the art students had created a national movement which impressed the NUS executive, given the largely dispersed and local nature of student protest in Britain. Finally, the art colleges – Hornsey and Guildford in particular – had received a great deal of attention in the press. See Nick Wright papers, brown folder labelled 'National Union of Students. Art Colleges Conference. Art Colleges Advisory Panel. . .', letter from Linda Tinckham, Executive Committee member responsible for art colleges, 16 Oct. 1968, to local branch presidents. See also in this folder much additional material including: 'Special Report on NUS Action over Art Colleges – A Summary of the Issues Under Discussion by the Advisory Panel' EW/82, 16 Oct. 1968;

'Minutes of the Art Colleges Advisory Panel Meeting', 18 Jan. 1969, chaired by Jack Straw, which note that the Secretary of State for Education, Edward Short, has rejected the Union's request for an enquiry into the occupations at Hornsey and Guildford; correspondence between the NUS and Alderman Cathles in Aug. and Sept. 1968 concerning the reopening of the college and assurances over 'no victimization'; ATTI South East Regional Conference of Art Teachers, Imperial College, 14 Feb. [1969? 1970?], 'Statement of policy on art education. First Draft'. (This recommends a comprehensive re-examination of higher education in art and design such as had 'not been held . . . since its origin in the nineteenth century'; the removal of art colleges from local authority control; the abolition of the GCE entrance requirement; renewed attention to the larger question of art's place in society; and the organization of vocational and diploma colleges and courses in a single unified system 'without differences of status or function'.) Conferences specifically devoted to art college issues were sponsored by the NUS at Oxford in 1968 and Swansea in 1969.

6   The outline of the Coldstream structure survives today. The NCDAD was merged with the Council for National Academic Awards in 1974 and the DipAD became a BA (Hons). The GCSE entrance requirement remains but the percentage of pupils attaining it is very much higher than in 1963. Academic work is still required, but the subjects have been transformed and the earlier benchmarks quietly lowered. Students are chiefly assessed on course-work and no longer take exams. The sweeping, year-long survey-courses of 'Mediaeval and Byzantine', 'Renaissance and Baroque', 'Modern and non-Western' have given way to modules grounded in design history or the 'new art history', or 'studies in visual culture' (including film). These new disciplines, or inter-disciplines, emerged primarily in polytechnics catering for art and design students, rather than in the established universities which only later, seeing a demand for them, took them up. My thanks to Ann Hulland and Phil Shaw for talking through with me their views on fine art and design education now. Both observed that these days students are rather bored with the Union and with the bureaucracy of representation – with 'module feedback forms' and 'boards of study'.

7   *The Hornsey Affair*, p.10. 'It will be evident that, far from committing any kind of outrage, we were merely fumbling towards the very minimal conditions of genuinely creative, "higher" education.' Richard Wollheim wrote that 'I personally cannot believe that in art schools things will be the same again, that what was said and thought in those weeks will not radically affect the system' ('Should Art be Respectable?', *Sunday Times*, 8 Sept. 1968, pp. 22–4, quotation p. 28). But he insisted that this depended on the resolution of two issues: first, that there should be no victimization of participants; and second, that Coldstream's *Joint Report* should emerge swiftly and clearly, taking on board the arguments about entrance qualifications, network systems, student participation and the end of written exams. Neither of these issues was resolved in the manner or to the degree that had been demanded.

8   Professor Peter Green, former head of Teacher Training at Hornsey and later Dean of the Faculty of Art and Design at Middlesex Polytechnic, believes that 'the new structure, administration and organization' of art education post-1968 owed a great deal to 'the student action which drew such effective attention to the inadequate and outdated way colleges across the country had [previously] been run' (communication, 15 Dec. 2005). In his *Memoir* (p. 58) Richard Robbins regretted 'the chaos and the level of

debate' in the sit-in, adding, 'that it drew attention to the college nationally and internationally I believe. I do now believe some benefits emerged but at what cost!'

9 One of several postscripts to the 'Hornsey Affair' was 'The Madingley Game', a 'management mixed-motive game for the public sector of higher education', devised by John Rae and David Warren Piper as a residential course for the Cambridge University Board of Extra-mural Studies in March 1969. David Joseph was director of studies and Alan Grant, Albert Hunt, Eric Robinson, Prue Bramwell-Davis and a slew of senior lecturers from regional art colleges took part in it. Game theory involves role-play, prediction, and the analysis of conflicts of interest. The Madingley Game had a value system, a set of roles, and a sequence of stages to be got through culminating in the students' graduation and a Summerson quinquennial review. Red tokens (resources and expertise), blue tokens (students' time), green tokens (kudos) and yellow tokens (power) were exchanged throughout the game by those in the roles of Principal, administrative and academic staff, students, representatives of the Students' Union, the local education authority, the Summerson Council, the press, the public and independent umpires. John Rae was amused to discover that those who did best were those who selected roles at the furthest remove from their everyday lives.

10 *The Hornsey Affair*, p. 215.

11 Judt (2005), p. 412. Judt concludes that the state's 'institutions were never seriously questioned (except the French university system, where it all began, which suffered sustained internal disruption and discredit without undergoing any significant reforms)'. Ross (2002) argues to the contrary that subsequent histories have rewritten the real political threat of the allied student-worker upheavals in France as something closer to a cultural blip.

12 *The Hornsey Affair*, p. 215. Sue Adams, now an artist and psychotherapist, puts it like this: 'Many of us . . . stimulated by the fertility of the sit-in, took the yeast of it into our lives and work. . . . The event continues to energize and inspire us. It was indeed the most truly educational experience I could have wished to have had.' Communication 14/10/2007.

13 Page, interview 11 Nov. 2005.

14 Rushton and Wood (1978), p. 4; Robin Blackburn, 'Student Reformers', review of *The Hornsey Affair*, *Listener*, 5 June 1969, pp. 793–4 (p. 793). Discussing the impact of 'Hornsey' on the established order, Blackburn expects that 'its impact on the Left will be just as great and just as necessary. With a few exceptions (Wilde, Morris) the British Left has shared the philistinism of society as a whole' (p. 794).

15 Walter Benjamin's model of history is that of the 'constellation' (rather than a sequence of events in continuously linear time), in which fragments of the past emerge into new configurations from the perspective of the present (like the patterns of the stars). See his 'Theses on the Philosophy of History' reprinted in *Illuminations* , ed. Hannah Arendt, transl. Harry Zohn, London: Fontana Collins, 1973, pp. 255–66. 'The true picture of the past flits by. The past can be seized only as an image which flashes up at the instant when it can be recognised and is never seen again' (p. 257). Benjamin saw history as double faced and in *The Arcades Project* quotes Maxime du Camp's aphorism: 'History is like Janus: it has two faces.' Benjamin, *The Arcades Project*, transl. Howard Eiland and Kevin Laughlin, based on the German volume ed. Rolf Tiedeman, Cambridge, Mass.: Belknap Press of Harvard University Press, 1999 (S1, 1) p. 543.

BIBLIOGRAPHY

Interviews and Correspondence

Prue Bramwell-Davis, 23/6/07
Stuart Brisley, 30/10/06
Steve Ehrlicher, 8/8/06
John Field, 21/1/07
Trevor Frankland, 17/2/07
John Goldschmidt, 5/6/07
Peter Green, correspondence during
　Dec. 2005
Kim Howells, 27/2/06
John Mitchell, 30/8/07
David Page, 11/11/05 and
　correspondence 2004–6
David Warren Piper, 23/11/05, 3/3/07,
　and correspondence 2006–7
John Rae, 1/12/05
Richard Robbins, 12/10/05, 21/11/05
Alex Roberts, 6/11/05
Fred Scott, 1/2/05
Denis Short and Eirian Short, 5/6/06
Jim Singh-Sandhu, correspondence
　during Feb. 2006
Marc Vaux, 14/2/07
Martin Walker, 21/6/06
Copies of interviews with David Page
　(17–18/1/02) and Nick Wright
　(23/8/01) conducted by Frederika
　Adam

Archives

Private

AR: Alex Roberts papers, loose,
　uncatalogued.
DP: David Page papers, eleven file boxes
　and an additional large envelope,
　uncatalogued.
DWP: David Warren Piper, filing-
cabinet drawer with Hornsey and
　NCDAD papers, uncatalogued.
Memoir: Richard Robbins, unpublished
　MS Memoir in two parts, 1985 and
　1992.
NW: Nick Wright papers, two file boxes,
　uncatalogued.

Public

Haringey Papers: Haringey Libraries,
　Archives and Museum Service, Bruce
　Castle Museum: Haringey Council
　Minutes including Education
　Committee Minutes (1/LBH/C14),
　Further Education Sub-Committee
　Minutes (1/LBH/C14/1), and bound
　volumes of Council Minutes (vol. 4,
　22 May 1967–29 April 1968; vol. 5,
　20 May 1968–6 May 1969; vol. 6, 19
　May 1969–6 May 1970).
HCA Archive: Hornsey College of Art
　Archive, Learning Resources,
　Middlesex University, uncatalogued:
　Boxes HCA/1/01/D; HCA/1/01/C/1;
　HCA Press Cuttings 1968; HCA/3/3
　(Ron Ingles's papers); Jack Procter's
　papers (uncoded); spiral-bound,
　photocopied press-cuttings inscribed
　'Jenny Cole scrapbooks' (unpaged); a
　loose copy of Gravy 21.
HHS Archive: Harold Shelton Papers,
　Victoria and Albert Museum
　Archives, AAD/1997/9,
　uncatalogued. Some boxes already
　have numbers, others were given
　temporary numbers by the archivist,
　Mrs Eva White, to ease citation.
Maurice de Sausmarez Papers, National
　Arts Education Archive, Bretton
　Hall, University of Leeds, BHDS$.

The NAEA also has material relating to Basic Design courses in the papers of Victor Pasmore and Richard Hamilton (King's College Newcastle), Harry Thubron (Leeds and Lancaster Colleges of Art) and Tom Hudson (Leeds, Leicester and Cardiff Colleges of Art).

Papers of the National Advisory Council on Art Education 1964–70 (the 'Coldstream Council'), National Archives ED206 together with a subseries within ED 46.

Papers of the National Council for Diplomas in Art and Design (the 'Summerson Council') and its panels, National Archives DB4.

Papers of the National Council for Diplomas in Art and Design, Modern Records Centre, University of Warwick, GB 152 MSS. 322/AD, uncatalogued.

Royal Watercolour Society Archives, Bankside Gallery (a few papers and posters donated by Trevor Frankland, ex-President of the RWS and a former lecturer at Hornsey College of Art).

Books and Catalogues

Adelstein, David, *Teach Yourself Student Power*, London: Radical Student Alliance, 1968.

Allthorpe-Guyton, Marjorie and John Stevens, *A Happy Eye: A School of Art in Norwich 1845–1982*, Norwich: Jarrold and Sons, 1982.

Art education: an international survey, Paris: UNESCO, 1972. See 'The education of the professional artist', pp. 65–6, on the UK.

Ashwin, Clive (ed.), *Art Education; Documents and Policies 1768–1975*, London: Society for Research into Higher Education, 1975.

Ashwin, Clive, *A Century of Art Education 1882–1982*, London: Middlesex Polytechnic, 1982.

Batchelor, David, *et al.* (eds.), *The Noises Within Echo from a Gimcrack, Remote and Ideologically Hollow Chamber of the Education Machine: Art School*, Edinburgh: School Press, 1979, financed by SCARP (Student Community Action Resources Programme).

Battcock, Gregory (ed.), *New Ideas in Art Education: A Critical Anthology*, New York: E. P. Dutton, 1973.

Bell, Quentin, *The Schools of Design*, London: Routledge and Kegan Paul, 1963.

Bird, Jon, *et al.* (eds.), *The Block Reader in Visual Culture*, London: Routledge, 1996.

Bonaventura, Paul and Stephen Farthing (eds.), *A Curriculum for Artists*, Oxford: The Laboratory, Ruskin School of Drawing and Fine Art, 2004.

Callen, Anthea, *Angel in the Studio: Women in the Arts and Crafts Movement, 1870–1914*, London: Astragal Books, 1979.

Cockburn, Alexander and Robin Blackburn (eds.), *Student Power: Problems, Diagnosis, Action*, Harmondsworth, Middlesex: Penguin, 1969 in association with *New Left Review*.

Crick, Bernard and William A. Robson (eds.), *Protest and Discontent*, Harmondsworth, Middlesex: Penguin, 1970.

Crouch, Colin, *The Student Revolt*, London: Bodley Head, 1970.

Davies, Ray, *X-Ray: The Unauthorized Autobiography*, London: Viking, 1994.

De Ville, Nicholas and Stephen Foster (eds.), *The Artist and the Academy: Issues in Fine Art Education and the Wider Cultural Context*, Southampton: John Hansard Gallery, 1994.

Douar, Fabrice, and Matthias Waschek (eds.), *Peut-on enseigner l'art?*, Paris: École Nationale Supérieure des Beaux-Arts, 2004.

Eisner, Elliot W. and David W. Ecker (eds.), *Readings in Art Education*, Waltham, Mass.: Ginn-Blaisdell, 1966.

Elkins, James, *Why Art Cannot be Taught: A Handbook for Art Students*, Urbana and Chicago: University of Illinois Press, 2001.

Field, Dick, *Change in Art Education*, London: Routledge and Kegan Paul, 1970.

Fraser, Ronald *et al.*, *1968: A Student Generation in Revolt*, London: Chatto & Windus, 1988.

Frayling, Christopher, *The Royal College of Art: One Hundred & Fifty Years of Art & Design*, London: Barrie and Jenkins, 1987.

Furlong, William, Polly Gould and Paul Hetherington (eds.), *Issues in Art and Education: The Dynamics of Now* [papers submitted at conferences 1995–8], London: Wimbledon School of Art in association with Tate Publishing.

Green, Jonathon, *Days in the Life: Voices from the English Underground 1961–1971*, London: Heinemann, 1988.

Green, Jonathon, *All Dressed Up: The Sixties and the Counterculture*, London: Jonathan Cape, 1998.

Hamilton, Richard, *Collected Words 1953–1982*, London and New York: Thames and Hudson, 1982.

Hannema, Sjoerd, *Fads, Fakes and Fantasies: The Crisis in the Art Schools and the Crisis in Art*, London: Macdonald, 1970.

Harrison, Charles, *Essays on Art and Language* [1991], Cambridge, Mass.: MIT Press, 2001.

Harrison, Charles and Fred Orton, *A Provisional History of Art & Language*, Paris: Editions E. Fabre, 1982.

Hetherington, Paul (ed.), *Artists in the 1990s: Their Education and Values*, London: Wimbledon School of Art in association with the Tate Gallery, 1994.

Hetherington, Paul (ed.), *Issues in Art and Education: Aspects of the Fine Art Curriculum*, London: Tate Publishing, 1996.

Hewison, Robert, *Too Much: Art and Society in the Sixties 1960–1975*, London: Methuen, 1986.

Hewison, Robert, *Culture and Consensus: England, Art and Politics since 1940*, London: Methuen, 1995.

Hornsey Affair, The see: 'Students and Staff of Hornsey College of Art'.

Judt, Tony, *Postwar: A History of Europe since 1945*, London: Heinemann, 2005.

Kurlansky, Mark, *1968: The Year that Rocked the World*, London: Jonathan Cape, 2004.

Kustow, Michael, *Tank: An Autobiographical Fiction*, London: Jonathan Cape, 1975.

Laughton, Bruce, *William Coldstream*, New Haven and London: Yale University Press for the Paul Mellon Centre for Studies in British Art, 2004. (Chapter 21 concerns the Coldstream Reports.)

Macdonald, Stuart, *The History and Philosophy of Art Education*, London: Faber and Faber, 1970. (Chapter 19 concerns Coldstream, Summerson and student unrest in 1968.)

Madge, Charles and Barbara Weinberger, *Art Students Observed*, London: Faber and Faber, 1973. (Coventry College of Art is thinly disguised as 'Midville College of Art'.)

Marwick, Arthur, *The Sixties*, Oxford: Oxford University Press, 1998.

Medley, Robert, *Drawn from the Life: a Memoir*, London and Boston: Faber and Faber, 1983.

Mellor, David, *The Sixties Art Scene in London*, exh. cat., Barbican Art Gallery, 11 Mar.-13 Jun. 1993, London: Phaidon in association with the Barbican Art Gallery, 1993.

Mellor, David Alan and Laurent Gervereau, with the collaboration of Sarah Wilson and Laurence Bertrand Dorléac, *The Sixties: Britain and France, 1962–1973: The Utopian Years*, London: Philip Wilson, 1997.

Miles, Barry, *In the Sixties*, London: Jonathan Cape, 2002.

Nagel, Julian ed., *Student Power*, London: Merlin Press, 1969.

Nuttall, Jeff, *Bomb Culture*, London: MacGibbon and Kee, 1968.

Papanek, Victor, *Design for the Real World* [1971], with an introduction by R. Buckminster Fuller, London and New York: Thames and Hudson, 1972.

Perry, Gill and Paul Wood (eds.), *Art of the 20th Century: Themes in Contemporary Art*, New Haven and London: Yale University Press in association with the Open University, 2004.

Pevsner, Nikolaus, *Academies of Art Past and Present* [1940], New York: Da Capo Press, 1973.

Piper, David Warren (ed.), *Readings in Art Education* – vol. 1, *After Hornsey*; vol. 2, *After Coldstream*, London: Davis-Poynter, 1973.

Robinson, Eric, *The New Polytechnics: A Radical Policy for Higher Education*, London: Cornmarket, 1968. Subsequently published as a Penguin Education Special, *The New Polytechnics: the People's Universities*,

Harmondsworth, Middlesex: Penguin, 1968. [Page references are to the Cornmarket edition.]

Ross, Kristin, *May '68 and its Afterlives*, Chicago: University of Chicago Press, 2002.

Roszack, Theodore, *The Making of a Counter-Culture: Reflections on the Technocratic Society and its Youthful Opposition*, London: Faber and Faber, 1970.

Rushton, Dave and Paul Wood (eds.), *Politics of Art Education*, London: Studio Trust , 1978.

Sampson, Anthony, *Anatomy of Britain Today*, London: Hodder and Stoughton, 1965 [first published as *Anatomy of Britain*, 1962].

Singerman, Howard, *Art Subjects: Making Artists in the American University*, Berkeley, Calif.: University of California Press, 1999.

Singerman, Howard (ed.), *Public Offerings*, exh. cat., Museum of Contemporary Art, Los Angeles, 1 Apr.-29 Jul. 2001, London and New York: Thames and Hudson, 2001.

Stephens, Chris and Katharine Stout (eds.), *Art & the 60s: This Was Tomorrow*, exh. cat., London: Tate Publishing, Tate Britain 30 Jun.-3 Oct. 2004 and touring.

Strand, Robert, *A Good Deal of Freedom: Art and Design in the public sector of higher education, 1960–1982*, London: Council for National Academic Awards, 1987.

Students and Staff of Hornsey College of Art, *The Hornsey Affair*, Harmondsworth, Middlesex: Penguin, 1969.

Taylor, Brandon, *Art for the Nation: Exhibitions and the London Public, 1747–2001*, Manchester: Manchester University Press, 1999.

Thistlewood, David, *A Continuing*

Process: The New Creativity in British Art Education 1955–1965, exh. cat, London: Institute of Contemporary Arts, 17 Mar.-19 Apr. 1981.

Thistlewood, David, *Histories of Art and Design Education: Cole to Coldstream*, Harlow: Longman in association with the National Society for Education in Art and Design, 1992.

Walker, John A., *Learning to Paint: A British Art Student and Art School 1956–61*, London: Institute of Artology, 2003.

When Attitudes Become Form, exh. cat., Kunsthalle Bern, 22 Mar.-27 Apr. 1969.

Wood, Paul (ed), *Exocet: The Humanities Code-Book*, Edinburgh: October Press, supported by the Edinburgh College of Art Students' Union, 1982.

Wood, Paul, 'Between God and the Saucepan: Some aspects of art education in England between the middle of the nineteenth century and the end of the twentieth', forthcoming in *The History of British Art – vol. 3, Art and the Modern World: From the Victorians to Now*, London: Tate Publishing, 2008.

Articles

Newspaper reports, including letters to *The Times*, the *Guardian*, the *Hornsey Journal* and many other sources, are too numerous to list separately and are cited in the notes.

Ascott, Roy, 'The Coldstream Report', *Studio International* vol. 181, Jan. 1971, p.6 (letter in response to Norbert Lynton).

Ashwin, Clive, 'Art Education and Success', *Studio International* vol. 188, Nov. 1974.

Askham, Elma and Harry Thubron, 'The Case for Polytechnics', *Studio International* vol. 174, Sept. 1967, pp. 82–3.

Askham, Elma and Harry Thubron, 'Art through Education', *Studio International*, vol. 176, July/Aug. 1968, pp. 5–6.

Association of Members of Hornsey College of Art, 'Hornsey – The Flower Breaks the Concrete', *IT* no. 34, 28 June-11 July 1968.

Association of Members of Hornsey College of Art, 'On the Reasons for a Revolution: a Study Paper by the Association of Members of Hornsey College of Art, England', *Leonardo* vol. 2, pp. 193–8, 1969.

Atkinson, Terry and Michael Baldwin, 'Art Teaching', *Art-Language* vol. 1 no.4 (Nov. 1971) pp. 25–50.

Baker-White, John, 'Students in Revolt: the Revolutionaries', *Twentieth Century* vol. 177 no. 1038, 1968, pp. 21–5.

Banham, Rayner, 'Representations in Protest', *New Society* 13 (8 May 1969), pp. 717–8.

Berry, P., K. Wright and P. Wood, 'Aspects of art education 2: Remarks on art education', *Studio International*, vol. 184, Nov. 1972, pp. 179–81.

Cornford, Christopher, 'Fine art and industrial design – the danger of an educational apartheid', *Studio International*, vol. 173, Mar. 1967, pp. 117–8.

Deacon, C. E. W., 'Hornsey's Revolution', *Listener*, 15 Aug. 1968, p.211.

Everitt, Anthony, 'Four Midland polytechnic fine art departments', 'Aspects of art education 2', *Studio International*, vol. 184, Nov. 1972, pp. 176–9.

Fausset, Shelley, 'Visits to Fourteen Colleges of Art', *Studio International*, vol. 178, Nov. 1969, pp. 148–9.

Francis, Clare, Harry Munn and David Page, correspondence re Hornsey in *Studio International*, vol. 176, July/Aug. 1968, p.7.

Gilbert, Richard, 'Wisdom Working', *Listener*, vol. 80, 4 July 1968, pp. 12–13.

Grant, Keith, 'Cost of the Hornsey Revolution', *Studio International*, vol. 176, Nov. 1968, pp. 179–80.

Gravy (Hornsey College of Art magazine), issues 21, 22, undated [1967–8].

Hall, Peter and Kay Hunt, 'Dismissals at Guildford Art School', *Studio International*, vol. 176, Dec. 1968, p. 239.

Harrison, Charles, 'Educating Artists', *Studio International*, vol. 183, May 1972, pp. 222–4.

Hewitt, John, 'Good Design in the Market Place. The Rise of Habitat Man', *Oxford Art Journal*, vol. 10, no. 2, 1987, pp. 28–42.

Hudson, Tom, '"Pure" and "applied" art – the need for the right balance in education', *Studio International*, vol. 173, Jan. 1967, pp. 4–5.

Hudson, Tom, 'Points in a reconstructive primer for the creative individual', *Studio International*, vol. 176, Sept. 1968, pp. 65–6.

Laurie, Peter and Roger Law, 'What Really Happened at Hornsey', *Sunday Times Magazine*, 13 Sept. 1970, pp. 36–47.

Litherland, R. H., 'Power without authority in art and design education', *Studio International*, vol. 182, Dec. 1971, pp. 224–5.

Litherland, R. H., 'The Future Development of Art Education', *The Technical Journal* [journal of the ATTI], vol. 7 no. 6, July 1969, pp. 17–19.

Lucie-Smith, Edward, 'The Talk at the Next Table' [reply to Harold Rosenberg], *Encounter*, vol. 29 no. 1, July 1967, pp. 54–5.

Lynton, Norbert, 'Waiting for Coldstream', *Studio International*, vol. 178, Sept. 1969, pp. 58–9.

Lynton, Norbert, 'Coldstream 1970', *Studio International* vol. 180, Nov. 1970, pp. 167–8.

Morgan, Geri, 'For and Against Polytechnics', *Studio International*, vol. 175, Jan. 1968, p.8 [letter in response to Askham and Thubron].

Morris, Linda, Digby Jacks, Charles Harrison, 'Some Concerns in Fine Art Education II', *Studio International* vol. 183, Nov. 1971, pp. 168–70.

Nairn, Tom, 'On the Subversiveness of Art Students', *Listener*, vol. 80, 17 Oct. 1968, pp. 491–2.

Page, David, 'Hornsey and After', *Twentieth Century*, vol. 177 no. 1038, 1968, pp. 21–5.

Page, David, 'Conference on Art and Design in Polytechnics', *Studio International*, vol. 183, Mar. 1972, p. 95.

Pilkington, Philip, Kevin Lole, David Rushton, 'Some concerns in fine art education', afterword by Charles Harrison, *Studio International*, vol. 183, Oct. 1971, pp. 120–2.

Piper, David Warren, 'Hornsey's Dissenting Voice – the Revolution at Hornsey College of Art', *Studio International*, vol. 176, July/Aug. 1968, pp. 6–7.

Piper, David Warren, 'Two Symposia', *Studio International*, vol. 181, Apr. 1971, pp. 145–6.

Piper, David Warren, 'Art and Design Education', *Studio International* vol. 181, May 1971, pp. 194–7.

Pollock, Griselda, 'Art, Art School, Culture: Individualism after the death of the artist', *Block* no.11, 1985/6, reprinted in *The BLOCK Reader in Visual Culture*, London and New York: Routledge 1996, pp.50–67.

Richardson, Gordon and Ted Hawkes (eds.), 'After art school?', *Studio International*, vol. 175, May 1968, pp. 238–40.

Rosenberg, Harold, 'Where to Begin', *Encounter* vol. 28 no.3, Mar. 1967, pp. 36–40.

Sampson, Anthony, 'Anatomy of the Student Revolt', *Observer*, 20 Oct. 1968, p.11.

Secrest, Meryl, 'An American at Leeds', *Studio International*, vol. 177, May 1969, pp. 206–7.

Shuttleworth, Martin, 'Art through Education', *Studio International*, vol. 176, July/Aug. 1968, pp. 4–5.

Sparrow, John, 'Revolting Students', *Listener*, vol. 80, 4 July 1968, pp. 1–4.

Walker, John, 'Radical Artists and Art Students versus Management and Bureaucracy in the 1970s', *International Journal of Art and Design Education*, vol. 20 no. 2, 2001, pp. 230–7.

Watkinson, Ray, 'Art Colleges and Polytechnics', *The Technical Journal* (journal of the ATTI), vol. 6 no. 5, June 1968, pp. 13–16.

Whitford, Frank, 'Is there anything wrong with art schools?', *Arts Review*, vol. 18, 16 Apr. 1966, p. 168.

Whiteley, Nigel, 'Towards a Throw-Away Culture. Consumerism, "Style Obsolescence" and Cultural Theory', *Oxford Art Journal*, vol. 10, no. 2, 1987, pp. 3–27.

Willing, Victor, 'What kind of art education?', *Studio International* vol. 172, Sept. 1966, pp. 131–9. Introduction and interviews with Richard Hamilton, Professor Misha Black and Sir Herbert Read. *Studio International* published follow-up pieces with the same title and various contributors in October (vol. 172, pp. 166–7) and November (vol. 172, pp. 226–7) 1966.

Wollheim, Richard, 'Should Art be Respectable?', *Sunday Times*, 8 Sept. 1968, pp. 22–4, 28.

Reports
(in chronological order)

Report on Proposed Changes in the Art Examinations and in the Length of the Diploma Course, National Advisory Committee on Art Examinations, London: HMSO, 1957.

First Report of the National Advisory Council on Art Education (First Coldstream Report), London: HMSO, 1960.

Second Report of the National Advisory Council on Art Education: 'Vocational Courses in Colleges and Schools of Art' (Second Coldstream Report), London: HMSO, 1962.

Third Report of the National Advisory Council on Art Education: 'Post-Diploma Studies in Art and Design' (Third Coldstream Report), London: HMSO, 1964.

First Report of the National Council for Diplomas in Art and Design (The Summerson Report), London: HMSO, 1964.

First Report of the National Advisory Council on Art Education: Addendum, 'Pre-Diploma Studies', London: HMSO, 1965.

A Plan for Polytechnics and Other Colleges: Higher Education in the Further Education System, White Paper on Education, Department of Education and Science, London: HMSO, 23 May 1966.

Unity and Variety: Current Problems in
Art and Design Education. Report of the
Hornsey Commission, Chairman Lord
Longford, undated [c.1968].

Report from the Select Committee on
Education and Science (Student
Relations), 25 July 1969. This includes
minutes of evidence and memoranda
from representatives of all the
interested parties: students, staff, the
Principal, governors, Haringey
Council, the ATTI and the NUS. On
Hornsey see vol. 1, Report; vol. 5,
Sub-committee B. Evidence and
Appendices; and Sub-Committee B.
Minutes of Evidence, 30 Jan. 1969.

Joint Report of the NACAE and the
NCDAD: 'The Structure of Art and
Design Education in the Further
Education Sector', London: HMSO,
1970.

Second Report of the National Council for
Diplomas in Art and Design, London:
HMSO, 1970.

The Employment of Art College Leavers,
Jane Ritchie assisted by Chris Frost
and Sue Dight, Office of Population
Censuses and Surveys (Social Survey
Division), London: HMSO, 1972.

Films

Our Live Experiment is Worth More than
Three Thousand Textbooks, directed by
John Goldschmidt, 1969. (Video
copy, 2005, supplied by ITN to
Middlesex University Learning
Resources.)

The Hornsey Film, directed by Patricia
Holland, 1970. (Viewing print, the
National Film and Television
Archive; video copy, Middlesex
University Learning Resources.)

Radio Broadcast

What's Wrong with Art Education?,
National Sound Archive, British
Library, London, NP1341R. Thirty
statements from interviews conducted
for BBC radio at the National
Conference for Rethinking Art and
Design Education organized by
MORADE at the Roundhouse, Chalk
Farm, July 1968. Recorded and
produced by Meg Sheffield and Tony
Gould, transmitted BBC Radio 4, 25
Sept. 1968. (This is a collage of
unidentified voices with no linking
narrative.)

Sound Tapes

Two reel-to-reel tapes in the possession
of John Rae, Staff Meeting, June 1968,
and Television Programme, 23 Sept.
1968 (currently unplayable but possibly
recoverable through digitization).

INDEX

Gordon, Colin (ed.): *Power/Knowledge*, 105n8

Gordon Walker, Patrick, 25, 116n27

Gould, Tony, 140n113

Gramsci, Antonio, 125n28

Grant, Alan: as speaker at 'critical seminar', 32; on polytechnic idea, 113n21; on student-staff relations, 123n14; and Select Committee, 148n34; on staff/student organization, 149n39; in General Studies Department, 156n71; resigns, 157n78, 160n89; on decline in service to students, 161n94; participates in Madingley Game, 184n9

Grant, Keith, 32, 142n6, 158n79, 180n78

Gravy (Hornsey College magazine), 23, 113n21, 117n31, 167n4

Green, Peter, 141n2, 143n9, 145n23, 183n8

Greenberg, Clement, 94, 132n74, 173n40, 174n43; *Art and Culture*, 92

Guardian (newspaper), 39, 44, 61

Guildford College of Art, 64, 66, 158n78, 161n99, 182n5

Gurling, Trudi, 96

H

Hailsham, Quintin McGarel Hogg, Baron, 107n12

Hamilton, Richard, 38, 49, 138n107, 163n101, 171n29, 172n32, 174n44

Hamilton, Vicky, 151n46, 157n78, 158n79, 182n3

Hamling, William, 115n25

Hancock, Bernard, 66, 148n34, 156n70, 157n77, 161n94

Hannema, Sjoerd, 137n99, 175n49

Haringey (Borough) Council: Education Authority, 21; opposed by Hornsey College over polytechnic status, 23–5; reconstituted as Borough Council (1965), 26, 75; Conservatives win control, 29; employs security firm to clear college, 54–5; on payment of student fees, 59; Education

Committee (Borough Council), 62; *see also* Bains, Alderman Laurence; Cathles, Alderman George

Harrison, Charles, 93–4, 174n43, 179n76

Hartley, Air Marshal Sir Christopher, 28

Harvey, Peter, 177n58

Hawes, M.W., 163n103

Hawser, Lewis, 27

Hayden, Roger, 38, 143n9, 170n24

Hayes, John, 156n71

Hayman, Peter, 29–30

Heath, Alec, 115n25

Hendon College of Technology, 21, 24

Henri, Adrian, 139n109

Hepworth, Barbara, 181n79

Heron, Patrick, 111n11

Hill, Tony, 95

Hilton, Kathy, 176n52

Hitchens, Councillor, 55, 143n9

Hockney, David, 138n107, 166n112

Hofmann, Hans, 98, 176n56

Holland, Patricia: *The Hornsey Film*, 121n1, 132n67, 133n77

Hornsey Affair, The (1969), 8, 40, 42, 51, 61, 64, 77, 87, 100, 102

Hornsey College of Art: grievances, 7, 32, 119n44; document declaring student occupation, 11; causes of occupation, 13–14; revolutionary importance, 13; curriculum, 15, 42, 50–3; and new Diploma in Art and Design, 16; liberal educational role, 17; part-time and full-time students, 17–18; recognised by Summerson Council, 19; proposed merger in new polytechnic, 20, 23–6; incorporated in Middlesex Polytechnic, 26, 101; under Haringey Borough Council (1965), 26; accommodation dispersed, 27–8; organisational inadequacies, 28–9; Students' Union funds frozen and released, 29; sit-in planned and put into effect, 31–3; students' mass discussions, 31–2; political implications and allegiances, 33, 67–70, 93, 168n7; governors agree to reforms, 34; staff and student bodies united as AMHCA, 35–6; seminars, 37–8; social work projects, 38–9, 88–9; working parties, 38; student demands and arguments for educational reform, 41–2, 45–6, 50; selection procedures, 44–5; vocational courses, 46; art history teaching, 47; steering committee and commission appointed, 53–5; executive committee of governors propose end to sit-in, 54–5; closed (12 July 1968), 56; reassessment of students, 59–60; reopening (autumn 1968), 59; staff-student commission, 60–2; decision-making structure proposed, 63; College Advisory Panel, 64; General Studies Department, 65–6, 72–5, 100, 161n94; Visual Research Department, 72, 74–5; quinquennial review renews DipAD status for two years (1969), 73–4, 77–9; departments merged, 74–5; Students' Union votes no confidence in Principal and administration, 79; sit-in assessed, 83–5, 92–5, 100–1; class, race and gender composition, 93–4; effects on participants, 101–2; founded, 105n5; Principals, 105n5; expansion, 117n30, 118n36; canteen, 122n5; Teacher Training Department, 138n56, 141n2; fine art students, 175n49

Hornsey Journal, 38
Hornsey Strikes Again (exhibition), 56
Horrocks, Anthony, 143n9
Howard, Graham, 178n66
Howells, Kim: speaks at mass discussion, 31; socio-political views and activism, 33, 68, 87, 153n53, 153n55, 175n49, 176n54; serves on working party, 38; living quarters, 122n7; on student/staff organization, 123n14; accused of haranguing students, 128n41; on composition of staff/student commission, 142n9; on debate about creativity, 150n42; on purpose and

conduct of sit-in, 150n44, 151n46; on LSE sit-in, 169n18; opposition to gallery system, 169n20, 171n31; suspended and reinstated, 179n69
Hoyland, John, 90
Hudson, Tom, 49, 163n101, 171n29, 172n32
Hunt, Albert, 184n9
Hussey, Harold, 145n23
Huxley, Paul, 174n45

I

Ingles, Ron, 32
Institute of Contemporary Arts, London (ICA), 56; exhibitions, 14, 56–7, 137n100, 171n29
Itten, Johannes, 134n84

J

Jacks, Digby, 31, 162n99, 166n112
Jackson, Donald, 104n2
Jackson, Ron, 149n39
Jerram, Roger, 123n14, 136n95, 147n31, 148n34
John, Gwen, 98
Johnston, William, 172n32
Joint Committee (of NACAE and NCDAD), 79–80, 165n109
Joint Report see Structure of Art and Design Education in the Further Education Sector
Jones, Gareth, 177n58
Joseph, David: speaks at meetings, 32; in General Studies Department, 72–3, 156n71; attitude to student protesters, 73; works on new curriculum, 73–4; as teacher, 104n2; on inclusion of art colleges in White Paper, 113n21; on accommodation problems, 118n39; on student/staff organization, 123n14; gives evidence to Select Committee, 124n21; resigns (1969), 132n67, 158n78, 158n79; supports proposed academic structure, 145n23; evidence to Select Committee, 148n34, 149n41; on conduct of sit-in, 150n44, 152n49;